Multilevel Analysis

Techniques and Applications

D0950210

QUANTITATIVE METHODOLOGY SERIES
Methodology for Business and Management

George A. Marcoulides, Series Editor

The purpose of this series is to present methodological techniques to investigators and students from all functional areas of business, although individuals from other disciplines will also find the series useful. Each volume in the series will focus on a specific method (e.g., Data Envelopment Analysis, Factor Analysis, Multilevel Analysis, Structural Equation Modeling). The goal is to provide an understanding and working knowledge of each method with a minimum of mathematical derivations.

Proposals are invited from all interested authors. Each proposal should consist of the following: (i) a brief description of the volume's focus and intended market, (ii) a table of contents with an outline of each chapter, and (iii) a curriculum vita. Materials may be sent to Dr. George A. Marcoulides, Department of Management Science, California State University, Fullerton, CA 92634.

Marcoulides • Modern Methods for Business Research

Duncan/Duncan/Strycker/Li/Alpert • An Introduction to Latent Variable Growth Curve Modeling: Concepts, Issues, and Applications

Heck/Thomas • An Introduction to Multilevel Modeling Techniques

Marcoulides/Moustaki • Latent Variable and Latent Structure Models

Hox • Multilevel Analysis: Techniques and Applications

Multilevel Analysis

Techniques and Applications

Joop Hox
Utrecht University, the Netherlands

2002

LAWRENCE ERLBAUM ASSOCIATES, PUBLISHERS
Mahwah, New Jersey   London

The camera ready copy for the text of this book was supplied by the author.

Copyright © 2002 by Lawrence Erlbaum Associates, Inc.
    All rights reserved. No part of this book may be reproduced in
    any form, by photostat, microform, retrieval system, or any other
    means, without the prior written permission of the publisher.

Lawrence Erlbaum Associates, Inc., Publishers
10 Industrial Avenue
Mahwah, New Jersey 07430

Cover Design by Kathryn Houghtaling Lacey

Library of Congress Cataloging-in-Publication Data

Hox, J.J.
    Multilevel analysis : techniques and applications / by Joop Hox.
        p.   cm.
    Includes bibliographical references and index.
    ISBN 0-8058-3218-1 (alk. paper) – ISBN 0-8058-3219-X (alk. paper)
      1. Social sciences–Statistical methods. 2. Analysis of variance.
      3. Regression analysis.
    I. Title.

HA29.H783 2002
001.4'22–dc21

                                                           2001057760

Printed in the United States of America
10 9 8 7 6 5 4 3 2 1

Contents

Preface

To err is human, to forgive divine;
but to include errors into your design is statistical.

—Leslie Kish

This book is intended as an introduction to multilevel analysis for applied researchers. The term 'multilevel' refers to a hierarchical or nested data structure, usually people within organizational groups, but the nesting may also consist of repeated measures within people, or respondents within clusters as in cluster sampling. The expression *multilevel model* or *multilevel analysis* is used as a generic term for all models for nested data. This book presents two multilevel models: the multilevel regression model and a model for multilevel covariance structures.

Multilevel modeling used to be only for specialists. However, in the past decade, multilevel analysis software has become available that is both powerful and relatively accessible for applied researchers. As a result, there is a surge of interest in multilevel analysis, as evidenced by the appearance of several reviews and monographs, applications in different fields ranging from psychology and sociology to medicine, and a thriving Internet discussion list with more than 1400 subscribers.

Despite it being an introduction, the book includes a discussion of many extensions and special applications. As an introduction, it should be useable in courses in a variety of fields, such as psychology, education, sociology and business. The various extensions and special applications should make it useful to researchers who work in applied or theoretical research, and to methodologists who have to consult with these researchers. The basic models and examples are discussed in non-technical terms; the emphasis is on understanding the methodological and statistical issues involved in using these models. Some of the extensions and special applications contain discussions that are more technical, either because that is necessary for understanding what the model does, or as a helpful introduction to more advanced treatments in other texts. Thus, in addition to its role as an introduction, the book should be useful as a standard reference for a large variety of applications. It assumes that readers have a basic knowledge of social science statistics, including analysis of variance and multiple regression analysis. The section about multilevel structural equation models assumes a basic understanding of ordinary structural equation modeling.

I thank Peter van der Heijden, Herbert Hoijtink, Bernet Sekasanvu Kato, Edith de Leeuw, George Marcoulides, Mirjam Moerbeek, Ian Plewis, Ken Rowe, Godfried van den Wittenboer and Bill Yeaton for their comments on earlier drafts.

I thank my colleagues at the Department of Methodology and Statistics of the Faculty of Social Sciences at Utrecht University for providing me with many discussions and a generally stimulating research environment. My research has also benefited from the lively discussions by the denizens of the Internet *Multilevel Modeling* and the *Structural Equations Modeling (SEMNET)* discussion lists. I also want to mention the Dutch NOSMO research committee on Multilevel Research (MULOG) for their continued interest in multilevel modeling. Finally, draft chapters of this book have been used in a multilevel course at the Summer Institute of the Social Research Center of the University of Michigan. I thank the Summer Institute students for their critical comments. As always, any errors remaining in the book are entirely my own responsibility.

                                                                          J.J. Hox

                                                                          Amsterdam

1

Introduction to Multilevel Analysis

Social research regularly involves problems that investigate the relationship between individual and society. The general concept is that individuals interact with the social contexts to which they belong, meaning that individual persons are influenced by the social groups or contexts to which they belong, and that the properties of those groups are in turn influenced by the individuals who make up that group. Generally, the individuals and the social groups are conceptualized as a hierarchical system of individuals and groups, with individuals and groups defined at separate levels of this hierarchical system. Naturally, such systems can be observed at different hierarchical levels, and variables may be defined at each level. This leads to research into the interaction between variables characterizing individuals and variables characterizing groups, a kind of research that is now often referred to as '*multilevel research*'.

In multilevel research, the data structure in the population is hierarchical, and the sample data are viewed as a multistage sample from this hierarchical population. Thus, in educational research, the population consists of schools and pupils within these schools, and the sampling procedure proceeds in two stages: first, we take a sample of schools, and next we take a sample of pupils within each school. Of course, in real research one may have a convenience sample at either level, or one may decide not to sample pupils but to study all available pupils in the sample of schools. Nevertheless, one should keep firmly in mind that the central statistical model in multilevel analysis is one of successive sampling from each level of a hierarchical population.

In this example, pupils are *nested* within schools. Other examples are cross-national studies where the individuals are nested within their national units, organizational research with individuals nested within departments within organizations, family research with family members within families and methodological research into interviewer effects with respondents nested within interviewers. Less obvious applications of multilevel models are longitudinal research and growth curve research, where a series of several distinct observations are viewed as nested within individuals, and meta-analysis where the subjects are nested within different studies. For simplicity, this book describes the multilevel models mostly in terms of individuals nested within groups, but note that the models apply to a much larger class of analysis problems.

In multilevel research, variables can be defined at any level of the hierarchy. Some of these variables may be measured directly at their 'own' natural level; for example, at the school level we may measure school size and denomination, and at the pupil level intelligence and school success. In addition, we may move variables from one level to another by aggregation or disaggregation. Aggregation means that the variables at a lower level are moved to a higher level, for instance, by assigning to the schools the school mean of the pupils' intelligence scores. Disaggregation means moving variables to a lower level, for instance by assigning to all pupils in the schools a variable that indicates the denomination of the school they belong to. Lazarsfeld and Menzel (1961) offer a typology to describe the relations between different types of variables, defined at different levels. A simplified scheme is presented below:

Level:	1		2		3	et cetera
Variable	global	$\Rightarrow$	analytical			
type:	relational	$\Rightarrow$	structural			
	contextual	$\Leftarrow$	global	$\Rightarrow$	analytical	
			relational	$\Rightarrow$	structural	
			contextual	$\Leftarrow$	global	$\Rightarrow$
					relational	$\Rightarrow$
					contextual	$\Leftarrow$

The lowest level (level 1) in this scheme is usually defined by the individuals. However, this is not always the case. Galtung (1969), for instance, defines roles within individuals as the lowest level, and in longitudinal designs, one can define repeated measures within individuals as the lowest level (Goldstein, 1986, 1989).

At each level in the hierarchy, we may have several types of variables. *Global* variables are variables that refer only to the level at which they are defined, without reference to other units or levels. A pupil's intelligence or gender would be a global variable at the pupil level. School size would be a global variable at the school level. *Relational* variables also belong to one single level, but they describe the relationships of a unit to the other units at the same level. Many sociometric indices, such as indices of popularity or the reciprocity of relationships, are relational variables. *Analytical* and *structural* variables are measured by referring to the sub-units at a lower level. Analytical variables are constructed from variables at a lower level, for example, in defining the school variable 'mean intelligence' as the mean intelligence of the pupils in that school. Using the mean of a lower-level variable as an explanatory variable at a higher level is a customary procedure in multilevel analysis. Other functions may also be valuable. For instance, using the standard deviation of a lower-level variable as an explanatory variable at a higher level could be used to test hypotheses about the effect of group heterogeneity on the outcome variable. Structural variables refer to the distribution of relational variables at the lower level; many social network indices are of this type. It is clear that constructing an analytical or structural variable from the lower-level data involves *aggregation* (which is indicated in the scheme by ⇒); data on lower-level units are aggregated into data on a smaller number of higher-level units. *Contextual* variables, on the other hand, refer to the super-units; all units at the lower level receive the value of a variable for the super-unit to which they belong at the higher level. For instance, we can assign to all pupils in a school the school size, or the mean intelligence, as a pupil level variable. This is called *disaggregation* (indicated in the scheme by ⇐); data on higher-level units are disaggregated into data on a larger number of lower-level units. The resulting variable is called a *contextual* variable, because it refers to the higher-level context of the units we are investigating.

In order to analyze multilevel models, it is not important to assign each variable to its proper place in the scheme given above. The benefit of the scheme is conceptual; it makes clear to which level a measurement properly belongs. Historically, multilevel problems led to analysis approaches that moved all variables by aggregation or disaggregation to one single level of interest followed by an ordinary multiple regression, analysis of variance, or some other 'standard' analysis method. However, analyzing variables from different levels at one single common level is inadequate, because it leads to two distinct problems.

The first problem is statistical. If data are aggregated, the result is that different data values from many sub-units are combined into fewer values for fewer higher-level units. As a result, much information is lost, and the statistical analysis loses power. On the other hand, if data are disaggregated, the result is that a few data values from a small number of super-units are 'blown up' into many more values for a much larger number of sub-units. Ordinary statistical tests treat all these disaggregated data values as independent information from the much larger sample of sub-units. The proper sample size for these variables is of course the number of higher-level units. Using the larger number of disaggregated cases for the sample size leads to significance tests that reject the null-hypothesis far more often than the nominal alpha level suggests. In other words: investigators come up with many 'significant' results that are totally spurious.

The second problem encountered is conceptual. If the analyst is not very careful in the interpretation of the results, s/he may commit the fallacy of the wrong level, which consists of analyzing the data at one level, and formulating conclusions at another level. Probably the best-known fallacy is the *ecological fallacy*, which is interpreting aggregated data at the individual level. It is also know as the 'Robinson effect' after Robinson (1950). Robinson presents aggregated data describing the relationship between the percentage of blacks and the illiteracy level in nine geographic regions in 1930. The *ecological correlation*, that is, the correlation between the aggregated variables at the region level is 0.95. In contrast, the individual-level correlation between these global variables is 0.20. Robinson concludes that in practice an ecological correlation is almost certainly not equal to its corresponding individual-level correlation. For a statistical explanation why this happens, see Robinson (1950) or Kreft and de Leeuw (1987). This problem occurs also the other way around. Formulating inferences at a higher level based on analyses performed at a lower level is just as misleading. This fallacy is known as the *atomistic fallacy*. A related but different fallacy is known as 'Simpson's Paradox' (see Lindley & Novick, 1981). Simpson's paradox refers to the problem that completely erroneous conclusions may be drawn if grouped data, drawn from heterogeneous populations, are collapsed and analyzed as if they came from a single homogeneous population. An extensive typology of such fallacies is given by Alker (1969). When aggregated data are the only available data, King (1997) presents some procedures that make it possible to estimate the corresponding individual relationships without committing the ecological fallacy.

A more general way to look at multilevel data is to realize that there is not one 'proper' level at which the data should be analyzed. Rather, all levels present in the data are important in their own way. This becomes clear when we investigate cross-level hypotheses, or *multilevel* problems. A multilevel problem is a problem that concerns the relationships between variables that are measured at a number of different hierarchical levels. For example, a common question is how a number of individual and group variables influence one single individual outcome variable. Typically, some of the higher-level explanatory variables may be the aggregated group means of lower-level individual variables. The goal of the analysis is to determine the direct effect of individual and group level explanatory variables, and to determine if the explanatory variables at the group level serve as moderators of individual-level relationships. If group level variables moderate lower-level relationships, this shows up as a statistical interaction between explanatory variables from different levels. In the past, such data were usually analyzed using conventional multiple regression analysis with one dependent variable at the lowest (individual) level and a collection of explanatory variables from all available levels (cf. Boyd & Iversen, 1979; Roberts & Burstein, 1980; van den Eeden & Hüttner, 1982). Since this approach analyzes all available data at one single level, it suffers from all of the conceptual and statistical problems mentioned above. Much research has been directed at developing more appropriate analysis methods for this hierarchical regression model, and at clarifying the associated conceptual and statistical issues.

1.1. WHY DO WE NEED SPECIAL MULTILEVEL ANALYSIS TECHNIQUES?

A multilevel problem concerns a population with a hierarchical structure. A sample from such a population can be described as a multistage sample: first, we take a sample of units from the higher level (e.g., schools), and next we sample the sub-units from the available units (e.g., we sample pupils from the schools). In such samples, the individual observations are in general not completely independent. For instance, pupils in the same school tend to be similar to each other, because of selection processes (for instance, some schools may attract pupils from higher social economic status (SES) levels, while others attract more lower SES pupils) and because of the common history the pupils share by going to the same school. As a result, the average correlation (expressed in the so-called *intraclass correlation*) between variables measured on pupils from the same school will be higher than the average correlation between variables measured on pupils from different schools. Standard statistical tests lean heavily on the assumption of independence of the observations. If this assumption is violated (and in multilevel data this is almost always the case) the estimates of the standard errors of conventional statistical tests are much too small, and this results in many spuriously 'significant' results.

The problem of dependencies between individual observations also occurs in survey research, if the sample is not taken at random but cluster sampling from geographical areas is used instead. For similar reasons as in the school example given above, respondents from the same geographical area will be more similar to each other than respondents from different geographical areas are. This leads again to estimates for standard errors that are too small and produce spurious 'significant' results. In survey research, this effect of cluster sampling is well known (cf. Kish, 1965, 1987). It is called a 'design effect', and various methods are used to deal with it. A convenient correction procedure is to compute the standard errors by ordinary analysis methods, estimate the intraclass correlation between respondents within clusters, and finally employ a correction formula to the standard errors. A correction described by Kish (1965: p. 259) corrects the standard error using $s.e._{eff} = s.e.\left(1+\left(n_{clus}-1\right)\rho\right)$, where $s.e._{eff}$ is the effective standard error, n_{clus} is the cluster size, and ρ is the intraclass correlation. The formula assumes equal group sizes, which is not always realistic. A variation of this formula computes the effective sample size in two-stage cluster sampling as $n_{eff} = n/\left[1+\left(n_{clus}-1\right)\rho\right]$, where n is the total sample size and n_{eff} is the effective sample size. Using this formula, we can simply calculate the effective sample size for different situations.[1] For instance, suppose that we take a sample of 10 classes,

---

[1] The formulas given here apply to two-stage cluster sampling. Other sampling schemes, such as stratified sampling, require different formulas. See Kish (1965, 1987) for details. The symbol ρ (the Greek letter rho) was introduced by Kish (1965, p. 161) who called it *roh* for 'rate of homogeneity'.

each with 20 pupils. This comes to a total sample size of 200, which is reasonable. Let us further suppose that we are interested in a variable, for which the intraclass correlation ρ is 0.10. This seems a rather low intraclass correlation. However, the effective sample size in this situation is $200/[1+(20-1)0.1]= 69.0$, which is much less than the apparent total sample size of 200! Gulliford, Ukoumunne and Chin (1999) give an overview of estimates of the intraclass correlation to aid in the design of complex health surveys. Their data include variables on a range of lifestyle risk factors and health outcomes, for respondents clustered at the household, postal code, and health authority district levels. They report between-cluster variation at each of these levels, with intraclass correlations ranging from 0.0-0.3 at the household level, and being mostly smaller than 0.05 at the postal code level, and below 0.01 at the district level. Since the design effect depends on both the intraclass correlation and the cluster sample size, the large household intraclass correlations are partly compensated by the small household sizes. Conversely, the small intraclass correlations at the higher levels are offset by the usually large cluster sizes at these levels. Groves (1989) also discusses the effects of cluster sampling on the standard errors, and concludes that the intraclass correlation is usually small, but in combination with the usual cluster size still can lead to substantial design effects.

Some of the correction procedures developed for cluster and other complex samples are quite powerful (cf. Skinner, Holt & Smith, 1989). Actually, in principle these correction procedures could also be applied in analyzing multilevel data, by adjusting the standard errors of the statistical tests. However, in general the intraclass correlation and hence the effective N is different for different variables. In addition, in most multilevel problems we have not only clustering of individuals within groups, but we also have variables measured at all available levels. Combining variables from different levels in one statistical model is a different and more complicated problem than estimating and correcting for design effects. Multilevel models are designed to analyze variables from different levels simultaneously, using a statistical model that properly includes the various dependencies.

For example, an explicitly multilevel or contextual theory in education is the so-called 'frog pond' theory, which refers to the idea that a specific individual frog may either be a small frog in a pond otherwise filled with large frogs, or a large frog in a pond otherwise filled with small frogs. Applied to education, this metaphor points out that the effect of an explanatory variable such as 'intelligence' on school career may depend on the average intelligence of the other pupils in the school. A moderately intelligent pupil in a highly intelligent context may become demotivated and thus become an underachiever, while the same pupil in a considerably less intelligent context may gain confidence and become an overachiever. Thus, the effect of an individual pupil's intelligence depends on the average intelligence of the other pupils. A popular approach in educational research to investigate 'frog pond' effects has been to aggregate variables like the pupils' IQ into group means, and then to disaggregate these group means again to the individual level. As a result, the data file contains both individual level (global) variables and higher-level (contextual) variables in the form of disaggregated group means. Cronbach (1976; cf. Cronbach & Webb, 1979) has suggested to express the individual scores as deviations from their respective group means, a procedure that has become known as *centering on the group mean*, or *group mean centering*. Centering on the group means makes very explicit that the individual scores should be interpreted relative to their group's mean. The example of the 'frog pond' theory and the corresponding practice of centering the predictor variables makes clear that combining and analyzing information from different levels within one statistical model is central to multilevel modeling.

1.2. MULTILEVEL THEORIES

Multilevel problems must be explained by multilevel theories, an area that seems underdeveloped compared to the advances made in the recently developed modeling and computing machinery (cf. Hüttner & van den Eeden, 1993). If there are effects of the social context on individuals, these effects must be mediated by intervening processes that depend on characteristics of the social context. Multilevel models so far require that the grouping criterion is clear, and that variables can be assigned unequivocally to their appropriate level. In reality, group boundaries are sometimes fuzzy and somewhat arbitrary, and the assignment of variables is not always obvious and simple. In multilevel problems, decisions about group membership and operationalizations involve a wide range of theoretical assumptions, and an equally wide range of specification problems for the auxiliary theory (Blalock, 1990). When the number of variables at the different levels is large, there is an enormous number of possible cross-level interactions. Ideally, a multilevel theory should specify which variables belong to which level, and which direct effects and cross-level interaction effects can be expected. Cross-level interaction effects between the individual and the context level require the specification of processes within individuals that cause those individuals to be differentially influenced by certain aspects of the context. Attempts to identify such processes have been made by, among others, Stinchcombe (1968), Erbring and Young (1979), and Chan (1998). The common core in these theories is that they all postulate one or more psychological processes that mediate between individual variables and group variables. Since a global explanation by 'group telepathy' is generally not acceptable, communication processes and the internal structure of groups become important concepts. These are often measured as a 'structural variable'. In spite of their theoretical relevance, structural variables are infrequently used in multilevel research. Another theoretical area that has been largely neglected by multilevel researchers is the influence of individuals on the group. This is already visible in Durkheim's concept of sociology as a science that focuses primarily on the constraints that a society can put on its members, and disregards the influence of individuals on their society. In multilevel modeling, the focus is on models where the outcome variable is at the lowest level. Models that investigate the influence of individual variables on group outcomes are scarce. For a review of this issue see DiPrete and Forristal (1994), an example is discussed by Alba and Logan (1992).

1.3. MODELS DESCRIBED IN THIS BOOK

This book treats two classes of multilevel models: multilevel regression models, and multilevel models for covariance structures.

Multilevel regression models are essentially a multilevel version of the familiar multiple regression model. As Cohen and Cohen (1983), Pedhazur (1997) and others have shown, the multiple regression model is very versatile. Using dummy coding for categorical variables, it can be used to analyze analysis of variance (ANOVA)-type of models as well as the more usual multiple regression models. Since the multilevel regression model is an extension of the classical multiple regression model, it too can be used in a wide variety of research problems. It has been used extensively in educational research (cf. the special issues of the *International Journal of Educational Research*, 1990 and the *Journal of Educational and Behavioral Statistics* in 1995). Other applications have been in the analysis of longitudinal and growth data (cf. Bryk & Raudenbush, 1987; Goldstein, 1989; DiPrete & Grusky, 1990; Goldstein, Healy & Rasbash, 1994), the analysis of interview survey data (Hox, de Leeuw & Kreft, 1991; Hox, 1994a; O'Muirchartaigh & Campanelli, 1999; Pickery & Loosveldt, 1998), data from surveys with complex sampling schemes with respondents nested within sampling units (Goldstein & Silver, 1989; Snijders, 2001), and data from factorial surveys and facet designs (Hox, Kreft & Hermkens, 1991; Hox & Lagerweij, 1993). Raudenbush and Bryk have introduced multilevel regression models in meta-analysis (cf. Raudenbush & Bryk, 1985, 1987; Hox & de Leeuw, 1994; Raudenbush, 1994). Multilevel regression models for binary and other non-normal data have been described by Wong and Mason (1985), Longford (1988), Mislevy and Bock (1989) and Goldstein (1991).

Chapter Two of this book contains a basic introduction to the multilevel regression model, also known as the hierarchical linear model, or the random coefficient model. Chapters Three and Four discuss estimation procedures, and a number of important methodological and statistical issues. It also discusses some technical issues that are not specific to multilevel regression analysis, such as coding categorical explanatory variables and interpreting interactions.

Chapter Five introduces the multilevel regression model for longitudinal data. The model is a straightforward extension of the standard multilevel regression model, but there are some specific complications, such as autocorrelated errors, which will be discussed.

Chapter Six treats the logistic model for dichotomous data and proportions. When the response (dependent) variable is dichotomous or a proportion, standard regression models should not be used. This chapter discusses the multilevel version of the logistic regression model.

Chapter Seven discusses cross-classified models. Some data are multilevel in nature, but do not have a neat hierarchical structure. Examples are longitudinal school research data, where pupils are nested within schools, but may switch to a different school in later measurements, and sociometric choice data. Multilevel models for such cross-classified data can be formulated, and estimated with standard software provided that it can handle restrictions on estimated parameters.

Chapter Eight describes a variant of the multilevel regression model that can be used in meta-analysis. It resembles the weighted regression model often recommended for meta-analysis. Using standard regression procedures, it is a flexible analysis tool.

Chapter Nine discusses multilevel regression models for multivariate outcomes. These can also be used to estimate models that resemble confirmative factor analysis, and to assess the reliability of multilevel measurements. A different approach to multilevel confirmative factor analysis is treated in chapter Eleven.

Chapter Ten deals with the sample size needed for multilevel modeling, and the problem of estimating the power of an analysis given a specific sample size. An obvious complication in multilevel power analysis is that there are different sample sizes at the distinct levels, which should be taken into account.

Chapter Eleven treats some advanced methods of estimation and assessing significance. It discusses the profile likelihood method, robust standard errors for establishing confidence intervals, and multilevel bootstrap methods for estimating bias-corrected point-estimates and confidence intervals. This chapter also contains an introduction into Bayesian (MCMC) methods for estimation and inference.

Multilevel models for covariance structures, or multilevel structural equation models (SEM), are a powerful tool for the analysis of multilevel data. Much fundamental work has been done on multilevel factor and path analysis (cf. Goldstein & McDonald, 1988; Muthén, 1989, 1990; McDonald & Goldstein, 1989). There is also a growing number of applications, for instance Härnqvist, Gustafsson, Muthén, and Nelson (1994), and Hox (1993). These applications require only conventional software for structural equation modeling (e.g., Amos, Eqs, Lisrel) with unusual setups.

Specialized software to analyze multilevel structural equation models is available as well (M*plus*, Muthén & Muthén, 1998). The general statistical model for multilevel covariance structure analysis is quite complicated. Chapter Twelve in this book describes a simplified statistical model proposed by Muthén (1990, 1994), and explains how multilevel confirmatory factor models can be estimated with either conventional SEM software or using specialized programs like M*plus*. It also describes a direct estimation approach, and deals with issues of calculating standardized coefficients and goodness-of-fit indices in multilevel structural models. Chapter Thirteen extends this to path models. Chapter Fourteen describes structural models for latent curve analysis. This is a SEM approach to analyzing longitudinal data, which is very similar to the multilevel regression models treated in Chapter Five.

This book is intended as an introduction to the world of multilevel analysis. Most of the chapters on multilevel regression analysis should be readable for social scientists who have a good general knowledge of analysis of variance and classical multiple regression analysis. Some of these chapters contain material that is more difficult, but this is generally a discussion of specialized problems, which can be skipped at first reading. An example is the chapter on longitudinal models, which contains a prolonged discussion of techniques to model specific structures for the covariances between adjacent time points. This discussion is not needed to understand the essentials of multilevel analysis of longitudinal data, but it may become important when one is actually analyzing such data. The chapters on multilevel structure equation modeling obviously require a strong background in multivariate statistics and some background in structural equation modeling, equivalent to, for example, the material covered in Tabachnick and Fidell's (1996) book. Conversely, in addition to an adequate background in structural equation modeling, the chapters on multilevel structural equation modeling do not require knowledge of advanced mathematical statistics. In all these cases, I have tried to keep the discussion of the more advanced statistical techniques theoretically sound, but non-technical.

Many of the techniques and their specific software implementations discussed in this book are the subject of active statistical and methodological research. In other words: both the statistical techniques and the software tools are evolving rapidly. As a result, increasing numbers of researchers will apply increasingly advanced models to their data. Of course, researchers still need to understand the models and techniques that they use. Therefore, in addition to being an introduction to multilevel analysis, this book aims to let the reader become acquainted with some advanced modeling techniques that might be used, such as bootstrapping and Bayesian estimation methods. At the time of writing, these are specialist tools, and certainly not part of the standard analysis toolkit. But they are developing rapidly, and are likely to become more popular in applied research as well.

2

The Basic Two-Level Regression Model: Introduction

The multilevel regression model has become known in the research literature under a variety of names, such as 'random coefficient model' (de Leeuw & Kreft, 1986; Longford, 1993), 'variance component model' (Longford, 1987), and 'hierarchical linear model' (Raudenbush & Bryk, 1986, 1988). Statically oriented publications tend to refer to this model as a mixed-effects or mixed model (Littell, Milliken, Stroup & Wolfinger, 1996). The models described in these publications are not *exactly* the same, but they are highly similar, and I will refer to them collectively as 'multilevel regression models'. They all assume that there is a hierarchical data set, with one single outcome or response variable that is measured at the lowest level, and explanatory variables at all existing levels. Conceptually, it is useful to view the multilevel regression model as a hierarchical system of regression equations. In this chapter, I will explain the multilevel regression model for two-level data. Regression models with more than two levels are used in later chapters.

2.1   EXAMPLE

Assume that we have data from J classes, with a different number of pupils n_j in each class. On the pupil level, we have the outcome variable 'popularity' (Y), measured by a self-rating scale that ranges from 0 (very unpopular) to 10 (very popular). We have one explanatory variable *gender* (X: 0=boy, 1=girl) on the pupil level, and one class level explanatory variable *teacher experience* (Z: in years). We have data from 2000 pupils from 100 classes, so the average class size is 20 pupils. The data are described in the Appendix.

To analyze these data, we can set up separate regression equations in each class to predict the outcome variable Y by the explanatory variable X as follows:

$$Y_{ij} = \beta_{0j} + \beta_{1j}X_{ij} + e_{ij} \tag{2.1}$$

Using variable labels instead of algebraic symbols, the equation reads:

$$popularity_{ij} = \beta_{0j} + \beta_{1j}gender_{ij} + e_{ij} \qquad\qquad (2.2)$$

In this regression equation, β_{0j} is the usual intercept, β_{1j} is the usual regression coefficient (regression slope) for the explanatory variable gender, and e_{ij} is the usual residual error term. The subscript j is for the classes (j=1...J) and the subscript i is for individual pupils (i=1...n_j). The difference with the usual regression model is that we assume that each class has a different intercept coefficient β_{0j}, and a different slope coefficient β_{1j}. This is indicated in equations (2.1) and (2.2) by attaching a subscript j to the regression coefficients. The residual errors e_{ij} are assumed to have a mean of zero, and a variance to be estimated. Most multilevel software assumes that the variance of the residual errors is the same in all classes. Different authors (cf. Bryk & Raudenbush, 1992; Goldstein, 1995) use different systems of notation. This book uses σ_e^2 to denote the variance of the lowest level residual errors.[1]

Since the intercept and slope coefficients are assumed to vary across the classes, they are often referred to as *random* coefficients.[2] In our example, the specific value for the intercept and the slope coefficient for the pupil variable 'gender' are a class characteristic. In general, a class with a high intercept is predicted to have more popular pupils than a class with a low value for the intercept. Similarly, differences in the slope coefficient for gender indicate that the relationship between the pupils' gender and their predicted popularity is not the same in all classes. Some classes have a high value for the slope coefficient of gender; in these classes, the difference between boys and girls is relatively large. Other classes have a low value for the slope coefficient of gender; in these classes, gender has a small effect on the popularity, which means that the difference between boys and girls is small.

Across all classes, the regression coefficients β_j have a distribution with some mean and variance. The next step in the hierarchical regression model is to explain the variation of the regression coefficients β_{0j} and β_{1j} by introducing explanatory variables at the class level, as follows:

$$\beta_{0j} = \gamma_{00} + \gamma_{01}Z_j + u_{0j} \qquad\qquad (2.3)$$

---

[1] At the end of this chapter, a section explains the difference between some commonly used notation systems. Models that are more complicated sometimes need a more complicated notation system, which is introduced in the relevant chapters.

[2] Of course, we hope to be able to explain at least some of the variation by introducing higher-level variables. Generally, we will not be able to explain all the variation, and there will be some unexplained residual variation. Hence the name 'random coefficient model': the regression coefficients (intercept and slopes) have some amount of (residual) random variation between groups. The name 'variance component model' refers to the statistical problem of estimating the amount of random variation.

and

$$\beta_{1j} = \gamma_{10} + \gamma_{11}Z_j + u_{1j} \tag{2.4}$$

Equation (2.3) predicts the average popularity in a class (the intercept β_{0j}) by the teacher's experience (Z). Thus, if γ_{01} is positive, the average popularity is higher in classes with a more experienced teacher. Conversely, if γ_{01} is negative, the average popularity is lower in classes with a more experienced teacher. The interpretation of equation (2.4) is a bit more complicated. Equation (2.4) states that the *relationship*, as expressed by the slope coefficient β_{1j}, between the popularity (Y) and the gender (X) of the pupil, depends upon the amount of experience of the teacher (Z). If γ_{11} is positive, the gender effect on popularity is larger with experienced teachers. Conversely, if γ_{11} is negative, the gender effect on popularity is smaller with experienced teachers. Thus, the amount of experience of the teacher acts as a *moderator variable* for the relationship between popularity and gender; this relationship varies according to the value of the moderator variable.

The u-terms u_{0j} and u_{1j} in equations (2.3) and (2.4) are (random) residual error terms at the class level. These residual errors u_j are assumed to have a mean of zero, and to be independent from the residual errors e_{ij} at the individual (pupil) level. The variance of the residual errors u_{0j} is specified as $\sigma_{u_0}^2$, and the variance of the residual errors u_{1j} is specified as $\sigma_{u_1}^2$. The *covariance* between the residual error terms u_{0j} and u_{1j} is $\sigma_{u_{01}}$, which is generally *not* assumed to be zero.

Note that in equations (2.3) and (2.4) the regression coefficients γ are not assumed to vary across classes. They therefore have no subscript j to indicate to which class they belong. Because they apply to *all* classes, they are referred to as *fixed* coefficients. All between-class variation left in the β coefficients, after predicting these with the class variable Z_j, is assumed to be residual error variation. This is captured by the residual error terms u_j, which do have subscripts j to indicate to which class they belong.

Our model with one pupil level and one class level explanatory variable can be written as a single complex regression equation by substituting equations (2.3) and (2.4) into equation (2.1). Rearranging terms gives:

$$Y_{ij} = \gamma_{00} + \gamma_{10}X_{ij} + \gamma_{01}Z_j + \gamma_{11}X_{ij}Z_j + u_{1j}X_{ij} + u_{0j} + e_{ij} \tag{2.5}$$

Using variable labels instead of algebraic symbols, we have

$$popularity_{ij} = \gamma_{00} + \gamma_{10}\ gender_{ij} + \gamma_{01}\ experience_j + \gamma_{11}\ experience_j \times gender_{ij}$$
$$+ u_{1j}\ gender_{ij} + u_{0j} + e_{ij}$$

The segment $[\gamma_{00} + \gamma_{10} X_{ij} + \gamma_{01} Z_j + \gamma_{11} Z_j X_{ij}]$ in equation (2.5) contains the fixed coefficients. It is often called the fixed (or deterministic) part of the model. The segment $[u_{0j} + u_{1j} X_{ij} + e_{ij}]$ in equation (2.5) contains the random error terms, and it is often called the random (or stochastic) part of the model. The term $Z_j X_{ij}$ is an interaction term that appears in the model as a consequence of modeling the varying regression slope β_{1j} of pupil level variable X_{ij} with the class level variable Z_j. Thus, the moderator effect of Z on the relationship between the dependent variable Y and the predictor X, is expressed in the single equation version of the model as a *cross-level interaction*. The interpretation of interaction terms in multiple regression analysis is complex, and this is treated in more detail in Chapter Three. In general, the point made in Chapter Three is that the substantive interpretation of the coefficients in models with interactions is much simpler if the variables making up the interaction are expressed as deviations from their respective means.

Note that the random error term u_{1j} is connected to X_{ij}. Since the explanatory variable X_{ij} and the error term u_{1j} are multiplied, the resulting total error will be different for different values of X_{ij}, a situation that in ordinary multiple regression analysis is called 'heteroscedasticity'. The usual multiple regression model assumes 'homoscedasticity', which means that the variance of the residual errors is independent of the values of the explanatory variables. If this assumption is not true, ordinary multiple regression does not work very well. This is another reason why analyzing multilevel data with ordinary multiple regression techniques does not work well.

As explained in the introduction in Chapter One, multilevel models are needed because with grouped data observations from the same group are generally more similar than the observations from different groups, which violates the assumption of independence of all observations. The amount of dependence can be expressed as a correlation coefficient: the intraclass correlation. The methodological literature contains a number of different formulas to estimate the intraclass correlation ρ. For example, if we use one-way analysis of variance with the grouping variable as independent variable to test the group effect on our outcome variable, the intraclass correlation is given by $\rho = [\text{MS}(A) - \text{MS}(error)]/[\text{MS}(A) + (n-1) \times \text{MS}(error)]$, where n is the common group size. Shrout and Fleiss (1979) give an overview of formulas for the intraclass correlation for a variety of research designs.

If we have simple hierarchical data, the multilevel regression model can also be used to produce an estimate of the intraclass correlation. The model used for this purpose is a model that contains no explanatory variables at all, the so-called *intercept-only* model. The intercept-only model is derived from equations (2.1) and (2.3) as follows. If there are no explanatory variables X at the lowest level, equation (2.1) reduces to

$$Y_{ij} = \beta_{0j} + e_{ij} \tag{2.6}$$

Likewise, if there are no explanatory variables Z at the highest level, equation (2.2) reduces to

$$\beta_{0j} = \gamma_{00} + u_{0j} \tag{2.7}$$

We find the single equation model by substituting (2.7) into (2.6):

$$Y_{ij} = \gamma_{00} + u_{0j} + e_{ij} \tag{2.8}$$

We could also have found equation (2.8) by removing all terms that contain an X or Z variable equation (2.5). The intercept-only model of equation (2.8) does not explain any variance in Y. It only decomposes the variance into two independent components: σ_e^2, which is the variance of the lowest-level errors e_{ij}, and σ_{u0}^2, which is the variance of the highest-level errors u_{0j}. Using this model, we can define the intraclass correlation ρ by the equation

$$\rho = \frac{\sigma_{u_0}^2}{\sigma_{u_0}^2 + \sigma_e^2} \tag{2.9}$$

The intraclass correlation ρ indicates the proportion of the variance explained by the grouping structure in the population. Equation (2.9) simply states that the intraclass correlation is the proportion of group level variance compared to the total variance.[1] The intraclass correlation ρ can also be interpreted as the expected correlation between two randomly chosen units that are in the same group.

2.2   AN EXTENDED EXAMPLE

Ordinary multiple regression analysis uses an estimation technique called Ordinary Least Squares, abbreviated as OLS. The statistical theory behind the multilevel regression model is more complex, however. Based on observed data, we want to estimate the parameters of the multilevel regression model: the regression coefficients and the variance components. The usual estimators in multilevel regression analysis are Maximum Likelihood (ML) estimators. Maximum Likelihood estimators estimate the

---

[1] Note that the intraclass correlation is an estimate of the proportion of explained variance *in the population*. The proportion of explained variance in the *sample* is given by the correlation ratio η^2 (eta-squared, cf. Tabachnick & Fidell, 1996, p. 335): η^2=SS(A)/SS(Total).

parameters of a model by providing estimated values for the population parameters that maximize the so-called Likelihood Function: the function that describes the probability of observing the sample data, given the specific values of the parameter estimates. Simply put, ML estimates are those parameter estimates that maximize the probability of finding the sample data that we have actually found. For an accessible introduction to maximum likelihood methods see Eliason (1993).

Maximum Likelihood estimation includes procedures to generate standard errors for most of the parameter estimates. These can be used in significance testing, by computing the test statistic Z: $Z=parameter/(st.error\ param.)$. This statistic is referred to the standard normal distribution, to establish a p-value for the null-hypothesis that the population value of that parameter is zero. The Maximum Likelihood procedure also produces a statistic called the *deviance*, which indicates how well the model fits the data. In general, models with a lower deviance fit better than models with a higher deviance. If two models are *nested*, meaning that a specific model can be derived from a more general model by removing parameters from that general model, the deviances of the two models can be used to compare their fit statistically. For nested models, the difference in deviance has a chi-square distribution with degrees of freedom equal to the difference in the number of parameters that are estimated in the two models. The deviance test can be used to perform a formal chi-square test, in order to test whether the more general model fits significantly better than the simpler model. The chi-square test of the deviances can also be used to good effect to explore the importance of a set of random effects, by comparing a model that contains these effects against a model that excludes them. If the models to be compared are not nested models, the principle that models should be as simple as possible (theories and models should be parsimonious) indicates that we should generally keep the simpler model.

The intercept-only model is useful as a null-model that serves as a benchmark with which other models are compared. For our example data, the intercept-only model is written as

$$Y_{ij} = \gamma_{00} + u_{0j} + e_{ij}$$

The model that includes pupil gender and teacher experience, but not the cross-level interaction between those two, is written as

$$Y_{ij} = \gamma_{00} + \gamma_{10} X_{ij} + \gamma_{01} Z_j + u_{1j} X_{ij} + u_{0j} + e_{ij}$$

or, using variable names instead of algebraic symbols,

$$popularity_{ij} = \gamma_{00} + \gamma_{10}\ gender_{ij} + \gamma_{01}\ experience_j + u_{1j}\ gender_{ij} + u_{0j} + e_{ij}$$

Table 2.1 Intercept-only and model with pupil gender and teacher experience				
Model:	M0: intercept-only		M1: + pup. gender and t. exp.	
Fixed part				
Predictor	coefficient	standard error	coefficient	standard error
intercept	5.31	0.10	3.34	0.16
pupil gender			0.84	0.06
teacher exp.			0.11	0.01
Random part				
σ^2_e	0.64	0.02	0.39	0.01
σ^2_{u0}	0.87	0.13	0.40	0.06
σ^2_{u1}			0.27	0.05
σ_{u01}			0.02	0.04
Deviance	5112.7		4261.2	

Table 2.1 presents the parameter estimates and standard errors for both models.[1] In this table, the intercept-only model estimates the intercept as 5.31, which is simply the average popularity across all schools and pupils. The variance of the pupil level residual errors, symbolized by σ^2_e, is estimated as 0.64. The variance of the class level residual errors, symbolized by σ^2_{u0}, is estimated as 0.87. All parameter estimates are much larger than the corresponding standard errors, and calculation of the Z-test shows that they are all significant at $p < 0.005$. The intraclass correlation, calculated by equation (2.9) $\rho = \sigma^2_{u0}/(\sigma^2_{u0} + \sigma^2_e)$, is 0.87/1.52, which equals 0.58. Thus, 58% of the variance of the popularity scores is at the group level, which is very high. Since the intercept-only model contains no explanatory variables, the residual variances represent unexplained error variance. The deviance reported in Table 2.1 is a measure of model misfit; when we add explanatory variables to the model, the deviance is expected to go down.

The second model includes pupil gender and teacher experience as explanatory variables. The regression coefficients for both variables are significant. The regression coefficient for pupil gender is 0.84. Since pupil gender is coded 0=boy, 1=girl, this means that on average the girls score 0.84 points higher on the popularity measure. The regression coefficient for teacher experience is 0.11, which means that for each year of experience of the teacher, the average popularity score of the class goes up with 0.11 points. This does not seem very much, but the teacher experience in our example data ranges from 2 to 25 years, so the predicted difference between the least experienced and

---

[1] For reasons to be explained later, different options that can be chosen for the details of the Maximum Likelihood procedure may result in slightly different estimates. So, if you re-analyze the example data from this book, your results may differ slightly from the results given here. However, these differences should never be so large that you would draw entirely different conclusions.

the most experienced teacher is (25-2=) 23×0.11=2.53 points on the popularity measure. We can use the standard errors of the regression coefficients reported in Table 2.1 to construct a 95% confidence interval. For the regression coefficient of pupil gender, the 95% confidence interval runs from 0.72 to 0.96, and the 95% confidence interval for the regression coefficient of teacher experience runs from 0.09 to 0.13.

The model with the explanatory variables includes a variance component for the regression coefficient of pupil gender, symbolized by σ_{u1}^2 in Table 2.1. The variance of the regression coefficients for pupil gender across classes is estimated as 0.27, with a standard error of 0.05. The covariance between the regression coefficient for pupil gender and the intercept is very small and obviously not significant.

The significant and quite large variance of the regression slopes for pupil gender implies that we should not interpret the estimated value of 0.84 without considering this variation. In an ordinary regression model, without multilevel structure, the value of 0.84 means that girls are expected to differ from boys by 0.84 points, for all pupils in all classes. In our multilevel model, the regression coefficient for pupil gender varies across the classes, and the value of 0.84 is just the expected value across all classes. In multilevel regression analysis, the varying regression coefficients are assumed to follow a normal distribution. The variance of this distribution is in our example estimated as 0.27. Interpretation of this variation is easier when we consider the standard deviation, which is the square root of the variance or 0.52 in our example data. A useful characteristic of the standard deviation is that with normally distributed observations about 67% of the observations lie between one standard deviation below and above the mean, and about 95% of the observations lie between two standard deviations below and above the mean. If we apply this to the regression coefficients for pupil gender, we conclude that about 67% of the regression coefficients are expected to lie between (0.84-0.52=) 0.32 and (0.84+0.52=) 1.36, and about 95% are expected to lie between (0.84-1.04=) –0.20 and (0.84+1.04=) 1.88. Using the more precise value of $Z_{.975}$=1.96 we calculate the limits of the 95% interval as –0.18 and 1.86. We can also use the standard normal distribution to estimate the percentage of regression coefficients that are negative. As it turns out, even if the mean regression coefficient for pupil gender is 0.84, about 5% of the classes are expected to have a regression coefficient that is actually negative. Note that the 95% interval computed here is totally different from the 95% confidence interval for the regression coefficient of pupil gender, which runs from 0.72 to 0.96. The 95% confidence interval applies to γ_{10}, the mean value of the regression coefficients across the classes. The 95% interval calculated here is the 95% *predictive interval*, which expresses that 95% of the regression coefficients of the variable 'pupil gender' in the classes are predicted to lie between –0.20 and 1.88.

Given the large and significant variance of the regression coefficient of pupil gender across the classes it is attractive to attempt to predict its variation using class level variables. We have one class level variable: teacher experience. The individual level regression equation for this example, using variable labels instead of symbols, is given by equation (2.2), which is repeated below:

$$popularity_{ij} = \beta_{0j} + \beta_{1j} \, gender_{ij} + e_{ij} \qquad \text{(2.2, repeated)}$$

The regression equations predicting β_{0j}, the intercept in class j, and β_{1j}, the regression slope of pupil gender in class j, are given by equation (2.3) and (2.4), which are rewritten below using variable labels

$$\beta_{0j} = \gamma_{00} + \gamma_{01} \, t.exp_j + u_{0j} \qquad (2.10)$$

$$\beta_{1j} = \gamma_{10} + \gamma_{11} \, t.exp_j + u_{1j} \qquad (2.11)$$

By substituting (2.10) and (2.11) into (2.2) we get

$$popularity_{ij} = \gamma_{00} + \gamma_{10} \, gender_{ij} + \gamma_{01} \, t.exp_j + \gamma_{11} \, gender_{ij} \times t.exp_j$$
$$+ u_{1j} \, gender_{ij} + u_{0j} + e_{ij} \qquad (2.12)$$

The algebraic manipulations of the equations above make clear that to explain the variance of the regression coefficients β_{1j}, we need to introduce an interaction term in the model. This interaction, between the variables pupil gender and teacher experience, is a cross-level interaction, because it involves explanatory variables from different levels. Table 2.2 presents the estimates from a model with this cross-level interaction. For comparison, the estimates for the model without this interaction are also included in Table 2.2.

The estimates for the fixed coefficients in Table 2.2 are similar for both models, except the regression slope for pupil gender, which is considerably larger in the cross-level model. The interpretation remains the same: girls are more popular than boys are. The regression coefficient for the cross-level interaction is –0.03, which is small but significant. This interaction is formed by multiplying the scores for the variables 'pupil gender' and 'teacher experience,' and the negative value means that with experienced teachers, the advantage of being a girl is smaller than expected from the direct effects only. Thus, the difference between boys and girls is smaller with more experienced teachers.

Table 2.2 Results pupil gender and teacher experience, cross-level interaction				
Model:	M1: + pup. gender and t. exp.		M2: + cross-level interaction	
Fixed part				
Predictor	coefficient	standard error	coefficient	standard error
intercept	3.34	0.16	3.31	0.16
pupil gender	0.84	0.06	1.33	0.13
teacher exp.	0.11	0.01	0.11	0.01
pup. gender ×				
teacher exp.			-.03	0.01
Random part				
σ^2_e	0.39	0.01	0.39	0.01
σ^2_{u0}	0.40	0.06	0.40	0.06
σ^2_{u1}	0.27	0.05	0.22	0.04
σ_{u01}	0.02	0.04	0.02	0.04
Deviance	4261.2		4245.9	

Comparison of the other results between the two models shows that the variance component for pupil gender goes down from 0.27 in the direct effects model to 0.22 in the cross-level model. Apparently, the cross-level model explains some of the variation of the slopes for pupil gender. The deviance also goes down, which indicates that the model fits better than the previous model.

The coefficients in Tables 2.1 and 2.2 are all unstandardized regression coefficients. To interpret them properly, we must take the scale of the explanatory variables into account. In multiple regression analysis, and structural equation models, for that matter, the regression coefficients are often standardized because that facilitates the interpretation when one wants to compare the effects of different variables within one sample. Only if the goal of the analysis is to compare parameter estimates from different samples to each other, should one always use unstandardized coefficients. To standardize the regression coefficients, as presented in Table 2.1 or Table 2.2, one could standardize all variables before putting them into the multilevel analysis. However, this would in general also change the estimates of the variance components. This may not be a bad thing in itself, because standardized variables are also centered on their overall mean. Centering explanatory variables has some distinct advantages, which are discussed in Chapter Four. Even so, it is also possible to derive the standardized regression coefficients from the unstandardized coefficients:

$$\text{Standardized coefficient} = \frac{(\text{unstandardized coeff.}) \times (\text{stand. dev. explanatory var.})}{\text{stand. dev. outcome variable}}$$

(2.13)

In our example data, the standard deviations are: 1.23 for popularity, 0.50 for gender, and 6.55 for teacher experience. Table 2.3 presents the unstandardized and standardized coefficients for the second model in Table 2.1. It also presents the estimates that we obtain if we first standardize all variables, and then carry out the analysis .

Table 2.3 Comparing unstandardized and standardized estimates				
Model:	Standardization after estimation		Using standardized variables	
Fixed part	unstandardized	standardized		
Predictor	coefficient s.e.	coefficient	coefficient s.e.	
intercept	3.34 0.16	-	-	-
pupil gender	0.84 0.06	0.34	0.34	0.02
teacher exp.	0.11 0.01	0.59	0.58	0.05
Random part				
σ^2_e	0.39 0.01		0.26	0.01
σ^2_{u0}	0.40 0.06		0.32	0.05
σ^2_{u1}	0.27 0.05		0.05	0.01
σ_{u01}	0.02 0.04		0.05	70.02
Deviance	4261.2		3446.5	

Table 2.3 shows that the standardized regression coefficients are almost the same as the coefficients estimated for standardized variables. The small differences in Table 2.3 are simply rounding errors. However, if we use standardized variables in our analysis, we find very different variance components. This is not only the effect of scaling the variables differently, which becomes clear if we realize that the covariance between the slope for pupil gender and the intercept is significant for the standardized variables. This kind of difference in results is general. The fixed part of the multilevel regression model is invariant for linear transformations, just as the regression coefficients in the ordinary single-level regression model. This means that if we change the scale of our explanatory variables, the regression coefficients and the corresponding standard errors change by the same multiplication factor, and all associated p-values remain exactly the same. However, the random part of the multilevel regression model is not invariant for

linear transformations. The estimates of the variance components in the random part can and do change, sometimes dramatically. This is discussed in more detail in section 4.2 in Chapter Four. The conclusion to be drawn here is that, if we have a complicated random part, including random components for regression slopes, we should think carefully about the scale of our explanatory variables. If our only goal is to present standardized coefficients in addition to the unstandardized coefficients, applying equation (2.13) is safer than transforming our variables. On the other hand, we may estimate the unstandardized results, including the random part and the deviance, and then re-analyze the data using standardized variables, merely using this analysis as a computational trick to obtain the standardized regression coefficients without having to do hand calculations.

2.3   INSPECTING RESIDUALS

Inspection of residuals is a standard tool in multiple regression analysis to examine whether assumptions of normality and linearity are met (cf. Stevens, 1996; Tabachnick & Fidell, 1996). Multilevel regression analysis also assumes normality and linearity, and inspection of the residuals can be used for the same goal. There is one important difference from ordinary regression analysis; we have more than one residual, in fact, we have residuals for each random effect in the model. Consequently, many different residuals plots can be made.

2.3.1 Examples of Residuals Plots

The equation below represents the one-equation version of the direct effects model for our example data. This is the multilevel model without the cross-level interaction.

$$popularity_{ij} = \gamma_{00} + \gamma_{10}\, gender_{ij} + \gamma_{01}\, experience_j + u_{1j}\, gender_{ij} + u_{0j} + e_{ij}$$

In this model, we have three residual error terms: e_{ij}, u_{0j}, and u_{1j}. The e_{ij} are the residual prediction errors at the individual level, similar to the prediction errors in ordinary single-level multiple regression. A simple boxplot of these residuals will enable us to identify extreme outliers. An assumption that is usually made in multilevel regression analysis is that the variance of the residual errors is the same in all groups. This can be assessed by computing a one-way analysis of variance of the groups on the absolute values of the residuals, which is the equivalent of Levene's test for equality of variances in Analysis of Variance (Stevens, 1996). Bryk and Raudenbush (1992) describe a chi-square test that can be used for the same purpose, which is an option in the program HLM (Raudenbush, Bryk, Cheong, & Congdon, 2000).

The u_{0j} are the residual prediction errors at the group level, which can be used in ways analogous to the analysis of the individual level residuals e_{ij}. The u_{1j} are the residuals of the regression slopes across the groups. By plotting the regression slopes for the various groups, we get a visual impression of how much the regression slopes actually differ, and we may also be able to identify groups which have a regression slope that is wildly different from the others.

To test the normality assumption, we can plot standardized residuals against their normal scores. If the residuals have a normal distribution, the plot should show a straight diagonal line. Figure 2.1 is a scatterplot of the standardized level-1 residuals (denoted by 'const' in the graph) against their normal scores. The graph indicates close conformity to normality, and no extreme outliers. Similar plots can be made for the level-2 residuals.

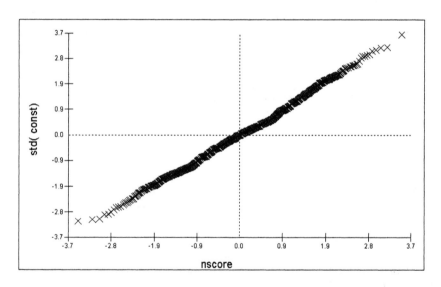

Figure 2.1. Plot of level 1 standardized residuals against normal scores

We obtain a different plot, if we plot the residuals against the predicted values of the outcome variable popularity, using the fixed part of the multilevel regression model for the prediction. Such a scatter plot of the residuals against the predicted values provides information about possible failure of normality, nonlinearity, and heteroscedasticity. If these assumptions are met, the plotted points should be evenly divided above and below their mean value of zero, with no strong structure (cf. Tabachnick & Fidell, 1996, p. 137). Figure 2.2 shows this scatter plot. For our example data, the scatter plot in Figure 2.2 does not indicate strong violations of the assumptions.

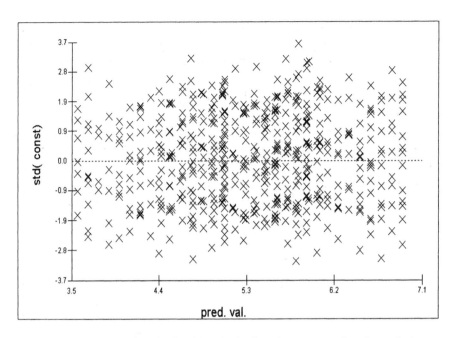

Figure 2.2. Level 1 standardized residuals plotted against predicted popularity

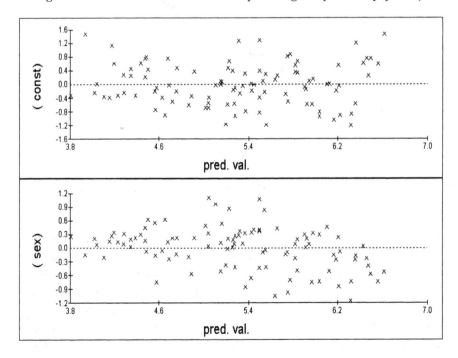

Figure 2.3. Level 2 residuals plotted against predicted popularity

Similar scatter plots can be made for the second level residuals for the intercept and the slope of the explanatory variable pupil gender. As an illustration, Figure 2.3 shows the scatterplots of the level-2 residuals around the average intercept (denoted 'const' in the graph) and around the average slope of pupil gender against the predicted values of the outcome variable popularity.

The spread of the plotted points for pupil gender (denoted 'sex' in the plot) around their mean value of 0.0 suggests some degree of heterogeneity for the residuals around the slope of pupil gender. In our case, this heterogeneity is caused by a misspecification of the model, which is the result of omitting the cross-level interaction to explain the variance of the regression slopes of pupil gender.

An interesting plot that can be made using the level-2 residuals, is a plot of the residuals against their rank order, with an added error bar. In Figure 2.4, an error bar surrounds each point estimate, and the classes are sorted in rank order of the residuals. The error bars represent the confidence interval around the individual estimate, constructed by multiplying its standard error by 1.39. This results in confidence intervals that have the property that two classes have significantly different residuals (at the 5% level), if their error bars do not overlap (Goldstein, 1995).

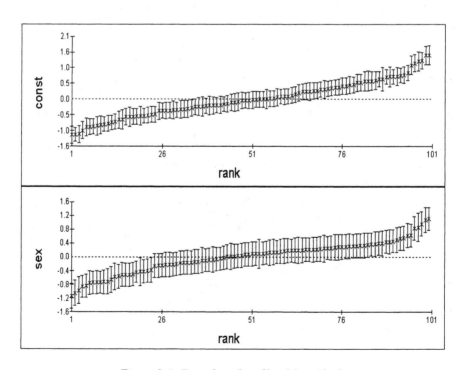

Figure 2.4. Error bar plot of level 2 residuals

In our example, we see large differences between the classes. A logical next step would be to identify the classes at the extremes of the rank order, and to seek for a post hoc interpretation of what makes these classes different. For a discussion of the construction and use of these error bars see Goldstein and Healy (1995) and Goldstein and Spiegelhalter (1996).

Examining residuals in multivariate models presents us with a problem. For instance, the residuals should show a nice normal distribution, which implies absence of extreme outliers. However, this applies to the residuals after including all important explanatory variables and relevant parameters in the model. If we analyze a sequence of models, we have a series of different residuals for each model, and scrutinizing them all at each step is not always practical. On the other hand, our decision to include a specific variable or parameter in our model might well be influenced by a violation of some assumption. Although there is no perfect solution to this dilemma, a reasonable approach is to examine the two residual terms in the intercept-only model, to find out if there are gross violations of the assumptions of the model. If there are, we should accommodate them, for instance by applying a normalizing transformation, by deleting certain individuals or groups from our data set, or by including a dummy variable that indicates a specific outlying individual or group. When we have determined our final model, we should make a more thorough examination of the various residuals. If we detect gross violations of assumptions, these should again be accommodated, and the model should be estimated again. Of course, after accommodating an extreme outlier, we might find that we should now change our model again. Procedures for model exploration and detection of violations in ordinary multiple regression are discussed, for instance, in Tabachnick and Fidell (1996) or Stevens (1996). In multilevel regression, the same procedures apply, but the analyses are more complicated because we have to examine more than one set of residuals, and must distinguish between multiple levels.

As mentioned in the beginning of this section, graphs can be useful in detecting outliers and nonlinear relations. However, an observation may have an undue effect on the outcome of a regression analysis without being an obvious outlier. Figure 2.5, a scatter plot of the so-called Anscombe data (Anscombe, 1973), illustrates this point. There is one data point in Figure 2.5, which by itself almost totally determines the regression line. Without this one observation, the regression line would be very different. Yet, it does not show up as an obvious outlier.

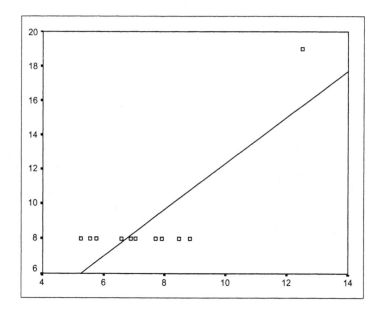

Figure 2.5. Regression line determined by one single observation

In ordinary regression analysis, various measures have been proposed to indicate the influence of individual observations on the outcome (cf. Tabachnick & Fidell, 1996). In general, such *influence* or *leverage* measures are based on a comparison of the estimates when a specific observation is included in the data or not. Langford and Lewis (1998) discuss extensions of these influence measures for the multilevel regression model. Since most of these measures are based on comparison of estimates with and without a specific observation, it is difficult to calculate them by hand. However, if the software offers the option to calculate influence measures, it is advisable to do so. If a unit (individual or group) has a large value for the influence measure, that specific unit has a large influence on the values of the regression coefficients. It is useful to inspect cases with extreme influence values for possible violations of assumptions, or even data errors.

2.3.2 Examining Slope Variation: OLS and Shrinkage Estimators

The residuals can be added to the average values of the intercept and slope, to produce predictions of the intercepts and slopes in different groups. These can also be plotted.

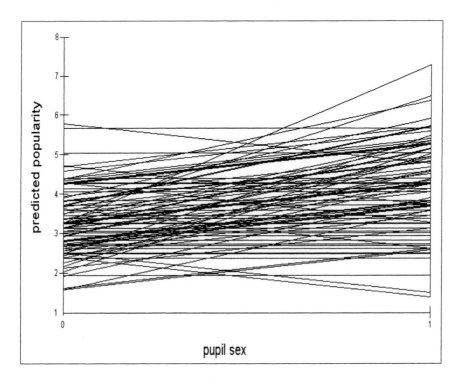

Figure 2.6. Plot of the 100 class regression slopes for pupil gender

For example, Figure 2.6 plots the 100 regression slopes for the explanatory variable pupil gender in the 100 classes. It is clear that for most classes the effect is positive: girls are more popular than boys are. It is also clear that in some classes the relationship is the opposite: boys are more popular than girls are. Most of the regression slopes are not very different from the others, although there is one slope that appears to be much steeper than the others are. It could be useful to examine the data for that one class in more detail, to find out if there is a reason for this steeper slope.

The predicted intercepts and slopes for the 100 classes are not identical to the values we would obtain, if we carry out 100 separate ordinary regression analyses in each of the 100 classes, using standard Ordinary Least Squares (OLS) techniques. If we would compare the results from 100 separate OLS regression analyses to the values obtained from a multilevel regression analysis, we would find that the results from the separate analyses are more variable. This is because the multilevel estimates of the regression coefficients of the 100 classes are weighted. They are so-called Empirical Bayes (EB) or *shrinkage* estimates; a weighted average of the specific OLS estimate in each class and the overall regression coefficient, estimated for all similar classes.

As a result, the regression coefficients are *shrunk* back towards the mean coefficient for the whole data set. The shrinkage weight depends on the reliability of the estimated coefficient. Coefficients that are estimated with small accuracy shrink more than very accurately estimated coefficients. Accuracy of estimation depends on two factors: the group sample size, and the distance between the group-based estimate and the overall estimate. Estimates in small groups are less reliable, and shrink more than estimates from large groups. Other things being equal, estimates that are very far from the overall estimate are assumed less reliable, and they shrink more than estimates that are close to the overall average. The statistical method used is called *empirical Bayes estimation*. Due to this shrinkage effect, empirical Bayes estimators are biased. However, they are often more precise, a property that is often more useful than being unbiased (cf. Kendall, 1959).

For instance, in an intercept-only model the equation to form the empirical Bayes estimate of the intercept is given in the equation

$$\hat{\beta}_{0j}^{EB} = \lambda_j \hat{\beta}_{0j}^{OLS} + \left(1 - \lambda_j\right)\gamma_{00} \qquad (2.14)$$

where λ_j is the reliability of the OLS estimate β_{0j}^{OLS} as an estimate of β_{0j}, which is given by the equation $\lambda_j = \sigma_{u_0}^2 / \left(\sigma_{u_0}^2 + \sigma_e^2 / n_j\right)$ (Bryk & Raudenbush, 1992, p. 39), and γ_{00} is the overall intercept. The reliability λ_j is close to 1.0 when the group sizes are large and/or the variability of the intercepts across groups is large. In these cases, the overall estimate γ_{00} is not a good indicator of each group's intercept. If the group sizes are small and have only small variation across groups, the reliability λ_j is close to 0.0, and more weight is put on the overall estimate γ_{00}. Equation (2.14) makes clear that, since the OLS estimates are unbiased, the empirical Bayes estimates β_{0j}^{EB} must be biased towards the overall estimate β_{00}. They are *shrunken* towards the average value γ_{00}. For that reason, the empirical Bayes estimators are also referred to as shrinkage estimators. Although the empirical Bayes or shrinkage estimators are biased, they are also in general closer to the (unknown) values of β_{0j} (Bryk & Raudenbush, 1992, p. 40). If the regression model includes a group level model, the shrinkage estimators are conditional on the group level model. The advantages of shrinkage estimators remain, *provided the group-level model is well specified* (Bryk & Raudenbush, 1992, p. 80). This is especially important if the estimated coefficients are used to describe specific groups. For instance, we can use estimates for the intercepts of the schools to rank order them on their average outcome. If this is used as an indicator of the quality of schools, the shrinkage estimators introduce a bias, because high scoring schools will be presented too negatively, and low scoring schools will be presented too positively. This is offset by the advantage of having a smaller standard error (Carlin & Louis, 1996; Lindley

& Smith, 1972). Bryk and Raudenbush discuss this problem in an example involving the effectiveness of organizations (Bryk & Raudenbush, 1992, chapter 5); see also the cautionary points made by Raudenbush and Willms (1991) and Snijders and Bosker (1999, pp. 58-63). All stress that the higher precision of the Empirical Bayes residuals is bought at the expense of a certain bias. The bias is largest when we inspect groups that are both small and far removed from the overall mean. In such cases, inspecting residuals should be supplemented with other procedures, such as comparing error bars for all schools (Goldstein & Healy, 1995). Error bars are illustrated in this chapter in Figure 2.4.

2.4   THREE- AND MORE-LEVEL REGRESSION MODELS

2.4.1 Multiple-level Models

In principle, the extension of the two-level regression model to three and more levels is straightforward. There is an outcome variable at the first, the lowest level. In addition, there may be explanatory variables at all higher levels. The problem is that three- and more-level models can become complicated very fast. In addition to the usual fixed regression coefficients, we must entertain the possibility that regression coefficients for first-level explanatory variables may vary across units of both the second and the third level. Regression coefficients for second-level explanatory variables may vary across units of the third level. To explain such variation, we must include cross-level interactions in the model. Regression slopes for the cross-level interaction between first-level and second-level variables may themselves vary across third-level units. To explain such variation, we need a second-order interaction involving variables at all three levels.

The equations for such models are complicated, especially when we do not use the more compact summation notation but write out the complete single equation-version of the model in an algebraic format (for a note on notation see section 2.5).

The resulting models are not only difficult to follow from a conceptual point of view, they may also be difficult to estimate in practice. The number of estimated parameters is considerable, and at the same time the highest level sample size tends to become relatively smaller. As DiPrete and Forristal (1994, p. 349) put it, the imagination of the researchers "…can easily outrun the capacity of the data, the computer, and current optimization techniques to provide robust estimates."

Having said that, three- and more-level models have their place in multilevel analysis. Intuitively, three-level structures such as pupils in classes in schools, or respondents nested within households, nested within regions, appear to be both conceptually and empirically manageable. If the lowest level is repeated measures over time, having repeated measures on pupils nested within schools again does not appear to be overly difficult. In such cases, the solution for the conceptual and statistical problems mentioned is to keep models reasonably small. Especially specification of the higher-level variances and covariances should be driven by theoretical considerations. A higher-level variance for a specific regression coefficient implies that this regression coefficient is assumed to vary across units at that level. A higher-level covariance between two specific regression coefficients implies that these regression coefficients are assumed to covary across units at that level. Especially when models become large and complicated, it is advisable to avoid higher-order interactions, and to include in the random part only those elements for which there is strong theoretical or empirical justification. This implies that an exhaustive search for second-order and higher-order interactions is not a good idea. In general, we should seek for higher-order interactions only if there is strong theoretical justification for their importance, or if an unusually large variance component for a regression slope calls for explanation. For the random part of the model, there are usually more convincing theoretical reasons for the higher-level variance components than for the covariance components. Especially if the covariances are small and insignificant, analysts sometimes do not include all possible covariances in the model. This is defensible, with some exceptions. First, it is recommended that the covariances between the intercept and the random slopes are always included. Second, it is recommended to include covariances corresponding to slopes of dummy-variables belonging to the same categorical variable, and for variables that are involved in an interaction or belong to the same polynomial expression (Longford, 1990, p. 79-80).

2.4.2 Intraclass-correlations in three-level models

In a two-level model, the intraclass correlation is calculated in the intercept-only model using equation (2.9), which is repeated below:

$$\rho = \frac{\sigma_{u_0}^2}{\sigma_{u_0}^2 + \sigma_e^2} \qquad \text{(2.9, repeated)}$$

The intraclass correlation is an indication of the proportion of variance at the second level, and it can also be interpreted as the expected correlation between two randomly chosen individuals within the same group.

If we have a three-level model, for instance pupils nested within classes, nested within schools, there are several ways to calculate the intraclass correlation. First, we estimate an intercept-only model for the three-level data, for which the single-equation model can be written as follows:

$$Y_{ijk} = \gamma_{000} + v_{0k} + u_{0jk} + e_{ijk} \tag{2.15}$$

The variances at the first, second, and third level are respectively σ_e^2, $\sigma_{u_0}^2$, and $\sigma_{v_0}^2$. The first method (cf. Davis & Scott, 1995) defines the intraclass correlations at the class and school level as

$$\rho_{class} = \frac{\sigma_{u_0}^2}{\sigma_{v_0}^2 + \sigma_{u_0}^2 + \sigma_e^2} \tag{2.16}$$

and

$$\rho_{school} = \frac{\sigma_{v_0}^2}{\sigma_{v_0}^2 + \sigma_{u_0}^2 + \sigma_e^2} \tag{2.17}$$

The second method (cf. Siddiqui, Hedeker, Flay & Hu, 1996) defines the intraclass correlations at the class and school level as

$$\rho_{class} = \frac{\sigma_{v_0}^2 + \sigma_{u_0}^2}{\sigma_{v_0}^2 + \sigma_{u_0}^2 + \sigma_e^2} \tag{2.18}$$

and

$$\rho_{school} = \frac{\sigma_{v_0}^2}{\sigma_{v_0}^2 + \sigma_{u_0}^2 + \sigma_e^2} \tag{2.19}$$

Actually, both methods are correct (Algina, 2000). The first method identifies the proportion of variance at the class and school level. This should be used if we are interested in a decomposition of the variance across the available levels, or if we are interested in how much variance is explained at each level (a topic discussed in section 4.4). The second method represents an estimate of the expected correlation between two randomly chosen elements in the same group. So ρ_{class} as calculated in equation (2.18) is the expected correlation between two pupils within the same class, and it correctly takes into account that two pupils who are in the same class must also be in the same school. For this reason, the variance components for classes and schools must both be in the numerator of equation (2.18). If the two sets of estimates are different, which may happen if the amount of variance at the school level is large, there is no contradiction involved. Both sets of equations express two different aspects of the data, which happen to coincide when there are only two levels.

2.5   A NOTE ABOUT NOTATION AND SOFTWARE

2.5.1 Notation

In general, there will be more than one explanatory variable at the lowest level and more than one explanatory variable at the highest level. Assume that we have P explanatory variables X at the lowest level, indicated by the subscript p ($p=1...P$). Likewise, we have Q explanatory variables Z at the highest level, indicated by the subscript q ($q=1...Q$). Then, equation (2.5) becomes the more general equation:

$$Y_{ij} = \gamma_{00} + \gamma_{p0} X_{pij} + \gamma_{0q} Z_{qj} + \gamma_{pq} Z_{qj} X_{pij} + u_{pj} X_{pij} + u_{0j} + e_{ij} \qquad (2.20)$$

Using summation notation, we can express the same equation as

$$Y_{ij} = \gamma_{00} + \sum_p \gamma_{p0} X_{pij} + \sum_q \gamma_{0q} Z_{qj} + \sum_p \sum_q \gamma_{pq} X_{pij} Z_{qj} + \sum_p u_{pj} X_{pij} + u_{0j} + e_{ij} \qquad (2.21)$$

The errors at the lowest level e_{ij} are assumed to have a normal distribution with a mean of zero and a common variance σ_e^2 in all groups. The u-terms u_{0j} and u_{pj} are the residual error terms at the highest level. They are assumed to be independent from the errors e_{ij} at the individual level, and to have a multivariate normal distribution with means of zero. The variance of the residual errors u_{0j} is the variance of the intercepts between the groups; it is symbolized by $\sigma_{u_0}^2$. The variances of the residual errors u_{pj} are the variances of the slopes between the groups; they are symbolized by $\sigma_{u_p}^2$. The *covariances* between the residual error terms $\sigma_{u_{pp'}}$ are generally not assumed to be zero; they are collected in the higher level variance/covariance matrix Ω.[1]

Note that in equation (2.15), γ_{00}, the regression coefficient for the intercept, is not associated with an explanatory variable. We can expand the equation by providing an explanatory variable that is a constant equal to one for all observed units. This yields the equation

$$Y_{ij} = \gamma_{p0} X_{pij} + \gamma_{pq} Z_{qj} X_{pij} + u_{pj} X_{pij} + e_{ij} \qquad (2.22)$$

where $X_{0ij}=1$, and $p=0...P$. Equation (2.22) makes clear that the intercept is a regression coefficient, just like the other regression coefficients in the equation. Some multilevel software, for instance HLM (Raudenbush, Bryk, Cheongh & Congdon, 2000) puts the

---

[1] We may attach a subscript to Ω to indicate to which level it belongs. As long as there is no risk of confusion, the simpler notation without the subscript is used.

intercept variable $X_0=1$ in the regression equation by default. Other multilevel software, for instance MLwiN (Goldstein et al., 1998), requires that the analyst includes a variable in the data set that equals one in all cases, which must be added explicitly to the regression equation. In some cases, being able to eliminate the intercept term from the regression equation is a convenient feature.

Equation (2.22) can be made very general if we let $\mathbf{X}$ be the matrix of all explanatory variables in the fixed part, symbolize the residual errors at all levels by $u^{(l)}$ with l denoting the level, and associate all error components with predictor variables $\mathbf{Z}$, which may or may not be equal to the $\mathbf{X}$. This produces the very general matrix formula $\mathbf{Y}=\mathbf{X}\boldsymbol{\beta}+\mathbf{Z}^{(l)}\mathbf{u}^{(l)}$ (cf. Goldstein, 1995, appendix 2.1). Since this book is more about applications than about mathematical statistics, it generally uses the algebraic notation, except when multivariate procedures such as structural equation modeling are discussed.

The notation used in this book is close to the notation used by Goldstein (1987, 1995), Hox (1995), and Kreft and de Leeuw (1998). The most important difference is that these authors indicate the higher-level variance by σ_{00} instead of our $\sigma_{u_0}^2$. The logic is that, if σ_{01} indicates the covariance between variables 0 and 1, then σ_{00} is the covariance of variable 0 with itself, which is its variance. Bryk and Raudenbush (1992), and Snijders and Bosker (1999) use a different notation; they denote the lowest level error terms by r_{ij}, and the higher-level error terms by u_j. The lowest level variance is σ^2 in their notation. The higher-level variances and covariances are indicated by the Greek letter *tau*; for instance, the intercept variance is given by τ_{00}. The τ_{pp} are collected in the matrix TAU, symbolized as T. The HLM program and manual in part use a different notation, for instance when discussing longitudinal and three-level models.

2.5.2 Software

Multilevel models can be formulated in two ways: (1) by presenting separate equations for each of the levels, and (2) by combining all equations by substitution into a single model-equation. The software HLM (Raudenbush et al., 2000) requires specification of the separate equations at each available level. Most other software (e.g., MLwiN; Rasbash et al., 2000), SAS Proc Mixed (Littell et al., 1996)) uses the single equation representation. Both representations have their advantages and disadvantages. The separate-equation representation has the advantage that it is always clear how the model is built up. The disadvantage is that it hides from view that modeling regression slopes by other variables results in adding an interaction to the model. As will be explained in Chapter Four, estimating and interpreting interactions correctly requires careful thinking. On the other hand, while the single-equation representation makes the existence of interactions obvious, it conceals the role of the complicated error components that are created by modeling varying slopes. In practice, to keep track of the model, it is recommended to start by writing the separate equations for the separate levels, and to use substitution to arrive at the single-equation representation.

To take a quote from Singer's excellent introduction to using SAS Proc Mixed for multilevel modeling (Singer, 1998, p. 350): "Statistical software does not a statistician make. That said, without software, few statisticians and even fewer empirical researchers would fit the kinds of sophisticated models being promulgated today." Indeed, software does not make a statistician, but the advent of powerful and user-friendly software for multilevel modeling has had a large impact in research fields as diverse as education, organizational research, demography, epidemiology, and medicine. This book focuses on the conceptual and statistical issues that arise in multilevel modeling of complex data structures. It assumes that researchers who apply these techniques have access to and familiarity with *some* software that can estimate these models. Software is mentioned in various places, especially when a technique is discussed that is only available in a specific program. In addition to the relevant program manuals, several software programs have been discussed in introductory articles. Using SAS Proc Mixed for multilevel and longitudinal data is discussed by Singer (1998). Both Arnold (1992), and Heck and Thomas (2000) discuss multilevel modeling using HLM as the software tool. Sullivan, Dukes and Losina (1999) discus HLM and SAS Proc Mixed. Hox (1995) applies the programs HLM, MLn and Varcl to the same data set, to highlight their similarities and differences. Kreft, de Leeuw and van der Leeden (1994) compare the programs BMDP-5V, Genmod, HLM, ML3 (a precursor to MLn/MLwiN) and Varcl on a variety of criteria, ranging from user-interface to statistical methods implemented. The multilevel procedure in SPSS s relatively new, and has not appeared in any published comparisons.

Since statistical software evolves rapidly, with new versions of the software coming out much faster than new editions of general handbooks such as this, I do not discuss software setups or output in detail. As a result, this book is more about the possibilities offered by the various techniques than about the specifics of how these things can be done in a specific software package. The various techniques are explained using analyses on small but realistic data sets, with examples of how the results could be presented and discussed. At the same time, if the analysis requires that the software used have some specific capacities, these are pointed out. This should enable interested readers to determine whether their software meets these requirements, and assist them in working out the software setups for their favorite package.

The data used in the various examples are described in the appendix, and are available through the Internet.

3

Estimation and Hypothesis Testing in Multilevel Regression

The usual method to estimate the values of the regression coefficients, and the intercept and slope variances, is the Maximum Likelihood method. This chapter gives a non-technical explanation of this estimation method, to enable analysts to make informed decisions on the estimation options presented by present software. Some alternatives to Maximum Likelihood estimation are briefly discussed. Recent developments, such as bootstrapping and Bayesian estimation methods, are also briefly introduced in this chapter. In addition, these are explained in more detail in Chapter Eleven. Finally, this chapter describes some procedures that can be used to test hypotheses about specific parameters.

3.1 WHICH ESTIMATION METHOD?

Estimation of parameters (regression coefficients and variance components) in multilevel modeling is mostly done by the Maximum Likelihood method. The Maximum Likelihood (ML) method is a general estimation procedure, which produces estimates for the population parameters that maximize the probability (produce the 'Maximum Likelihood') of observing the data that are actually observed, given the model (cf. Eliason, 1993). Other estimation methods that have been used in multilevel modeling are Generalized Least Squares (GLS), Generalized Estimating Equations (GEE), and Bayesian methods such as Markov Chain Monte Carlo (MCMC). Bootstrapping methods (cf. Mooney & Duval, 1993) can be used to improve the parameter estimates and the standard errors. In this section, I will discuss these methods briefly.

3.1.1 Maximum Likelihood

Maximum Likelihood (ML) is the most commonly used estimation method in multilevel modeling. An advantage of the Maximum Likelihood estimation method is that it is generally robust, and produces estimates that are asymptotically efficient and consistent. With large samples, ML estimates are usually robust against mild violations of the assumptions, such as having non-normal errors. Maximum Likelihood estimation proceeds by maximizing a function called the Likelihood Function. Two different Likelihood functions are used in multilevel regression modeling. One is called Full Maximum Likelihood (FML); in this method, both the regression coefficients and the variance components are included in the likelihood function. The other method is called Restricted Maximum Likelihood (RML); here only the variance components are included in the likelihood function, and the regression coefficients are estimated in a second estimation step. Both methods produce parameter estimates with associated standard errors and an overall model *deviance*, which is a function of the Likelihood. FML treats the regression coefficients as fixed but unknown quantities when the variance components are estimated, but does not take into account the degrees of freedom lost by estimating the fixed effects. RML estimates the variance components after removing the fixed effects from the model (cf. Searle, Casella & McCulloch, 1992, chapter 6). As a result, FML estimates of the variance components are biased; they are generally too small. RML estimates have less bias (Longford, 1993). RML also has the property, that if the groups are balanced (have equal group sizes), the RML estimates are equivalent to Anova estimates, which are optimal (Searle, Casella & McCulloch, 1992, p. 254). Since RML is more realistic, it should, in theory, lead to better estimates, especially when the number of groups is small (Bryk & Raudenbush, 1992; Longford, 1993). In practice, the differences between the two methods are usually not large (cf. Hox, 1998; Kreft & de Leeuw, 1998). For example, if we compare the FML estimates for our example data in Table 2.1 with the corresponding RML estimates, the only difference within two decimals is the intercept variance at level-2. FML estimates this as 0.40, and RML as 0.41. The size of this difference is absolutely trivial. If nontrivial differences are found, the RML method usually performs better (Browne, 1998). FML still continues to be used, because it has two advantages over RML. Firstly, the computations are generally easier, and secondly, since the regression coefficients are included in the likelihood function, an overall chi-square test based on the likelihood can be used to compare two models that differ in the fixed part (the regression coefficients). With RML, only differences in the random part (the variance components) can be compared with this test.

   Computing the Maximum Likelihood estimates requires an *iterative* procedure. At the beginning, the computer program generates reasonable starting values for the various parameters (in multilevel regression analysis these are usually based on single level regression estimates). In the next step, an ingenious computation procedure tries to improve upon the starting values, to produce better estimates. This second step is repeated (iterated) many times. After each iteration, the program inspects how much the estimates actually changed compared to the previous step. If the changes are very small, the program concludes that the estimation procedure has *converged* and that it is finished. Using multilevel software, we generally take the computational details for granted. However, computational problems do sometimes occur. A problem common to programs using an iterative Maximum Likelihood procedure is that the iterative process is not *guaranteed* to stop. There are models and data sets for which the program goes through an endless sequence of iterations, which can only be stopped by reaching for the <reset> switch on the computer. Because of this, most programs set a built-in limit to the maximum number of iterations. If convergence is not reached within this limit, the computations can be repeated with a higher limit. If the computations do not converge after an extremely large number of iterations, we suspect that they may never converge.[1] The problem is how one should interpret a model that does not converge. The usual interpretation is that a model for which convergence cannot be reached is a bad model, using the simple argument that if estimates cannot be found, this disqualifies the model. However, the problem may also lie with the data. Especially with small samples, the estimation procedure may fail even if the model is valid. In addition, it is even possible that, if only we had a better computer algorithm, or better starting values, we could find acceptable estimates. Still, experience shows that if a program does not converge with a data set of reasonable size, the problem often is a badly misspecified model. In multilevel analysis, non-convergence often occurs when we try to estimate too many random (variance) components that are actually close or equal to zero. The solution is to simplify the model by leaving out some random components; often the results from the non-converged solution provide an indication which random components can be omitted.

3.1.2 Generalized Least Squares

Generalized Least Squares (GLS) estimates can be obtained from a Maximum Likelihood procedure by restricting the number of iterations to one. GLS estimates approximate ML estimates, and they are asymptotically equivalent. Asymptotic equivalence means that in very large samples they are in practice indistinguishable. Since GLS estimates are obviously faster to compute than full ML estimates, they can be used as a stand-in for ML estimates in computationally intensive procedures such as extremely large data sets, or when bootstrapping is used. They can also be used when ML procedures fail to converge; inspecting the GLS results may help to diagnose the problem. Furthermore, since GLS estimates are respectable statistical estimates in their own right, in such situations one can report the GLS estimates instead of the more usual ML estimates. However, simulation research shows that, in general, GLS estimates are less efficient, and the GLS-derived standard errors are rather inaccurate (cf. Hox, 1998;

---

[1] Some programs allow the analyst to monitor the iterations, to observe whether the computations are going somewhere, or are just moving back and forth without improving the likelihood function.

van der Leeden & Busing, 1994; Kreft, 1996). Therefore, in general, ML estimation should be preferred.

3.1.3 Generalized Estimating Equations

The Generalized Estimating Equations method (GEE, cf. Liang & Zeger, 1986) estimates the variances and covariances in the random part of the multilevel model directly from the residuals, which makes them faster to compute than full ML estimates. After the GEE estimates for the variance components are obtained, GLS is used to estimate the fixed regression coefficients. The GEE approach is used by the program HLM (Bryk, Raudenbush & Congdon, 1996) to estimate a *population average model*, where the emphasis is on comparing the group level units. The GEE estimates are different from the ML estimates when a nonlinear model is estimated. Bryk, Raudenbush and Congdon (1996, p. 129) describe the distinction between GEE and ML as 'tricky'. For a discussion, I refer to Zeger, Liang and Albert (1988). According to Goldstein (1995, p. 23), GEE estimates are less efficient than full ML estimates, but they make weaker assumptions about the structure of the random part of the multilevel model. If the model for the random part is correct, ML estimators are more efficient, and the model-based (ML) standard errors are generally smaller than the GEE-based standard errors. If the model for the random part is incorrect, the GEE-based estimates and standard errors are still consistent. So, provided the sample size is reasonably large, GEE estimators are robust against misspecificaation of the model, including violations of the normality assumption. Given the general robustness of ML methods, it is probably preferable to use ML methods, and use robust estimators or bootstrap corrections when there is serious doubt about the assumptions of the ML method. Robust estimators, which are related to GEE estimators (Burton, Gurrin & Sly, 1998), and bootstrapping are treated in more detail in Chapter Eleven of this book.

3.1.4 Bootstrapping

In bootstrapping, random samples are repeatedly drawn with replacement from the observed data. In each of these random samples, the model parameters are estimated, generally using either FML or RML maximum likelihood estimation. This process is repeated b times. For each model parameter, this results in a set of b parameter estimates. The variance of these b estimates is used as an indicator of the sampling variance associated with the parameter estimate obtained from the full sample. Since the bootstrap samples are obtained by resampling from the total sample, bootstrapping falls under the general term of resampling methods (cf. Good, 1999). Bootstrapping can be used to improve both the point estimates and the standard errors. Typically, 500 to 1000 bootstrap samples are needed for sufficient accuracy. This makes the method computationally demanding, but less so than the Bayesian methods treated in the next section. Since bootstrapping has its own complications, it is discussed in more detail in Chapter Eleven. If we execute a bootstrap estimation for our example data, the results are almost identical to the asymptotic FML results reported in Table 2.1. Some standard errors are a bit higher: for example, the standard error for teacher experience is 0.06 for the bootstrap estimate, and 0.05 for the asymptotic estimate. This difference is trivial. Bootstrap estimates are most attractive when we have reasons to suspect the asymptotic results, for example because we have a small sample size, or because we have non-normal data.

3.1.5 Bayesian methods

In Bayesian statistics, we express our uncertainty about the population values of the model parameters by assigning to them a distribution of possible values. This distribution is called the *prior* distribution, because it is specified independently from the data. The prior distribution is combined with the Likelihood of the data to produce a *posterior* distribution, which describes our uncertainty about the population values after observing the data. Typically, the variance of the posterior distribution is smaller than the variance of the prior distribution, which means that observing the data has reduced our uncertainty about the possible population values. For the prior distribution, we have a fundamental choice between using an informative prior or an uninformative prior. An informative prior is a peaked distribution with a small variance, which expresses a strong belief about the unknown population parameter. An informative prior will, of course, strongly influence the posterior distribution, and hence our conclusions. For this reason, many statisticians prefer an uninformative or diffuse prior, which has very little influence on the posterior, and only serves to produce the posterior. An example of an uninformative prior is the uniform distribution, which simply states that the unknown parameter value is a number between minus and plus infinity, with all values equally likely.

If the posterior distribution has a mathematically simple form, for instance a normal distribution, we can use this distribution to produce a point estimate and a confidence interval for the population parameter. However, in complex multivariate models, the posterior is generally a complex multivariate distribution, which makes it difficult to establish confidence intervals. Therefore, simulation techniques are used to generate random samples from the posterior distribution. The simulated posterior distribution is then used to provide a point estimate (typically the mode or median of the simulated values) and a confidence interval.

Bayesian methods can provide accurate estimates of the parameters and the uncertainty associated with them (Goldstein, 1995). However, they are computationally demanding, and the simulation procedure must be monitored to insure that it is working properly. Bayesian estimation methods are treated in more detail in Chapter Eleven.

3.2 SIGNIFICANCE TESTING AND CONFIDENCE INTERVALS

This section discusses procedures for testing significance and constructing confidence intervals for the regression coefficients and variance components. There is also a global test based on the Likelihood that can be used to compare two nested models. Finally, contrasts of regression coefficients or variances are described, and constraints which can be used to fix regression coefficients or variance components at specific values.

3.2.1 Testing regression coefficients and variance components

Maximum Likelihood procedures produce standard errors for the estimated parameters. These can be used to carry out a significance test of the form $Z=(estimate)/(standard\ error\ of\ estimate)$, where Z is referred to the standard normal distribution. This test is known as the *Wald test* (Wald, 1943). The standard errors are asymptotic, which means that they are valid for large samples. As usual, it is not precisely known when a sample is large enough to be confident about the precision of the estimates. Simulation research suggests that for accurate standard errors for level-2 variances, a relatively large level-two sample size is needed. For instance, simulations by Van der Leeden, Busing and Meijer (1997) suggest that with fewer than 100 groups, ML estimates of variances and their standard errors are not very accurate. In ordinary regression analysis, a rule of thumb is to require $104+p$ observations, where p is the number of explanatory variables (Green, 1991). In multilevel regression, the relevant sample size for higher-level coefficients and variance components is the number of groups, which is often not very large. Green's rule of thumb and Van der Leeden et al.'s simulation results agree on a preferred group level sample size of at least 100. Additional simulation research (Maas & Hox, 2001) suggests that if the interest lies mostly in the fixed part of the model, far fewer groups are sufficient, especially for the lowest level regression coefficients. The issue of the sample sizes needed to produce accurate estimates and standard errors is taken up in more detail in Chapter Ten.

It should be noted that the *p*-values and confidence intervals produced by the program HLM (Raudenbush et al., 2000) differ from those obtained from most other programs. Most multilevel analysis programs produce as part of their output parameter estimates and asymptotic standard errors for these estimates, all obtained from the maximum likelihood estimation procedure. The usual significance test is the Wald test, with Z evaluated against the standard normal distribution. Bryk and Raudenbush (1992, p. 50), referring to a simulation study by Fotiu (1989), argue that for the fixed effects it is better to refer this ratio to a *t*-distribution on *J-p-1* degrees of freedom, where *J* is the number of second level units, and *p* is the total number of explanatory variables in the model. Likewise, they argue that the *Z*-test is not appropriate for the variances, because it assumes a normal distribution, while the sampling distribution of variances is skewed (Bryk & Raudenbush, 1992, p. 47, 55), especially when the variance is small. Instead, they propose to use a chi-square test of the residuals. This chi-square is computed by

$$\chi^2 = \sum \left(\hat{\beta}_j - \beta \right)^2 / \hat{V}_j \tag{3.1}$$

where $\hat{\beta}_j$ is the OLS estimate of a regression coefficient computed separately in group *j*, β its overall estimate, and V_j its estimated sampling variance in group *j*. The number of degrees of freedom is given by $df=J-p-1$, where *J* is the number of second level units, and *p* is the total number of explanatory variables in the model.

The *p*-values produced by the program HLM (Bryk, Raudenbush & Congdon, 1996) are based on these tests rather than the more common Wald tests. When the number of groups *J* is large, the difference between the asymptotic Wald test and the alternative Student-*t* test is very small. However, when the number of groups is small, the differences may become important. Since referring the result of the *Z*-test on the regression coefficients to a Student *t*-distribution is conservative, this procedure should provide a better protection against type I errors. Simulation research on the Wald test for a variance component (van der Leeden, Busing & Meijer, 1997) and the alternative chi-square test (Harwell, 1997; Sánchez-Meca & Marín-Martínez, 1997) suggest that with small numbers of groups both tests suffer from a very low power. If the data are normal, a test that compares a model with and without the parameters under consideration, using the chi-square model test described in the next section, is generally better (Goldstein, 1995). For large samples and non-normal data, the Wald test is preferred. Note that if the Wald test is used to test a variance component, a one-sided test is the appropriate one. When we have both a small sample of groups and a variance component close to zero, the distribution of the Wald statistic is clearly non-normal. In that case, using the chi-square test is more appropriate. However, bootstrap and Bayesian estimation methods appear to be superior in such circumstances (Browne, 1998).

3.2.2 Comparing nested models

From the Likelihood function we can calculate a statistic called the *deviance* that indicates how well the model fits the data. The deviance is defined as -2×LN(Likelihood), where *Likelihood* is the value of the Likelihood function at convergence, and LN is the natural logarithm. In general, models with a lower deviance fit better than models with a higher deviance. If two models are *nested*, which means that a specific model can be derived from a more general model by removing parameters from the general model, we can compare them statistically using their deviances. The difference of the deviances for two nested models has a chi-square distribution, with degrees of freedom equal to the difference in the number of parameters estimated in the two models. This can be used to perform a formal chi-square test to test whether the more general model fits significantly better than the simpler model. The chi-square test of the deviances can be used to good effect to explore the importance of random effects, by comparing a model that contains these effects with a model that excludes them.

Table 2.1 Intercept-only and model with pupil gender and teacher experience				
Model:	M0: intercept-only		M1: + pup. gender and t. exp.	
Fixed part				
Predictor	coefficient	standard error	coefficient	standard error
intercept	5.31	0.10	3.34	0.16
pupil gender			0.84	0.06
teacher exp.			0.11	0.01
Random part				
σ^2_e	0.64	0.02	0.39	0.01
σ^2_{u0}	0.87	0.13	0.40	0.06
σ^2_{u1}			0.27	0.05
σ_{u01}			0.02	0.04
Deviance	5112.7		4261.2	

Table 2.1, which is repeated here, presents two models for the pupil popularity data used as an example in Chapter 2. The first model contains only an intercept. The second model adds a pupil-level and a teacher-level variable, with the pupil-level variable having random slopes at the second (class) level. To test the difference between the two models using the chi-square deviance test, we first must establish that the two models are indeed nested. This is clearly the case, since we can reach the first model M0 by restricting the added regression coefficients and variance components to zero. Accordingly, we may apply the chi-square deviance test. Since the regression coefficients are included in the test, we must use Full Maximum Likelihood estimation. The difference between the two deviances in Table 2.1 is 851.5. Under the null-hypothesis of no difference between the two models, this difference has a chi-square distribution with degrees of freedom the difference in the number of parameters of the

two models. Model M1 estimates two more regression coefficients, one variance for the slopes of pupil sex, and one covariance between the slopes and the intercepts. In total 4 more parameters are estimated, so we have a chi-square of 851.5 with 4 degrees of freedom. This is obviously significant (p <0.001), and we conclude that model M1 has a better fit to the data than model M0.

Asymptotically, the Wald test and the test using the chi-square difference are equivalent. In practice, the Wald test and the chi-square difference test do not always lead to the same conclusion. If a variance component is tested, the chi-square difference test is clearly better, except when models are estimated where the likelihood function is only an approximation, as in the logistic models discussed in Chapter Six. When the chi-square difference test is used to test a variance component, it should be noted that the standard application is equivalent to a two-sided Wald test. Since the null-hypothesis for a variance component is tested against a one-sided alternative (variances cannot be negative), the p-value from the chi-square difference test must be divided by two if a variance component is tested (Berkhof & Snijders, 2001). If a fixed regression coefficient is tested, the chi-square difference test is still superior. The reason is that the Wald test is to some degree sensitive to the parameterization of the model and the specific restrictions to be tested (Davidson & MacKinnon, 1993, chapter 13.5-13.6). The chi-square difference test is invariant under reparametrization of the model. Since the Wald test is more convenient, it is in practice used the most. Even so, if there is a discrepancy between the result of a chi-square difference test and the equivalent Wald test, the chi-square difference test is generally the preferred one.

3.2.3 Comparing non-nested models

If the models to be compared are not nested models, the principle that models should be as simple as possible (theories and models should be parsimonious), indicates that we should generally keep the simpler model. A general fit index to compare the fit of statistical models is Akaike's Information Criterion AIC (Akaike, 1987), which was developed to compare non-nested models, adjusting for the number of parameters estimated. The AIC for multilevel regression models is most conveniently calculated from the deviance d, and the number of estimated parameters q:

$$AIC = d + 2q \qquad (3.2)$$

The AIC is a very general fit-index that assumes that we are comparing models that are fit to the same data set, using the same estimation method. A fit index similar to the AIC is Schwarz's Bayesian Information Criterion BIC (Schwarz, 1978), which is given by

$$BIC = d + q \text{ LN(N)} \tag{3.3}$$

When the deviance goes down, indicating a better fit, both the AIC and the BIC also tend to go down. However, the AIC and the BIC also include a penalty function based on the number of estimated parameters q. When the number of estimated parameters goes up, the AIC and BIC tend to go up too. For most sample sizes, the BIC places a larger penalty on complex models, which leads to a preference for smaller models. Since multilevel data have a different sample size at different levels, the AIC is more straightforward than the BIC, and therefore the recommended choice. The AIC and BIC are typically used to compare a range of competing models, and the model(s) with the lowest AIC or BIC value are considered the most attractive. It should be noted that the AIC and BIC are based on the Likelihood function. With FML estimation, the AIC and BIC can be used to compare models that differ either in the fixed part or in the random part. If RML estimation is used, it can only be used to compare models that differ in the random part. Since RML effectively partials out the fixed part, before the random part is estimated, the RML Likelihood may still change if the fixed part is changed. Therefore, if Likelihood based procedures are used to compare models using RML estimation, the fixed part of the model should be kept constant. Most current software does not produce the AIC or BIC (SAS *Proc Mixed* does), but they can be calculated using the formulas given earlier.

3.3 CONTRASTS AND CONSTRAINTS

It is possible to define a *contrast* for a set of regression coefficients or variance components. A contrast is a composite hypothesis on a set of parameters, for example, that they are equal, or that a set of parameters are all equal to zero. In general, a contrast has the form

$$H_0: \; \mathbf{Cp=k} \tag{3.4}$$

where $\mathbf{C}$ is a contrast matrix that specifies the composite hypothesis, $\mathbf{p}$ is the vector of parameters that is involved, and k is a vector of contrast values. An example makes clear how this works. Table 2.1, which was repeated above, presents the results of analyzing the popularity data. There were 2000 pupils in 100 classes. The intercept-only model lists two random parameters: the intercept variance at level-1, which is estimated as 0.64, and the intercept variance at level-2, which is estimated as 0.87. Suppose that we want to evaluate the null-hypothesis that these variance components are equal. Thus, the null-hypothesis is: $\sigma^2_e - \sigma^2_{u0} = 0$. The parameter vector $\mathbf{p}$ is

$$\mathbf{p} = \left\{ \begin{matrix} \sigma_e^2 \\ \sigma_{u0}^2 \end{matrix} \right\} \tag{3.5}$$

We can write the null-hypothesis as

$$\{1,-1\} \left\{ \begin{matrix} \sigma_e^2 \\ \sigma_{u0}^2 \end{matrix} \right\} = \{0\} \tag{3.6}$$

or, in simple algebraic notation

$$1 \times \sigma_e^2 - 1 \times \sigma_{u0}^2 = 0 \tag{3.7}$$

Contrasts are tested using an asymptotic chi-square test (Bryk & Raudenbush, 1992, pp. 51-52) If we test the null-hypothesis represented by contrast (3.9) on the example data, we obtain a chi-square of 3.28 with one degree of freedom, and a p-value of 0.07. The null-hypothesis of equal variances at both levels is not rejected.

Sometimes we have a composite hypothesis that is more complicated, and we may require more than one contrast vector. For example, suppose that we want to test the null-hypothesis that all three of the regression coefficients in Table 2.1 are equal. The coefficients are: the intercept, the regression coefficient for pupil sex, and the regression coefficient for teacher experience. Our composite null hypothesis is H_0: $\gamma_1 = \gamma_2 = \gamma_3$. This is a composite null hypothesis, which can be expressed by having two simple null hypotheses: $\gamma_1 - \gamma_2 = 0$ and $\gamma_2 - \gamma_3 = 0$. In matrix formulation, replacing the gamma's by the corresponding variable names, we have

$$\left\{ \begin{matrix} 1 & -1 & 0 \\ 0 & 1 & -1 \end{matrix} \right\} \left\{ \begin{matrix} intercept \\ pup.sex \\ teach.exper. \end{matrix} \right\} = \left\{ \begin{matrix} 0 \\ 0 \end{matrix} \right\} \tag{3.8}$$

Equation (3.8) represents the two contrasts given by $1 \times \gamma_1 + (-1) \times \gamma_2 + 0 \times \gamma_3 = 0$ and $0 \times \gamma_1 + 1 \times \gamma_2 + (-1) \times \gamma_3 = 0$, or more simply $\gamma_1 = \gamma_2$ and $\gamma_2 = \gamma_3$. If we test this composite null-hypothesis on the example data, we obtain a chi-square of 462.1 with two degrees of freedom (one for each row of the contrast matrix), and a p-value of 0.00. The null hypothesis is clearly untenable.

In these examples, the null-hypothesis is not very interesting. Contrast tests on parameters are theoretically informative when we can use them to compare regression coefficients or variance components that refer to similar variables. For instance, in a multivariate multilevel analysis, where we have two or more outcome variables, we can use contrasts to test if a predictor variable has the same effect on both outcome variables. Alternatively, if we have two comparable predictor variables, we can test if they both have the same effect on a single outcome variable. Contrast tests are also useful when categorical variables are represented by a set of dummies. Using complex contrasts, we can replace a set of separate Wald tests by one single omnibus test on the full set of dummies.

Some software allows putting *constraints* on a set of parameters. Simple constraints are constraining a single parameter to be equal to zero or one. This is used, for instance, in multilevel models for meta-analysis, which is treated in Chapter Eight. Complex constraints are similar to complex contrasts, and allow constraining a set of parameters to be equal. A useful application is in models with dummy variables that identify groups. We can use a constraint matrix to specify that the variances for the group identification must be equal. This is used in models for cross-classified data, which is treated in Chapter Seven.

Constraints are similar to contrasts, but do not specify a value for the contrast. If we compare models with and without constraints using the deviance chi-square test, we have a test that is asymptotically identical to the equivalent composite test using contrasts. The composite contrast test on model parameters is a composite Wald test (cf. Goldstein, 1995, chap. 2). The global model comparison using deviances is a likelihood ratio test. With normal data, the global likelihood ratio test is generally considered more accurate, especially when variance components are tested. With non-normal data, the Likelihood is often approximated, and then the composite Wald test is preferred.

4

Some Important
Methodological and Statistical Issues

The multilevel regression model is more complicated than the standard single-level multiple regression model. One difference is the number of parameters, which is much larger in the multilevel model. This poses problems when models are fitted that have many parameters, and also in model exploration. Another difference is that multilevel models often contain interaction effects in the form of cross-level interactions. Interaction effects are tricky, and analysts should deal with them carefully. Finally, the multilevel model contains several different residual variances, and no single number can be interpreted as *the* amount of explained variance. These issues are treated in this chapter.

4.1 ANALYSIS STRATEGY

The number of parameters in a multilevel regression model can easily become very large. If there are p explanatory variables at the lowest level and q explanatory variables at the highest level, the multilevel regression model for two levels is given by equation (4.1)

$$Y_{ij} = \gamma_{00} + \gamma_{p0} X_{pij} + \gamma_{0q} Z_{qj} + \gamma_{pq} Z_{qj} X_{pij} + u_{pj} X_{pij} + u_{0j} + e_{ij} \qquad (4.1)$$

The number of estimated parameters in the model described by equation (4.1) is given by the following list:

parameters:	number:
intercept	1
lowest level error variance	1
fixed slopes for the lowest level predictors	p
highest level error variances for these slopes	p
highest level covariances of the intercept with all slopes	p
highest level covariances between all slopes	$p(p-1)/2$
fixed slopes for the highest level predictors	q
slopes for cross-level interactions	$p \times q$

An ordinary single-level regression model for the same data would estimate only the intercept, one error variance, and $p+q$ regression slopes. The superiority of the multilevel regression model is clear, if we consider that the data are clustered in groups. If we have 100 groups, estimating an ordinary multiple regression model in each group separately requires estimating 100 × (1 regression intercept + 1 residual variance + p regression slopes) plus possible interactions with the q group level variables. Multilevel regression replaces estimating 100 intercepts by estimating an average intercept plus its residual variance across groups, assuming a normal distribution for these residuals. Thus, multilevel regression analysis replaces estimating 100 separate intercepts by estimating two parameters (the mean and variance of the intercepts), plus a normality assumption. The same simplification is used for the regression slopes. Instead of estimating 100 slopes for the explanatory variable pupil gender, we estimate the average slope along with its variance across groups, and assume that the distribution of the residuals is normal. Nevertheless, even with a modest number of explanatory variables, multilevel regression analysis implies a complicated model. Generally, we do not want to estimate the complete model, firstly because this is likely to get us into computational problems, but also because it is very difficult to interpret such a complex model. We prefer more limited models that include only those parameters that have proven their worth in previous research, or are of special interest for our theoretical problem.

If we have no strong theories, we can use an exploratory procedure to select a model. An attractive procedure is to start with the simplest possible model, the intercept-only model, and to add the various types of parameters step by step. At each step, we inspect the results to see which parameters are significant, and how much residual error is left at the two distinct levels. Since we have larger sample sizes at the lowest level, it makes sense to build up the model from there. In addition, since fixed parameters are typically estimated with much more precision than random parameters, we start with the fixed regression coefficients, and add variance components at a later stage. The different steps of such a selection procedure are given below.

Step 1:
Analyze a model with no explanatory variables. This model, the *intercept-only model*, is given by the model of equation (2.8), which is repeated here:

$$Y_{ij} = \gamma_{00} + u_{0j} + e_{ij} \tag{4.2}$$

In equation (4.2), γ_{00} is the regression intercept, and u_{0j} and e_{ij} are the usual residuals at the group and the individual level. The intercept-only model is useful because it gives us an estimate of the intra-class correlation ρ by applying equation (2.9), which is repeated here:

$$\sigma_{u0}^2 / \left(\sigma_{u0}^2 + \sigma_e^2 \right) \tag{4.3}$$

where σ_{u0}^2 is the variance of the group level residuals u_{0j}, and σ_e^2 is the variance of the individual level residuals e_{ij}. The intercept-only model also gives us a benchmark value of the deviance, which is a measure of the degree of misfit of the model (cf. McCullagh & Nelder, 1989), and which can be used to compare models as described in Chapter Three.

Step 2:
Analyze a model with all lower level explanatory variables fixed. This means that the corresponding variance components of the slopes are fixed at zero. This model is written as:

$$Y_{ij} = \gamma_{00} + \gamma_{p0} X_{pij} + u_{0j} + e_{ij} \tag{4.4}$$

where the X_{pij} are the p explanatory variables at the individual level. In this step, we assess the contribution of each individual level explanatory variable. If we use the FML estimation method, we can test the improvement of the final model chosen in this step by computing the difference of the deviance of this model and the previous model (the intercept-only model). This difference approximates a chi-square with as degrees of freedom the difference in the number of parameters of both models (cf. 3.1.1). In this case, the degrees of freedom are simply the number of explanatory variables added in step 2.

Step 3:
Add the higher-level explanatory variables:

$$Y_{ij} = \gamma_{00} + \gamma_{p0} X_{pij} + \gamma_{0q} Z_{qj} + u_{0j} + e_{ij} \tag{4.5}$$

where the Z_{qj} are the q explanatory variables at the group level. This model allows us to examine whether the group level explanatory variables explain between group variation in the dependent variable. Again, if we use FML estimation, we can use the global chi-square test to formally test the improvement of fit. If there are more than two levels, this step is executed on a level-by-level basis.

The models in steps 2 and 3 are often denoted as *variance component* models, because they decompose the intercept variance into different variance components for each hierarchical level. In a variance component model, the regression intercept is assumed to vary across the groups, but the regression slopes are assumed fixed. If there are no higher level explanatory variables, this model is equivalent to a random effects analysis of covariance (ANCOVA); the grouping variable is the usual factor, and the lowest level explanatory variables are the covariates (cf. Bryk & Raudenbush, 1992, p. 18; Kreft & de Leeuw, 1998, p. 30). There is a difference in estimation method: ANCOVA uses OLS techniques and multilevel regression uses ML estimation. Nevertheless, both models are highly similar, and if the groups have all equal sizes, it is even possible to compute the usual ANCOVA statistics from the multilevel program output (Raudenbush, 1993a). The reason to start with models that include only fixed regression coefficients is that we generally have more information on these coefficients; they can be estimated with more precision than the variance components. When we are confident that we have a well-fitting model for the fixed part, we turn to modeling the random part.

Step 4:
Assess whether any of the slopes of any of the explanatory variables has a significant variance component between the groups. This model, the *random coefficient model* is given by:

$$Y_{ij} = \gamma_{00} + \gamma_{p0} X_{pij} + \gamma_{0q} Z_{qj} + u_{pj} X_{pij} + u_{0j} + e_{ij} \qquad (4.6)$$

where the u_{pj} are the group level residuals of the slopes of the individual level explanatory variables X_{pij}.

   Testing for random slope variation is best done on a variable-by-variable basis. When we start by including all possible variance components in a model, the result is most likely a model with serious estimation problems, such as convergence problems or extremely slow computations. Variables that were omitted in the previous step may be analyzed again in this step; it is quite possible for an explanatory variable to have no significant average regression slope (as tested in step 2), but to have a significant variance component for this slope.

After deciding which of the slopes have a significant variance between groups, we add all these variance components simultaneously in a final model, and use the chi-square test based on the deviances to test whether the final model of step 4 fits better than the final model of step 3. Since we are now introducing changes in the random part of the model, the chi-square test can also be used with RML estimation (cf. 3.1.1). When counting the number of parameters added, remember that step 3 also includes the covariances between the slopes!

If there are more than two levels, this step is repeated on a level-by-level basis.

Step 5:

Add cross-level interactions between explanatory group level variables and those individual level explanatory variables that had significant slope variation in step 4. This leads to the full model already formulated in equation (2.15):

$$Y_{ij} = \gamma_{00} + \gamma_{p0} X_{pij} + \gamma_{0q} Z_{qj} + \gamma_{pq} Z_{qj}X_{pij} + u_{pj} X_{pij} + u_{0j} + e_{ij} \qquad (4.7)$$

Again, if we use FML estimation, we can use the global chi-square test to formally test the improvement of fit.

If we use an exploratory procedure to arrive at a 'good' model, there is always the possibility that some decisions that have led to this model are based on chance. We may end up overfitting the model by following peculiarities of our specific sample, rather than characteristics of the population. If the sample is large enough, a good strategy is to split it at random in two, use one half for our model exploration and the other half for cross-validation of the final model. See Camstra and Boomsma (1992) for a review of several cross-validation strategies. If the sample is not large enough to permit splitting it up in an exploration and validation sample, we can apply a Bonferroni correction to the individual tests performed in the fixed part at each step. The Bonferroni correction multiplies each p-value by the number of tests performed, and requires the inflated p-value to be significant at the usual level.[1]

At each step, we decide which regression coefficients or (co)variances to keep on the basis of the significance tests, the change in the deviance, and changes in the variance components. Specifically, if we introduce explanatory variables in step 2, we expect that the lowest-level variance σ_e^2 goes down. If the composition of the groups

---

[1] The usual Bonferroni correction is to keep the p-values, and divide the formal alpha level by the number of tests. However, if we have many tests in various steps, we end up with many different significance criteria. It is simpler to correct by appropriately inflating the p-values, and use one alpha criterion for all analysis steps. Both procedures are equivalent, but inflating the p-values makes for a simpler presentation of the results. Holm (1979) describes a more powerful variation of the Bonferroni. If k tests are performed, the Holm correction would multiply the smallest p-value by k, the next smallest p-value by k-1, and so on.

with respect to the explanatory variables is not exactly identical for all groups, we expect that the higher-level variance σ_{u0}^2 also goes down. Thus, the individual level explanatory variables explain part of the individual and part of the group variance. The higher level explanatory variables added in step 3 can explain only group level variance. It is tempting to compute the analogue of a multiple correlation coefficient to indicate how much variance is actually explained at each level (cf. Bryk & Raudenbush, 1992). However, this 'multiple correlation' is at best an approximation, and it is quite possible for it to become smaller when we add explanatory variables, which is impossible with a real multiple correlation. This problem is taken up in section 4.5.

4.2 CENTERING AND STANDARDIZING EXPLANATORY VARIABLES

In ordinary multiple regression analysis, linear transformations of the explanatory variables do not change the essence of the regression estimates. If we divide an explanatory variable by two, its new regression slope equals the old one multiplied by two, and the standard error is also multiplied by two, and a significance test for the regression slope gives exactly the same result. Most importantly, the proportion of unexplained residual variance and hence the multiple correlation does not change either. This is summed up in the statement that the multiple regression model is invariant under linear transformations: if we transform the variables, the estimated parameters change in a similar way, and it is always possible to recalculate the untransformed estimates.

In multilevel regression analysis, the model is only invariant for linear transformations if there are no random regression slopes, that is, if the slopes do not vary across the groups. To understand why this is the case, consider first a simple data set with only one explanatory variable and three groups. Figure 4.1 plots the three regression slopes when there is no slope variance across the groups. In this situation, the slopes are parallel lines. The variance of the intercept is the variance of the slopes at the point where the slopes cut through the Y-axis, which is at the point where the explanatory variable X is equal to zero. It is clear from Figure 4.1 that, if we shift the scale of X to X^* by adding or subtracting a certain amount, we merely shift the location of the Y-axis, without altering the spread of the intercepts. In this case, the variance of the slope is clearly invariant for shifts on the X-axis, which we produce by adding or subtracting a constant from X.

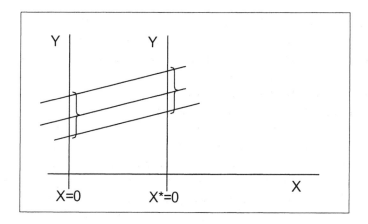

Figure 4.1. Parallel regression lines, with shift on X

The variance of the regression slopes is not invariant for such a transformation if the regression slopes vary across the groups, which is the case if we have group level slope variance. Figure 4.2 shows the situation with three different slope coefficients. This figure shows clearly that with random regression slopes the variance of the intercept changes when we shift the scale of the explanatory variables. It also makes clear how the slope variance should be interpreted: it is the variance of the slopes at the point where the explanatory variable X is equal to zero.

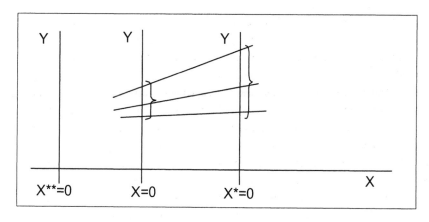

Figure 4.2. Varying regression lines, with shifts on X

It is clear from Figure 4.2 that, if we shift the scale of X to X^* or X^{**} by adding or subtracting a certain amount, the spread of the intercepts changes. If we shift the scale of the X-axis to X^*, the variation of the intercepts is considerable. If we shift the scale of the X-axis to X^{**} and extrapolate the regression slopes, the variation of the intercepts is very small and probably not statistically significant.

In multiple regression analysis, multilevel or single-level, the intercept is interpreted as the expected value of the outcome variable, when all explanatory variables have the value zero. The problem, illustrated in Figure 4.2 by the transformation of the X-scale to X^{**}, is that in many cases 'zero' may not even be a possible value. For instance, if we have an explanatory variable 'gender' coded as 1=male, 2=female, zero is not in the possible score range, and as a consequence the value of the intercept is meaningless. To handle this problem, it is useful to perform a transformation of the X-variables that make 'zero' a legitimate, observable value.

A linear transformation that is often applied to achieve this is *centering* the explanatory variables. The usual practice is that the overall or grand mean is subtracted from all values of a variable, which is called centering on the grand mean, or grand mean centering in short. If we apply grand mean centering, we solve the problem, because now the intercept in the regression equation is always interpretable as the expected value of the outcome variable, when all explanatory variables have their mean value. Grand mean centering is most often used, but it is also possible to center on a different value, e.g., on the median, or on a theoretically interesting value. For example, if we have an explanatory variable 'gender' coded as 1=male, 2=female, the value of the mean could be 1.6, reflecting that we have 60% females in our sample and 40% males. We can center on the sample mean of 1.6, but we may prefer to center on the mean of a theoretical population with 50% males and 50% females. To accomplish this, we would center on the population mean of 1.5, which effectively leads to a code of -0.5 for male and +0.5 for female. Although we center on a value that as such does not and even cannot exist in the population, the intercept is still interpretable as the expected outcome for the average person, disregarding gender.

In multilevel modeling, centering the explanatory variables has the additional advantage that variances of the intercept and the slopes now have a clear interpretation. They are the expected variances when all explanatory variables are equal to zero, in other words: the expected variances for the 'average' subject.

Centering is also important if the multiple regression model includes interactions. For each of the two explanatory variables involved in an interaction, the interpretation of its slope is that it is the expected value of the slope when the other variable has the value zero. Again, since 'zero' may not even be a possible value, the value of the slope may not be interpretable at all. Since many multilevel regression models include cross-level interactions, this is a serious interpretation problem. When both variables in the interaction are centered on their grand mean, the problem disappears. The problem of interpreting interactions in multilevel regression models is discussed in more detail in the next section.

We will consider the issue of centering in a simple example, using the data from our example in Chapter Two, and including only pupil gender as explanatory variable. We compare the estimates for pupil gender as a raw and as a grand mean centered variable, both for a variance component model (fixed slope for pupil gender) and for a random coefficient model (varying slope for pupil gender). The table also shows the estimates that result when we standardize the variable pupil gender. Standardization is a linear transformation that implies grand mean centering, but adds a multiplicative transformation to achieve a standard deviation of one.

Table 4.1	Model with pupil gender, raw and centered explanatory variables			
Model:	pupil gender fixed coefficient		pupil gender random coefficient	
Fixed part	raw	centered	raw	centered
Predictor	coeff. (s.e.)	coeff. (s.e.)	coeff. (s.e.)	coeff. (s.e.)
intercept	4.90 (.10)	5.31 (.09)	4.89 (.10)	5.30 (.09)
pup. gender	0.84 (.03)	0.84 (.03)	0.84 (.06)	0.84 (.06)
Random part				
σ_e^2	0.46 (.02)	0.46 (.02)	0.39 (.01)	0.39 (.01)
σ_{u0}^2	0.86 (.13)	0.86 (.13)	0.93 (.14)	0.86 (.12)
σ_{u1}^2	-	-	0.27 (.05)	0.27 (.05)
Deviance	4484.9	4484.9	4329.6	4329.6

As Table 4.1 shows, for a model without random slopes, grand mean centering of the variable pupil gender results only in a change in the intercept. All the other estimates remain the same. Standardizing changes the scale of pupil gender, but the effect of this transformation on the slope of pupil gender is easily understandable. Since the standard deviation of pupil gender is about 0.5, standardization means that this variable is multiplied by two. Consequently, its slope coefficient is divided by two. Everything else remains the same. However, this does not hold for the random coefficient model. Here, the estimates for the higher level intercept variance also change. The deviance remains the same, which indicates that all three random coefficient models fit the data equally well. In fact, all three models are equivalent. Equivalent models have the same fit, and produce the same residuals. The parameter estimates are not all identical, but the estimates for one model can be transformed to the estimates of the other model. Thus, grand mean centering and overall standardization do not really complicate the interpretation of the results. In addition, grand mean centering and standardization do have some advantages. One advantage is that the intercept becomes a meaningful value. The value of the higher-level intercept variance also becomes meaningful; it is the expected variance at the mean of all explanatory variables. A second advantage is that with centered explanatory variables the calculations tend to go faster, and encounter fewer convergence problems. Especially when explanatory variables vary widely in their means and variances, grand mean centering or standardization may be necessary to reach convergence, or even to be able to start the computations at all. Since grand mean centering only affects the intercept, which is often not interpreted anyway, it is preferred above standardization, which will also affect the interpretation of the regression slopes and the residual variances.

Some multilevel analysts advocate a totally different way of centering, called group mean centering. Group mean centering means that the group mean is subtracted from the corresponding individual scores. Since different values are subtracted from different scores, this is not the same as centering on some overall value, such as the grand mean. This form of centering will be discussed in the next section.

4.3 INTERPRETING INTERACTIONS

Whenever there are interactions in a multiple regression analysis (whether these are a cross-level interaction in a multilevel regression analysis or an interaction in an ordinary single-level regression analysis does not matter), there are two important technical points to be made. Both stem from the methodological principle, that in the presence of a significant interaction the effect of the interaction variable and the direct effects of the explanatory variables that make up that interaction must be interpreted together as a system (Jaccard, Turrisi & Wan, 1990; Aiken & West, 1991).

The first point is that if the interaction is significant, it is best to include both direct effects in the regression too, even if they are not significant.

The second point is that in a model with an interaction effect, the regression coefficients of the simple or direct variables that make up that interaction carry a different meaning than in a model without this interaction effect. If there is an interaction, then the regression coefficient of one of the direct variables is the expected value of the regression slope for the case that the other variable is equal to zero, and vice versa. If for one variable the value 'zero' is widely beyond the range of values that have been observed, as in age varying from 18 to 55, or if the value 'zero' is in fact impossible, as in gender coded male=1, female=2, the result is that the regression coefficient for the other variable has no substantive interpretation. In many such cases, if we compare different models, the regression coefficient for at least one of the variables making up the interaction will be very different from the corresponding coefficient in the model without interaction. *But this change does not mean anything.*

One remedy is to take care that the value 'zero' is meaningful and actually occurs in the data. One can accomplish this by centering both explanatory variables on their overall mean.[1] After centering, the value 'zero' refers to the mean of the centered variable; in this case the regression coefficients do not change when the interaction is added to the model. When the explanatory variables are centered, the regression coefficient of one of the variables in an interaction can be interpreted as the regression coefficient for individuals with an 'average' score on the other variable. If all explanatory variables are centered, the intercept is equal to the grand mean of the dependent variable.

In practice, to interpret an interaction, it is helpful to write out the regression equation for one explanatory variable for various values of the other explanatory variable. When both explanatory variables are continuous, we write out the regression equation for the lower level explanatory variable, for a choice of values for the explanatory variable at the higher level. Good choices are the mean, maximum and minimum, or the median and the 25th and 75th percentile. A plot of these regression lines clarifies the meaning of the interaction. If one of the explanatory variables is dichotomous, we write the regression equation for the continuous variable, for both values of the dichotomous variable.

In the example we have used so far, there is a cross-level interaction between pupil gender and teacher experience. In the corresponding data file, pupil gender is scored 0=male, and 1=female, and teacher experience is recorded in years, with the amount of experience ranging from 3 to 25 years. Since there are no teachers with zero experience, this explains why adding the cross-level interaction between pupil gender and teacher experience to the model results in an appreciable change in the regression slope of pupil gender from 0.84 to 1.33. In the model without the interaction, the regression slope of pupil gender is independent from teacher experience. Therefore, it can be said to apply to the average class, with an average teacher having an amount of experience somewhere in the middle between 3 and 25 years. In the model with the interaction, the pupil gender slope now refers to a class with a teacher who has zero years of experience. This is an extreme value, which is not even observed in the data. Following the same reasoning, we can conclude that the teacher experience slope refers to pupil gender = 0, which are the boys. Since 'zero' is a value that does occur in the data, the interpretation of the effect of teacher experience is straightforward.

---

[1] Standardizing the explanatory variables has the same effect. In this case, it is recommended not to standardize the interaction variable itself (which is possible in programs like MLwiN, where it must be included explicitly, because that makes it difficult to compute predictions or plot interactions. Standardized regression weights for the interaction term can always be determined using equation (2.13).

Table 4.2   Cross-level interactions, raw and centered explanatory variables

Model:	raw explanatory variables		centered explanatory variables	
Fixed part	no interact.	interaction	no interact.	interaction
Predictor	coeff. (s.e.)	coeff. (s.e.)	coeff. (s.e.)	coeff. (s.e.)
intercept	3.34 (.16)	3.31 (.16)	5.30 (.07)	5.30 (.07)
pup. gender	0.84 (.06)	1.33 (.13)	0.84 (.06)	0.84 (.06)
teach. exp	0.11 (.01)	0.11 (.01)	0.11 (.01)	0.09 (.01)
pup. gender × teach. exp	-	-.03 (.01)	-	-.03 (.01)
Random part				
σ_e^2	0.39 (.01)	0.39 (.01)	0.39 (.01)	0.39 (.01)
σ_{u0}^2	0.40 (.13)	0.40 (.13)	0.49 (.14)	0.87 (.13)
σ_{u1}^2	0.27 (.05)	0.22 (.04)	0.27 (.05)	0.22 (.04)
σ_{u01}	0.02 (.04)	0.02 (.04)	0.15 (.04)	0.13 (.04)
Deviance	4261.2	4245.9	4261.2	4445.9

The estimates for the centered explanatory variables in Table 4.2 are much more comparable across different models than the estimates for the uncentered variables (the small difference between 0.11 and 0.09 for teacher experience is due to rounding). To interpret the cross-level interaction, it helps to work out the regression equations for the boys and girls separately. Using the uncentered variables, the regression equation for boys is: *popularity* = 3.31 + 1.33 × *pupil gender* (=0) + 0.11 × *teacher experience* – 0.03 × *pupil gender* (=0) × *teacher experience*. For girls the regression equation is: *popularity* = 3.31 + 1.33 × *pupil gender* (=1) + 0.11 × *teacher experience* – 0.03 × *pupil gender* (=1) × *teacher experience*. Thus, for boys we get: *popularity* = 3.31 + 0.11 × *teacher experience*. For girls we get: *popularity* = 3.31 + 1.33 + 0.11 × *teacher experience* – 0.03 × *teacher experience*, which simplifies to *popularity* = 4.64 + 0.08 × *teacher experience*. From these two regression equations, we can conclude that for teachers with zero experience, boys are expected to have a popularity score of 3.31, which is lower than the girls' expected popularity score of 4.64. With each extra year of teacher experience, the boys' popularity is higher by 0.11, and the girls' by 0.08. So, for more experienced teachers, the difference between boys and girls becomes smaller.

Another way to make interactions easier to interpret is to plot the regression slopes for one of the explanatory variables for some values of the other. Figure 4.3 presents a plot of the regression lines for boys and girls in one picture.

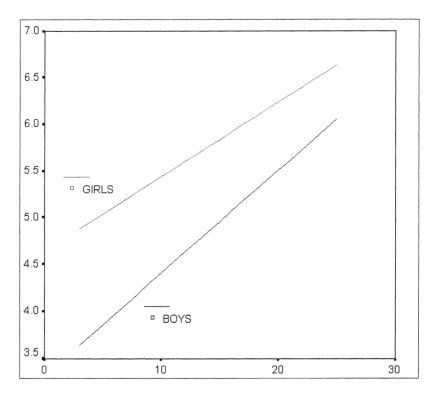

*Figure 4.3. Regression lines for popularity of girls and boys,
predicted by teacher experience*

It is clear that girls have a higher expected popularity score than boys, and although the difference is smaller with more experienced teachers, it does not disappear entirely. If we use the centered scores for the plot, the scale of the X-axis, which represents teacher experience, would change, but the picture would not. Centering explanatory variables is especially attractive when we want to interpret the meaning of an interaction by inspecting the regression coefficients in the table. As Figure 4.3 shows, plotting the interaction over the range of observed values of the explanatory variables is always an effective way to convey its meaning, even if we work with raw variables.

As mentioned in the previous section, some multilevel analysts prefer to use group mean centering, where the group's mean is subtracted from the corresponding individual scores. This is sometimes done, because it can be used to represent a specific hypothesis. For instance, in educational research there is a hypothesis called the 'frog pond effect.' This simply means that for the same frog the effect of being in a pond filled with big frogs is different than being in a pond filled with small frogs. In educational terms, pupils of average intelligence in a class with very smart pupils may find themselves unable to cope, and give up. Conversely, pupils of average intelligence in a class with very unintelligent pupils, are relatively smart, and may become stimulated to perform really well. The frog pond hypothesis states, that the effect of intelligence on school success depends on the relative standing of the pupils in their own class. A simple indicator of the pupils' relative standing can be constructed by computing the individual deviation score, by subtracting from the pupil's intelligence score the average intelligence in their class. Group mean centering is a direct translation of the frog pond mechanism in terms of the explanatory variables.

Unfortunately, group mean centering changes the meaning of the entire regression model in a complicated way. If we use grand mean centering, we get different regression slopes for the centered variables, and different variance components, but we have an equivalent model, with identical deviance and residual errors. Another way to describe this situation is to state that we have specified a different *parameterization* for our model, meaning that we have essentially the same model, but transformed in a way that makes it easier to interpret. Using straightforward algebra, we can transform the grand mean centered estimates back to the values we would have found by analyzing the raw scores. Group mean centering, on the contrary, is *not* a simple reparameterization of a model, but a completely different model. Transforming parameters back to the corresponding raw score estimates is not possible. The reason is that we have subtracted not one single value, but a collection of different values from the raw scores. The technical details that govern the relations between parameter estimates using raw scores, grand mean centered scores, and group mean scores, are complicated; they are discussed in detail in Kreft, de Leeuw and Aiken (1995), and in more general terms in Kreft and de Leeuw (1998) and in Hofman and Gavin (1998).

As Kreft, de Leeuw and Aiken (1995) show, models become complicated when group mean centering is considered. Group mean centering of an explanatory variable implies less effective modeling than using raw scores, simply because all information concerning differences between groups is removed from that variable. It would seem reasonable to restore this information by adding the group mean again as an additional group level explanatory variable. But this adds extra information about the group structure, which is not present in the raw scores, and therefore we will obtain a model that fits better than the raw score model. If we consider the effect of group mean centering in detail, it appears that group mean centering is an implicit, complicated way to change the meaning of individual and group level effects, including the interpretation of cross-level interactions. The conclusion is, that novice users of multilevel models should apply a good deal of caution in using group mean centering. If the theory behind the modeling strongly suggests 'frog pond' or similar effects (cf. Hofmann & Gavin, 1998), which are best modeled using group centering, using group mean centering may be advantageous, but the users should be keenly aware of the issues they are facing in interpretation.

4.4 HOW MUCH VARIANCE IS EXPLAINED?

An important statistic in ordinary multiple regression analysis is the multiple correlation R, or the squared multiple correlation R^2, which is interpreted as the proportion of variance modeled by the explanatory variables. In multilevel regression analysis, the issue of modeled or explained variance is a complex one. First, there is unexplained variance at several levels to contend with. This alone makes the proportion of explained variance a more complicated concept than in single level regression analysis. Second, if there are random slopes, the model is inherently more complex, and the concept of explained variance has no unique definition anymore. Various approaches have been proposed to indicate how well we are predicting the outcomes in a multilevel model.

Table 4.3	**Models for pupil popularity data**				
Model:	intercept only	level-1 fixed predictor	level-2 predictor	random coefficient	cross-level interaction
Fixed part					
Predictor	coefficient	coefficient	coefficient	coefficient	coefficient
intercept	5.31	4.90	3.56	3.34	3.31
pup. gender		0.84	0.85	0.84	1.33
teach. exp			0.09	0.11	0.11
gender × exp					-.03
Random part					
σ_e^2	0.64	0.46	0.46	0.39	0.39
σ_{u0}^2	0.87	0.85	0.48	0.40	0.40
σ_{u1}^2		-		0.27	0.22
σ_{u01}		-		0.02	0.02
Deviance	5112.7	4484.9	4428.6	4261.2	4245.9

A straightforward approach to examining the proportion of explained variance consists of examining the residual error variances in a sequence of models, such as the sequence proposed in Chapter Three. Table 4.3 presents for such a sequence of models the parameter estimates (regression coefficients and variance components) plus the deviance, using FML estimation. The first model is the intercept-only model. This is a useful baseline model, because it does not introduce any explanatory variables (except the constant intercept term) and decomposes the total variance of the outcome variable into two levels. Thus, the individual level variance of the popularity scores is 0.64, the class level variance is 0.87, and the total variance is the sum of the two: 1.51. Since there are no explanatory variables in the model, it is reasonable to interpret these variances as the error variances.

In the first 'real' model, the pupil level explanatory variable 'pupil gender' is introduced. As a result, the first level residual error variance goes down to 0.46, and the second level variance goes down to 0.85. Again, it is reasonable to interpret the difference as the amount of variance explained by introducing the variable 'pupil gender'. To calculate a statistic analogous to the multiple R^2, we must express this difference as a proportion of the total error variance. It appears most informative if we do this separately level-by-level. For the proportion of variance explained at the first level we use (cf. Bryk & Raudenbush, 1992, p. 68):

$$R_1^2 = \left(\frac{\sigma_{e|b}^2 - \sigma_{e|m}^2}{\sigma_{e|b}^2} \right) \tag{4.8}$$

where $\sigma_{e|b}^2$ is the lowest level residual variance for the baseline model, which is the intercept-only model, and $\sigma_{e|m}^2$ is the lowest level residual variance for the comparison model. For the pupil popularity data this calculates the proportion explained variance at the pupil level for the model with pupil gender as:

$$R_1^2 = \left(\frac{0.64 - 0.46}{0.64} \right) = 0.28$$

For the proportion of variance explained at the second level (cf Bryk & Raudenbush, 1992, p65) we use:

$$R_2^2 = \left(\frac{\sigma_{u0|b}^2 - \sigma_{u0|m}^2}{\sigma_{u0|b}^2} \right) \tag{4.9}$$

where $\sigma_{u0|b}^2$ is the second-level residual variance for the baseline model, which is the intercept-only model, and $\sigma_{u0|m}^2$ is the second-level residual variance for the comparison model. For the pupil popularity data this calculates the proportion explained variance at the class level as:

$$R_2^2 = \left(\frac{0.87 - 0.85}{0.87} \right) = 0.02$$

This is a small number, but it may come as a surprise that a pupil level variable like 'pupil gender' is able to explain variance at the class level at all. The explanation is straightforward. If the proportion of girls is not exactly the same in all classes, the classes do differ in their average number of girls, and this variation can explain some of the class level variance in average popularity between classes. In our example, the amount of variance explained by pupil gender at the class level is very small, which reflects the fact that both sexes are distributed almost equally across all classes. The results could have been different; explanatory variables that are divided very selectively across the groups can often explain a fair amount of group level variance. The interpretation would generally be that this does not reflect a real contextual effect, but rather the unequal composition of the groups.

Assessing the effect of adding the school level explanatory variable 'teacher experience' to the model follows the same reasoning. The residual variance at the first level does not change at all. This is as it should be, because class level variables cannot predict individual level variation. The class level residual variance goes down to 0.48, so the class level R-square becomes

$$R_2^2 = \left(\frac{0.87 - 0.48}{0.87} \right) = 0.45$$

which means that 45% of the variance at the class level is explained by the pupil gender and teacher experience. A comparison with the previous $R_2^2 = 0.02$ makes clear that most of the predictive power stems from the teacher experience.

The next model is the random coefficient model, where the regression slope for pupil gender is assumed to vary across schools. In the random coefficient model, the variance of the slopes for pupil gender is estimated as 0.27. Since the model contains no cross-level interactions with pupil gender, this variance is not modeled, and it is analogous to the error variance of the intercept at the class level. The cross-level model includes the interaction of pupil gender with teacher experience, and estimates the variance for the pupil gender slopes as 0.22. Hence, the explained variance in these slopes is given by (cf. Bryk & Raudenbush, 1992, p. 74):

$$R_{\beta_1}^2 = \left(\frac{\sigma_{u1|b}^2 - \sigma_{u1|m}^2}{\sigma_{u1|b}^2} \right) \tag{4.10}$$

where $\sigma^2_{u1|b}$ is the variance of the slopes for pupil gender in the baseline model, and $\sigma^2_{u1|m}$ is the variance of the slopes for pupil gender in the comparison model. For our example data, comparing the random coefficient model as a baseline model with the cross-level interaction model, we obtain:

$$R^2_{t.exp2} = \left(\frac{0.27 - 0.22}{0.27} \right) = 0.19$$

Using one explanatory variable at the school level, we can explain 19% of the variance of the pupil gender slopes.

All this appears straightforward, but there are two major problems. First, by using these formulas it is quite possible to arrive at the conclusion that a specific explanatory variable has a negative contribution to the explained variance. In fact, it is possible to arrive at a negative R^2. This is unfortunate, to say the least. Snijders and Bosker (1994) explain why these seemingly anomalous results in fact *must* happen under some circumstances A second problem is that, in models with random slopes, the estimated variances depend on the scale of the explanatory variables. This has been explained in section 4.2 of this chapter, in the discussion of the effects of centering and standardization. This means that the explained variance changes if we change the scale of the explanatory variables that have varying slopes.

To understand how variables can have a negative contribution to the explained variance, as computed by equations (4.8) to (4.10), we must investigate the effect of including an explanatory variable on the various variance components. Intuitively, the argument relies on the assumption of multilevel modeling that the sample is obtained by simple random sampling at all levels. The underlying assumption of the model is that the groups are sampled at random from a population of groups, and that the individuals are sampled at random within these groups.

Assume that we sample N individuals, and randomly assign them to J groups, all with equal group size n. For any variable X with mean μ and variance σ^2, the distribution of the group means is approximately normal with mean μ and variance:

$$\sigma^2_\mu = \sigma^2 / n \qquad (4.11)$$

This is a well-known statistical theorem, which is the basis of the familiar F-test in the Analysis of Variance. In analysis of variance, we estimate the population variance σ^2 using s^2_{PW}, the pooled within groups variance. A second estimate of σ^2 is given by ns^2_m, using (4.11) and filling in the observed means m for the population means μ. This is used in the familiar F-test, $F = ns^2_m / s^2_{PW}$, for the null-hypothesis that there are no real differences between the groups. If there are real group differences, there is a real group level variance, and ns_m^2 is an estimator of $\left(\sigma^2 + \sigma_\mu^2/n\right)$. Thus, in general, in grouped data some of the information about the population within groups variance is in the observed between-groups variance, and the between groups variance calculated in the sample is an upwardly biased estimator of the population between groups variance. This also means that, even if the between groups variance in the population is zero, the observed between groups variance is not expected to be zero, but to be equal to σ^2/n.

Thus, for an individual level variable sampled via a simple multilevel sampling process, we expect that it will show some between-group variability, even if there are no group effects in the population. For such variables, the approximate R-square formulas defined above should do reasonably well. But in some situations we have variables that have (almost) no variation at one of the levels. This occurs when we use as explanatory variable a group mean centered variable, from which all group information is removed, or the group averages, which have no variation at all at the individual level. In an implicit way this occurs when we have data with a strong selection process, or time series designs. For instance, if we carry out an educational experiment, we might assign pupils to classes to achieve an exactly equal gender ratio of 50% boys and 50% girls in each class. If we do this, we have no between class variation in average gender, which is *less* than expected by simple random sampling of boys and girls. In a similar way, in many studies where we have as the lowest level a series of repeated observations at different occasions, all subjects have exactly the same series of time points, because they were measured at the same occasions. Here again we have no variation of time points across subjects. In these cases, using the simple formulas given above may produce the result that the explanatory variable 'gender' or 'occasion' appears to explain negative variance.

Snijders and Bosker (1994) explain the problem in detail. First, let us consider a model that contains no random effects for the slopes. We could base an estimate of σ_e^2 on the pooled within groups variance. This would be inefficient, because it ignores the information we have about σ_e^2 in the between groups variance. Furthermore, the observed between groups variance must be corrected for the within groups variance to produce an accurate estimator for σ_{u0}^2. As a result, the maximum likelihood estimators of σ_e^2 and σ_{u0}^2 are a complex weighted function of the pooled within groups and the between groups variances.

Assume that we start by estimating an intercept-only model, which gives us baseline estimates for the two variance components σ_e^2 and σ_{u0}^2. First, we introduce a 'normal' first-level explanatory variable, like pupil gender in our example. As explained above, the expected between groups variation for such a variable is not zero, but σ^2/n. So, this variable will in general reduce both the within groups variance, and the between group variance. The correction implicit in the ML estimators insures that both σ_e^2 and σ_{u0}^2 are reduced by the correct amount. Since σ_{u0}^2 is corrected for a 'normal' explanatory variable, it should not change, unless our explanatory variable explains some real group-level variation as well. If we add a group-level variable to the model, this will reduce only the between groups variance, and not the within group variance. As a result, the estimate for the population variance σ_{u0}^2 goes up. Since most of the information about the lowest level variance comes from the within groups variance, the estimate σ_e^2 will usually not change much, but it may also go up. In ordinary multiple regression analysis such a thing cannot occur. Now, consider what happens if we add an explanatory variable that is group mean centered, which means that all group level information has been removed. This can reduce only the within groups variance, and leaves the between group variance unchanged. The correction implicit in the ML estimator of σ_{u0}^2 will now correct for the smaller amount of within groups variance, and as a result the estimate of the apparent between groups variance σ_{u0}^2 goes up. Using equation (4.8), we get a negative estimate for the explained variance at the group level, which makes no sense.

With this knowledge in mind, let us look again at the formulas for explained variance. For the lowest level, we repeat the equation here:

$$R_1^2 = \left(\frac{\sigma_{e|b}^2 - \sigma_{e|m}^2}{\sigma_{e|b}^2} \right)$$

(4.8, repeated)

Provided that σ_e^2 is an unbiased estimator, this formula is correct. But, as we have seen, adding group level variables to the model may lead to incorrect estimates, because the estimation procedure does not combine the information from the two levels correctly. Snijders and Bosker (1994) propose to remedy this by replacing σ_e^2 in (4.8) by the sum $\sigma_e^2 + \sigma_{u0}^2$. This will use all available information about the within group variance in a consistent way.

The formula for the second level explained variance is given by

$$R_2^2 = \left(\frac{\sigma_{u0|b}^2 - \sigma_{u0|m}^2}{\sigma_{u0|b}^2} \right)$$

(4.9, repeated)

Snijders and Bosker (1994) propose to replace σ_{u0}^2 in (4.9) by $\sigma_{u0}^2 + \sigma_e^2/n$. For unequal group sizes, the simplest solution is to replace the common group size n by the average group size. A more elaborate option proposed by Snijders and Bosker (1994) is to replace n by the harmonic group mean defined by $\left\{ (1/N)\sum_j (1/n_j) \right\}^{-1}$. The ad hoc estimator proposed by Muthén (1994), given by $c = \left[N^2 - \sum_j n_j^2 \right] / \left[N(J-1) \right]^{-1}$, is

components, it appears prudent to center all explanatory variables that have varying slopes on their overall mean. Given that the estimates of the variance components may depend on the explanatory variables, this at least insures that we get these estimates for values of the explanatory variables that actually exist, and reflect some average sampling unit. This would apply to both the approximate and the Snijders & Bosker approach to estimating explained variance.

5

Analyzing Longitudinal Data

Longitudinal data, or repeated measures data, can be viewed as multilevel data, with repeated measurements nested within individuals. In its simplest form, this leads to a two-level model, with the series of repeated measures at the lowest level, and the individual persons at the highest level. Longitudinal measures can be taken at fixed or at varying occasions. Multilevel analysis for longitudinal data can handle both situations. Since multilevel modeling does not require balanced data, it is not a problem if the number of available measurements is not the same for all individuals. This is an important benefit if there is panel dropout, or other forms of missing measurements within individuals. Since longitudinal data collected at fixed occasions is the simplest situation, this chapter starts with fixed occasions, and discusses varying occasions later.

If the data are collected to analyze individual change over time, the constructs under study must be measured on a comparable scale at each occasion (cf. Plewis, 1985, 1996; Taris, 2000). When the time span is short, this does not pose complicated problems. For instance, Tate and Hokanson (1993) report on a longitudinal study where the scores of students on the Beck Depression scale were collected at three occasions during the academic year. In such an application, we may assume that the research instrument remains constant for the duration of the study. On the other hand, in a study that examines improvements in reading skill in school children from ages 5-12, it is clear that we cannot use the same instrument to measure reading skill at such different age levels. Here, we must make sure that the different measurement instruments are calibrated, meaning that a specific score has the same psychometric meaning at all age levels, independent of the actual reading test that is used. The issues are the same as the issues in cross-cultural comparison (cf. Bechger, van Schooten, de Glopper, & Hox, 1998). Another requirement is that there is sufficient time between the measurements that memory effects are not a problem. In some applications, this may not be the case. For instance, if data are collected that are closely spaced in time, we may expect considerable correlation between measurements collected at occasions that are close together, partly because of memory effects. These effects should then be included in the model, which leads to models with correlated errors. Formulating multilevel models for such situations can be quite complex. Some multilevel software has built-in provisions for modeling correlated errors. These are discussed in the last part of this chapter.

The models discussed in this chapter are all models for data that have repeated measures on individuals over time. Within the framework of multilevel modeling, we can also analyze data where the repeated measures are on higher levels, e.g., data where we follow the same set of schools over a number of years, with of course in each year a different set of pupils. Models for such data are similar to the models discussed in this chapter. Such repeated cross-sectional data are discussed by DiPrete and Grusky (1990) and Raudenbush and Chan (1993).

Multilevel analysis of repeated measures most often applied to data from large-scale panel surveys. In addition, it can also be a valuable analysis tool in a variety of experimental designs. If we have a pretest-posttest design, the usual analysis is an analysis of covariance (Ancova) with the experimental and control groups as the factor and the pretest as the covariate. In the multilevel framework, we analyze the slopes of the change over time, using an experimental group/control group dummy variable to predict differences in the slopes. If we have just a pretest-posttest design this does not offer much more than the usual analysis of covariance. However, in the multilevel framework it makes sense to add more measurement occasions between the pretest and the posttest. Willett (1989) and Maxwell (1998) show that the power of the test can be increased dramatically by adding only a few additional waves of data collection.

5.1   FIXED AND VARYING OCCASIONS

It is useful to distinguish between repeated measures that are collected at fixed or varying occasions. If the measurements are taken at fixed occasions, all individuals provide measurements at the same set of occasions, usually regularly spaced, such as every year. When occasions are varying, we have a different set of measures taken at different points in time for different individuals. Such data occur, for instance, in growth studies, where physical or psychological characteristics are studied for a set of individuals at different moments in their development. The data collection could be at fixed moments in the year, but the individuals would have different ages at that moment. Alternatively, the original design is a fixed occasion design, but due to planning problems, the data collection does not take place at the intended moments. For a multilevel analysis of the resulting data, the difference between fixed and varying occasions is not very important. For fixed occasion designs, especially when the occasions are regularly spaced and there are no missing data, repeated measures analysis of variance is a viable alternative for multilevel analysis. A comparison of the analysis of variance approach and multilevel analysis is given in section 5.2.

Another possibility in such designs is latent curve analysis, also known as latent growth curve analysis. This is a structural equation model (cf. Willett & Sayer, 1994; Duncan & Duncan, 1995) that models a repeated measures polynomial analysis of variance. Latent growth curve models are treated in Chapter Fourteen. Multilevel models for longitudinal data are discussed by, among others, Bryk and Raudenbush (1987, 1992) and Goldstein (1987, 1995); for introductory articles see Snijders (1996), Cnaan, Laird and Slasor (1997), and Van der Leeden (1998).

5.2   EXAMPLE WITH FIXED OCCASIONS

The example data are a longitudinal data set from 200 college students. The students' Grade Point Average (GPA) has been recorded for six successive semesters. At the same time, it was recorded whether the student held a job in that semester, and for how many hours. This is recorded in a variable 'job' (with categories 0=no job, 1=1 hour, 2=2 hours, 3=3 hours, 4=4 or more hours), which for the purpose of this example is treated as an interval level variable. In this example, we also use the student variables high school GPA and gender (1=male, 2=female), which of course remain constant for each student across the six time points.

1:student		1												
	student	sex	highgpa	gpa1	gpa2	gpa3	gpa4	gpa5	gpa6	job1	job2	job3	job4	job5	job6
1	1	2	2.8	2.3	2.1	3.0	3.0	3.0	3.3	2	2	2	2	2	2
2	2	1	2.5	2.2	2.5	2.6	2.6	3.0	2.8	2	3	2	2	2	2
3	3	2	2.5	2.4	2.9	3.0	2.8	3.3	3.4	2	2	2	3	2	2
4	4	1	3.8	2.5	2.7	2.4	2.7	2.9	2.7	3	2	2	2	2	2
5	5	1	3.1	2.8	2.8	2.8	3.0	2.9	3.1	2	2	2	2	2	2
6	6	2	2.9	2.5	2.4	2.4	2.3	2.7	2.8	2	3	3	2	3	3
7	7	1	2.3	2.4	2.4	2.8	2.6	3.0	3.0	3	2	3	2	2	2
8	8	2	3.9	2.8	2.8	3.1	3.3	3.3	3.4	2	2	2	2	2	2
9	9	1	2.0	2.8	2.7	2.7	3.1	3.1	3.5	2	2	3	2	2	2
10	10	1	2.8	2.8	2.8	3.0	2.7	3.0	3.0	2	2	2	3	2	2
11	11	2	3.9	2.6	2.9	3.2	3.6	3.6	3.8	2	3	2	2	2	2
12	12	2	2.9	2.6	3.0	2.3	2.9	3.1	3.3	3	2	2	2	2	2
13	13	1	3.7	2.8	3.1	3.5	3.6	3.9	3.9	2	2	2	2	2	2
14	14	2	3.5	2.4	3.0	2.9	3.0	3.3	3.4	2	2	2	2	2	2

Figure 5.1. Repeated measures data structure in SPSS

In a statistical package such as SPSS or SAS, such data are typically stored with the students defining the cases, and the repeated measurements as a series of variables, such as GPA1, GPA2,..., GPA6, and JOB1, JOB2,..., JOB6. For example, in SPSS the data structure would be as shown in Figure 5.1.

The data structure for a multilevel analysis of these data is generally different, depending on the specific program that is used. Most multilevel software requires that the data is structured with the measurement occasions defining the cases, and student level variables repeated over the cases. For instance, the programs MLwiN or MixReg require that the data structure is as shown in Figure 5.2. In Figure 5.2, each row in the data set represents a separate occasion, with repeated measurements resulting in a series of rows for each student. Although Figure 5.2 does not show them, missing occasions simply result in students with less than the full set of six occasions in the data file. As a result, missing occasions are very simple to handle in a multilevel model.

1:student		1				
	student	occasion	gpa	job	sex	highgpa
1	1	1	2.3	2	2	2.8
2	1	2	2.1	2	2	2.8
3	1	3	3.0	2	2	2.8
4	1	4	3.0	2	2	2.8
5	1	5	3.0	2	2	2.8
6	1	6	3.3	2	2	2.8
7	2	1	2.2	2	1	2.5
8	2	2	2.5	3	1	2.5
9	2	3	2.6	2	1	2.5
10	2	4	2.6	2	1	2.5
11	2	5	3.0	2	1	2.5
12	2	6	2.8	2	1	2.5
13	3	1	2.4	2	2	2.5
14	3	2	2.9	2	2	2.5

Figure 5.2. Repeated measures data structure for multilevel analysis

The multilevel regression model for longitudinal data is a straightforward application of the multilevel regression model described in Chapter Two. It can also be written as a sequence of models for each level. At the lowest, the repeated measures level, we have:

$$Y_{ti} = \pi_{0i} + \pi_{1i}T_{ti} + \pi_{2i}X_{ti} + e_{ti} \tag{5.1}$$

In repeated measures applications, the coefficients at the lowest level are often indicated by the Greek letter π. This has the advantage that the person level coefficients, which are in repeated measures modeling at the second level, can be represented by the usual Greek letter β, and so on. In equation (5.1), Y_{ti} is the response variable of individual i measured at time point t, T is the time variable that indicates the time point, and X_{ti} is a *time varying covariate*. For example, Y_{ti} could be the GPA of a student at time point t, T_{ti} indicates the occasion at which the GPA is measured, and X_{ti} the job status of the student at time t. Student characteristics, such as gender, are *time invariant covariates*, which enter the equation at the second level:

$$\pi_{0i} = \beta_{00} + \beta_{01}Z_i + u_{0i} \tag{5.2}$$

$$\pi_{1i} = \beta_{10} + \beta_{11}Z_i + u_{1i} \tag{5.3}$$

$$\pi_{2i} = \beta_{20} + \beta_{21}Z_i + u_{2i} \tag{5.4}$$

By substitution, we get the single equation model:

$$Y_{ti} = \beta_{00} + \beta_{10}T_{ti} + \beta_{20}X_{ti} + \beta_{01}Z_i + \beta_{11}Z_iT_{ti} + \beta_{21}Z_iX_{ti} + \\ u_{1i}T_{ti} + u_{2i}X_{ti} + u_{0i} + e_{ti} \tag{5.5}$$

Using variable labels instead of letters, the equation becomes

$$GPA_{tj} = \beta_{00} + \beta_{10}Time_{ti} + \beta_{20}Job_{ti} + \beta_{01}Sex_i + \beta_{11}Sex_iTime_{ti} + \beta_{21}Sex_iJob_{ti} + \\ u_{1i}Time_{ti} + u_{2i}Job_{ti} + u_{0i} + e_{ti} \tag{5.6}$$

In longitudinal research, we sometimes have repeated measurements of individuals, who are all measured together on a small number of fixed occasions. This is typically the case with experimental designs involving repeated measures and panel research. If we simply want to test the null hypothesis that the means are equal for all occasions, we can use repeated measures Analysis of Variance. If we use repeated measures univariate analysis of variance (Stevens, 1996, p. 455), we must assume *sphericity*. Sphericity means that there are complex restrictions on the variances and covariances between the repeated measures, for details see Stevens (1996, chapter 13). A specific form of sphericity, which is easily understood, is *compound symmetry*, sometimes referred to as *uniformity*. Compound symmetry requires that all population variances of the repeated measures are equal, and that all population covariances of the repeated measures are equal. If sphericity is not met, the *F*-ratio used in Analysis of Variance is positively biased, and we reject the null hypothesis too often. An alternative approach is to specify the repeated measures as observations on a multivariate response vector and use Multivariate Analysis of Variance (MANOVA). This does not require sphericity, and is considered the preferred approach if analysis of variance is used on repeated measures (O'Brien & Kaiser, 1985; Stevens, 1996). However, the multivariate test is more complicated, because it is based on a transformation of the repeated measures, and what is tested are actually contrasts among the repeated measures.

A MANOVA analysis of the example data using the General Linear Model in SPSS (SPSS Inc., 1997) cannot easily incorporate a time-varying covariate such as job status. But MANOVA can be used to test the trend over time of the repeated GPA measures by specifying polynomial contrasts for the time variable, and to test the fixed effects of gender and high school GPA. Gender is a dichotomous variable, which is entered as a factor, and high school GPA is a continuous variable that is entered as a covariate. Table 5.1 presents the results of the significance tests.

Table 5.1 MANOVA significance tests on GPA example data			
Effect tested:	F	df	*p*
GPA (categorical)	4.53	5/193	.001
GPA (linear trend)	12.77	1/197	.000
GPA*HighGPA	0.87	5/193	.505
GPA*Gender	1.42	5/193	.220
HighGPA	9.16	1/197	.003
Gender	7.23	1/197	.000

The MANOVA results indicate that there is a significant linear trend for the GPA measures. Both Gender and High school GPA have significant effects. The higher polynomial trends, which are not in the Table, are not significant, and the interactions of between GPA and High school GPA and gender are not significant. Table 5.2 presents the GPA means, rounded to one decimal, for the six occasions, for male and female students.

Table 5.2 makes clear that there is a linear upward trend of about 0.1 for each successive GPA measurement. Female students have a GPA that is consistently higher than the GPA of the male students. Finally, the SPSS output also contains the regression coefficient for the High school GPA at the six occasions; this coefficient (not given in the table) varies across the six occasions, but it is generally positive, which indicates that students, who have a high GPA in High school, generally have a relatively high GPA in college.

Table 5.2 GPA means at six occasions, for male and female students							
Occasion:	1	2	3	4	5	6	Total
Male	2.6	2.7	2.7	2.8	2.9	3.0	2.8
Female	2.6	2.8	2.9	3.0	3.1	3.2	2.9
All students	2.6	2.7	2.8	2.9	3.0	3.1	2.9

In the multilevel regression model, the development over time is often modeled by a linear regression equation, which may have different regression coefficients for different individuals. Thus, each individual can have their own regression curve, specified by the individual regression coefficients that in turn may depend on individual attributes. Quadratic and higher functions can be used to model nonlinear dependencies on time, and both time varying and person level covariates can be added to the model. Although the measurement occasions will usually be thought of as occasion one, two, et cetera, it is useful to code the time points T as $t = 0, 1, 2, 3, 4, 5$. As a result, the intercept can be interpreted as the expected outcome on the first occasion. Using time points $t = 1, 2, 3, 4, 5, 6$ would be completely equivalent, but more difficult to interpret, because the value zero is not in the range of observed time points.[1] If the explanatory variable is not time points but, for instance, calendar age, setting the first observation to zero is not the best solution. In that case, it is usual to center on the mean or median age, or on a rounded-off value close to the mean or median.

Before we start the analysis, we examine the distribution of the outcome variable GPA in the disaggregated data file with 200x6=1200 observations. The histogram with embedded best fitting normal curve is in Figure 5.3. The distribution appears quite normal, so we proceed with the analysis.

---

[1] The importance of centering explanatory variables on their overall mean or a similar value is discussed in Chapter Four.

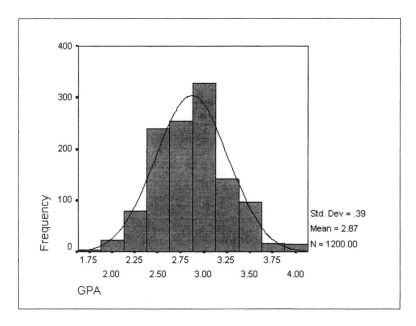

Figure 5.3. Histogram of GPA values in disaggregated data file

Table 5.3 presents the results of a multilevel analysis of these longitudinal data. Model (1) is a model that contains only an intercept term. The intercept of 2.87 in this model is simply the average GPA across all individuals and occasions. The intercept-only model estimates the repeated measures variance as 0.098, and the person level variance as 0.057 (because these numbers are so small, they are given in 3 decimals). This estimates the total GPA variance as 0.155. Using equation (2.9), the intraclass correlation or the proportion variance at the person level is estimated as $\rho = 0.057/0.155 = 0.37$. About one-third of the variance of the GPA measures is variance between individuals, and about two-thirds is variance within individuals across time.

In model (2), the Time variable is added as a linear predictor with the same coefficient for all persons. The model predicts a value of 2.60 at the first occasion, which increases by 0.11 on each succeeding occasion. Just as in the MANOVA analysis, adding higher order polynomial trends for Time to the model does not improve prediction. Model (3) adds the time varying covariate Job status to the model. The effect of Job status is clearly significant; the more hours are worked, the lower the GPA. Model (4) adds the person level (time invariant) predictors High school GPA and Sex. Both effects are significant; high school GPA correlates with average GPA in college, and female students perform better than male students.

Table 5.3   Results multilevel analysis of GPA, fixed effects only

Model:	M1: null model		M2: + time		M3: + job status		M4: + high school GPA & gender	
Fixed part								
Predictor	coeff.	s.e.	coeff.	s.e.	coeff.	s.e.	coeff.	s.e.
intercept	2.87	.02	2.60	.02	2.97	.04	2.49	.11
time			0.11	.00	0.10	.00	0.10	.00
job status					-0.17	.02	-0.17	.02
high GPA							0.09	.03
gender							0.15	.03
Random part								
σ_e^2	0.098	.004	0.058	.003	0.055	.002	0.055	.002
σ_{u0}^2	0.057	.007	0.063	.007	0.052	.006	0.045	.005
Deviance	913.5		393.7		308.4		282.8	
AIC	919.5		401.7		318.4		296.8	

If we compare the variance components of model (1) and model (2), we see that entering the time variable has decreased the occasion level variance considerably, while increasing the person level variance by 11%. This seems strange, but it is in fact typical for multilevel analysis of repeated measures. It makes it impossible to use the residual error variance of the intercept-only model as a benchmark, and to examine how much this goes down when explanatory variables are added to the model. In Table 5.3, this strategy leads to inconsistencies, because in model (2) the second-level residual error variance for the intercept actually goes up when the time variable is added to the model! As a result we estimate a negative value for the amount of explained variance.

The reason for this apparent anomaly is, as is discussed in detail in Chapter Four, that the 'amount of variance explained at a specific level' is not a simple concept in multilevel models (cf. Snijders & Bosker, 1994). The problem arises because the statistical model behind multilevel models is a hierarchical sampling model: groups are sampled at the higher level, and at the lower level individuals are sampled within groups. This sampling process creates some variability in all variables between the groups, even if there are in fact no real group differences. In time series, the lowest level is a series of measurements. In many cases, the data collection design is set up to make sure that the repeated measurements are evenly spaced and the data are collected at the same time for all individuals in the sample. As a result, the variability between persons in the time series variable is usually *much* higher than the hierarchical sampling model assumes. Consequently, the intercept-only model overestimates the variance at the occasion level, and underestimates the variance at the person level. The time variable model (2) models the occasion level variance in the dependent variable GPA. Conditional upon this effect, the variance estimated at the person level is much more realistic.

Chapter Four in this book describes procedures based on Snijders and Bosker (1994) to correct the problem. A simple approximation is to use as a benchmark for the occasion level variance the variance component estimated in the intercept only model (model 1). For the person level variance, we use the variance component of the model that includes a model for the time variable (model 2).[1] Then we observe that the error variance at the occasion level goes down from 0.098 to 0.058, which means that the time variable explains about (0.098-0.058)/0.098 = 0.41 (41%) of the GPA variance between the occasions. To see how much variance the time varying covariate Job status explains, we compare the occasion level variance components from models (3) and (1), which shows that model (3) explains about (0.098-0.055)/0.098 = 0.44 (44%) of the occasion level variance. Thus, job status explains an additional three percent of the variation across occasions. Clearly, the effect of the linear trend is much stronger than the effect of Job status.

To assess the effects on the person level variables, we view the person level intercept variance of 0.063 in model (2) as the error variance, and observe that in model (3) this variance decreases to 0.052. This means that adding Job status to the model explains about (0.063-0.052)/0.063 = 0.18 (18%) of the GPA differences across persons. Since the time variate is centered on the first occasion (occasion one is coded 0), this actually applies to the relationship between Job status and GPA at the first occasion. Apparently, although Job status is a time-varying covariate, it explains more variation between different persons in the same semester, than within the same persons from one semester to the next. In model (4) the variance estimate goes down to 0.045. Model (4) explains about (0.063-0.045)/0.063 = 0.29 (29%) of the person level variance. Thus, at the person level, the covariates High school GPA and Gender explain an additional 11% of the variation between the persons.

The models presented in Table 5.3 all assume that the rate of change is the same for all individuals. In the models presented in Table 5.4, the regression coefficient of the Time variable is assumed to vary across individuals.

---

[1] The baseline model including the time variable(s) should have a good fit. This means that higher order polynomials or other effects should be included if needed. The fit of the model for time can be assessed by estimating a saturated model over time, using procedures described later in this chapter, and using the chi-square test on the deviances to test any simpler model that is considered.

Table 5.4	Results multilevel analysis of GPA, including random slopes				
Model:	M5: + Time random		M6:+ cross level interaction		
Fixed part					
Predictor	coeff.	s.e.	coeff.	s.e.	stand.coeff.
intercept	2.44	.10	2.51	.11	
time	0.10	.01	0.06	.02	0.26
job status	-0.13	.02	-0.13	.02	-0.19
high GPA	0.09	.03	0.09	.03	0.14
gender	0.12	.03	0.08	.04	0.10
time*gender			0.03	.01	0.23
Random part					
σ_e^2	0.042	.002	0.042	.002	
σ_{u0}^2	0.038	.006	0.038	.006	
σ_{u1}^2	0.004	.001	0.004	.001	
σ_{u01}	-0.002	.002	-0.002	.001	
$r_{int*time}$	-0.21		-0.19		
Deviance	170.1		163.0		
AIC	188.1		183.0		

In model (5) in Table 5.4, the slope of the time variable is allowed to vary across individuals. In this model, the variance components for the intercept and the regression slope for the time variable are both significant. The significant intercept variance of 0.038 means that individuals have different initial states, and the significant slope variance of 0.004 means that individuals also have different rates of change. In model (6), the interaction of the time variable with the person level predictor Gender is added to the model. The interaction is significant, but including it does not decrease the slope variance for the time variable. Since gender in this example is coded 1 (male) and 2 (female), including the interaction changes the value of the regression coefficient for the time trend. As discussed in Chapter Four, this regression coefficient now reflects the expected time-effect for respondents with value zero on the gender variable. Since such respondents do not exist, the value of 0.06 for the regression coefficient of time does not mean much. This again illustrates the advantage of centering explanatory variables when random slopes or interactions are present.

The variance component of 0.038 for the slopes of the Time variable does not seem large. However, multilevel models assume a normal distribution for these slopes (or, equivalently, for the slope residuals u_1), for which the standard deviation is estimated in model (5) and (6) as $\sqrt{0.038} = 0.195$. Compared to the value of 0.10 for the average time slope in model (5), this is not small. There is appreciable variation among the time slopes, which is not modeled well by the available student variables.

In both model (5) and (6) there is a small negative covariance σ_{u01} between the initial status and the growth rate; students who start with a relatively low value of their GPA, increase their GPA faster than the other students. It is easier to interpret this covariance if it is presented as a correlation between the intercept and slope residuals. Note that the correlation $r_{int*time}$ between the intercept and slope is slightly different in model (5) and (6); the covariances seem equal because of rounding. In a model without other predictors except the time variable, this correlation can be interpreted as an ordinary correlation, but in models (5) and (6) it is a partial correlation, conditional on the predictors in the model.

To facilitate interpretation, standardized regression coefficients are calculated for the last model (model 6) in Table 5.4 using equation (2.13). The standardized regression coefficients indicate that the change over time is the largest effect. Job status also seems important, and the interaction seems more important now. To investigate this further, we can construct the regression equation of the time variable separately for both male and female students. Substituting the mean for all other explanatory variables in the equation for model (6), we get for male students the regression equation: GPA = 2.58 + (0.06+0.03=) 0.09 * Time, and for female students the regression equation GPA = (2.58+0.08=) 2.66 + (0.06+2×0.03=) 0.12 * Time.

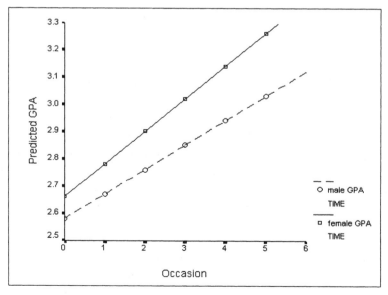

Figure 5.4. Regression lines for Time, separate for male and female students

Figure 5.4 presents a plot of these regression lines. The expected difference between male and female students, which is 0.08 in the first semester, increases to 0.23 in the second semester.

Since the time variable is coded in such a way that the first occasion is coded as zero, the negative correlation between the intercepts and slopes refers to the situation on the first measurement. As is explained in section 4.2 of chapter 4, the estimates of the variance components in the random part can change if the scale of the time variable is changed. In many models, this is not a real problem, because the interest is mostly in estimation and interpretation of the regression coefficients in the fixed part of the model. In repeated measures analysis, the correlation between the intercepts and the slopes of the time variable is often an interesting parameter, to be interpreted along with the regression coefficients. In this case, it is important to realize that the correlation is *not* invariant; it changes if the scale of the time variable is changed. In fact, one can show that by using extremely different scalings for the time variable, we can give the correlation between the intercepts and slopes any desired value (Stoel & van den Wittenboer, 2001).

Table 5.5 Results model 5 for different time scalings						
Model:	M5a		M5b		M5c	
	1st occasion= 0		last occasion= 0		time centered	
Fixed part						
Predictor	coeff.	set.	coeff.	s.e.	coeff.	s.e.
intercept	2.44	.10	2.96	.11	2.70	.10
time	0.10	.01	0.10	.01	0.10	.01
job status	-.13	.02	-.13	.02	-.13	.02
high GPA	0.09	.03	0.09	.03	0.09	.03
gender	0.12	.03	0.12	.03	0.12	.03
Random part						
σ_e^2	0.042	.002	0.042	.002	0.042	.002
σ_{u0}^2	0.038	.006	0.109	.013	0.050	.006
σ_{u1}^2	0.004	.001	0.004	.001	0.004	.001
σ_{u01}	-0.002	.002	0.017	.003	0.007	.001
$r_{int*time}$	-0.21		0.82		0.51	
Deviance	170.1		170.1		170.1	
AIC	188.1		188.1		188.1	

Table 5.5 illustrates this point. In Table 5.5, we have the parameter estimates for model (5) in Table 5.4, for different scalings of the time variable. In model 5a, the time variable is scaled as in all our analyses so far, with the first occasion coded as zero. In model 5b, the time variable is coded with the last occasion coded as zero, and the earlier occasions with negative values –5, …, -1. In model 5c, the time variable is centered on its overall mean.

From the correlations between the intercepts and slopes for the time-variable, we conclude in model 5b that students who end with a relatively high GPA, on average have a steeper GPA increase over time. In the centered model, 5c, this correlation is lower, but still quite clear. If we inspect the first model 5a, which codes the first occasion as zero, we see a negative correlation, meaning that persons with a relatively low initial GPA have a steeper growth rate. It is clear that we cannot interpret the correlation between the intercept and slopes directly. This correlation can only be interpreted in combination with the scale on which the occasion variable is defined.

Note that the three models in Table 5.5 have exactly identical estimates for all parameters that do not involve time, and exactly the same deviance. The models are in fact equivalent. The different ways that time is coded lead to what statisticians call a *re-parameterization* of the model. The three models all describe the data equally well, and are equally valid. Nevertheless, they are not identical. The situation is comparable to viewing a landscape from different angles. The landscape does not change, but some views are more interesting than others are. The important lesson here is that in repeated measures analysis, careful thought must be given to the coding of the time variable. As stated, by a judicious choice of scale, we can give the correlation between the intercept and slope residuals any value that we want. If the zero-point is far outside the observed values, for instance if we code the occasions as 1995, 1996, 1997, 1998, 1999 and 2000, which does make some sense, we will get an extreme correlation. If we want to interpret the correlation between the intercepts and slopes, we must make sure that the zero-point has a strong substantive meaning. Adding a graphical display of the slopes for different individuals may help to interpret the results.[1]

5.3   EXAMPLE WITH VARYING OCCASIONS

The data in the next example are a study of children's vocabulary development (Huttenlocher, Haight, Bryk & Seltzer, 1991), which is included with the HLM program (Raudenbush et al., 2000), and discussed at length by Bryk and Raudenbush (1992). The data set combines data from two studies. In the first study, children were observed on six or seven occasions between 12 to 26 months of age. In the second

---

[1] In large data sets this display will be confusing, and it is better to present a plot of a random or selected subsample of the individuals.

study, children were observed on four occasions between 12 and 24 months of age. For some cases, the 14-month occasion is missing. On each occasion, the vocabulary size was measured. In addition, we have the children's gender (coded 0 for male and 1 for female), and the amount of maternal speech measured at the 16-month data point (Bryk & Raudenbush, 1992, p. 141).[1]

Table 5.6 Data structure of children's vocabulary data							
Age-point (months) 12	14	16	18	20	22	24	26
Number of children 22	5	22	11	22	11	22	11

Although the measures are taken at regular ages, combining two studies and having missing data at one time point results in an unbalanced data file, as shown in Table 5.6. The total number of observations in these data is 126, on 22 children, or about 5.7 occasions per child. As a result, the sample size at both the child and the occasion level is rather small. In addition, for 11 children we have data on four occasions only.

Most MANOVA software removes all incomplete cases from the analysis, which for the data in Table 5.6 would result in removal of 17 out of 22 cases, leaving only five children for the analysis. In multilevel analysis, different numbers of observations at different time intervals pose no special problems, and all cases can be retained in the analysis. Since growth generally follows a nonlinear pattern, in the following analyses the square of the child's age is added to the explanatory variables.

The children's vocabulary data illustrate a number of points that are important in multilevel analysis of longitudinal data. Since the data are a combination of data collected in two separate studies, a dummy variable S_i is added to the data to indicate the study, to model possible differences between the studies that may result from differences in the research procedures. This dummy variable is coded −0.5 for the first study, and +0.5 for the second study. This coding implies that the intercept and the variance components, which are estimated for the value zero on this explanatory variable, refer to the average study result, disregarding the different number of observations for each study. Since the difference between −0.5 and +0.5 equals 1.0, the regression coefficient for the study variable indicates the difference between the two studies.

The study indicator variable is a control variable that is included in every model, including the null model, to statistically control for possible differences between the two studies. Because different children originate from one of the two

---

[1] The vocabulary growth data here differ slightly from the description in Bryk & Raudenbush (1992). Bryk & Raudenbush give the number of occasions for the second study as three, while the data set included with HLM actually contains four occasions.

studies, the study variable is a time invariant covariate at the child level. Thus, at the lowest level, we have

$$Y_{ti} = \pi_{0i} + e_{ti} \tag{5.7}$$

Including the study indicator S_i gives

$$\pi_{0i} = \beta_{00} + \beta_{01}S_i + u_{0i}$$

or

$$Y_{ti} = \beta_{00} + \beta_{01}S_i + u_{0i} + e_{ti} \tag{5.8}$$

or, using verbal labels for the variables:

$$Vocabulary_{ti} = \beta_{00} + \beta_{01} Study_i + u_{0i} + e_{ti}$$

If we fit the intercept-only model of equation (5.8), adding the study-indicator, the intercept is estimated as 132, which means that the average child in our data, at the average age in our data, knows about 132 words. If we add Age as a raw variable to the equation, the intercept is estimated as –420! As explained earlier, in a regression equation, the intercept is the expected outcome when all explanatory variables have the value zero. Thus, the intercept of –420 indicates that at age-point zero the children's vocabulary size is negative. This is clearly impossible, which illustrates the importance of using a zero-point for the time scale that is conceptually meaningful in the context of the study. Although an age of zero months is conceptually simple, it does not make sense in a study on vocabulary growth. For the moment, we decide to center the age variable on its overall mean of 18.9 months. The quadratic trend in the subsequent analyses is modeled by the square of the centered age-variable. To indicate that age is centered, it will be written in **bold** in the equations.

Thus, at the lowest level, we now have

$$Y_{ti} = \pi_{0i} + \pi_{1i} \, \mathbf{age}_{ti} + \pi_{2i} \, \mathbf{age}^2_{ti} + e_{ti} \tag{5.9}$$

Including the study indicator gives

$$\pi_{0i} = \beta_{00} + \beta_{01} Study_i + u_{0i}$$

Allowing random regression slopes for age, and keeping age-squared fixed, gives

$$\pi_{1i} = \beta_{10} + u_{1i}$$

and

$$\pi_{2i} = \beta_{20}$$

By substitution we arrive at the single equation version of the model:

$$Y_{ti} = \beta_{00} + \beta_{01} \, Study_i + \beta_{10} \, age_{ti} + \beta_{20} \, age^2_{ti} + u_{0i} + u_{1i} \, age_{ti} + e_{ti} \qquad (5.10)$$

Table 5.7 presents the results of a sequence of models for the centered age variables. The sequence of models 1-3 shows again, that the interpretation of variance components in a multilevel model is not as straightforward as that of variances of raw data. In model (1), the intercept-only model, the child-level residual variance is estimated as 2403. In model (2), which includes the centered age variable as a predictor variable, the child-level residual variance *increases* to 4878. In model (3), which adds the squared trend for age, the child level variance increases again to 5169. We have observed the same effect in the previous example using the GPA data, although here the increase in the variance is much larger.

Table 5.7	Results vocabulary data, occasion level only, age centered on mean							
Model:	M1		M2		M3		M4	
	Intercept only		+ age		+ age squared		+ age random	
Fixed part								
Predictor	coeff.	s.e.	coeff.	s.e.	coeff.	s.e.	coeff.	s.e.
intercept	132	20	138	18	85	19	88	17
study	-111	39	-70	35	-68	35	-4	5
age (cent.)			30	2	31	2	28	3
age^2					2.6	0.4	2.6	.2
Random part								
σ_e^2	31073	4290	10379	1437	7721	1071	940	140
σ_{u0}^2	2403	2459	4878	2075	5169	1994	6344	1948
σ_{u1}^2							236	73
σ_{u01}							1246	376
$r_{int*age}$							1.02	
Deviance	1669		1551		1519		1290	
AIC	1677		1561		1531		1304	

The reason for this anomalous result is, as is explained previously in this chapter and at more length in Chapter Four, that in multilevel models with random coefficients the notion of 'amount of variance explained at a specific level' is not a simple concept. In repeated measures models, the intercept-only model overestimates the occasion level variance, and underestimates the child level variance. Including the age variable, which models the occasion level variance in the vocabulary measures, results in much more realistic estimates for both the occasion level and the child-level variances. Adding the squared trend for the age variable improves the estimates again. Adding higher order trends does not improve prediction significantly.

In section 5.2, which discusses fixed occasion data, the advice is to use as a benchmark for the occasion level variance the variance component estimated in the intercept only model (model 1), and for the person level variance the variance component of the model that includes the time variable. This example illustrates the importance of having a good model for the time variable. If there are quadratic and higher trends, the benchmark for the person level variance must be the residual variance in the model that includes these time effects, in our example model (3).

Model (4) models the age effect as a random coefficient, as in equation (5.10). The variance of the slope coefficient for age itself is significant. Model (5) allows the slopes for the squared age variable to vary too, which leads to a model that does not converge. In model (4), the correlation between the slope and intercept residuals is estimated as 1.02, which is not an admissible value. It is close to the range of admissible values, so for the moment we can accept the estimated value, and interpret this result as an indication that the correlation in the population is high, close to 1.00.[1]

Before going on by adding child level explanatory variables, we will repeat the analysis with a slightly different parameterization. In their extensive analysis of this data set, Bryk and Raudenbush (1992, pp. 141-147) argue that, since children generally begin to utter their first words around the age of 12 months, it makes sense to express the age variable as centered on the age of 12 months. As a result, the estimated values of the intercept and the variances in the intercept-only model refer to the situation at the age of 12 months, when the vocabulary size is almost zero, and little variation exists between the children.

The same sequence of models as in Table 5.7, but now for age centered at 12 months, and age squared computed from the age variable centered at age 12 produces the results shown in Table 5.8.

---

[1] If the software allows it, a better solution is to constrain the covariance between the intercept and slope to a value that implies a correlation of 1.00 or 0.99.

Table 5.8 Results vocabulary data, age centered on 12 months								
Model:	M1		M2		M3		M4	
	Intercept only		+ age		+ age squared		+ age random	
Fixed part								
Predictor	coeff.	s.e.	coeff.	s.e.	coeff.	s.e.	coeff.	s.e.
intercept	132	20	-66	22	-5	23	-2	7
study	-111	39	-70	35	-68	35	-4	5
age (12)			30	2	4.6	5.9	-2.1	7.3
age^2					2.6	0.4	2.2	0.2
Random part								
σ_e^2	31073	4290	10377	1438	7721	1071	940	140
σ_{u0}^2	2403	2459	4882	2067	5169	1994	399	274
σ_{u1}^2							240	75
σ_{u01}							-388	137
$r_{int*age}$							-1.25	
Deviance	1669		1551		1519		1290	
AIC	1677		1561		1531		1304	

The results in Table 5.8 resemble those in Table 5.7. In the final model, the intercept is very small and insignificant, indicating that at age 12 months the average vocabulary size is indeed close to zero. The variance around the intercept is also insignificant. The coefficient for age is now also insignificant, which indicates that at age 12 months the vocabulary growth is almost zero, which in a graph would give almost a horizontal line. The age-squared variable, which indicates the acceleration in growth, is significant at 2.2. Each month, the number of words learned increases by a factor of 2.2 times the squared difference. So at 14 months, the expected vocabulary growth is 8.8 or about 9 words, at 16 months it is 35, at 18 months it is 79 words, and so on.

The vocabulary growth data are included as an example with the HLM program, and are discussed at length by Bryk and Raudenbush (1992). For reasons to be explained further on, it is instructive to compare the values in Table 5.8, which are estimated using MLwiN (version 1.10), to values estimated using HLM (version 5.0). The HLM-results are presented in Table 5.9.

One of the differences between Table 5.8 and Table 5.9 is the significance test on the variance components: MLwiN produces a standard error for the variances, while HLM carries out a chi-square test (these and other tests are discussed in Chapter Four).

Table 5.9 Vocabulary data, occasion level only, age centered on 12 months (HLM)

Model:	M1 Intercept only		M2 + age		M3 + age squared		M4 + age random		M5 + age, age² random	
Fixed part										
Predictor	coef.	s.e.	coef.	s.e.	coef.	s.e.	coef.	s.e.	coef.	s.e.
intercept	132	20	-66	22	-5	6	-3	8	-4	6
study	-111	40	-70	37	-68	36	-5	8	-1	7
age (12)			30	2	2.6	0.4	-1.8	4	-0.4	2
age²					2.6	0.4	2.2	0.2	2.0	0.2
Random part		χ^2_{20}		χ^2_{19}		χ^2_{18}		χ^2_{18}		χ^2_{18}
σ_e^2	31209	-	10498	-	7883	-	888	-	678	-
σ_{u0}^2	2994	28.9	5471	87.9	5749	117.0	817	40.1	120	6.5
σ_{u1}^2							257	75	56	33.2
σ_{u01}									0.5	48.7
Deviance	1656		1536		1507		1297		1272	
AIC	1670		1540		1511		1305		1286	

More important differences in this case are that HLM does not experience convergence problems, estimates somewhat different variance components, and is able to fit a model with both intercepts and slopes for age and age-squared varying across children. These differences are not the result of using Restricted ML estimation (default in HLM), rather than Full ML (default in MLwiN). If we use RML estimation in MLwiN, we obtain estimates close to the earlier MLwiN estimates in Table 5.8. The most likely cause for the difference between the MLwiN and HLM results is the difference in the algorithm used. HLM uses the EM algorithm, which is sometimes slow, but has the advantage that it is very stable, and cannot produce estimates that are outside the acceptable parameter space. This means that the correlation between the slopes and intercepts, for which MLwiN estimates the impossible value of -1.25, will always be kept within admissible bounds by HLM. HLM estimates this correlation as –0.99, which is very close to -1.00, but it is an acceptable value. As a result, the variances are also estimated somewhat differently. In model (5) in Table 5.9, which MLwiN cannot estimate, the correlations between the random coefficients range from 0.84 to 0.98. This indicates a high collinearity for these parameters. Apparently, the collinearity poses a problem for the estimation method used in MLwiN. In general, noticeable differences between the various estimation methods are rare (cf. Kreft, de Leeuw &

van der Leeden, 1994). Note that if we are only interested in the fixed effects, the regression coefficients estimated by MLwiN and HLM will carry the same substantive interpretation.

5.4 ADVANTAGES OF MULTILEVEL ANALYSIS
FOR LONGITUDINAL DATA

Using multilevel models to analyze repeated measures data has several advantages. Bryk and Raudenbush (1992) mention five key points. First, by modeling varying regression coefficients at the occasion level, we have growth curves that are different for each person. This fits in with the way individual development is generally conceptualized (cf. Willett, 1988). Second, the number of repeated measures and their spacing may differ across persons. Other analysis methods for longitudinal data cannot handle such data well. Third, the covariances between the repeated measures can be modeled as well, by specifying a specific structure for the variances and covariances at either level. Fourth, if we have balanced data and use RML estimation, the usual Analysis of Variance based F-tests and t-tests can be derived from the multilevel regression results (cf. Raudenbush, 1993a). This shows that Analysis of Variance on repeated measures is a special case of the more general multilevel regression model. Fifth, in the multilevel model it is simple to add higher levels, to investigate the effect of family or social groups on individual development. A sixth advantage, not mentioned by Bryk and Raudenbush, is that it is straightforward to include time varying or time constant explanatory variables to the model, which allows us to model both the average group development and the development of different individuals.

5.5 SOME STATISTICAL ISSUES IN LONGITUDINAL ANALYSIS

5.5.1 Investigating and Analyzing Patterns of Change

In the previous sections, polynomial curves were used to model the pattern of change over time. Polynomial curves are often used for estimating developmental curves. They are convenient, because they can be estimated using standard linear modeling procedures, and they are very flexible. If there are k measurement occasions, these can always be fitted exactly using a polynomial of degree k-1. In general, in the interest of parsimony, a polynomial of a lower degree would be preferred. Another advantage of polynomial approximation is that many inherently nonlinear functions can be approximated very well by a polynomial function. Nevertheless, modeling inherently nonlinear functions directly is sometimes preferable, because it may reflect some 'true' developmental process. For instance, Burchinal and Appelbaum (1991) consider the logistic growth curve and the exponential curve of special interest for developmental models. The logistic curve describes a developmental curve where the rate of development changes slowly in the beginning, accelerates in the middle, and slows again at the end. In the light of the example data used in section 5.3, it is interesting to note that Burchinal and Appelbaum explicitly mention vocabulary growth in children as an example of logistic growth. "...where children initially acquire new words slowly, beginning at about 1 year of age, then quickly increase the rate of acquisition until later in the preschool years when this rate begins to slow down again." (Burchinal & Appelbaum, 1991, pp. 29-29). A logistic growth function is inherently nonlinear, because there is no transformation that makes it possible to model it as a linear model. It is harder to estimate than linear functions, because the solution must be found using iterative estimation methods. In multilevel modeling, this becomes even more difficult, because these iterations must be carried out nested within the normal iterations of the multilevel estimation method. Estimating the nonlinear function itself rather than a polynomial approximation is attractive from a theoretical point of view, because the estimated parameters have a direct interpretation in terms of the hypothesized growth process. An alternative is to use polynomial functions to approximate the true development function. Logistic and exponential functions can be well approximated by a cubic polynomial. However, the parameters of the polynomial model have no direct interpretation in terms of the growth process, and interpretation must be based on inspection of plots of the average or some typical individual growth curves. Burchinal and Appelbaum (1991) discuss these issues with examples from the field of child development. Since the available multilevel software does not support this kind of estimation, in practice polynomial approximations are commonly used.

A general problem with polynomial functions is that they often have very high correlations. The resulting collinearity problem may cause numerical problems in the estimation. If the occasions are evenly spaced and there are no missing data, transforming the polynomials to orthogonal polynomials offers a perfect solution. Tables for orthogonal polynomials are given in most handbooks on Analysis of Variance procedures (e.g., Hays, 1994). Even if the data are not nicely balanced, using orthogonal polynomials usually reduces the collinearity problem. If the occasions are unevenly spaced, or we want to use continuous time measurements, it often helps to center the time measures in such a way that the zero point is well within the range of the observed data points.

Although polynomial curves are very flexible, other ways of specifying the change over time may be preferable. Snijders and Bosker (1999) discuss the use of piecewise linear functions and spline functions, which are functions that break up the development curve in different adjacent pieces, each with its own development model.

Pan and Goldstein (1998) present an example of a multilevel analysis of repeated data using spline functions.

If there are k fixed occasions, and there is no hypothesis involving specific trends over time, we can model the differences between the occasions perfectly using k-1 polynomial curves. However, in this case it is much more attractive to use simple dummy variables. The usual way to indicate k categories with dummy variables is to specify k-1 dummy variables, with an arbitrary category as the reference category. In the case of fixed occasion data, it is preferable to remove the intercept term from the regression, and use k dummy variables to refer to the k occasions. This is taken up in more detail in Chapter Nine.

5.5.2 Handling Missing Data and Panel Dropout

An often-cited advantage of multilevel analysis of longitudinal data is the ability to handle missing data (Bryk & Raudenbush, 1992; Snijders, 1996; Cnaan, Laird & Slasor, 1997; van der Leeden, 1998). More accurately, this refers to the ability to handle models with varying time points. In a fixed occasions model, observations may be missing because at some time points respondents were not measured. In MANOVA, the usual treatment of missing time points is to remove the case from the analysis, and analyze only the complete cases. Multilevel regression models do not assume equal numbers of observations, or even fixed time points, so respondents with missing observations pose no special problems here, and all cases can remain in the analysis. This is an advantage because larger samples increase the precision of the estimates and the power of the statistical tests. However, this advantage of multilevel modeling does not extend to missing observations on the explanatory variables. If explanatory variables are missing, the usual treatment is again to remove the case completely from the analysis.

The capacity to include incomplete cases in the analysis is a very important advantage. Little and Rubin (1987, 1989) distinguish between data that are missing completely at random (MCAR) and data that are missing at random (MAR). In both cases, the failure to observe a certain data point is assumed independent of the unobserved (missing) value. With MCAR data, the missingness must be completely independent of all other variables as well. With MAR data, the missingness may depend on other variables in the model, and through these be correlated with the unobserved values. It is clear that MCAR is a much more restrictive assumption than MAR. In longitudinal research, a major problem is the occurrence of panel attrition: individuals who after one or more measurement occasions drop out of the study altogether. Panel attrition is generally not random; some types of individuals are more prone to drop out than other individuals do. In panel attrition, we typically have much information about the dropouts from earlier measurement occasions. In this case, it appears reasonable to assume that, conditional on these variables (which includes the score on the outcome variable on earlier occasions), the missingness is random (MAR). The complete cases method used in MANOVA assumes that data are missing completely at random (MCAR). Little (1995) shows that multilevel modeling of repeated measures with missing data assumes that the data are missing at random (MAR), provided that Maximum Likelihood estimation is used. Thus, when the repeated measures data is MAR, but not MCAR, MANOVA leads to biased estimates, but multilevel analysis leads to unbiased estimates. Hox (2000) presents an analysis of repeated measures data where some data points were removed according to a simulated MAR attrition process. In this example, MANOVA estimates were quite different from the corresponding estimates obtained from the complete data set, while the multilevel results were very close to the corresponding complete estimates. Hedeker and Gibbons (1997) present a more elaborate way to incorporate the missingness mechanism in the model. Using multilevel analysis for repeated measures, they first divide the data into groups according to their missingness pattern. Subsequently, variables that indicate these groups are included in the multilevel model as explanatory variables. The resulting *pattern mixture model* makes it possible to investigate if there is an effect of the different missing data patterns on the outcome, and to estimate an overall outcome across the missingness patterns.

5.6 COMPLEX COVARIANCE STRUCTURES

If multilevel modeling is used to analyze longitudinal data, the variances and covariances between different occasions have a very specific structure. The variance at any occasion has the value $\sigma_e^2 + \sigma_{u_0}^2$, and the covariance between any two occasions has the value $\sigma_{u_0}^2$. Thus, for the GPA example data, a simple linear trend model as specified by equation (5.11) is

$$GPA_{ti} = \beta_{00} + \beta_{10}Time_{ti} + u_{0i} + e_{ti} \tag{5.11}$$

where the residual variance on the occasion level is given by σ_e^2, and the residual error on the person level is given by $\sigma_{u_0}^2$. For this and similar models without additional random effects, the matrix of variances and covariances among the occasions is given by (Goldstein, 1995; Bryk & Raudenbush, 1992):

$$\Sigma\,(Y) = \begin{pmatrix} \sigma_e^2 + \sigma_{u_0}^2 & \sigma_{u_0}^2 & \sigma_{u_0}^2 & \cdots & \sigma_{u_0}^2 \\ \sigma_{u_0}^2 & \sigma_e^2 + \sigma_{u_0}^2 & \sigma_{u_0}^2 & \cdots & \sigma_{u_0}^2 \\ \sigma_{u_0}^2 & \sigma_{u_0}^2 & \sigma_e^2 + \sigma_{u_0}^2 & \cdots & \sigma_{u_0}^2 \\ \vdots & \vdots & \vdots & \ddots & \vdots \\ \sigma_{u_0}^2 & \sigma_{u_0}^2 & \sigma_{u_0}^2 & \cdots & \sigma_e^2 + \sigma_{u_0}^2 \end{pmatrix} \qquad (5.12)$$

In the covariance matrix (5.12) all variances are equal, and all covariances are equal. This shows that using a standard multilevel model, assuming that the residual errors e_{ti} are independent and have constant variance over time, assumes *compound symmetry*, the same restrictive assumption that is made in univariate analysis of variance for repeated measures. According to Stevens (1996), if the assumption of compound symmetry is violated, the standard ANOVA significance tests are too lenient, and reject the null hypothesis more often than is warranted. Therefore, multivariate analysis of variance is preferred, which estimates all variances and covariances among occasions without restrictions.

Bryk and Raudenbush (1992, p. 132) argue that uncorrelated errors may be appropriate in short time series. However, the assumption of uncorrelated errors is not essential, because the multilevel regression model can easily be extended to include an unconstrained covariance matrix at the lowest level (Goldstein, 1995). To model correlated errors, we use a multivariate response model (treated in more detail in Chapter Nine in this book) with dummy variables indicating the different occasions. This, if we have p measurement occasions, we have p dummy variables, one for each occasion. The intercept term is removed from the model, so the lowest level is empty. The dummy variables are all allowed to have random slopes at the second level. Thus, for our grade point example with six occasions, we have six dummy variables O_1, O_2, ..., O_6, and the equation for a model without further explanatory variables becomes:

$$\begin{aligned} Y_{ti} = {} & \beta_{10}O_{1i} + \beta_{20}O_{2i} + \beta_{30}O_{3i} + \beta_{40}O_{4i} + \beta_{50}O_{5i} + \beta_{60}O_{6i} + \\ & u_{10}O_{1i} + u_{20}O_{2i} + u_{30}O_{3i} + u_{40}O_{4i} + u_{50}O_{5i} + u_{60}O_{6i} \end{aligned} \qquad (5.13)$$

Having six random slopes at level two provides us with a 6×6 covariance matrix for the six occasions. The regression slopes β_{10} to β_{60} are simply the estimated means at the six occasions. Equation (5.13) defines a multilevel model that is equivalent to the MANOVA approach. Maas and Snijders (2002) discuss model (5.13) at length, and show how the familiar F-ratio's from the MANOVA approach can be calculated from the multilevel software output. An attractive property of the multilevel approach here is that it is not affected by missing data. Delucchi and Bostrom (1999) compare the MANOVA and the multilevel approach to longitudinal data using small samples with missing data. Using simulation, they conclude that the multilevel approach is more accurate than the MANOVA approach.

The model in equation (5.13) is equivalent to a MANOVA model. Since the covariances between the occasions are estimated without restrictions, it does not assume compound symmetry. However, the fixed part is fully saturated; it estimates the six means at the six time points. To model a linear trend over time, we must replace the fixed part of model (5.13) with the fixed part of the linear trend in model (5.11). This gives us the following model:

$$GPA_{ti} = \beta_{00} + \beta_{10}T_{ti} + u_{10}O_{1i} + u_{20}O_{2i} + u_{30}O_{3i} + u_{40}O_{4i} + u_{50}O_{5i} + u_{60}O_{6i} \quad (5.14)$$

To specify model (5.14) in standard multilevel software we must specify an intercept term that has no second-level variance component and six dummy variables for the occasions that have no fixed coefficients. Unless the software has built-in facilities for longitudinal modeling, this requires that the regression coefficients for the occasion dummies are restricted to zero, while their slopes are still allowed to vary across individuals. At the same time, an intercept and a linear time trend is added, which may not vary across individuals. The covariance matrix between the residual errors for the six occasions has no restrictions. If we impose the restriction that all variances are equal, and that all covariances are equal, we have again the compound symmetry model. This shows that the simple linear trend model in (5.11) is one way to impose the compound symmetry structure on the random part of the model. Consequently, we can use the overall chi-square test based on the deviance of the two models to test if the assumption of compound symmetry is tenable.

Models with a residual error structure over time as in (5.14) are very complex, because they assume a saturated model for the error structure. If there are k time points, the number of elements in the covariance matrix for the occasions is $k(k+1)/2$. So, with six occasions, we have 21 elements to be estimated. If the assumption of compound symmetry is tenable, models based on this model (cf. equation 5.11) are preferable, because they are more compact. Their random part requires only two elements to be estimated. The advantage is not only that smaller models are more parsimonious, but also they are easier to estimate. However, the compound symmetry model is very restrictive, because it assumes that there is one single value for all correlations between time points. This assumption is in many cases not very realistic, because the error term contains all omitted sources of variation (including measurement errors), which may be correlated over time. Different assumptions about the *autocorrelation* over time lead to different assumptions for the structure of the covariance matrix across the occasions. For instance, it is reasonable to assume that occasions that are close together in time have a higher correlation than occasions that are far apart. Accordingly, the elements in covariance matrix Σ should become smaller, the further away they are from the diagonal. Such a correlation structure is called a *simplex*. A more restricted version of the simplex is to assume that the autocorrelation between the occasions follow the model

$$e_t = \rho\, e_{t-1} + \varepsilon \tag{5.15}$$

where e_t is the error term at occasion t, ρ is the autocorrelation, and ε is a residual error with variance σ_ε^2. The error structure in equation (5.15) is a first order autoregressive process. This leads to a covariance matrix of the form:

$$\Sigma\,(Y) = \frac{\sigma_\varepsilon^2}{\left(1-\rho^2\right)} \begin{pmatrix} 1 & \rho & \rho^2 & \cdots & \rho^{k-1} \\ \rho & 1 & \rho & \cdots & \rho^{k-2} \\ \rho^2 & \rho & 1 & \cdots & \rho^{k-3} \\ \vdots & \vdots & \vdots & \ddots & \vdots \\ \rho^{k-1} & \rho^{k-2} & \rho^{k-3} & \cdots & 1 \end{pmatrix} \tag{5.16}$$

The first term $\sigma_\varepsilon^2/(1-\rho^2)$ is a constant, and the autocorrelation coefficient ρ is between -1 and $+1$, but typically positive. It is possible to have second order autoregressive processes, and other models for the error structure over time. The first order autoregressive model that produces the simplex in (5.16), estimates two variances plus an autocorrelation. This is almost as parsimonious as the compound symmetry model, but does not assume constant variances and covariances.

Another attractive and very general model for the covariances across time is to assume that each lag has its own autocorrelation. So, all occasions that are 1 time point apart share a specific autocorrelation, all occasions that are 2 time points apart share a different autocorrelation, and so on. This leads to a covariance matrix for the occasions that is called a Toeplitz matrix:

$$\Sigma\,(Y) = \sigma_e^2 \begin{pmatrix} 1 & \rho_1 & \rho_2 & \cdots & \rho_{k-1} \\ \rho_1 & 1 & \rho_1 & \cdots & \rho_{k-2} \\ \rho_2 & \rho_1 & 1 & \cdots & \rho_{k-3} \\ \vdots & \vdots & \vdots & \ddots & \vdots \\ \rho_{k-1} & \rho_{k-2} & \rho_{k-3} & \cdots & 1 \end{pmatrix} \tag{5.17}$$

The Toeplitz model poses $k-1$ unique autocorrelations. Typically, the autocorrelations with large lags are small, so they can be removed from the model.

It should be noted that allowing random slopes for the time trend variables (e.g., for the linear trend), also models a less restricted covariance matrix for the occasions.

As a result, if the *Time* variable, or one of its polynomials, has a random slope, it is not possible to add a completely saturated MANOVA model for the covariances across time, as in equations (5.13) and (5.14). In fact, if we have k occasions, and use k polynomials with random slopes, we simply have used an alternative way to specify the saturated MANOVA model of equation (5.13).

The implication is that the restrictive assumption of compound symmetry, which is implied in the straightforward multilevel analysis of repeated measures, is also diminished when random components are allowed for the trends over time. For instance, in a model with a randomly varying linear time variable, the variance of any specific occasion at time point t is given by

$$\text{var}\left(Y_t\right) = \sigma_{u_0}^2 + \sigma_{u_{01}}\left(t - t_0\right) + \sigma_{u_1}^2\left(t - t_0\right) + \sigma_e^2 \tag{5.18}$$

and the covariance between any two specific occasions at time points t and s is given by

$$\text{cov}\left(Y_t, Y_s\right) = \sigma_{u_0}^2 + \sigma_{u_{01}}\left[\left(t - t_0\right) + \left(s - s_0\right)\right] + \sigma_{u_1}^2\left(t - t_0\right)\left(s - s_0\right) \tag{5.19}$$

where s_0/t_0 is the value on which the time variable is centered (if the time variable is already centered, t_0 and s_0 may be omitted from the equation). Such models usually do not produce the simple structure of a simplex or other autoregressive model, but their random part can be more easily interpreted in terms of unexplained variations in developmental curves or growth trajectories. In contrast, complex random structures such as the simplex or the Toeplitz are usually interpreted in terms of underlying but unknown disturbances.

The important point is that, in longitudinal data, there are many interesting models between the extremes of the very restricted compound symmetry model and the saturated MANOVA model. In general, if there are k time points, any model that estimates fewer than $k(k+1)/2$ (co)variances for the occasions represents a restriction on the full MANOVA model. Thus, any such model can be tested against the MANOVA model using the chi-square deviance test. If the chi-square test is significant, there are correlations across occasions that are not modeled adequately. In general, if our interest is mostly on the regression coefficients in the fixed parts, the variances in the random part are not extremely important. A simulation study by Verbeke and Lesaffre (1997) shows that estimates of the fixed regression coefficients are not severely compromised when the random part is mildly misspecified.

Table 5.10	Results model 5 with different random parts					
Model:	Time fixed comp symm.		Time random, comp. symm.		Time fixed, MANOVA	
Fixed part						
Predictor	coeff.	s.e.	coeff.	s.e.	coeff.	s.e.
intercept	2.49	.11	2.44	.10	2.39	.10
time	0.10	.00	0.10	.01	0.10	.01
job status	-0.17	.02	-0.13	.02	-0.10	.01
high GPA	0.09	.03	0.09	.03	0.08	.03
sex	0.15	.03	0.12	.03	0.12	.03
Random part						
σ_e^2	0.055	.002	0.042	.002		
σ_{u0}^2	0.045	.005	0.038	.013		
σ_{u1}^2			0.004	.001		
σ_{u01}			-.002	.002		
σ_{O1}^2					0.09	.01
σ_{O2}^2					0.10	.01
σ_{O3}^2					0.10	.01
σ_{O4}^2					0.11	.01
σ_{O5}^2					0.10	.01
σ_{O6}^2					0.12	.01
Deviance	282.8		170.1		-10.7	
AIC	296.8		188.1		41.3	

Table 5.10 presents three different models using the GPA example data. The first model has a fixed slope for the time variable. The second model has a random slope for the time variable, and the third model has no random effects for the intercept or the time variable, but models a saturated covariance matrix across the time points. For simplicity, the table only shows the variances at the six occasions, and not the covariances.

From a comparison of the deviances, it is clear that the saturated model fits better. However, the random time model estimates only four terms in the random part, and the saturated model estimates 21 terms. It would seem attractive to seek a more parsimonious model for the random part. We can also conclude that although the saturated model leads to slightly different estimates in the fixed part, the substantive conclusions are the same. Unless great precision is needed, we may decide to ignore the better fit of the saturated model, and present the model with the random slope for time instead.

5.7 SOME SOFTWARE ISSUES

The models that include complex covariance structures require multilevel software that allows restrictions on the random and fixed part. Some programs (MixReg, Hedeker & Gibbons, 1996b, or Prelis 2.3, Jöreskog, Sörbom, du Toit & du Toit, 1999) recognize the existence of longitudinal data, and allow direct specification of various types of autocorrelation structures. For a discussion of some of these structures in the context of multilevel longitudinal models, see Hedeker and Gibbons (1996b). If there are many different and differently spaced occasions, MANOVA and related models become impractical. With varying occasions, it is still possible to specify an autocorrelation structure, but it is more difficult to interpret than with fixed occasions. The program MLwiN (Goldstein et al., 2000) can model very general autocorrelation structures using macros available from the Multilevel Modelling Project at the University of London (Yang, Rasbash & Goldstein, 1998). Examples of such analyses are given by Goldstein, Healy and Rasbash (1994) and Barbosa and Goldstein (2000). The program HLM (version 5, Raudenbush et al., 2000) includes some provisions for structured time data. It should be noted that many of these programs, when the time structure is generated automatically, number the occasions starting at one. Since this makes 'zero' a non-existent value for the time variable, this is an unfortunate choice. If this happens, software users should override it with a choice that makes better sense given their substantive question.

6

The Logistic Model
for Dichotomous Data and Proportions

The models discussed so far assume a continuous dependent variable and a normal error distribution. If the dependent variable is a scale in which the responses to a large number of questions are summated to one score, the data generally approximate normality. However, there are situations in which the assumption of normality is clearly violated. For instance, in cases where the dependent variable is a single dichotomous variable, both the assumption of continuous scores and the normality assumption are obviously untrue. If the dependent variable is a proportion, the problems are less severe, but both the assumptions of continuous scores and normality are still violated. Also, in both cases, the assumption of homoscedastic errors is violated. This chapter treats multilevel models for this kind of data.

6.1   GENERALIZED LINEAR MODELS

The classical approach to the problem of non-normally distributed variables and heteroscedastic errors is to apply a transformation to achieve normality and reduce the heteroscedasticity, followed by a straightforward analysis with ANOVA or multiple regression. To distinguish this approach from the generalized linear modeling approach explained later in this chapter, where the transformation is part of the statistical model, it is often referred to as an empirical transformation. Some general guidelines for choosing a suitable transformation have been suggested for situations in which a specific transformation is often successful (e.g., Kirk, 1968; Mosteller & Tukey, 1977). For instance, for the proportion p some recommended transformations are: the arcsine transformation that is given by $f(p) = 2\arcsin\left(\sqrt{p}\right)$, the logit transformation $f(p) = \text{logit}(p) = \ln\left(p/(1-p)\right)$, where ln is the natural logarithm, and the probit or inverse Normal transformation $f(p) = \Phi^{-1}(p)$, where Φ^{-1} is the inverse of the standard Normal distribution. Thus, for proportions, we can use the logit transformation, and use standard regression procedures on the transformed variable:

$$\text{logit}(p) = \beta_0 + \beta_1 X_1 + \beta_2 X_2 + e \tag{6.1}$$

When the dependent variable is a frequency count of events with a small probability, such as the number of errors made in a school essay, the data tend to follow a Poisson distribution, which can often be normalized by taking the square root of the scores: $f(x) = \sqrt{x}$. When the data are highly skewed, which is usually the case if, for instance, reaction time is the dependent variable, a logarithmic transformation is often used: $f(x) = \ln(x)$, or the reciprocal transformation: $f(x) = 1/x$. For reaction times the reciprocal transformation has the nice property that it transforms a variable with an obvious interpretation: reaction time, into another variable with an equally obvious interpretation: reaction speed.

Empirical transformations have the disadvantage that they are ad hoc, and may encounter problems in specific situations. For instance, if we model dichotomous data, which are simply the observed proportions in a sample of size one, both the logistic and the probit transformations break down, because these functions are not defined for values 0 and 1. In fact, *no* empirical transformation can ever transform a dichotomous variable, which takes on only two values, into any resemblance of a normal distribution.

The modern approach to the problem of non-normally distributed variables is to include the necessary transformation and the choice of the appropriate error distribution (not necessarily a normal distribution) explicitly in the statistical model. This class of statistical models is called *generalized linear models* (Gill, 2000; McCullagh & Nelder, 1989). Generalized linear models are defined by three components:

1. an outcome variable y with a specific error distribution that has mean μ and variance σ^2,
2. a linear additive regression equation that produces a predictor η of the outcome variable y,
3. a *link function* that links the expected values of the outcome variable y to the predicted values for η: $\eta = f(\mu)$ (McCullagh & Nelder, 1989, p. 27).

If the link function is the identity function ($f(x) = x$) and the error distribution is normal, the generalized linear model simplifies to standard multiple regression analysis. This means that the familiar multiple regression model can be expressed as a special case of the generalized linear model (cf. Aitkin, Anderson, Francis & Hinde, 1989, chapter 2) by stating that:

1. the probability distribution is Normal with mean μ and variance σ^2, usually formulated as $y \sim N(\mu, \sigma^2)$,
2. the linear predictor is the multiple regression equation for η, e.g., $\eta = \beta_0 + \beta_1 X_1 + \beta_2 X_2$,
3. the link function is the identity function given by $\eta = \mu$.

The generalized linear model separates the error distribution from the link function. As a result, generalized linear models make it possible to extend standard regression models in two different ways: by choosing a non-normal error distribution, or by using nonlinear link functions. This is nearly the same as carrying out an empirical transformation on the response variable. However, if we carry out a standard regression analysis after transforming the outcome variable, we automatically assume that the error distribution is normal on the transformed scale. But the error distribution may not be simple, or the variance may depend on the mean. Generalized linear models can deal with such situations without problems. For instance, a generalized linear model for dichotomous data is given by:

1. the probability distribution is binomial (μ) with mean μ,
2. the linear predictor is the multiple regression equation for η,
   e.g., $\eta = \beta_0 + \beta_1 X_1 + \beta_2 X_2$,
3. the link function is the logit function given by $\eta = \text{logit}(\mu)$.

Note that this specification does not include a term for the variance of the error distribution. In the binomial distribution, the variance is a function of the mean, and it cannot be estimated separately.

The estimation method in generalized linear models is a maximum likelihood procedure that uses the inverse of the link function to predict the response variable. The inverse function for the logit used above for binomial data is the logistic transformation given by $g(x) = e^x / (1 + e^x)$. The corresponding regression model is usually written as:

$$y = \frac{e^{(\beta_0 + \beta_1 X_1 + \beta_2 X_2)}}{1 + e^{(\beta_0 + \beta_1 X_1 + \beta_2 X_2)}}.$$

It is much simpler to write this regression equation as $y = \text{logistic } (\beta_0 + \beta_1 X_1 + \beta_2 X_2)$. However, this does not show that the outcome has a binomial distribution, and in reporting the results of an analysis with a generalized linear model, it is usual to list the three components of the generalized linear model explicitly. Using the regression equation $y = \text{logistic } (\beta_0 + \beta_1 X_1 + \beta_2 X_2)$ for estimation makes clear why modeling dichotomous data now works. Generalized linear modeling does not attempt to apply a logit transformation to the observed values 0 and 1, which is impossible, but applies the inverse logistic transformation to the expected values, which does work.

In principle, many different error distributions can be used with any link function. Many distributions have a specific link function for which sufficient statistics exist, which is called the *canonical link* function. Table 6.1 presents some canonical link functions and the corresponding error distribution. The canonical link has some desirable statistical properties, and McCullagh and Nelder (1989, chapter 2) express a mild preference for using canonical links. However, there is no compelling reason to confine oneself to canonical link functions Other link functions may even be better in some circumstances. For instance, although the logit link function is an appropriate choice for proportions and dichotomous data, we have the choice to specify other functions, such as the probit or the log-log-function.

Table 6.1 Some canonical link functions and corresponding error distribution			
Response	**link**	**name**	**distribution**
continuous	$\eta=\mu$	identity	Normal
proportion	$\eta=\ln(\mu/(1-\mu))$	logit	binomial
count	$\eta=\ln(\mu)$	log	Poisson
positive	$\eta=\mu^{-1}$	inverse	gamma

Figure 6.1 shows the relation between the values of the proportion p and the transformed values using a either a logit or a probit transformation.

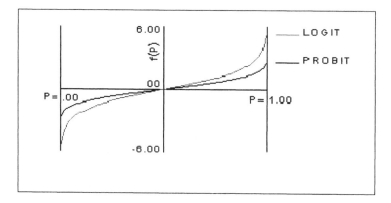

Figure 6.1. Plot of logit and probit transformed proportions

It shows that the logit transformation spreads the proportions close to 0.00 or 1.00 over a wider range of the transformed scale than the probit transformation. If the proportions are close to zero or one, and the interest is focused on these extreme proportions, the logit is a better transformation, because it differentiates better between extreme proportions. Other transformations, such as the log-log transformation, which is given by $f(p) = -\log(-\log(p))$, and the complementary log-log transformation, which is given by $f(p) = \log(-\log(1-p))$, are sometimes used as well. These functions are asymmetric. For instance, if the proportions are larger than 0.5, the log-log function behaves much like the logit, while for proportions smaller than 0.5, it behaves more like the probit. The complementary log-log function behaves in the opposite way. McCullagh & Nelder (1989) and Aitkin et al. (1989) discuss a broad range of link functions and error distributions for various modeling problems. Again, McCullagh and Nelder (1989, pp. 108-110) have a mild preference for the canonical logit link function. Agresti (1984) discusses substantive reasons for preferring certain link functions and distributions. In many cases, the choice is unimportant. When the modeled proportions are all between 0.1 and 0.9, the differences between these link functions are in practice negligible.

6.2   MULTILEVEL GENERALIZED LINEAR MODELS

Wong and Mason (1985), Mislevy and Bock (1989), Longford (1993) and Goldstein (1991, 1995) describe the multilevel extension of generalized linear models. In generalized linear multilevel models, the multilevel structure appears in the linear regression equation of the generalized linear model. Thus, a two-level model for proportions is written as follows (cf. equation 2.5):

$$Y_{ij} = \pi_{ij} ; \qquad\qquad \pi \sim \text{Binomial } (n_{ij}, \mu) \qquad\qquad (6.2)$$
$$\pi_{ij} = \text{logistic } (\gamma_{00} + \gamma_{10} X_{ij} + \gamma_{01} Z_j + \gamma_{11} Z_j X_{ij} + u_{1j} X_{ij} + u_{0j}) \qquad (6.3)$$

These equations state that our outcome variable is a proportion π_{ij}, that we use a logit link function, and that conditional on the predictor variables, we assume that π_{ij} has a binomial error distribution, with expected value μ, and sample size n_{ij}. If all sample sizes n_{ij} are equal to one, the possible outcomes are 0 and 1, and we are modeling dichotomous data. This specific case of the binomial distribution is called the *Bernoulli* distribution. Note that the usual lowest-level residual variance e_{ij} is not in the model equation, because it is part of the specification of the error distribution. If the error distribution is binomial, the residual error variance is a function of the population proportion π_{ij}: $\sigma^2 = (\pi_{ij}/(1-\pi_{ij})$ and it does not have to be estimated separately. Some software allows the estimation of a scale factor for the lowest level variance. If the scale factor is set to one, the assumption is made that the observed errors follow the theoretical binomial error distribution exactly. If the scale factor is significantly higher or lower than one, there is *overdispersion* or *underdispersion*. Underdispersion often indicates a misspecification of the model, such as the omission of large interaction effects. Overdispersion can occur if there are extreme outliers, or if we omit an entire level in a multilevel model. Very small group sizes (around three or less) also lead to overdispersion (Wright, 1997). Although the inclusion of a scale factor for under- or overdispersion improves the model fit in such cases, and in this way takes care of the problem, it does not identify the cause of the misfit. If the scale factor is very different from one, it is good practice to examine the problem, and to attempt to deal with it in a more explicit manner by modifying the model.

6.2.1 Estimating generalized multilevel models

The parameters of generalized linear models are estimated using maximum likelihood methods. Multilevel models are also generally estimated using maximum likelihood methods, and combining multilevel and generalized linear models leads to complex models and estimation procedures. The prevailing approach, implemented e.g., in MLwiN, HLM, and Prelis, is to approximate the nonlinear link by a nearly linear function, and to embed the multilevel estimation in the generalized linear model. This approach is a quasi-likelihood approach, and it confronts us with two choices that must be made. The nonlinear function is linearized using an approximation known as Taylor series expansion. Taylor series expansion approximates a nonlinear function by an infinite series of terms. Often only the first term of the series is used, which is referred to as a first order Taylor approximation. When the second term is also used, we have a second order Taylor approximation, which is generally better. So the first choice is whether to use a first order or a second order approximation. The second choice also involves the Taylor series expansion. Taylor series linearization of a nonlinear function depends on the values of its parameters. The maximum likelihood estimation procedure in multilevel modeling proceeds iteratively, starting with approximate parameter values, which are improved in each successive iteration. Thus, the estimated parameter values change during the iterations. In consequence, the Taylor series expansion must be repeated after each run of the multilevel estimation procedure, using the current estimated values of the multilevel model parameters. And this presents us with the second choice: the Taylor series expansion can use the current values of the fixed part only, which is referred to as marginal quasi-likelihood (MQL), or it can be improved by using the current values of the fixed part plus the residuals, which is referred to as penalized (or predictive) quasi-likelihood (PQL).

Estimation procedures for generalized multilevel models that are based on Taylor series expansion are discussed by Goldstein (1995, chapters 5 & 7), including procedures to model extra variation at the lowest level. In simulated data sets with a dichotomous response variable, Rodriguez and Goldman (1995) show that if the groups at the lowest level are small and the random effects are large, both the fixed and the random effects are severely underestimated by the first order MQL method. Goldstein and Rasbash (1996) demonstrate that using PQL and second order estimates in such situations leads to much better estimates that are still too small, but have a much smaller bias. Browne (1998) has repeated their analysis, using a much larger simulation setup. The amount of bias in the Taylor expansion approach can be judged from Table 6.2, which summarizes some of Browne's findings.

Table 6.2 Simulation comparing MQL and PQL (Browne, 1998)		
True value	**MQL – 1**	**PQL – 2**
$\beta_0=0.65$	0.47	0.61
$\beta_1=1.00$	0.74	0.95
$\beta_2=1.00$	0.75	0.96
$\beta_3=1.00$	0.73	0.94
$\sigma_e^2=1.00$	0.55	0.89
$\sigma_u^2=1.00$	0.03	0.57

From the results in Table 6.2, first order MQL estimation appears almost worthless, especially regarding the second level variance estimate. However, Goldstein and Rasbash (1996) point out that the data structure of this specific simulation is extreme, because there are very large variances in combination with very small groups. In less extreme data sets, the bias is much smaller, and then even first order MQL produces acceptable estimates. Goldstein (1995) also mentions that using second order PQL may encounter estimation problems. This explains our choice problem. If second order estimation and penalized quasi-likelihood are always better, then why not always use these? The reason is that complex models or small data sets may pose convergence problems, and we may be forced to use first order MQL. Goldstein and Rasbash (1996) suggest using bootstrap methods to improve the quasi-likelihood estimates, and Browne (1998) explores bootstrap and Bayesian methods. These approaches will be treated extensively in Chapter Eleven. Rodriguez and Goldman (2001) compare MQL and PQL to an exact estimation approach, bootstrapping and Bayesian methods. They conclude that PQL is a considerable improvement on MQL, and that bootstrapping or Bayesian methods can eliminate the bias. However, bootstrapping or Bayesian methods are computationally intensive, and they recommend continuing to use PQL for exploratory purposes.

It is important to note that the Taylor series approach is a quasi-likelihood method. Since the likelihood that is maximized is not the real likelihood, the test statistics based on comparing the deviances of the model (which equal minus 2 times the log likelihood) are not very accurate. The AIC and BIC indices are also based on the likelihood, and should also not be used. For testing parameter estimates when Taylor series linearization is used, the Wald test or procedures based on bootstrap or Bayesian methods are preferred.

Some software does not use the quasi-likelihood approach, but uses numerical integration of the complex Likelihood function. Using Taylor series approximation evades this difficult computing problem by maximizing an approximate likelihood. Numerical integration maximizes the correct likelihood (Schall, 1991; Wolfinger, 1993). So, when full maximum likelihood estimation with numerical integration is used, the test procedures and goodness of fit indices based on the deviance are appropriate. The multilevel software developed by Hedeker and Gibbons (cf. Hedeker & Gibbons, 1996a, 1996b), and the aML program developed by Lillard and Panis (Lillard & Panis, 2000) use numerical integration. HLM 5.0 has the option of using numerical integration for dichotomous data only (Raudenbush, Yang & Yosef, 2000). Simulation research (Hartford & Davidian, 2000; Rodriguez & Goldman, 2001) suggests that when both approaches are feasible, the numerical integration method achieves more precise estimates. Just like second order PQL estimation, however, the numerical integration method may encounter convergence problems with certain data (Lesaffre & Spiessens, 2001). If numerical integration is used, it helps if the user supplies good starting values, and it is recommended to check carefully if the algorithm has indeed converged (Lesaffre & Spiessens, 2001).

6.3   EXAMPLE: ANALYZING DICHOTOMOUS DATA

The program HLM (Raudenbush et al., 2000) includes an example file that contains data with a dichotomous outcome variable. These *Thailand education data* stem from a national survey of primary education in Thailand (Raudenbush & Bhumirat, 1992, cf. Raudenbush et al., 2000, p. 134). The outcome variable 'repeat' is a dichotomous variable indicating whether a pupil has repeated a grade during primary education. In this example, we use a child gender (0=female, 1=male) as predictor variable at the child level. As outlined in the previous section, the generalized linear model has three distinct components: (1) a specific error distribution, (2) a linear regression equation, and (3) a link function. The customary link function for binomial data is the *logit* function: $\text{logit}(p) = \ln(p/(1-p))$. The corresponding canonical error distribution is the binomial distribution. Following the logic of the generalized linear model, we write:

$$Repeat_{ij} = \pi_{ij} \; ; \qquad\qquad \pi \sim Binomial\,(\mu) \qquad\qquad (6.4)$$

$$\pi_{ij} = logistic\,(\eta_{ij}) \qquad\qquad (6.5)$$

$$\eta_{ij} = \gamma_{00} + \gamma_{10}\,Sex_{ij} + u_{0j} \qquad\qquad (6.6)$$

Or, more concisely

$$\pi_{ij} = logistic\,(\gamma_{00} + \gamma_{10}\,Sex_{ij} + u_{0j}) \qquad\qquad (6.7)$$

Equation (6.4) to (6.6) and equation (6.7) describe a generalized linear model with a dichotomous outcome *repeat*, which is assumed to have a binomial distribution with mean μ.[1] We use a logit link function, which implies that the mean μ of this distribution is predicted using a logistic regression model. In our case, this logistic regression model includes a pupil level variable *pupil gender* and a school level residual variance term u_{0j}. The parameters of this model can be estimated using the quasi-likelihood procedure involving the Taylor series expansion approach outlined above, or using the full maximum likelihood procedure with numerical integration of the likelihood function. Table 6.1 presents the results of both approaches, with first order MQL and second order PQL using MLwiN, and numerical integration using HLM.

Table 6.1 Thai educational data: predicting repeating a grade					
Model:	1st order MQL (FML)		2nd order PQL (FML)		Full ML (RML)
Predictor	coefficient (s.e.)		coefficient (s.e.)		coefficient (s.e.)
intercept	-1.96	(.07)	-2.45	(.09)	-2.52	(.10)
pupil gender	0.47	(.06)	0.55	(.07)	0.54	(.07)
σ^2_e (scale factor)	1		1		1	
σ^2_{u0}	1.14	(.11)	1.58	(.16)	1.74	(.16)

As Table 6.1 shows, the different methods produce estimates that are certainly not identical. First order MQL appears to underestimate both the frequency of repeats and the effect of being a male pupil, while second order PQL estimation and full maximum likelihood produce regression coefficients that are reasonably similar. Full maximum likelihood produces the largest estimate for the school level variance. Given the known

---

[1] Binary or dichotomous data follow a binomial distribution with $n=1$ for the sample size. This special case of the binomial distribution is sometimes referred to as the *Bernoulli* distribution.

tendency for the quasi-likelihood approach to underestimate regression coefficients and variance components, we assume that the full maximum likelihood estimates using numerical integration, which are presented in the last column in Table 6.1, are the most accurate.

The data analyzed are dichotomous. They can also be aggregated to groups of male and female students in different schools. In that case the outcome variable is 0aggregated to a proportion. If the same analysis is carried out on these proportions, we get effectively the same results. Since the data file has become smaller, the analysis proceeds a little faster. However, since HLM 5 does not provide the numerical integration option for proportions, if we aggregate the data we lose the choice of using that estimation method.

It is important to understand that the interpretation of the regression parameters reported in Table 6.1 is *not* in terms of the dichotomous outcome variable *repeat*. Instead, it is in terms of the underlying variate η defined by the logit transformation $\eta = \text{logit}(p) = \ln (p/(1-p))$. The predicted values for η are on a scale that ranges from $-\infty$ to $+\infty$. The logistic function transforms these predictions into values between 0 and 1, which can be interpreted as the predicted probability that an individual pupil has repeated a class. For a quick examination of the analysis results we can simply inspect the regression parameters as calculated by the program. To understand the implications of the regression coefficients for the proportions we are modeling, it is helpful to transform the predicted logit values back to the proportion scale. For example, the results in Table 6.1 show that boys repeat grades more often than girls. But, what do the intercept of -2.52 and the regression slope of 0.54 actually mean? They predict a repeat score of -2.52 for the girls and $(-2.52+0.54=)$ -1.98 for the boys. This is on the underlying continuous scale. Applying the logistic transformation $g(x) = e^x / (1 + e^x)$ to these estimates produces an estimated repeat rate of 7.4% for the girls and 12.1% for the boys.

6.4   EXAMPLE: ANALYZING PROPORTIONS

The second example uses data from a meta-analysis of studies that compared face-to-face, telephone, and mail surveys on various indicators of data quality (de Leeuw, 1992; for a more thorough analysis see Hox & de Leeuw, 1994). One of these indicators is the response rate; the number of completed interviews divided by the total number of eligible sample units. Overall, the response rates differ between the three data collection methods. In addition, the response rates differ also across studies. This makes it interesting to analyze what study characteristics account for these differences.

The data of this meta-analysis have a multilevel structure. The lowest level is the 'condition-level,' and the higher level is the 'study-level.' There are three variables at the condition level: the proportion of completed interviews in that specific condition, the number of potential respondents who are approached in that condition and a categorical variable indicating the data collection method used. The categorical data collection variable has three categories: 'face-to-face,' 'telephone' and 'mail' survey. To use it in the regression equation, it is recoded into two dummy variables: a 'telephone-dummy' and a 'mail-dummy'. In the mail survey condition, the mail-dummy equals one, and in the other two conditions it equals zero. In the telephone survey condition, the telephone-dummy equals one, and in the other two conditions it equals zero. The face-to-face survey condition is the reference category, indicated by a zero for both the telephone- and the mail-dummy. There are three variables at the study level: the year of publication (0 = 1947, the oldest study), the saliency of the questionnaire topic (0 = not salient, 2 = highly salient), and the way the response has been calculated. If the response is calculated by dividing the response by the total sample size, we have the completion rate. If the response rate is calculated by dividing by the sample size corrected for sampling frame errors, we have the response rate. Most studies compared only two of the three data collection methods; a few compared all three. Omitting missing values, there are 47 studies, in which a total of 105 data collection methods are compared. The data set is described in the appendix.

The dependent variable is the response. This variable is a proportion: the number of completed interviews divided by the number of potential respondents. If we had the original data sets at the individual respondents' level, we would analyze them as dichotomous data, using full maximum likelihood analysis with numerical integration. However, the studies in the meta-analysis report the aggregated results, and we have only proportions to work with. If we would model these proportions directly by normal regression methods, we would encounter two critical problems. The first problem is that proportions do not have a normal distribution, but a binomial distribution, which (especially with extreme proportions and/or small samples) invalidates several assumptions of the normal regression method. The second problem is that a normal regression equation might easily predict values larger than 1 or smaller than 0 for the response, which are impossible values for proportions. Using the generalized linear (regression) model for the proportion p of potential respondents that are responding to a survey solves both problems, which makes it an appropriate model for these data.

The hierarchical generalized linear model for our response data can be described as follows. In each condition i of study j we have a number of individuals who may or may not respond. Each condition i of study j is viewed as a draw from a specific binomial distribution. So, for each individual r in each condition i of study j the probability of responding is the same, and the proportion of respondents in condition i of study j is π_{ij}. Note that we could have a model where each individual's probability of responding varies, with individual level covariates to model this variation. Then, we would model this as a three-level model, with binary outcomes at the lowest (individual) level. Since in this meta-analysis example we do not have access to the individual data, the lowest level is the condition-level, with conditions (data collection methods) nested within studies.

Let p_{ij} be the observed proportion of respondents in condition i of study j. At the lowest level, we use a linear regression equation to predict logit (π_{ij}). The simplest model, corresponding to the intercept-only model in ordinary multilevel regression analysis is given by:

$$\pi_{ij} = \text{logistic} \ (\beta_{0j}) \tag{6.8}$$

which is sometimes written as

$$\text{logit} \ (\pi_{ij}) = \beta_{0j} \tag{6.9}$$

Equation (6.9) suggests that we are actually using a logit transformation on the proportions, which is precisely what the generalized linear model avoids doing, so equation (6.8) is a better representation of our model. Note again that the usual lowest level error term e_{ij} is not included in equation (6.8). In the binomial distribution the variance of the observed proportion depends only on the population proportion π_{ij}. As a consequence, in the model described by equation (6.8), the lowest level variance is determined completely by the estimated value for π_{ij}, and therefore it does not enter the model as a separate term.[1] In most current software, the variance of π is modeled by

$$\text{VAR}(\pi_{ij}) = \sigma^2 \ (\pi_{ij} \ (1 - \pi_{ij})) \ / \ n_{ij} \tag{6.10}$$

In equation (6.10), σ^2 is not a variance, but a scale factor. Choosing the binomial distribution fixes σ^2 to a default value of 1.00. This means that the binomial model is assumed to hold precisely, and the value 1.00 reported for σ^2 need not be interpreted. Given the specification of the variance in equation (6.10), we have the option to estimate the scale factor σ^2, which allows us to model under- or overdispersion.

The model in equation (6.8) can be extended with an explanatory variable X_{ij} at the condition level (e.g., a variable describing the condition as a mail or as a face-to-face survey):

$$\pi_{ij} = \text{logistic} \ (\beta_{0j} + \beta_{1j} \ X_{ij}) \tag{6.11}$$

---

[1]This is similar to the meta-analysis model in chapter 8. In both cases the lowest level variance is known. However, in the meta-analysis model this variance must be supplied with the data, while in the model for proportions it is automatically available because it is a function of the estimate for π_{ij}.

The regression coefficients β are assumed to vary across studies, and this variation is modeled by the study level variable Z_j in the usual second level regression equations:

$$\beta_{0j} = \gamma_{00} + \gamma_{01} Z_j + u_{0j} \qquad (6.12)$$
$$\beta_{1j} = \gamma_{10} + \gamma_{11} Z_j + u_{1j} \qquad (6.13)$$

Substituting (6.12) and (6.13) into (6.11), we get the multilevel model:

$$\pi_{ij} = \text{logistic } (\gamma_{00} + \gamma_{10}X_{ij} + \gamma_{01}Z_j + \gamma_{11}X_{ij} Z_j + u_{0j} + u_{1j}X_{ij}) \qquad (6.14)$$

Again, the interpretation of the regression parameters in (6.14) is *not* in terms of the response proportions we want to analyze, but in terms of the underlying variate defined by the logit transformation $\text{logit}(p) = \ln (p/(1-p))$. The logit link function transforms the proportions (between 0.00 and 1.00 by definition) into values on a logit scale ranging from $-\infty$ to $+\infty$. The logit link is nonlinear, and in effect it assumes that it becomes more difficult to produce a change in the outcome variable (the proportion) near the extremes of 0.00 and 1.00, as is illustrated in Figure 6.1. For a quick examination of the analysis results, we can simply inspect the regression parameters calculated by the program. To understand the implications of the regression coefficients for the proportions we are modeling, the predicted logit values must be transformed back to the proportion scale.

In our meta-analysis, we analyze survey response rates when available, and if these are not available, the completion rate is used. Therefore the appropriate null model for our example data is not the 'intercept-only' model, but a model with a dummy variable indicating whether the response proportion is a response rate or a completion rate. The lowest level regression model is therefore:

$$\pi_{ij} = \text{logistic } (\beta_{0j} + \beta_{1j} \, resptype) \qquad (6.15)$$

where the random intercept coefficient β_{0j} is modeled by

$$\beta_{0j} = \gamma_{00} + u_{0j} \qquad (6.16)$$

and the slope for the variable *resptype* by

$$\beta_{1j} = \gamma_{10} \qquad (6.17)$$

which leads by substitution to:

$$\pi_{ij} = \text{logistic } (\gamma_{00} + \gamma_{10} \, resptype + u_{0j}) \qquad (6.18)$$

Since the accurate estimation of the variance terms is an important goal in meta-analysis, the estimation method uses the restricted maximum likelihood method with second order PQL approximation. For the purpose of comparison, Table 6.2 presents for the model given by equation (6.18) the first order MQL parameter estimates in addition to the preferred second order PQL approximation.

Table 6.2 Null model for response rates		
Fixed part	**MQL - 1**	**PQL – 2**
Predictor	coeff. (s.e.)	coeff. (s.e.)
intercept	0.45 (.12)	0.59 (.15)
resptype	0.68 (.06)	0.71 (.06)
Random part		
σ^2_e (scale factor)	1.00	1.00
σ^2_{u0}	0.67 (.14)	0.93 (.20)

The PQL-2 method estimates the expected response rate as (0.45+0.68=) 1.30, and the MQL-1 methods as 1.13. As noted before, this refers to the underlying distribution established by the logit link function, and *not* to the proportions themselves. To determine the expected proportion, we must use the inverse transformation, the logistic function, given by $g(x) = e^x/(1+e^x)$. Using this transformation, we find an expected response rate of 0.79 for PQL-2 estimation, and 0.76 for MQL-1 estimation. This is not exactly equal to the value of 0.78 that we get as the mean of the response rates, weighted by sample size. However, this is as it should be, for we are using a nonlinear link function, and the value of the intercept refers to the intercept of the underlying variate. Transforming that value back to a proportion is *not* the same as computing the intercept for the proportions themselves. Nevertheless, the difference is usually rather small when the proportions are not too close to 1 or 0.

The value of precisely 1.00 for the variance at the lowest level looks peculiar. In the binomial distribution (and also in the Poisson and gamma distributions), the lowest level variance is completely determined when the mean (which in the binomial case is the proportion) is known. Therefore, σ^2_e has no useful interpretation in these models; it is used to define the scale of the underlying normal variate. By default, σ^2_e is fixed at 1.00, which is equivalent to the assumption that the binomial (Poisson, gamma) distribution holds *exactly*. In some applications, the variance of the error distribution turns out to be much larger than expected; there is *overdispersion* (cf Aitkin et al.,

1989; McCullagh & Nelder, 1989). In fact, if we allow σ_e^2 to be estimated for our meta-analysis data, we find a value of 21.9 with a corresponding standard error of 2.12. This value for the scale factor is simply enormous. It indicates a gross misspecification of the model. This is indeed the case, since the model does not contain important explanatory variables, such as the data collection method. Taking into account the small samples at the condition level (on average 2.2 conditions per study), the large estimate for the extrabinomial variation is probably not very accurate (Wright, 1997). For the moment, we ignore the extrabinomial variation.

It is tempting to use the value of 1.00 as a variance estimate to calculate the intraclass correlation for the null model in Table 6.3. However, the value of 1.00 is just a scale factor. The variance of a logistic distribution with scale factor 1 is $\pi^2/3 \approx 3.29$ (with $\pi \approx 3.14$, cf. Evans, Hastings & Peacock, 1993). So the intraclass correlation for the null-model is $\rho = 0.93/(0.93+3.29) = 0.22$.

The next model adds the condition level dummy variables for the telephone and the mail condition, assuming fixed regression slopes. The equation at the lowest (condition) level is:

$$\pi_{ij} = \text{logistic} \left(\beta_{0j} + \beta_{1j}\, resptype_{ij} + \beta_{2j}\, tel_{ij} + \beta_{3j}\, mail_{ij} \right) \tag{6.19}$$

and at the study level:

$$\beta_{0j} = \gamma_{00} + u_{0j} \tag{6.20}$$
$$\beta_{1j} = \gamma_{10} \tag{6.21}$$
$$\beta_{2j} = \gamma_{20} \tag{6.22}$$
$$\beta_{3j} = \gamma_{30} \tag{6.23}$$

Substituting (6.20) to (6.23) into (6.19) we obtain:

$$\pi_{ij} = \text{logistic} \left(\gamma_{00} + \gamma_{10}\, resptype_{ij} + \gamma_{20}\, tel_{ij} + \gamma_{30}\, mail_{ij} + u_{0j} \right) \tag{6.24}$$

Until now, the two dummy variables are treated as fixed. One even could argue that it does not make sense to model them as random, since the dummy variables are simple dichotomies that code for our three experimental conditions. The experimental conditions are under control of the investigator, and there is no reason to expect their effect to vary from one experiment to another. But some more thought leads to the conclusion that the situation is more complex. If we conduct a series of experiments, we would expect identical results only if the research subjects were all sampled from exactly the same population, and if the operations defining the experimental conditions were all carried out in exactly the same way. In the present case, both assumptions are questionable. In fact, some studies have sampled from the general population, while others sample from special populations such as college students. Similarly, although most articles give only a short description of the procedures that were actually used to implement the data collection methods, it is highly likely that they were not all identical. Even if we do not know all the details about the populations sampled and the procedures used, we may expect a lot of variation between the conditions as they were actually implemented. This would result in varying regression coefficients in our model. Thus, we analyze a model in which the slope coefficients of the dummy variables for the telephone and the mail condition are assumed to vary across studies. This model is given by

$$\beta_{0j} = \gamma_{00} + u_{0j}$$
$$\beta_{1j} = \gamma_{10}$$
$$\beta_{2j} = \gamma_{20} + u_{2j}$$
$$\beta_{3j} = \gamma_{30} + u_{3j}$$

which gives

$$\pi_{ij} = \text{logistic} \left(\gamma_{00} + \gamma_{10}\, resptype_{ij} + \gamma_{20}\, tel_{ij} + \gamma_{30}\, mail_{ij} + u_{0j} + u_{2j}\, tel_{ij} + u_{3j}\, mail_{ij} \right) \quad (6.25)$$

Results for the models specified by (6.24) and (6.25), estimated by second order PQL, are given in Table 6.3.

Table 6.3 Models for response rates in different conditions		
Fixed part	**conditions fixed**	**conditions random**
Predictor	coeff. (s.e.)	coeff. (s.e.)
intercept	0.90 (.14)	1.17 (.21)
resptype	0.53 (.06)	0.20 (.23)
telephone	-0.16 (.02)	-0.20 (.10)
mail	-0.49 (.03)	-0.58 (.16)
Random part		
σ^2_e (scale factor)	1.00	1.00
σ^2_{u0}	0.86 (.18)	0.87 (.20)
σ^2_{u2}		0.26 (.08)
σ^2_{u3}		0.59 (.20)

The intercept represents the condition in which all explanatory variables are zero. When the telephone-dummy and the mail-dummy are both zero, we have the face-to-face condition. Thus, the values for the intercept in Table 6.3 estimate the expected response in the face-to-face condition, 0.90 in the fixed model. The variable *resptype* indicates whether the response is a completion rate (*resptype* =0) or a response rate (*resptype*=1). The intercept plus the slope for *resptype* equals 1.43 in the final model. These values on the logit scale translate to an expected completion rate of 0.71 and an expected response rate of 0.81 for the average face-to-face survey. The negative values of the slope coefficients for the telephone and mail dummy-variables indicate that the expected response is lower in these conditions. To find out how much lower, we must use the regression equation to predict the response in the three conditions, and transform these values (which refer to the underlying logit-variate) back to proportions. For the telephone conditions, we expect an outcome of 1.26, and for the mail condition 0.94. These values on the logit scale translate to an expected response rate of 0.78 for the telephone survey and 0.72 for the mail survey.

The study level variances of the intercept and the conditions are obviously significant, and we may attempt to explain these using the known differences between the studies. In the example data, we have two study level explanatory variables: year of publication, and the salience of the questionnaire topic. Since not all studies compare all three data collection methods, it is quite possible that study level variables also explain between condition variance. For instance, if older studies tend to have a higher response rate, and the telephone method is included only in the more recent studies (telephone interviewing is, after all, a relatively new method), the telephone condition may seem characterized by low response rates. After correcting for the year of publication, in that case the telephone response rates should look better. We cannot inspect the condition level variance to investigate whether the higher level variables explain condition level variability. In the logistic regression model used here, the lowest-level (condition-level) variance term is automatically fixed at 1.00 in each model, so it remains the same in all analyses.

Both study-level variables make a significant contribution to the regression equation, but only the year of publication interacts with the two conditions. Thus, the final model for these data is given by

$$\pi_{ij} = \text{logistic} \ (\beta_{0j} + \beta_{1j} \ resptype_{ij} + \beta_{2j} \ tel_{ij} + \beta_{3j} \ mail_{ij})$$

at the lowest (condition) level, and at the study level:

$$\beta_{0i} = \gamma_{00} + \gamma_{01} \ year_j + \gamma_{02} \ saliency_j + u_{0j}$$
$$\beta_{1j} = \gamma_{10}$$
$$\beta_{2j} = \gamma_{20} + \gamma_{21} \ year_j + u_{2j}$$
$$\beta_{3j} = \gamma_{30} + \gamma_{31} \ year_j + u_{3j}$$

which produces the combined equation

$$\pi_{ij} = \text{logistic}\,(\gamma_{00} + \gamma_{10}\,resptype_{ij} + \gamma_{20}\,tel_{ij} + \gamma_{30}\,mail_{ij} + \gamma_{01}\,year_j + \gamma_{02}\,saliency_j +$$
$$\gamma_{21}\,tel_{ij}\,year_j + \gamma_{31}\,mail_{ij}\,year_j + u_{0j} + u_{2j}\,tel_{ij} + u_{3j}\,mail_{ij}\,) \qquad (6.26)$$

Results for the model specified by equation (6.26) are given in Table 6.4.

Table 6.4 Models for response rates in different conditions, with random slopes and cross-level interactions		
Fixed part	no interactions	with interactions
Predictor	coeff. (s.e.)	coeff. (s.e.)
intercept	0.93 (.43)	1.26 (.46)
resptype	0.33 (.21)	0.28 (.21)
telephone	-0.17 (.10)	-0.91 (.34)
mail	-0.58 (.15)	-1.45 (.46)
year	-0.02 (.01)	-0.03 (.01)
saliency	0.63 (.17)	0.64 (.17)
tel * year		0.02 (.01)
mail * year		0.03 (.01)
Random part		
σ^2_e (scale factor)	1.00	1.00
σ^2_{u0}	0.63 (.14)	0.63 (.14)
σ^2_{u2}	0.26 (.07)	0.24 (.07)
σ^2_{u3}	0.57 (.19)	0.43 (.15)

Compared to the earlier results, the regression coefficients are about the same in the model without the interactions, but some values are different in the model including the cross-level interactions. This does not have a substantive meaning, because the slopes for the conditions are involved in an interaction with the year of publication, and the effects of these predictor variables should therefore be considered together.

The regression coefficients in Table 6.4 must be interpreted in terms of the underlying variate. Moreover, the logit transformation implies that raising the response becomes more difficult as we approach the limit of 1.00. To show what this means the predicted response for the three methods is presented in Table 6.5 as logits (in parentheses) and proportions, both for a very salient (saliency=2) and a non-salient (saliency=0) questionnaire topic. To compute these numbers we must construct the regression equation implied by the last column of Table 6.4, and then use the inverse logistic transformation given earlier to transform the predicted logits back to proportions. The year 1947 is coded in the data-file as zero, but for the calculations in Table 6.5 the year was set at 1990 (year=43). As the expected response rates in Table 6.5 show, in 1990 the expected differences between the three data collection modes are small, while the effect of the saliency of the topic is much larger.

Table 6.5 Predicted response rates (logits) in 1990, based on cross-level interaction model			
Topic	face-to-face	telephone	mail
not salient	0.56 (.25)	0.55 (.20)	0.52 (.09)
salient	0.71 (.89)	0.70 (.84)	0.68 (.73)

To gain a better understanding of the development of the response rates over the years, it is useful to predict the response rates from the model and to plot these predictions over the years. This is done by filling in the regression equation implied by the final model for the three survey conditions, for the year varying from 1947 to 1998, with all other predictor variables fixed at their overall mean.

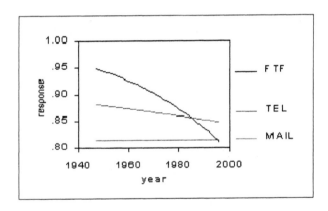

Figure 6.2. Predicted response rates over the years

Figure 6.2 presents such predictions for the response rates, based on the cross-level interaction model, with the saliency variable set to intermediate. The oldest study was published in 1947, the latest in 1992, so the values after 1992 are an extrapolation. At the beginning, in 1947, the cross level model implies that the differences between the three data collection modes were large. After that, the response rates for face-to-face and telephone surveys declined, while those for mail surveys remained stable. As a result, the response rates for the three data collection modes have become more similar in recent years.

6.5   ANALYZING EVENT COUNTS AND OTHER NONLINEAR MODELS

Nonlinear relations may also result if we analyze data that are event counts. If we count the occurrences of relatively rare events, such as fires in precincts or accidents on road stretches, the data often follow a Poisson distribution. In a generalized linear model, such data are usually analyzed using a Poisson error distribution, and a logarithmic link function. The issues in analyzing count models are much the same as in analyzing proportions. The usual approach is to apply quasi-likelihood estimation with Taylor linearization, with some software allowing a choice between first order or second order Taylor linearization, MQL or PQL estimation, and modeling overdispersion. An alternative to the Poisson error distribution is the negative binomial distribution, which can incorporate overdispersion directly by estimating an extra parameter in the variance function (cf. McCullagh & Nelder, 1989, p. 373). Note that the Poisson distribution assumes relatively rare events. Counts of relatively frequent events, such as the number of cigarettes smoked by heavy smokers, have different properties. The most important property of event counts is that they are always positive integers. If the count data are not rare, but do not follow a normal distribution, the usual link function is the inverse function, coupled with a gamma error distribution. An example of modeling counts using generalized multilevel models is a study of Pickery and Loosveldt (1998), who use a generalized multilevel model to analyze the effect of respondent and interviewer characteristics on the number of questions missed in an interview. Since missing a question is a relatively rare event, the count of missed questions follows a Poisson distribution nicely.

Other generalized regression models can be used to analyze data where the outcome variable is ordinal (Fielding, 1999), or where the outcome variable is a multinomial (categorical) variable. A discussion of these and other generalized regression models can be found in Long (1997). Current multilevel software does not support all these nonlinear models. The program aML is probably the most flexible multilevel software in this respect, but many nonlinear models can be specified in MLwiN and HLM. In most cases, the software relies on linearizing the model using a Taylor series approximation, but some software supports using exact likelihood methods. The methodological issues and analysis choices to be made are similar to the issues and choices discussed in this chapter in the context of multilevel logistic regression analysis.

7

Cross-Classified Multilevel Models

Not all multilevel data are purely hierarchical. For example, pupils can be nested within the schools they attend, and within the neighborhoods in which they live. However, the nesting structure may be less clear when we consider the schools and neighborhoods. It is likely that there is a tendency for pupils to attend schools in their own neighborhood, but there will be exceptions. Some pupils will attend schools in other neighborhoods than the one they live in, and especially schools that are located close to the border of two neighborhoods may be expected to draw pupils from several neighborhoods. As a result, it is not possible to set up an unambiguous nesting of pupils within schools within neighborhoods. We could, of course, arbitrarily set up such a model structure, but to do so we would have to include several schools more than once, because they appear in different neighborhoods.

Whenever we encounter this kind of problem, chances are that we are dealing with a cross-classified data structure. In the schools and neighborhoods example, pupils are nested within schools, and also within neighborhoods, but schools and neighborhoods are *crossed* with each other. If we study educational achievement, we may assume that achievement can be influenced by both schools and neighborhoods. Consequently, we should incorporate both schools and neighborhoods as sources of variation in achievement, with pupils nested in the cross-classification of both schools and neighborhoods.

Cross-classified data structures can occur at any level of a hierarchical data set. If we have pupils nested within the cross-classification of schools and neighborhoods, the schools and neighborhoods are nested at the second level. However, it is also possible to have a cross-classification at the lowest level. Consider the example of students who have to carry out a set of complicated analysis tasks in a computer class. There are several parallel classes, taught by different teachers. To keep the grading policy equivalent for all students, all computer exercises are graded by all available teachers. As a result, at the student level we would have grades for several different exercises, given by several different teachers. One way to view this, is to distinguish the class level as the highest level, with students below this level, with the teachers at the next lower level, and the exercises as the lowest level below the teachers. This constitutes a nicely hierarchical four-level data structure. On the other hand, we could also distinguish the class level as the highest level, with students below this level, the exercises at the next lower level, and the teachers as the lowest level below the exercises. This also constitutes a nicely four-level hierarchical data structure. It appears that we can model this data using two contradictory data structures. Again, whenever we have this kind of problem, it indicates that we are probably dealing with a cross-classified data structure. In the grading example, we have pupils nested within classes, with a cross-classification of teachers (graders) and exercises nested within the classes.

Since we may expect differences between classes and pupils, this cross-classification of exercises and teachers would be defined at the lowest level, nested within pupils within classes. The reliability of the combined grade of the student in such situations can be modeled using generalizability theory (Cronbach, Gleser, Nanda & Rajaratnam, 1972). To assess the generalizability of the students' combined grade across exercises and teachers using generalizability theory, we must partition the total variation of the assigned grades as the sum of contributions from classes, students, exercises and teachers. Cross-classified multilevel analysis is a good way to obtain the required estimates for the various variance components in such a partition.

Cross-classified multilevel models are applicable to a variety of situations. The examples given so far are from the field of education. Other applications are models for nonresponse in longitudinal research, where respondents are visited repeatedly, sometimes by the same interviewer, sometimes by a different interviewer. Interviewer characteristics may affect the respondents' cooperation, which is analyzed with a multilevel model with respondents nested within interviewers (Hox, de Leeuw & Kreft, 1991). In longitudinal studies, the previous interviewer may also be relevant, and as a result, we have a cross-classified structure, with respondents nested within the cross-classification of the current and the previous interviewer. Examples of multilevel cross-classified analyses in panel interview studies are the studies by Pickery and Loosveldt (1998), O'Muircheartaigh and Campanelli (1999) and Pickery, Loosveldt and Carton (2001). Cross-classified multilevel models have also been applied to sociometric choice data, where members of groups both give popularity ratings to and receive ratings from other group members (Van Duijn, van Bussbach & Snijders, 1999). For other examples see Raudenbush (1993b) and Rasbash and Goldstein (1994).

7.1   EXAMPLE OF CROSS-CLASSIFIED DATA: PUPILS NESTED WITHIN (PRIMARY AND SECONDARY SCHOOLS)

For example, assume that we have data from 1000 pupils who have attended 100 different primary schools, and subsequently went on to 30 secondary schools. Similar to the situation where we have pupils within schools and neighborhoods, we have a cross-classified structure. Pupils are nested within primary and within secondary schools, with primary and secondary schools crossed. In other words: pupils are nested within the cross-classification of primary and secondary schools. Goldstein (1994) introduces a formal description of these models, which will be followed here. In our example, we have a response variable *achievement* which is measured in secondary school. We have two explanatory variables at the pupil level: *pupil gender* (0=male, 1=female) and a six-point scale for pupil social-economic status, *pupil ses*. We have at the school level a dichotomous variable that indicates if the school is public (denom=0) or denominational (denom=1). Since we have both primary and secondary schools, we have two such variables (named *pdenom* for the primary school and *sdenom* for the secondary school).

At the pupil level, we can write an intercept-only model as

$$Y_{i(jk)} = \beta_{0(jk)} + e_{i(jk)} \tag{7.1}$$

Where the achievement score of pupil $Y_{i(jk)}$ of pupil i within the cross-classification of primary school j and secondary school k is modeled by the intercept (the overall mean) $\beta_{0(jk)}$ and a residual error term $e_{i(jk)}$. The subscripts (jk) are written between parentheses to indicate that they are conceptually at the same level: the $(jk)^{th}$ primary/secondary school combination in the cross-classification of primary and secondary schools.

The subscripts (jk) indicate that we assume that the intercept $\beta_{0(jk)}$ varies independently across both primary and secondary schools. Thus, we can model the intercept using the second level equation

$$\beta_{0(jk)} = \gamma_{00} + u_{0j} + v_{0k} \tag{7.2}$$

In equation (7.2) u_{0j} is the residual error term for the primary schools, and v_{0k} is the residual error term for the secondary schools. After substitution, this produces the intercept-only model:

$$Y_{i(jk)} = \gamma_{00} + u_{0j} + v_{0k} + e_{i(jk)} \tag{7.3}$$

where the outcome variable is modeled with an overall intercept γ_{00}, together with a residual error term u_{0j} for primary school j and a residual error term v_{0k} for secondary school k, and the individual residual error term $e_{i(jk)}$ for pupil i in the cross-classification of primary school j and secondary school k.

Individual level explanatory variables can be added to the equation, and their regression slopes may be allowed to vary across primary and/or secondary schools. School level variables can also be added, and used to explain variation in the slopes of individual level variables across schools, in a manner similar to ordinary multilevel regression models. However, at the time of writing, some complicated computational tricks are needed to specify a cross-classified model in standard multilevel regression software. The implementation details differ depending on the software; some comments on software use are given in the last section of this chapter.

Ignoring the secondary school level, we can specify the individual and primary school level as usual. To create a place to specify the crossed effects of the secondary school level, we introduce a third 'dummy'-level, with only one unit that covers the entire data set. At the pupil level, we specify dummy variables to indicate the secondary schools. In our example, we need 30 such dummy variables to indicate our 30 secondary schools. The fixed coefficients of these dummies are excluded from the model, but their slopes are allowed to vary at the third, the 'dummy'-level. In addition, the covariances between these dummies are all constrained to zero, and the variances are all constrained to be equal. Thus, we estimate one variance component for the secondary schools, and by putting the secondary schools in a separate level, we assure that there are no covariances between residuals for the primary and the secondary schools.

Although the analysis is set up using three separate levels, it should be clear that conceptually we have two levels, with primary and secondary schools crossed at the second level. The third level is just a computational device to allow estimation using standard multilevel software. For that reason, the third level is sometimes referred to as a 'dummy'-level, and not the 'secondary school'-level. There is no implication that the primary schools are nested within the secondary schools.

By way of example, Figure 7.1 shows part of the equations window of MLwiN for a cross-classified analysis of our example data. The equations in Figure 7.1 are the MLwiN-equivalent of the cross-classified intercept-only model in equation (7.3).

$$achiev_{ijk} \sim N(XB, \Omega)$$

$$achiev_{ijk} = \beta_{30j}const + v_{0k}c101_{ijk} + v_{1k}c102_{ijk} + v_{2k}c103_{ijk} + v_{3k}c104_{ijk} + v_{4k}c105_{ijk} + v_{5k}c106_{ijk} + v_{6k}c107_{ijk} + v_{7k}c108_{ijk}$$
$$+ v_{8k}c109_{ijk} + v_{9k}c110_{ijk} + v_{10k}c111_{ijk} + v_{11k}c112_{ijk} + v_{12k}c113_{ijk} + v_{13k}c114_{ijk} + v_{14k}c115_{ijk} + v_{15k}c116_{ijk}$$
$$+ v_{16k}c117_{ijk} + v_{17k}c118_{ijk} + v_{18k}c119_{ijk} + v_{19k}c120_{ijk} + v_{20k}c121_{ijk} + v_{21k}c122_{ijk} + v_{22k}c123_{ijk} + v_{23k}c124_{ijk}$$
$$+ v_{24k}c125_{ijk} + v_{25k}c126_{ijk} + v_{26k}c127_{ijk} + v_{27k}c128_{ijk} + v_{28k}c129_{ijk} + v_{29k}c130_{ijk}$$

$$\beta_{30j} = 6.349(0.078) + u_{30jk} + e_{30ijk}$$

$$\begin{bmatrix} v_{0k} \\ v_{1k} \\ v_{2k} \\ v_{3k} \\ v_{4k} \\ v_{5k} \end{bmatrix} \quad \begin{bmatrix} 0.065(0.022) & & & & & \\ 0 & 0.065(0.022) & & & & \\ 0 & 0 & 0.065(0.022) & & & \\ 0 & 0 & 0 & 0.065(0.022) & & \\ 0 & 0 & 0 & 0 & 0.065(0.022) & \\ 0 & 0 & 0 & 0 & 0 & 0.065(0.022) \end{bmatrix}$$

Figure 7.1. (Part of) MLwiN specification of cross-classified, intercept-only model

The first line in Figure 7.1 specifies a normal distribution for the outcome variable *achievement*. The second line and its continuation specify the fixed part of the multilevel regression model. The model is the intercept-only model, and we see a term β_{ij} CONST for the intercept (for simplicity, we ignore the subscript *30* for the sequence number of the regression coefficient that corresponds to the intercept). The line $\beta_{ij} =$ 6.349 (0.078) + u_{jk} + e_{ijk} (again ignoring in our notation the subscript *30*) gives the estimate for the intercept and its standard error, and shows that we assume two residual error terms: e_{ijk} at the individual level, and u_{jj} at the primary school level. What is not immediately clear in the equations window is that the 30 dummies for the secondary schools, labeled *c101* to *c130*, are not in the fixed part of the regression model. The regression coefficients for *v101* to *v130* are not estimated, which is the same as stating that they are constrained to be zero. What is estimated is the variance of the residual error term v_k at the secondary school level. We find this in the covariance matrix at the third, the dummy-level. Part of that 30×30 matrix is visible in Figure 7.1, and we can see that the off-diagonal elements are all constrained to be zero, and that the variance estimates on the diagonal are all constrained to be equal. The common variance estimate for the 30 dummies of 0.065 (s.e. 0.022) is the estimate for the variance of v_{0k} at the secondary school level.

Table 7.1 Cross-classified model achievement in primary and secondary schools

Model:	intercept-only coeff. (s.e.)	+ pupil vars coeff. (s.e.)	+ school vars coef. (s.e.)	+ *ses* random coeff. (s.e.)
Fixed part				
Predictor				
intercept	6.35 (.08)	5.76 (.11)	5.52 (.19)	5.53 (.14)
pupil gender		0.26 (.05)	0.26 (.05)	0.25 (.05)
pupil ses		0.11 (.02)	0.11 (.02)	0.11 (.02)
primary denom			0.20 (.12)	0.20 (.12)
secondary denom			0.18 (.10)	0.17 (.09)
Random part				
$\sigma^2_{int/pupil}$	0.51 (.02)	0.47 (.02)	0.47 (.02)	0.46 (.02)
$\sigma^2_{int/primary}$	0.17 (.04)	0.17 (.04)	0.16 (.04)	0.14 (.08)
$\sigma^2_{int/secondary}$	0.07 (.02)	0.06 (.02)	0.06 (.02)	0.05 (.02)
$\sigma^2_{ses/primary}$				0.008 (.004)
Deviance	2317.8	2243.5	2237.5	2224.5
AIC	2325.8	2255.5	2253.5	2244.5

The results of a series of models on the cross-classified data set are presented in Table 7.1 in a more conventional form. The first column in Table 7.1 presents the results for the intercept-only model. Since cross-classified models usually contain more than two levels, which are not all unambiguously nested, the table does not use the usual sigma-terms ($\sigma_e^2, \sigma_{u0}^2$, and so on) for the variance components, but names that correspond to the proper variable and level. Therefore, the term $\sigma^2_{\text{int/pupil}}$ corresponds to the usual term σ_e^2 in the model equation and $\sigma^2_{\text{int/primary}}$ to the usual term σ_{u0}^2. The term $\sigma^2_{\text{ses/primary}}$ corresponds to the usual term σ_{v0}^2 for a third level intercept variance. When a model contains many variance components, indicating these in the results tables by proper names instead of symbols often makes interpretation easier.

Since the levels of the primary and secondary school are independent, we can add the estimated variances in the intercept-only model (the first column in Table 7.1) for a total variance of 0.75. The intraclass correlation for the primary school level is 0.17/0.75= 0.23, and the intraclass correlation for the secondary school level is 0.07/0.75= 0.09. So, twenty-three percent of the total variance is accounted for by the primary schools, and nine percent by the secondary schools. Taken together, the schools account for (0.17+0.07)/0.75= 0.32 of the total variance.

The pupil level variables pupil gender and pupil ses have a significant contribution. The effect of either the primary or the secondary school being denominational is of borderline significance. The difference between the deviances of the second and the third model is 5.85, with two more parameters estimated in the third model. A chi-square test for this difference is also of borderline significance ($\chi_2^2 = 5.85, p = 0.054$). The AIC indicates that we should prefer model three. The conclusion is that, although there is apparently an effect of both school levels, the denomination of the school does not explain the school level variance very well. The fourth column in Table 7.1 shows the estimates for the model where we allow for variation in the slope for pupil ses across primary schools. This is indicated by the term $\sigma^2_{\text{ses/primary}}$ that in the interest of legibility is used instead of the symbol σ_{v0}^2. There is a small but significant slope variance for *ses* at the primary school level. The slope variance at the secondary school level (not shown in the table) is negligible.

7.2   EXAMPLE OF CROSS-CLASSIFIED DATA: (SOCIOMETRIC RATINGS) IN SMALL GROUPS

In the previous example, the cross-classification is at the higher levels, with pupils nested within the cross-classification of primary and secondary schools. The cross-classification can also be at lower levels. An example is the following model for sociometric ratings. Sociometric ratings can be collected by asking all members of a group to rate all other members, typically on a seven- or nine-point scale that indicates how much they would like to share some activity with the rated person. Figure 7.2 presents an example of a sociometric rating data set for three small groups, as it would look in standard statistical software.

	group	child	age	sex	grsize	rating1	rating2	rating3	rating4	rating5	rating6	rating7	rating8	rating9
1	1	1	8	1	7	.	3	6	4	4	7	6	.	.
2	1	2	10	1	7	5	.	6	4	5	7	5	.	.
3	1	3	11	1	7	4	6	.	4	5	7	6	.	.
4	1	4	9	0	7	4	4	6	.	5	7	5	.	.
5	1	5	11	0	7	5	5	6	5	.	7	6	.	.
6	1	6	10	1	7	4	5	6	3	4	.	6	.	.
7	1	7	10	1	7	3	5	6	5	3	6	.	.	.
8	2	1	9	0	9	.	3	5	3	4	6	6	4	5
9	2	2	9	0	9	2	.	4	5	6	5	4	4	5
10	2	3	9	0	9	5	3	.	4	3	6	5	4	6
11	2	4	8	1	9	3	2	5	.	6	6	5	3	4
12	2	5	9	1	9	4	4	5	5	.	5	7	4	5
13	2	6	9	0	9	3	4	4	4	4	.	5	4	5
14	2	7	9	1	9	4	4	6	5	6	5	.	4	5
15	2	8	11	0	9	3	4	5	4	5	6	6	.	5
16	2	9	8	1	9	3	4	5	5	4	6	7	5	.
17	3	1	11	0	5	.	5	7	5	6	.	.	.	.
18	3	2	11	0	5	5	.	7	6	6	.	.	.	.
19	3	3	13	1	5	5	5	.	6	8	.	.	.	.
20	3	4	12	1	5	4	4	6	.	6	.	.	.	.

Figure 7.2. Sociometric rating data for three small groups

In Figure 7.2, we see the sociometric ratings for a group of seven and a group of nine children, and part of the data of a third group of five children. High numbers indicate a positive rating. One way to collect such data is to give each child a questionnaire with a list of names for all children, and ask them to write their rating after each name. Therefore, each row in the table in Figure 7.2 consists of the sociometric ratings given by a specific child. The columns (variables) labeled *rating1*, *rating2*, …, *rating11* are the ratings received by child number 1, 2,…, 11. Figure 7.2 makes clear that network data, of which these sociometric ratings are an example, have a complicated structure that does not fit well in the rectangular data matrix assumed by most statistical software. The groups do not have the same size, so *rating6* to *rating11* have all missing values for group three, which has only five children. The children do not rate themselves, so these ratings also have missing values in the data matrix. The data also include the pupil characteristic *age* and *gender* and the group characteristic *group size*.

Special models have been proposed for network data (for an extensive introduction see Wasserman & Faust, 1994), and specialized software is available for the analysis of network data. Van Duijn (1995) shows that one can also use multilevel regression models to analyze network data. In the example of the sociometric ratings, we would view the ratings as an outcome variable that is nested within the cross-classification of the *senders* and the *receivers* of sociometric ratings. At the lowest level we have the separate ratings that belong to specific sender-receiver pairs. This is nested within the cross-classification of senders and receivers at the second level level, which in turn can be nested, for example within a sample of groups.

	group	sender	receiver	rating	agesend	sexsend	agerec	sexrec	grsize
1	1	1	2	3	8	1	10	1	7
2	1	1	3	6	8	1	11	1	7
3	1	1	4	4	8	1	9	0	7
4	1	1	5	4	8	1	11	0	7
5	1	1	6	7	8	1	10	1	7
6	1	1	7	6	8	1	10	1	7
7	1	2	1	5	10	1	8	1	7
8	1	2	3	6	10	1	11	1	7
9	1	2	4	4	10	1	9	0	7
10	1	2	5	5	10	1	11	0	7
11	1	2	6	7	10	1	10	1	7
12	1	2	7	5	10	1	10	1	7
13	1	3	1	4	11	1	8	1	7
14	1	3	2	6	11	1	10	1	7
15	1	3	4	4	11	1	9	0	7
16	1	3	5	5	11	1	11	0	7
17	1	3	6	7	11	1	10	1	7
18	1	3	7	6	11	1	10	1	7
19	1	4	1	4	9	0	8	1	7
20	1	4	2	4	9	0	10	1	7

Figure 7.3. Sociometric data rearranged for multilevel analysis, first four senders

To analyze sociometric choice data using multilevel techniques, the data must be arranged in a different format than the one shown in Figure 7.2. In the new data file, the individual rows must refer to the separate ratings, with associated child identification codes to identify the sender and receiver in that particular rating, and the variables that characterize the sender and receiver of information. Such a data set looks like the one depicted in Figure 7.3. This figure illustrates clearly how the distinct ratings are nested below both senders and receivers, who in turn are nested below the sociometric groups.

As the data set in Figure 7.3 illustrates, the cross-classification is here at the second level. We have ratings of senders and receiver pairs, which form a cross-classification nested within the groups. At the lowest level are the separate ratings. At the second level, we have the explanatory variables *age* and *gender* for the senders and receivers of ratings, and at the group level, we have the group characteristic *group size*.

The data in Figure 7.2 and 7.3 are part of a data set that contains sociometric data from twenty groups of children, with group sizes varying between four and eleven. At the lowest level, we can write the intercept-only model as follows:

$$Y_{i(jk)l} = \beta_{0(jk)l} + e_{i(jk)l} \tag{7.4}$$

In equation (7.4), rating i of sender j and receiver k is modeled by an intercept $\beta_{0(jk)l}$. At the lowest level, the ratings level, we have residual random errors $e_{i(jk)l}$, which indicates that we do not assume that all variation between ratings can be explained by differences between senders and receivers. These residual errors could be the result of random measurement errors, but they could also reflect unmodeled interactions between senders and receivers. The cross-classification of senders and receivers is nested within the groups, indicated by l. Again, parentheses are used to indicate a cross-classification of factors that are conceptually at the same level: the $(jk)^{\text{th}}$ sender/receiver combination, which is nested within groups l.

Note that we use subscripts on the intercept term β_0 to indicate that we assume that the intercept varies across both senders and receivers. Models involving cross-classified levels tend to have many distinct levels, and the practice of assigning a different Greek letter to regression coefficients at each level leads in such cases to a confusing array of Greek letters. In this chapter, the Greek letter β is used for regression coefficients that are assumed to vary across some level(s), with subscripts indicating these levels, and the Greek letter γ is used to denote fixed regression coefficients. So, the subscripts j, k and l on the regression coefficient $\beta_{0(jk)l}$ indicate that we assume that the intercept $\beta_{0(jk)l}$ varies across the cross-classification of senders and receivers nested within groups. Thus, we can model this intercept variance using the second level equation

$$\beta_{0(jk)l} = \beta_{0l} + u_{0j} + v_{0kl} \tag{7.5}$$

The subscript l on the regression coefficient β_{0l} indicates that we assume that the intercept β_{0l} varies across groups. We can further model the intercept variance using the third level equation

$$\beta_{0l} = \gamma_{00} + f_{0l} \tag{7.6}$$

After substitution, this produces

$$Y_{i(jk)l} = \gamma_{00} + f_{0l} + u_{0jl} + v_{0kl} + e_{i(jk)l} \tag{7.7}$$

where the outcome variable is modeled with an overall intercept γ_{00}, together with a residual error term f_l for group l, the individual level residual error terms u_{jl} for sender j in group l, and v_{kl} for receiver k in group l, and the measurement level error term $e_{i(jk)l}$.

It is immaterial whether we use the dummies to indicate the senders or the receivers. This time, the crossed effects of the receiver level are incorporated using dummies. At the lowest level, the ratings, we specify dummy variables that indicate the receivers. In our example data, the largest group consists of eleven pupils, so we need eleven dummy variables. The fixed coefficients of these dummies are excluded from the model, but their slopes are allowed to vary. Since the cross-classification is nested within the sociometric groups, the slopes of the dummy variables are set to vary at a third group level defined by the group identification variable. In addition, the covariances between the receiver dummies are constrained to zero, and the variances are constrained to be equal. Thus, we estimate one variance component for the receivers, and by putting the receivers in a separate level, we assure that there are no covariances between the residuals for the sender and the receiver level. Both sender and receiver characteristics like *age* and *gender* and group characteristics like *group size* can be added to the model as predictors, and child characteristics may be allowed to have random slopes at the group level. The analysis proceeds along exactly the same lines as outlined for the cross-classification of primary and secondary schools.

Since the third 'group' level is already used to specify the random variation for the receiver-dummies, we must make sure that the intercept and possible slope variation at the 'real' group level is not correlated with the dummies. This can be accomplished by adding the appropriate constraints to the model. When the software supports more than three levels (e.g., MLwiN (Rasbash et al., 2000), and aML (Lillard & Panis, 2000)), the same result can be accomplished more conveniently by adding a fourth level to the model, also for the groups, which is used for the random part at the real group level. Once more, it should be emphasized that, although the analysis is then set up using four separate levels, conceptually we have three levels, with senders and receivers crossed at the second level. The fourth level, the duplicated group level, is just a computational device to allow simple estimation of these very complex models using standard multilevel software.

To analyze our sociometric data, we decide to define the senders as an ordinary level in the standard manner, and the receivers at the third, the 'dummy' group level, using dummies. The first model is the intercept-only model of (7.7) written with variable names rather than symbols.

$$Rating_{i(jk)l} = \gamma_{00} + f_{0l} + u_{0jl} + v_{0kl} + e_{i(jk)l} \qquad (7.8)$$

Table 7.2 Results cross-classified model sociometric ratings in groups

Model:	intercept-only coeff. (s.e.)	+ all vars fixed coeff. (s.e.)	+sender gender random coef. (s.e.)	+ interaction gender send/rec coeff. (s.e.)
Fixed part				
Predictor				
intercept	5.03 (.22)	1.56 (1.17)	1.00 (1.00)	1.00 (1.00)
sender age		0.23 (.03)	0.22 (.03)	0.22 (.03)
sender gender		-0.16 (.07)	-0.12 (.13)	-0.37 (.14)
receiver age		0.21 (.06)	0.21 (.06)	0.22 (.06)
receiver gender		0.74 (.13)	0.73 (.13)	0.49 (.13)
interact.				0.51 (.09)
gender/gender				
Group size		-0.17 (.10)	-0.08 (.07)	-0.08 (.07)
Random part				
$\sigma^2_{int/ratings}$	0.41 (.02)	0.42 (.02)	0.42 (.02)	0.40 (.02)
$\sigma^2_{int/senders}$	0.15 (.03)	0.09 (.01)	0.02 (.01)	0.02 (.01)
$\sigma^2_{int/receivers}$	0.65 (.09)	0.49 (.07)	0.49 (.07)	0.48 (.07)
$\sigma^2_{int/groups}$	0.84 (.30)	0.42 (.16)	0.23 (.10)	0.23 (.10)
$\sigma^2_{send.gend//groups}$			0.28 (.11)	0.30 (.11)
$\sigma_{send.gend-int/groups}$			0.17 (.08)	0.18 (.08)
Deviance	2772.4	2677.0	2613.7	2580.3
AIC	2782.4	2697.3	2637.7	2606.2

This produces an estimate for the overall intercept, and the variance components σ^2_e for the variance of the ratings, $\sigma^2_{u_0}$ and $\sigma^2_{v_0}$ for the senders and the receivers, plus $\sigma^2_{f_0}$ for the variance at the group level. The estimates are in the first column of Table 7.2.

For the sake of readability, the variance components in the random part are indicated by proper variable and level names instead of the usual symbols. From the intercept-only model in the first column, it appears that 20% of the total variance is at the lowest (ratings) level, only 7% of the total variance is variance between the senders, 32% of the total variance is variance between the receivers, and 41% is variance between groups. Apparently, there are strong group effects.

The model in the second column of Table 7.2 adds all available explanatory variables as fixed predictors. Using abbreviated variable names, it can be written as:

$$rating_{i(jk)l} = \gamma_{00} + \gamma_{10}\, send.age_{jl} + \gamma_{20}\, send.gender_{jl} + \gamma_{30} rec.age_{kl} + \gamma_{40}\, rec.gender_{kl}$$
$$+ \gamma_{01}\, groupsize_l + f_{0l} + u_{0jl} + v_{0kl} + e_{i(jk)l} \qquad (7.9)$$

From the regression coefficients estimated in the second column of Table 7.2 we conclude that age of sender and receiver have a small positive effect on the ratings. In larger groups, the ratings are a bit lower, but this effect is not significant. The effect of the children's gender is more complicated. *Gender* is coded 0 for male, 1 for female, and Table 7.2 shows that female senders give lower ratings, while female receivers get higher ratings.

Only one explanatory variable, *sender gender*, has a significant slope variation on the group level. This model can be written as:

$$rating_{i(jk)l} = \gamma_{00} + \gamma_{10}\, send.age_{jl} + \gamma_{20}\, send.gender_{jl} + \gamma_{30} rec.age_{kl} + \gamma_{40}\, rec.gender_{kl}$$
$$+ \gamma_{01}\, groupsize_l + f_{1l}\, send.gender_{jl} + f_{0l} + u_{0jl} + v_{0kl} + e_{i(jk)l} \qquad (7.10)$$

Apart from having two residual error terms at the second level, one for the senders and one for the receivers, equation (7.10) represents an ordinary multilevel regression model with one varying slope at the group level, and no cross-level interactions. The estimates for this model are in the third column of Table 7.2. The variance of the slopes for sender gender is substantial, which indicates that the effect of the gender of the senders differs considerably across groups.

The only group level variable available to explain the variation of the *sender gender* slopes is group size. However, if we enter that in the model by forming the cross-level interaction between the variables *sender gender* and *group size*, it turns out to be nonsignificant.

The different effects of sender and receiver gender suggest looking in more detail at the effect of the explanatory variable *gender*. The last model in Table 7.2 includes an interaction effect for sender gender and receiver gender. This interaction, which is an ordinary interaction and not a cross-level interaction, is indeed significant. To interpret this interaction, it is useful to graph it. Figure 7.3 shows the interaction. It is clear that, in addition to the direct effects of sender gender (girls give on average lower ratings than boys), and receiver gender (girls receive on average higher ratings than boys), there is an interaction effect: both boys and girls give higher ratings to other children from their own gender.

Snijders and Bosker (1999, chapter 11) discuss a number of extensions of multilevel models for sociometric data. For instance, it may be useful to insert a second level that defines the *dyads*, the sender-receiver pairs. For each pair there are two ratings. The amount of variance at the dyad level indicates the degree of reciprocity in the ratings. For other extensions to the multilevel analysis of network data see Snijders and Kenny (1999) and van Duijn, van Busschbach, and Snijders (1999). The analysis of so-called ego-centered network data, which have a simple nesting structure, is discussed by Snijders, Spreen, and Zwaagstra (1994), Spreen and Zwaagstra (1994) and by Kef, Habekothé and Hox (2000).

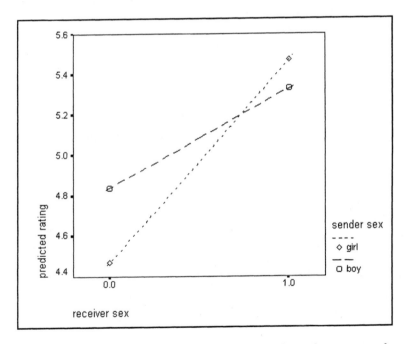

Figure 7.3. Graph of interaction between sender gender and receiver gender

7.3 STATISTICAL AND COMPUTATIONAL ISSUES

It is clear that for cross-classified models we need software that allows creating a highest level with just one unit, and imposing zero- and equality constraints on the highest level variances and covariances. What may not be immediately clear, though, is the fact that we are going to have large and complicated models. For instance, in our example with the cross-classification of primary and secondary schools, we are modeling a single variance component for the secondary school level using 30 dummy variables. For the random variance of the intercept at the secondary school level, we need therefore a covariance matrix for the random intercept of $30{\times}30{=}900$ elements. This covariance matrix must have equality constraints on the 30 variances on the diagonal, and zero constraints on the 435 covariances. If we add a pupil level variable, for instance *pupil ses*, and allow its slope to vary across secondary schools, the model becomes even more complicated. To create the secondary school level dummies for this variance component, we must create 30 new *pupil ses* dummies that are the product of the 30 secondary school dummies and the value of *pupil ses*. These dummies are then added to the model, and allowed to vary at the highest, the 'dummy'-level. We now have a covariance matrix at the secondary school level of $60{\times}60{=}3600$ elements. We must constrain the 30 variances of the intercept dummies to be equal, and their 435 covariances to be zero. In addition, we must constrain the 30 variances of the slopes of the *ses* dummies to be equal, and their 435 covariances to be zero. In general, we assume that the covariance between the intercepts and slopes at a higher level is not zero, which means that we must estimate in our example a common value by imposing equality constraints on the $30{\times}30{=}900$ covariances between intercept- and slope dummies. This is an intimidating prospect, and even more so if we had, say, 100 secondary schools.

It is clear that there are practical limits to what can be done in standard multilevel software. For the model, it does not matter whether we define a dummy level for the primary or the secondary schools. The way the cross-classified model is set up, they are completely exchangeable, and we should get the same estimates either way. In practice, if we specify the 100 primary schools as a dummy level, we need 100 dummy variables. It is clear that in general we would prefer to use the dummy level for the smallest classification, which in our example is the secondary school level. To specify the 30 secondary schools as a dummy level, we need only 30 dummy variables.

Given the complexity and size of cross-classified models, it is advisable to carry out preliminary analyses using standard multilevel models, leaving out one of the cross-classified factors in turn. This provides a rough indication of which variance components are important at which level. This is only a rough indication, because if the two classifications are correlated, leaving one out will lead to upwardly biased variance estimates for the other classification. Nevertheless, it will provide some indication of which classification has the largest variance components. Since specifying varying slopes on the dummy level is complicated and time consuming, it is best to use the standard specification for the classification with the largest number of random effects, and specify the other classification as a dummy level. In fact, if we carry out 3-level analyses on our sociometric ratings data, with ratings at the lowest level, either sender or receiver at the second level, and groups at the third level, we find that sender-level variables appear to have significant variance components at the group level, while receiver-level variables appear to have only fixed effects. This preliminary result justifies our decision to use a regular level for the senders, and model the receivers using a dummy-level.

Specifying cross-classified models is straightforward in MLwiN (version 1.1, Rasbash et al., 2000), because it contains a command SETX that carries out the tedious details. Later versions of MLwiN will probably have a graphical interface for cross-classified models. Other multilevel programs can be used, provided that they have facilities to impose constraints on the covariances and variances of the dummies. For instance, the program Prelis 2.3 (Jöreskog et al., 1999), contains the command COVPAT to impose a specific pattern of constraints on the covariance matrix at the dummy level, and it is simple to use this to specify that all diagonal elements must be equal and all off-diagonal elements must be zero. The program aML (Lillard & Panis, 2000) also allows complex constraints on the covariance matrices. The program HLM after version 6.0 will also have options for cross-classified data, which do not require that the user creates and manages all the dummy variables and constraints.

As mentioned above, the size of a cross-classified model and hence its computational demands can become very large. In principle, it does not make any difference in our example whether we put the primary schools or the secondary schools at the third 'dummy'-level. In practice, if we put the primary schools at the dummy-level, we must specify 100 dummies, and if we put the secondary schools at the dummy-level, we must specify 30 dummies. It is clear that the model is much smaller if we put the secondary schools at the dummy-level. In general, computations are simpler and go faster if we put at the dummy-level that factor that has the fewest random effects. To find out which factor of a cross-classification should be specified as a dummy-level, it is advisable to carry out some exploratory analyses first, using conventional two- and three-level models.

There is a second way to simplify a cross-classified model. Our 30 secondary schools could be crossed with the primary schools in such a way, that we can distinguish, for instance, three groups of each 10 secondary schools that receive pupils from, say, 34, 33 and 33 of the primary schools, in such a way that this structure is completely nested. That is, the first group of secondary schools takes only pupils from the first 34 primary schools; the second group takes only pupils from the following 33 primary schools, and the third group takes only pupils from the last 33 primary schools.

This means that we can split the data set on the secondary school level into three separate groups. If we can do this, we can simplify the model by specifying the third level as the secondary school-group level. We now need only 10 dummies for the secondary schools (the largest number of secondary schools in any of the groups so made), and the covariance matrix reduces to a size of $10 \times 10 = 100$ elements, instead of the 900 we had earlier. If we add the *ses* slope, we now need a covariance matrix of $20 \times 20 = 400$ elements, instead of 3600. Finding such groupings dramatically reduces the size of the model. In fact, if there is no such separate grouping structure, but we can create it by deleting a few stray pupils from the data set, it may well be worth it. MLwiN contains a command to search for such groupings, with other programs one has to tabulate the 100×30 cross-tabulation of the primary and secondary schools to search visually for separable groupings.

The examples all use 0/1 dummies to indicate group membership. If an individual is a member of more than one group, or if group membership is unknown for some individuals, it is possible to 'spread' the dummy-value of 1.0 over several groups, for instance giving each of two possible groups a dummy value of 0.5. This kind of model, which is useful when group membership is fuzzy (cf. Blalock, 1990), is discussed by Hill and Goldstein (1998).

8

The Multilevel Approach to Meta-Analysis

Meta-analysis is a systematic approach towards summarizing the findings of a collection of independently conducted studies on a specific research problem. In meta-analysis, statistical analyses are carried out on the published results of empirical studies on a specific research question. This chapter shows that multilevel regression models are attractive for analyzing meta-analytic data.

8.1 META-ANALYSIS AND MULTILEVEL MODELING

Meta-analysis is a systematic approach towards the synthesis of a large number of results from empirical studies (cf. Glass, 1976). The goal is to summarize the findings of a collection of independently conducted studies on a specific research problem. For instance, the research question might be: 'What is the effect of social skills training on socially anxious children?' In a meta-analysis, one would collect reports of experiments concerning this question, explicitly code the reported outcomes, and integrate the outcomes statistically into a combined 'super outcome'. Often the focus is not so much on integrating or summarizing the outcomes, but on more detailed questions such as: 'What is the effect of different durations for the training sessions?' or 'Are there differences between different training methods?' In these cases, the meta-analyst not only codes the study outcomes, but also codes study characteristics. These study characteristics are potential explanatory variables to explain differences in the study outcomes. Meta-analysis is not just the collection of statistical methods used to achieve integration. It is the application of systematic scientific strategies to the literature review (Cornell & Mulrow, 1999; Light & Pillemer, 1984). For a brief introduction to general meta-analysis I refer to Cornell and Mulrow (1999), and Lipsey and Wilson (2001). A thorough and complete treatment of methodological and statistical issues in meta-analysis, including a chapter on using multilevel regression methods (Raudenbush, 1994) can be found in Cooper and Hedges (1994) and in Sutton et al. (2000).

The core of meta-analysis is that statistical analyses are carried out on the published results of a collection of empirical studies on a specific research question. One approach is to combine the p-values of all the collected studies into one combined *p*-value. This is a simple matter, but does not provide much information. A very general model for meta-analysis is the random-effects model (Hedges & Olkin, 1985, p. 198). In this model, the focus is not on establishing the statistical significance of a combined outcome, but on analyzing the size of the effects found in the different studies. The random-effects model for meta-analysis assumes that study outcomes vary across studies, not only because of random sampling effects, but also because there are real differences between the studies. For instance, study outcomes may vary because the different studies employ different sampling methods, use different experimental manipulations, or measure the outcome with different instruments. The random-effects model is used to decompose the variance of the study outcomes into two components: one component that is the result of sampling variation, and a second component that reflects real differences between the studies. Hedges and Olkin (1985) describe procedures that can be used to decompose the total variance of the study outcomes into random sampling variance and systematic between-studies variance, and to test the significance of the between studies variance. If the between studies variance is large and significant, the study outcomes are regarded as *heterogeneous*. This means that the studies do not all provide the same outcome. One procedure to investigate the differences between the studies is to form clusters of studies, which differ in their outcomes between the clusters, but which are homogeneous within the clusters. The next goal is to identify study characteristics that explain differences between the clusters. Variables that affect the study outcomes are in fact moderator variables: variables that interact with the independent variable.

Meta-analysis can be viewed as a special case of multilevel analysis. We have a hierarchical data set, with subjects within studies at the first level, and studies at the second level. If the raw data of all the studies would be available, we could carry out a standard multilevel analysis, predicting the outcome variable using the available individual and study level explanatory variables. In our example on the effect of social skills training of children, we would have one outcome variable, for instance the result on a test measuring social skill, and one explanatory variable which is a dummy variable that indicates whether the subject is in the experimental or the control group. On the individual level, we have a linear regression model that relates the outcome to the experimental/control-group variable. The general multilevel regression model assumes that each study has its own regression model. If we have access to all the original data, standard multilevel analysis can be used to estimate the mean and variance of the regression coefficients across the studies. If the variance of the regression slopes of the experimental/control-group variable is large and significant, we have heterogeneous results. In that case, we can use the available study characteristics as explanatory variables to predict the differences of the regression coefficients.

These analyses can be carried out using standard multilevel regression methods and using standard multilevel software. However, in meta-analysis we usually do *not* have access to the original raw data. Instead, we have the published results in the form of *p*-values, means, standard deviations or correlation coefficients. Classical meta-analysis has developed a large variety of methods to integrate these statistics into one overall outcome, and to test whether the outcomes should be regarded as homogeneous or heterogeneous. Hunter and Schmidt (1990) discuss these methods in detail, and Hedges and Olkin (1985) discuss the statistical models on which these methods are based. Hedges and Olkin (1985) also describe a weighted regression model that can be used to model the effect of study characteristics on the outcomes, and Lipsey and Wilson (2001) show how conventional software for weighted regression analysis can be used to analyze meta-analytic data.

Even without access to the raw data, it is often possible to carry out a multilevel meta-analysis on the summary statistics that are available data for the meta-analysis. Raudenbush and Bryk (Bryk & Raudenbush, 1992; Raudenbush & Bryk, 1985) view the random-effects model for meta-analysis as a special case of the multilevel regression model. The analysis is performed on sufficient statistics instead of raw data, and as a result, some specific restrictions must be imposed on the model. The major advantage of using multilevel analysis instead of classical meta-analysis methods is flexibility (Hox & de Leeuw, 2002). In multilevel meta-analysis, it is simple to include study characteristics as explanatory variables in the model. If we have hypotheses about study characteristics that influence the outcomes, we can code these and include them on a priori grounds in the analysis. Alternatively, after we have concluded that the study outcomes are heterogeneous, we can explore the available study variables in an attempt to explain the heterogeneity.

8.2 THE VARIANCE-KNOWN MODEL

In a typical meta-analysis, the various studies found in the literature employ different instruments and use different statistical tests. To make the outcomes comparable, the study results must be transformed into a standardized measure of the effect, such as a correlation coefficient or the standardized difference between two means. For instance, if we perform a meta-analysis on studies that compare an experimental group to a control group, an appropriate measure for the effect size is the standardized difference between two means g, which is given by $g = \left(\overline{Y}_E - \overline{Y}_C \right) / s$. Since the standardized difference g has a small bias, it is usually transformed to the effect size indicator $d = (1-3/(4(n_E+n_C)-9))g$, which is unbiased.

However, the bias correction is often negligible, and in practice d is therefore often simply defined as $d = (\overline{Y}_E - \overline{Y}_C)/s$, ignoring the correction.

The general model for the study outcomes, ignoring possible study-level explanatory variables, is given by

$$d_j = \delta_j + e_j \qquad\qquad\qquad (8.1)$$

In equation (8.1), d_j is the outcome of study j ($j=1, \ldots, J$), δ_j is the corresponding population value, and e_j is the sampling error for this specific study. It is assumed that the e_j have a normal distribution with a known variance σ_j^2. If the sample sizes of the individual studies are not too small, for instance between 20 (Hedges & Olkin, 1985, p. 175) to 30 (Bryk & Raudenbush, 1992, p. 157), it is reasonable to assume that the sampling distribution of the outcomes is normal. The assumption of underlying normality is not unique for multilevel meta-analysis; most classical meta-analysis methods also assume normality (cf. Hedges & Olkin, 1985). The variance of the sampling distribution of the outcome measures is assumed known from statistical theory. In some cases, the outcomes must be transformed to achieve normality and known sampling variance.

Table 8.1 Some effect measures, their transformation and sampling variance

measure	estimator	transformation	sampling variance
mean	$\overline{x}$	-	s^2/n
diff. 2 means	$d = (\overline{y}_E - \overline{y}_C)/s$	-	$(n_E + n_C)/(n_E n_C) +$ $d^2/(2(n_E + n_C))$
stand. dev,	s	$s^* = \mathrm{LN}(s) + 0.5df$	$0.5df$
correlation	r	$z = 0.5\,\mathrm{LN}((1+r)/(1-r))$	$1/(n-3)$
proportion	p	$\mathrm{logit} = \mathrm{LN}\,(p/1-p)$	$1/(np(1-p))$
diff. 2 prop.	$d \approx Z_{p1} - Z_{p2}$	-	$\dfrac{2\pi p_1\left(1 - p_1\right)e^{Z_{p1}^2}}{n_1} + $ $\dfrac{2\pi p_2\left(1 - p_2\right)e^{Z_{p2}^2}}{n_2}$

To obtain a good approximation to a normal sampling distribution, a transformation of the original effect size statistic is often needed. For instance, since the sampling distribution of a standard deviation is only approximately normal, it should not be used with small samples. The transformation $s^* = \mathrm{LN}(s) + 0.5df$ of the standard deviation improves the normal approximation. The usual transformation for the correlation coefficient r is the familiar Fisher-Z transformation, and for the proportion it is the logit. Note that, if we need to perform a meta-analysis on logits, the procedures outlined in Chapter Six are generally more accurate. Usually, if a confidence interval is constructed for the transformed variable, the end-points are translated back to the scale of the original estimator. Table 8.1 lists some common effect size measures, the usual transformation if one is needed, and the sampling variance (of the transformed outcome if applicable) (Lipsey & Wilson, 2001; Raudenbush & Bryk, 1985; Rosenthal, 1994).

Equation (1) shows that the parameter δ_j, the study outcome, is assumed to vary across the studies. The variance of the δ_j is explained by the regression model

$$\delta_j = \gamma_0 + \gamma_1 Z_{1j} + \gamma_2 Z_{2j} + \ldots + \gamma_p Z_{pj} + u_j \tag{8.2}$$

where $Z_1 \ldots Z_p$ are study characteristics, $\gamma_1 \ldots \gamma_p$ are the regression coefficients, and u_j is the residual error term, which is assumed to have a normal distribution with variance σ_u^2. By substituting (8.2) into (8.1) we obtain the complete model

$$d_j = \gamma_0 + \gamma_1 Z_{1j} + \gamma_2 Z_{2j} + \ldots + \gamma_p Z_{pj} + u_j + e_j \tag{8.3}$$

If there are no explanatory variables, the model reduces to

$$d_j = \gamma_0 + u_j + e_j \tag{8.4}$$

Model (8.4), which is the 'intercept only' or 'empty' model, is equivalent to the random-effects model for meta-analysis described by Hedges and Olkin (1985).

In model (8.4), the intercept γ_0 is the estimate for the mean outcome across all studies. The variance of the outcomes across studies, σ_u^2, indicates how much these outcomes vary across studies. Thus, testing if the study outcomes are homogeneous is equivalent to testing the null-hypothesis that the variance of the residual errors u_j, indicated by σ_u^2, is equal to zero. If the test of σ_u^2 is significant, the study outcomes are considered heterogeneous. The proportion of systematic between-study variance can be estimated by the intraclass correlation $\rho = \sigma_u^2/(\sigma_u^2 + \sigma_e^2)$.

The general model (8.3) includes study characteristics Z_{pj} to explain differences in the studies' outcomes. In model (8.3), σ_u^2 is the residual between-study variance after the explanatory variables are included in the model. The statistical test on σ_u^2 now tests whether the explanatory variables in the model explain all the variation in the studies' outcomes, or if there still is unexplained systematic variance left in the outcomes. The difference between the between-studies variance σ_u^2 in the empty model and in the model that includes the explanatory variables Z_{pj}, can be interpreted as the amount of variance explained by the explanatory variables, that is, by the coded study characteristics.

The multilevel meta-analysis model given by equation (8.3) is similar to the general weighted regression model for fixed effects described by Hedges and Olkin (1985, chapter 8). In our notation, their model is given by

$$d_j = \gamma_0 + \gamma_1 Z_{1j} + \gamma_2 Z_{2j} + \ldots + \gamma_p Z_{pj} + e_j \qquad (8.5)$$

Compared to model (8.3), model (8.5) lacks the study-level residual error term u_j. Thus, the general model for fixed effects described by Hedges and Olkin is a special case of the multilevel meta-analysis model. Omitting the study-level residual error term u_j implies assuming that the explanatory variables in the model explain all the variance among the studies. Thus, if the residual between-study variance is zero, a fixed-effect model is appropriate (Hedges & Vevea, 1998). However, this assumption is not very realistic. For instance, Hunter and Schmidt (1990) argue that the between-studies heterogeneity is partly produced by some unavoidable artifacts encountered in meta-analysis. Examples of such artifacts are the (usually untestable) assumption of a normal distribution for the sampling errors e_j, the correctness of statistical assumptions made in the original analyses, differences in reliability of instruments used in different studies, coder unreliability, et cetera. It is unlikely that the available study level variables cover all these artifacts. Generally, the amount of detail in the input for the meta-analysis, the research reports, papers and articles, is not enough to code all these study characteristics for all of the studies. Therefore, heterogeneous results are to be expected (cf. Engels, Schmidt, Terrin, Olkin & Lau, 2000). Since heterogeneous results are common, Hunter and Schmidt recommend as rule of thumb that the study-level variance should be larger than 25% of all variance to merit closer inspection.

Since there is as a rule unexplained variance in a meta-analysis, random-effects models should be preferred over fixed-effect models. Lipsey and Wilson (2001) describe a Weighted Least Squares regression procedure for estimating the model parameters, which can be applied using standard statistical software for weighted regression. Just like multilevel meta-analysis this is a powerful approach, because one can include explanatory variables in the model. However, in the weighted regression approach the investigators must supply an estimate of the residual between-study variance. This variance is estimated before the weighted regression analysis, and the estimated value is then plugged into the weighted regression analysis (Lipsey & Wilson, 2001). Multilevel analysis programs estimate this variance component, typically using iterative Maximum Likelihood estimation, taking into account the information contained in the explanatory variables in the model, which in general is more precise and efficient. In practice, both approaches usually produce very similar parameter estimates. The multilevel approach has the additional advantage that it offers more flexibility, for example, by using a three-level model for multivariate outcomes. Compared to the fixed effect model, if random effects models are used in the presence of significant between-study variance, this appears to lead to larger average effect estimates, with wider confidence intervals (Villar, Mackey, Carroli & Donner, 2001). If fixed effect models are used in the presence of significant between-study variance, the resulting confidence intervals are much too small (Villar, Mackey, Carroli & Donner, 2001; Brockwell & Gordon, 2001).

8.3 EXAMPLE AND COMPARISON WITH CLASSICAL META-ANALYSIS

In this section we analyze an example data set using classical meta-analysis methods as implemented in the program META by Schwarzer (1989). This program is based on methods and procedures described by Rosenthal (1984), Hunter and Schmidt (1990) and Hedges and Olkin (1985). The (simulated) data set consists of 20 studies that compare an experimental group and a control group.

Let us return to our example on the effect of social skills training on socially anxious children. We collect reports of experiments concerning this question. If we compare the means of an experimental and a control group, an appropriate outcome measure is the standardized difference between the experimental and the control group, originally proposed by Glass (1976) and defined by Hedges and Olkin as $g = \left(\overline{Y}_E - \overline{Y}_C\right)/s$, where s is the pooled standard deviation of the two groups. Because g is not an unbiased estimator of the population effect $\delta = (\mu_E - \mu_C)/\sigma$, Hedges and Olkin prefer a corrected effect measure d: $d = (1-3/(4(n_E+n_C)-9))g$. The sampling variance of the effect estimator d is $(n_E + n_C)/(n_E n_C) + d^2/(2(n_E + n_C))$ (Hedges & Olkin, 1985, p. 86).

Table 8.2 is a summary of the outcomes from a collection of 20 studies. The studies are presented in increasing order of their effect sizes (g, d). Table 8.2 presents both g and d for all 20 studies, with some study characteristics described later. With commonly used sample sizes, the difference between g and d is very small. Table 8.2 also presents the sampling variance of the effect sizes d (var(d)), the one-sided p-value of the t-test for the difference of the two means (p), the number of cases in the experimental (n_{exp}) and control group(n_{con}), and the reliability (r_{ii}) of the outcome measure used in the study. The example data set contains several study level explanatory variables. A theoretically motivated explanatory variable is the duration in number of weeks of the experimental intervention. It is plausible to assume that longer interventions lead to a larger effect. In addition we have the reliability of the outcome measure (r_{ii}), and the size of the experimental and control group.

Table 8.2	Example meta-analytic data from 20 studies							
study	weeks	g	d	var(d)	p	n_{exp}	n_{con}	r_{ii}
1	3	-.268	-.264	.086	.810	23	24	.90
2	1	-.235	-.230	.106	.756	18	20	.75
3	2	.168	.166	.055	.243	33	41	.75
4	4	.176	.173	.084	.279	26	22	.90
5	3	.228	.225	.071	.204	29	28	.75
6	6	.295	.291	.078	.155	30	23	.75
7	7	.312	.309	.051	.093	37	43	.90
8	9	.442	.435	.093	.085	35	16	.90
9	3	.448	.476	.149	.116	22	10	.75
10	6	.628	.617	.095	.030	18	28	.75
11	6	.660	.651	.110	.032	44	12	.75
12	7	.725	.718	.054	.003	41	38	.90
13	9	.751	.740	.081	.009	22	33	.75
14	5	.756	.745	.084	.009	25	26	.90
15	6	.768	.758	.087	.010	42	17	.90
16	5	.938	.922	.103	.005	17	39	.90
17	5	.955	.938	.113	.006	14	31	.75
18	7	.976	.962	.083	.002	28	26	.90
19	9	1.541	1.522	.100	.0001	50	16	.90
20	9	1.877	1.844	.141	.00005	31	14	.75

8.3.1 Classical Meta-analysis

Classical meta-analysis includes a variety of approaches that complement each other. For instance, several different formulas are available for combining *p*-values. A classic procedure is the so-called Stouffer method (Rosenthal, 1984). In the Stouffer method, each individual *p* is converted to the corresponding standard normal Z-score. The Z-scores are then combined using $Z = \left(\sum Z_j \right) / \sqrt{k}$, where Z_j is the Z-value of study *j*, and *k* is the number of studies. For our example data, the Stouffer method gives a combined Z of 7.73, which is highly significant ($p < 0.001$).

The combined *p*-value gives us proof that an effect exists, but no information on the size of the experimental effect. The next step in classical meta-analysis is to combine the effect sizes of the studies into one overall effect size, and to establish the significance or a confidence interval for the combined effect. Considering the possibility that the effects may differ across the studies, the random-effects model is used to combine the studies. A meta-analysis of the effect sizes in Table 8.2, using the random-effects model, estimates the overall effect as $\delta=0.58$, with a standard error of 0.11. Using this information, we can carry out a null-hypothesis test by computing $Z=0.58/0.11=5.27$ ($p<0.001$). The 95% confidence interval for the overall effect size is $0.36<\delta<0.80$. The usual significance test of the between-study variance used in meta-analysis is a chi-square test on the residuals, which for our example data leads to $\chi_{19}^2 = 48.9$, ($p <0.001$). As this is clearly significant, we have heterogeneous outcomes. This means that the overall effect 0.58 is not the estimate of a fixed population value, but an average of the distribution of effects in the population. The Z-value of 5.27 computed using the random-effects model is not the same as the Z-value of 7.73 computed using the Stouffer method. Since the difference is due to the inclusion of between-study variance in the random-effects model, which is significant, the Z-value of 5.27 is more appropriate.

The parameter variance σ_u^2 is estimated as 0.17, and the proportion of systematic variance is 0.65. This is much larger than the 0.25 that Hunter and Schmidt (1990) consider a lower limit for examining differences between studies. The conclusion is that the between-study variance is not only significant, but also large enough to merit further analysis using the study characteristics at our disposal. The usual follow-up approach in classical meta-analysis is to divide the studies into clusters that have different average effect sizes, while being internally homogeneous.

8.3.2 Multilevel Meta-analysis

A multilevel meta-analysis of the 20 studies using the empty 'intercept only' model produces virtually the same results as the classical meta-analysis. Since in meta-analysis we are strongly interested in the size of the between-study variance component, Restricted Maximum Likelihood (RML) estimation is the best approach. Using RML, the intercept, which in the absence of other explanatory variables is the overall outcome, is estimated as $\gamma_0=0.58$, with a standard error of 0.11 ($Z=5.25$, $p<0.001$). The null hypothesis of homogeneous outcomes is rejected, but the parameter variance is estimated a bit lower than in the classical meta-analysis. The parameter variance σ_u^2 is estimated as 0.14, and the proportion of systematic variance is 0.61. This again is much larger than 0.25, the lower limit for examining differences between studies (Hunter & Schmidt, 1990). The small differences between these results and the results computed using

The power of multilevel meta-analysis becomes apparent when we attempt to model the differences in the study outcomes, which is expressed in the parameter variance. We simply include the duration of the experimental intervention as an explanatory variable in the regression model. The multilevel meta-analysis model can be written as

$$d_j = \gamma_0 + \gamma_1 DURATION_{1j} + u_j + e_j \qquad (8.6)$$

The results of the multilevel meta-analysis are summarized in Table 8.3, which presents the results for both the empty (null) model and the model that includes duration and the results obtained by the classical (random-effects) meta-analysis.

Table 8.3 Random-effects model and multilevel analyses on example data			
Model:	classical meta-analysis	multilevel intercept-only	multilevel regression
delta/intercept	.58 (.11)	.58 (.11)	-.22 (.20)
duration			.14 (.03)
σ_u^2	.17	.14	.04
p-value χ^2 test	$p < 0.001$	$p < 0.001$	$p = 0.09$

After including duration as explanatory variable in the model, the residual between-study variance is much smaller, and no longer significant. The regression coefficient for the duration is 0.14 (p <0.001), which means that for each additional week the expected gain in study outcome is 0.14. The intercept in this model is –0.22, with a standard error of 0.20 (p =0.20). The intercept is not significant, which is logical, because it refers to the expected outcome of a hypothetical experiment with duration of zero weeks. If we center the duration variable by subtracting its overall mean, the intercept does not change from one model to the next, and reflects the expected outcome of the average study. The residual variance in the last model is 0.04, which is not significant. If we compare this with the parameter variance of 0.14 in the empty model, we conclude that 71% of the between-studies variance can be explained by including 'duration' as the explanatory variable in the model.

Note that in the multilevel analyses reported in Table 8.3, RML estimation is used, and the residual variance is tested for significance using the chi-square test proposed by Bryk and Raudenbush (1992), and not using the asymptotic Wald test (cf. Chapter Three). There are two important reasons for these choices. Firstly, in standard applications of multilevel analysis, the variances are often viewed as nuisance parameters. It is important to include them in the model, but their specific value is not very important, because they are not interpreted. In meta-analysis, the question whether all the studies report essentially the same outcome is a central issue, and its answer depends on the decision about the significance of the between-studies variance. Therefore, it is very important to have a good estimate of the between-studies variance and its significance. For this reason, Restricted Maximum Likelihood (RML) estimation is used instead of Full Maximum Likelihood (FML). Generally, FML and RML estimation lead to very similar variance estimates, but if they do not, using RML provides better estimates (Browne, 1998). Secondly, the asymptotic Wald test on the variance computes the test statistic Z by dividing the variance estimate by its standard error. This assumes a normal sampling distribution for the variance. This assumption is not justified, because variances are known to have a chi-square sampling distribution. An additional reason for using the chi-square test on the variance is more practical; the chi-square test proposed by Bryk and Raudenbush (1992) follows the same logic as the chi-square test on the residuals in classic random-effects meta-analysis, which facilitates comparison.

Since the study outcome depends in part on the duration of the experiment, reporting an overall outcome for the twenty studies does not convey all the relevant information. We could report the expected outcome for different duration, or calculate which duration is minimally needed to obtain a significant outcome. This can be accomplished by centering the explanatory variable on different values. For instance, if we center the duration around two weeks, the intercept can be interpreted as the expected outcome at two weeks. Some multilevel analysis programs can produce predicted values with their expected error variance, which is also useful to describe the expected outcome for experiments with a different duration.

8.4 CORRECTING FOR ARTIFACTS

Hunter and Schmidt (1990, 1994) encourage correcting study-outcomes for a variety of artifacts. It is common to correct the outcome for the attenuation that results from unreliability of the measure used. The correction simply divides the outcome measure by the square root of the reliability, for instance $d^* = d / \sqrt{r_{ii}}$, after which the analysis is carried out as usual. This is the same correction as the classical correction for attenuation of the correlation coefficient in psychometric theory (cf. Nunnally & Bernstein, 1994). Hunter and Schmidt (1994) describe many more corrections. All these corrections share major methodological and statistical problems. One problem is that the majority of corrections always result in larger effect sizes. For instance, if the studies use instruments with a low reliability, the corrected effect size is much larger than the original effect size. If the reported reliability is incorrect, so will be the correction. Because the large effects have in fact not been observed, routinely carrying out such corrections is controversial. For that reason, Schwarzer (1989, p56) advises to always report the original values in addition to the corrected results. A second problem with all these corrections is that they influence the standard error of the outcome-measure. Lipsey and Wilson (2001) present proper standard errors for some corrections. However, if the values used to correct outcomes are themselves subject to sampling error, the sampling variance of the outcome measure becomes still larger. Especially if many corrections are performed, their cumulative effect on the bias and accuracy of the outcome-measures is totally unclear.

A different approach to correcting artifacts is to include them as covariates in the multilevel regression analysis. For reliability of the outcome measure, this is still not optimal, because the proper correction is a nonlinear model (cf. Nunnally & Bernstein, 1994), and regression analysis is additive. However, if the range of reliabilities is not extreme, a linear model is a reasonable approximation, and we can always include quadratic or cubic trends in the analysis if that is needed. The advantage is that the effect of unreliability on the study outcomes is estimated based on the available data and not by a priori corrections. Another advantage is that we can test if the correction has a significant contribution to the regression equation. Lastly, if we suspect that a certain covariate, for instance poor experimental design, has an effect on the variability of the outcomes we can include it only in the random part of the model, where it affects the between studies variance, but not the average outcome.

A variation on correcting for artifacts is controlling for the effect of study size. An important problem in meta-analysis is the so-called *file drawer problem*. The data for a meta-analysis are the results from previously published studies. Studies that find significant results may have a greater probability to get published. As a result, a sample of published studies can be biased in the direction of reporting large effects. In classical meta-analysis, one way is to carry out a fail-safe analysis. This answers the question how many unpublished insignificant papers must lie in various researchers' file drawers to render the combined results of the available studies insignificant. If the fail-safe number is high, we assume it is unlikely that the file drawer problem affects our analysis. An alternative approach to the file drawer problem is drawing a *funnel plot*. The funnel plot is a plot of the effect size versus the total sample size (Light & Pillemer, 1984; Light, Singer & Willet, 1994; Lipsey & Wilson, 2001). If the sample of available studies is 'well-behaved' this plot should have the shape of a funnel. The outcomes from smaller studies are more variable, but estimate the same underlying population parameter. If large effects are found predominantly in smaller studies, this indicates the possibility of publication bias, and the possibility of many other insignificant small studies remaining unpublished in file drawers. In addition to a funnel plot, the effect of study sample size can be investigated by including the total sample size of the studies as an explanatory variable in a multilevel meta-analysis. This variable should *not* be related to the outcomes. Macaskill, Walter and Irwig (2001) recommend using the inverse of the sampling variance instead of the studies' sample size, because this is a more direct indicator of a study's expected variability.

The example data in Table 8.2 have an entry for the reliability of the outcome measure (r_{ii}). These (fictitious) data on the effect of social skills training assume that two different instruments were used to measure the outcome of interest; some studies used one instrument, some studies used another instrument. These instruments, in this example tests for social anxiety in children, differ in their reliability as reported in the test manual. If we use classical psychometric methods to correct for attenuation by unreliability, followed by classical meta-analysis using the random-effects model, the combined effect size is estimated as 0.64 instead of the value of 0.58 found earlier. The parameter variance is estimated as 0.23 instead of the earlier value of 0.17.

If we include the reliability and the sample size as explanatory variables in the regression model, we obtain the results presented in Table 8.4.

Table 8.4 Random-effects model and multilevel meta-analyses on example data					
Model:	intercept-only	+ N_{tot}	+ reliability	+ duration	+ all
intercept	.58 (.11)	.50 (.05)	.15 (1.23)	-.22 (.20)	.42 (.92)
N_{tot}		.001 (.01)			-.004(.01)
reliability			.51 (1.47)		-.51(1.18)
duration				.14 (.03)	.15 (.04)
σ_u^2	.14	.16	.16	.04	.05
p-value χ^2 test	$p < .001$	$p < .001$	$p < .001$	$p = .09$	$p = .07$

The first model in Table 8.4 is the empty 'intercept only' model presented earlier. The second model, which follows equation (8.2), includes the total sample size as a predictor. The third model includes the reliability of the outcome measure. The fourth model includes the duration of the experiment, and the fifth includes all available predictors. Both the univariate and the multivariate analyses show that only the duration has a significant effect on the study outcomes. Differences in measurement reliability and study size are no major threat to our substantive conclusion about the effect of duration. Since there is no relation between the study size and the reported outcome, the existence of a file drawer problem is unlikely.

The last model that includes all predictor variables simultaneously is instructive. The (insignificant) regression coefficient for reliability is negative. This is counterintuitive. This is also in the opposite direction of the regression coefficient in the model (3) with reliability as the only predictor. It is the result of a so-called 'repressor' effect caused by the correlations (from 0.25 to 0.33) among the predictor variables. Since in meta-analysis the number of available studies is often small, such effects are likely to occur if we include too many explanatory study-level variables. In the univariate model (8.3), the regression coefficient of reliability is 0.51. This implies that, if the reliability goes from 0.75 to 0.90, the expected outcome increases by (0.15×0.51=) 0.08. This is reasonably close to the correction of 0.06 that results from applying the classical correction for attenuation. However, the large standard error for reliability in model (8.3) suggests that this correction is not needed. Thus, the corrected results using classical methods may well be misleading.

An interesting extension of the multilevel regression model for meta-analysis is allowing for more than two levels. For instance, we may have a situation in which there are several outcome measures for each study. The approach in classical meta-analysis is to either combine these into one single outcome per study, or to carry out separate meta-analyses for each different outcome. In a multilevel model, it is possible to specify a multivariate outcome model. When all studies report all available outcome measures, the multivariate multilevel model is a straightforward extension of the univariate model (cf. Raudenbush & Bryk, 1985). When some studies do not report on all available outcomes, we have a missing data problem. This extension leads to a more complicated model, which still can be estimated using standard multilevel software. Multivariate multilevel models are treated in Chapter Nine of this book, for details on multivariate multilevel meta-analysis see Kalaian and Raudenbush (1996) and Goldstein (1995). An example of a multivariate multilevel meta-analysis is discussed by Berkey et al. (Berkey, Hoaglin, Antczak-Bouckoms, Mosteller & Colditz, 1998). Another interesting extension arises when we have access to the raw data for at least some of the studies. This situation leads to a multilevel model that combines both sufficient statistics, as in standard meta-analysis, and raw data to estimate a single effect size parameter. Higgins et al. (Higgins, Whitehead, Turner, Omar & Thompson, 2001) describe the general framework for this hybrid meta-analysis, and discuss classical and Bayesian analysis methods. Examples of such hybrid meta-analyses are the studies by Goldstein et al. (Goldstein, Yang, Omar, Turner & Thompson, 2000) and Turner et al. (Turner, Omar, Yang, Goldstein & Thompson, 2000).

8.5 STATISTICAL AND SOFTWARE ISSUES

The program HLM (Raudenbush et al., 2000) has a built-in provision for meta-analysis, which is restricted to two-levels. If we need three levels, we can use the standard HLM/3L software, using an adapted program setup. Other software can be used, provided it is possible to put restrictions on the random part. MLwiN (Rasbash et al., 2000) and Proc Mixed in SAS (Littell et al., 1996) all have this capacity, and can therefore be used for meta-analysis, again with an adapted setup. Ways of tweaking HLM and MLwiN for meta-analysis are discussed in the Appendix to this chapter.

There are some minor differences between the programs. HLM uses by default an estimator based on Restricted Maximum Likelihood (RML), while MLwiN by default uses Full Maximum Likelihood (FML, called IGLS in MLwiN). Since RML is theoretically better, especially in situations where we have small samples and are interested in the variances, for meta-analysis we should prefer RML (called RIGLS in MLwiN). The results reported in this chapter have been computed using RML.

An important difference between HLM and other multilevel analysis software is the test used to assess the significance of the variances. HLM by default uses the variance test based on a chi-square test of the residuals (Bryk & Raudenbush, 1992, cf. Chapter Three of this book). MLwiN estimates a standard error for each variance, which can be used for a Z-test of the variance. In meta-analysis applications, this Z-test is problematic. Firstly, it is based on the assumption of normality, and variances have a chi-square distribution. Secondly, it is a large-sample test, and with small sample sizes and small variances the Z-test is inaccurate. In meta-analysis the sample size is the number of studies that are located, and it is quite common to have at most 20 studies. An additional advantage of the chi-square test on the residuals is that for the empty model this test is equivalent to the chi-square variance test in classical meta-analysis (Hedges & Olkin, 1985). The variance tests reported in this chapter use the chi-square test on the residuals. MLwiN does not offer this test, but it can be produced using the MLwiN macro language.

It should be noted that the standard errors that are used to test the significance of the regression coefficients and to establish confidence intervals are also asymptotic. With the small samples common in meta-analysis, they lead to confidence intervals that are too small, and p-values that are spuriously low (Brockwell & Gordon, 2001). It appears prudent not to use the standard normal distribution, but the Student t-distribution with degrees of freedom equal to $k-p-1$, where k is the number of studies and p the number of study-level explanatory variables in the model. In HLM this is the standard test for the regression coefficients. In simulations by Berkey at al. (Berkey et al., 1998) this provided correct *p*-values. Brockwell and Gordon (2001) recommend profile likelihood methods and bootstrapping. These are treated in Chapter Eleven in this book. For estimating complex models, Bayesian procedures are promising and coming into use (cf. Sutton et al., 2000). These use computer-intensive methods such as Markov Chain Monte Carlo (MCMC) methods to estimate the parameters and their sampling distributions. These methods are attractive for meta-analysis (DuMouchel 1980, 1994; Smith, Spiegelhalter & Thomas, 1995) because they are less sensitive to the problems that arise when we model small variances in small samples. Bayesian models can be extended by including a prior distribution. This prior distribution can be used to reflect a-priori beliefs about the likelihood of publication bias. In principle, this is an elegant method to investigate the effect of publication bias. An example of such an analysis is Biggerstaff, Tweedy and Mengersen (1994). Although the software MLwiN includes Bayesian methods, at present these cannot analyze meta-analytic models, and more complicated software is needed, such as the general Bayesian modeling program BUGS (Spiegelhalter, 1994).

Appendix

Software Implementations
The simplest program for multilevel meta-analysis is VKHLM, which is part of the software HLM. HLM expects for each study a row of data containing the study ID, an outcome measure, its sampling variance, followed by the explanatory variables. If the empty model is specified, the results from HLM are close to the classical meta-analysis results produced by Schwarzer's program META, provided one realizes that META reads effect sizes *g* and transforms these internally into *d*'s.

Using MLn or MLwiN is more complicated. The data structure is analogous to HLM: we need a study ID, the effect size, its standard error (the square root of the sampling variance), the regression constant (HLM includes this automatically), and the explanatory variables. To set up the analysis, we distinguish two levels: the outcomes are the first level, and the studies the second. Usually we have one outcome per study, so there is no real nesting. The predictor 'sampling error' is included only in the random part on level 1, with a coefficient fixed at 1 (MLn uses the command RCON for this). The regression constant is included in the fixed part, and in the random part at level 2. Explanatory variables are included in the fixed part only. MLwiN does not produce the chi-square test on the variances. The formula for the chi-square test is $\chi^2 = \sum \left(\left(d_j - \hat{d}_j \right) / s.e.\left(d_j \right) \right)^2$, which is the sum of the squared residuals divided by their sampling variances. The degrees of freedom are given by $df = J\text{-}q\text{-}1$, where J is the number of studies, and q the number of explanatory variables in the model. Assuming that the outcomes are denoted by 'd', and the standard errors of the d's by 'sed', the sequence of MLWIN commands for computing the chi-square is: PRED C50; CALC C50=(('d'-C50)/'sed')^2; SUM C50 to B1; CPRO B1 df. This code assumes that the spreadsheet column C50 is unused.

If we need more than two levels in HLM, we must use HLM/3L, which does not include the VKHLM option. For HLM/3L we also need a special setup. In this case, we include the inverse of the standard errors as a weighting variable at the lowest level. We must instruct the program *not* to normalize the weights, which is the default option, and constrain the lowest level variance to be equal to 1.

To apply multilevel models in meta-analysis in other software, such as SAS Proc Mixed, the software must have options to set up a model using constraints as specified for MLn or for HLM/3L. This means that it must be possible to have a complex lower-level variance structure, as in MLWIN, or to constrain the lowest-level variance to 1 and to add a weight variable, as in HLM/3L. So far, public domain software for multilevel analysis does not offer these options.

The freeware program META is available from Ralph Schwarzer at the Internet location <http://userpage.fu-berlin.de/~health/author.htm>. It comes with a program manual that also explains the basic elements of meta-analysis.

9

Multivariate Multilevel Regression Models

Multivariate multilevel regression models are multilevel regression models that contain more than one response variable. As such, they are comparable to classical multivariate analysis of variance (MANOVA) models, where we also have several outcome measures. The reason to use a multivariate model is usually because the researchers have decided to use multiple measurements of one underlying construct, to achieve a better construct validity. A classic example is in medical research when diseases manifest themselves in a *syndrome* that leads to a pattern of related effects (Sammel, Lin & Ryan, 1999). By using several outcome measures, researchers can obtain a better and more complete description of what is affected by changes in the predictor variables (cf. Tabachnick & Fidell, 1996). Simply carrying out a series of univariate analyses, one for each response measure, seems inadequate. One manifest advantage of multivariate analysis is that carrying out a series of univariate statistical tests inflates the type I error rate, which is better controlled in a multivariate analysis. A second advantage of multivariate analysis is that it often has a better power. On each individual response measure, the differences may be small and insignificant, but for the total set of response measures, the joint effect may produce a significant effect (Stevens, 1996; Tabachnick & Fidell, 1996). However, the disadvantage of multivariate models is that they are more complicated, and that their interpretation is more ambiguous.

In multilevel analysis, using multiple outcome measures leads to some very powerful analysis tools. First, like in analysis of variance, using several response variables may lead to more power. Since multilevel analysis does not assume that all response measures are available for all individuals, it may be used as an alternative for MANOVA when there are missing values on some of the response variables. Most software for MANOVA cannot cope with missing data on the response variables, while for multilevel analysis this poses no special problem. Since the multilevel model is much more flexible than MANOVA, there are some additional advantages to multivariate multilevel modeling. For instance, since multivariate multilevel analysis combines multiple response variables in one model, it is possible to test the equality of their regression coefficients or variance components by imposing equality constraints. Also, the covariances between the dependent variables can be decomposed over the separate levels, which is one way to obtain the covariance matrices needed for multilevel factor analysis or structural equation modeling (see Chapter Twelve and

Thirteen for details). Finally, it is possible to construct multilevel measurement models, by including a set of questions that form a scale as multivariate responses in a multilevel model.

9.1 THE BASIC MODEL

In multivariate multilevel models, the different measures are the lowest-level units. In most applications, the different measures would be the first level, the individuals the second level, and if there are groups, these form the third level. Therefore, if we have p response variables, Y_{hij} is the response on measure h of individual i in group j.

Ignoring possible missing responses, at the lowest level (the variable level) we have p 'cases,' which in fact are the p response variables. Each case has a single response, which is the response of person i to question h. One way to deal with the different outcome variables would be to define p-1 dummy variables that indicate the variables 2, ..., P. In this scheme, variable 1 would be the base category, indicated by the value 0 for all dummy variables. However, this would give the first variable a special position. A much better way to indicate the multiple response variables is to define p dummy variables, one for each response variable. Thus, we have p dummy variables d_{phij}, defined for $p=1$, ..., P by

$$d_{phij} = \begin{cases} 1 & p = h \\ 0 & p \neq h \end{cases} \tag{9.1}$$

To use these p dummy variables in a model, we must exclude the usual intercept from the model. Hence, on the lowest level we have

$$Y_{hij} = \pi_{1ij}d_{1ij} + \pi_{2ij}d_{2ij} + \ldots + \pi_{pij}d_{pij} \tag{9.2}$$

We use an extra level, the *dummy-variable* level, to specify a multivariate model using software that is essentially developed for univariate analyses. There is no lowest-level error term in equation (9.2); the lowest level exists solely to define the multivariate response structure.[1] For the moment, we assume no explanatory variables, and we have the equivalent of the intercept-only model. Then, at the individual level (the second level in the multivariate model), we have

$$\pi_{pij} = \beta_{pj} + u_{pij} \tag{9.3}$$

---

[1] The symbol π is used for the lowest-level regression coefficients, so we can continue to employ the usual β for the individual level and γ for the group level regression coefficients.

At the group level (the third level in the multivariate model), we have

$$\beta_{pj} = \gamma_p + u_{pj} \tag{9.4}$$

By substitution we obtain

$$Y_{hij} = \gamma_1 d_{1ij} + \gamma_2 d_{2ij} + \ldots + \gamma_p d_{pij}$$
$$+ u_{1ij} d_{1ij} + u_{2ij} d_{2ij} + \ldots + u_{pij} d_{pij} + u_{1j} d_{1ij} + u_{2j} d_{2ij} + \ldots + u_{pj} d_{pij} \tag{9.5}$$

In the univariate intercept-only model, the fixed part contains only the intercept, which is the overall mean, and the random part contains two variances, which are the variance at the individual and the group level. In the equivalent multivariate model, the fixed part contains P regression coefficients for the dummy variables, which are the P overall means for the P outcome variables. The random part contains two covariance matrices, Ω_{ij} and Ω_j, which contain the variances and the covariances of the regression slopes for the dummies on the individual and the group level. Since equation (9.5) is complicated, especially if we have many response variables, it is often expressed using sum notation:

$$Y_{hij} = \sum_{h=1}^{P} \gamma_h d_{hij} + \sum_{h=1}^{P} u_{hij} d_{hij} + \sum_{h=1}^{P} u_{hj} d_{hij} \tag{9.6}$$

Just as in univariate modeling, explanatory variables at the individual or the group level can be added to the model. In the general case, if we add an individual level explanatory variable X_{ij} or a group level variable Z_j to the model by multiplying it by all p dummy variables, and adding all p resulting interaction-variables to the equation. Since the dummy variables are equal to zero whenever $p \neq h$, these terms disappear from the model. Thus there are p distinct contributions to the multilevel regression equation, each specific to one of the p response variables.

We can specify random slopes for the individual level explanatory variables at the group level, and add cross-level interactions to explain random variation, completely analogous to adding explanatory variables and cross-level interactions to the univariate models discussed in Chapter Two. If we multiply each explanatory variable with all of the dummy variables, we allow each regression coefficient in the model to be different for each response variable. It would simplify the model considerably, if we could impose an equality constraint across all response variables, assuming that the effects are equal for all response variables. There are two ways to accomplish this. For simplicity, let us assume that we have two response variables Y_1

and Y_2, only one explanatory variable X, and no group structure. Equation (9.2) now becomes

$$Y_{hi} = \pi_{1i}d_{1i} + \pi_{2i}d_{2i}$$ (9.7)

and equation (9.5) simplifies to

$$Y_{hi} = \gamma_1 d_{1i} + \gamma_2 d_{2i} + u_{1i}d_{1i} + u_{2i}d_{2i}$$ (9.8)

Suppose we add explanatory variable X_i to the model, multiplying it with each dummy variable. This produces

$$Y_{hi} = \gamma_{01}d_{1i} + \gamma_{02}d_{2i} + \gamma_{11}d_{1i}X_i + \gamma_{12}d_{2i}X_i + u_{1i}d_{1i} + u_{2i}d_{2i}$$ (9.9)

If we force the two regression coefficients for Y_1 and Y_2 to be equal by adding the constraint that $\gamma_{11} = \gamma_{12} = \gamma^*$, we get

$$Y_{hi} = \gamma_{01}d_{1i} + \gamma_{02}d_{2i} + \gamma^* d_{1i}X_i + \gamma^* d_{2i}X_i + u_{1i}d_{1i} + u_{2i}d_{2i}$$ (9.10)

which can also be written as

$$Y_{hi} = \gamma_{01}d_{1i} + \gamma_{02}d_{2i} + \gamma^*[d_{1i}X_i + d_{2i}X_i] + u_{1i}d_{1i} + u_{2i}d_{2i}$$ (9.11)

Since the two dummies that indicate the separate response variables are mutually exclusive, only one dummy variable will be equal to one for each specific response variable Y_{hi}, and the other is equal to zero. Therefore, equation (9.11) can also be written as

$$Y_{hi} = \gamma_{01}d_{1i} + \gamma_{02}d_{2i} + \gamma^* X_i + u_{1i}d_{1i} + u_{2i}d_{2i}$$ (9.12)

This makes clear that imposing an equality constraint across all regression slopes for a specific explanatory variable is equal to adding this explanatory variable directly, without multiplying it with all the available dummies. This also implies that the model of equation (9.12) is nested within the model of equation (9.9). As a result, we can test whether simplifying model (9.9) to model (9.12) is justified, using the chi-square test on the deviances, with $p-1$ degrees of freedom. The example given here involves changes to the fixed part, so we can use the deviance test only if we use FML estimation. If the explanatory variable X has random slopes at the group level, a similar argument would apply to the random part of the model. Adding a random slope for one single explanatory variable X to the model implies estimating one variance component. Adding a random slope to each of the explanatory variables constructed by multiplying X with each of the dummies implies adding a $p \times p$ (co)variance matrix to the model. This adds $p(p-1)/2$ parameter estimates to the model, and the degrees of freedom for the corresponding simultaneous chi-square difference test is $(p(p-1)/2)-1$.

9.2 EXAMPLE OF MULTIVARIATE MULTILEVEL ANALYSIS: MULTIPLE RESPONSE VARIABLES

Chapter Six discusses an example that analyzes response rates on face-to-face, telephone, and mail surveys, as reported in 47 studies over a series of years (Hox & de Leeuw, 1994). In this example, there are two indicators of survey response. The first is the completion rate, which is the number of completed interviews divided by the total number of persons approached. The second is the response rate, which is the number of completed interviews divided by the total number of persons approached *minus* the number of persons that are considered sampling frame errors (address incorrect, deceased). Some studies report the completion rate, some the response rate, and some both. The analysis reported in Chapter Six analyzes response rates where available, and otherwise completion rates, with a dummy variable indicating when the completion rate is used. Since some studies report both the response rate and the completion rate, this approach is wasteful because it ignores part of the available information. Furthermore, it is an interesting question by itself, whether the response rate and completion rate behave similarly or differently over time. Using a multivariate model we can include all information, and carry out a multivariate meta-analysis to investigate the similarity between response rate and completion rate.

In Chapter Six, the model is a two-level model, with data collection conditions (face-to-face, telephone, and mail) as the lowest level, and the 47 studies the second level. For the multivariate model, we specify the response as the lowest level, with conditions the second and studies the third level. Since the response variable is a proportion, we use a generalized linear model with a logit link and a binomial error distribution (for details on multilevel generalized linear models see Chapter Six). Let p_{hij} be the observed proportions of respondents on the response rate or completion rate in condition i of study j. At the response indicator level, we have two explanatory variables, COMP and RESP, which are dummies that indicate whether the response is a completion rate or a response rate. The multivariate empty model can now be written as

$$P_{hij} = \text{logistic}\left(\pi_{1ij} comp_{ij} + \pi_{2ij} resp_{ij}\right) \qquad (9.13)$$

The empty model for these data is

$$P_{hij} = \text{logistic}\begin{pmatrix} \gamma_{01}comp_{ij} + \gamma_{02}resp_{ij} \\ +u_{1ij}comp_{ij} + u_{2ij}resp_{ij} + u_{1j}comp_{ij} + u_{2j}resp_{ij} \end{pmatrix} \tag{9.14}$$

The model of equation (9.14) provides us with estimates (on the logit scale) of the average completion rate and response rate, and the covariance matrix on the condition and study level.

Table 9.1	Results survey response data			
Model:	M0: intercepts for comp. and resp. rate		M1: M0 + condition indicators	
Fixed part				
Predictor	coefficient	s. e.	coefficient	s. e.
comprate	0.84	0.13	1.15	0.16
resprate	1.28	0.15	1.40	0.16
tel_comp			-0.34	0.15
tel_resp			-0.10	0.11
mail_comp			-0.69	0.16
mail_resp			-0.40	0.13
Random part				
$\sigma^2_{comp/cond}$	0.41	0.09	0.31	0.07
$\sigma^2_{resp/cond}$	0.20	0.05	0.18	0.04
$r_{cr/cond}$	0.96		0.97	
$\sigma^2_{comp/cstudy}$	0.53	0.17	0.61	0.17
$\sigma^2_{resp/study}$	0.89	0.22	0.83	0.21
$r_{cr/study}$	0.99		0.95	

The parameter estimates (using RML with PQL estimation and second-order Taylor linearization, cf. Chapter Six) are in Table 9.1. The first column shows the parameter estimates for the empty model. It produces two intercept estimates, indicated by 'comprate' and 'resprate,' one for the completion rate and one for the response rate. Note that these estimates are not necessarily the same as the estimates we would get from two separate univariate analyses. If there is a tendency, for instance, to report only the completion rate when the survey response is disappointing, because that looks better in the report, the omitted values for the response rate are not missing completely at random. The univariate analysis has no way to correct for this bias; it assumes that any absent values are missing completely at random (MCAR). The multivariate model contains the covariance between the response rate and the completion rate. Hence, it can correct for the bias in reporting the response rate; it assumes that any absent values are missing at random (MAR), which is a weaker assumption. Because of this implicit correction, the intercepts and other regression coefficients in the multivariate model can be different from those estimated separately in univariate analyses. This is similar to the situation in multilevel longitudinal modeling (cf. Chapter Five), where panel dropout in the multilevel model is assumed to be Missing At Random (MAR). For an accessible discussion of the differences between MAR and MCAR see Little and Rubin (1989). As in multilevel longitudinal modeling, the fact that the multivariate multilevel model assumes that any absent outcome variables are MAR rather than MCAR is an important advantage when we have incomplete data. The usual practice in MANOVA to analyze only complete cases assumes MCAR, which is a much stronger assumption than MAR.

The second column in Table 9.1 shows the parameter estimates for the model where the dummy variables that indicate the data collection conditions are added separately for the completion rate and the response rate. The face-to-face condition is the reference category, and two dummy variables are added which indicate the telephone and mail condition. We do not assume that the effect of the conditions is the same for both completion and response rate. Therefore, the two condition dummies are entered as interactions with the dummies that indicate the completion and response rate. Thus, the model equation is

$$P_{hij} = \text{logistic} \begin{pmatrix} \gamma_{01}comp_{ij} + \gamma_{02}resp_{ij} \\ +\gamma_{03}tel_{ij}comp_{ij} + \gamma_{04}tel_{ij}resp_{ij} + \gamma_{05}mail_{ij}comp_{ij} + \gamma_{06}mail_{ij}resp_{ij} \\ +u_{1ij}comp_{ij} + u_{2ij}resp_{ij} + u_{1j}comp_{ij} + u_{2j}resp_{ij} \end{pmatrix} \quad (9.15)$$

Both the two 'intercepts' for the completion rate and the response rate, and the regression slopes for the effect of the telephone and mail condition on the completion rate and the response rate seem to be quite different in Table 9.1. We can formally test the null-hypothesis that they are equal by testing the appropriate contrast. Testing the intercepts of COMP and RESP for equality, using the procedures described in Chapter Three, produces a chi-square of 6.82, which with one degree of freedom has a p-value of 0.01. The same test produces for the telephone condition variables a chi-square of 6.81, with one degree of freedom and a p-value of 0.01. For the mail condition, we get a chi-square of 8.94, with one degree of freedom and a p-value of 0.00. Clearly, the different data collection conditions affect the completion rate and the response rate in a different way.

The variance components are indicated in Table 9.1 by $\sigma^2_{comp/cond}$ for the intercept variance for the completion rate on the condition level, and $\sigma^2_{comp/study}$ for the intercept variance for the completion rate on the study level. Likewise, $\sigma^2_{resp/cond}$ indicates the intercept variance for the response rate on the condition level, and $\sigma^2_{resp/study}$ for the intercept variance for the response rate on the study level. Note that Table 9.1 does not give a value for the deviance. The estimation is based on the quasi-likelihood approach described in Chapter Six, and therefore the deviance is approximate. For that reason, it is not included in the table.

Table 9.2	Results survey response data, model comparison			
Model:	year and saliency as interaction terms		year and saliency directly	
Fixed part				
Predictor	coefficient	s. e.	coefficient	s. e.
comprate	0.83	0.43	0.83	0.43
resprate	1.06	0.43	1.06	0.43
tel_comp	-0.32	0.15	-0.32	0.15
tel_resp	-0.41	0.11	-0.41	0.11
mail_comp	-0.71	.16	-0.71	0.16
mail_resp	-0.40	0.13	-0.40	0.13
year_comp[a]	-0.01	0.01		n/a
year_resp[a]	-0.01	0.01		n/a
sali_comp[b]	0.69	0.17		n/a
sali_resp[b]	0.69	0.17		n/a
year		n/a	-0.01	0.01
saliency		n/a	0.69	0.17
Random part				
$\sigma^2_{comp/cond}$	0.31	0.07	0.31	0.07
$\sigma^2_{resp/cond}$	0.18	0.04	0.18	0.04
$r_{cr/cond}$	0.97		0.97	
$\sigma^2_{comp/cstudy}$	0.45	0.14	0.45	0.14
$\sigma^2_{resp/study}$	0.52	0.14	0.52	0.14
$r_{cr/study}$	0.91		0.91	

[a,b] Slopes constrained to be equal.

If we add the explanatory variables publication year and saliency of survey topic, contrast tests show that these have similar effects on both the completion rate and the response rate. As a result, we can either add them to the regression equation as interactions with the completion and response rate dummies, constraining the equivalent regression slopes to be equal (cf. equation 9.9-9.11), or as a direct effect of the explanatory variables year and saliency (cf. equation 9.12). Table 9.2 presents the parameter estimates for both model specifications.

Both models produce the same value for the parameter estimates and the corresponding standard errors for the explanatory variables 'year' and 'saliency.' The model that includes the explanatory variables directly is given by

$$
P_{hij} = \text{logistic} \left(\begin{array}{l} \gamma_{01}comp_{ij} + \gamma_{02}resp_{ij} \\ +\gamma_{03}tel_{ij}comp_{ij} + \gamma_{04}tel_{ij}resp_{ij} + \gamma_{05}mail_{ij}comp_{ij} + \gamma_{06}mail_{ij}resp_{ij} \\ +\gamma_{07}year_{j} + \gamma_{08}saliency_{j} \\ +u_{1ij}comp_{ij} + u_{2ij}resp_{ij} + u_{1j}comp_{ij} + u_{2j}resp_{ij} \end{array} \right) \quad (9.16)
$$

The model that includes these explanatory variables as interactions including two equality constraints, indicated by the superscripts a and b, is given by

$$
P_{hij} = \text{logistic} \left(\begin{array}{l} \gamma_{01}comp_{ij} + \gamma_{02}resp_{ij} \\ +\gamma_{03}tel_{ij}comp_{ij} + \gamma_{04}tel_{ij}resp_{ij} + \gamma_{05}mail_{ij}comp_{ij} + \gamma_{06}mail_{ij}resp_{ij} \\ +\gamma_{07}^{a}year_{j} \cdot comp_{ij} + \gamma_{08}^{a}year_{j} \cdot resp_{ij} \\ +\gamma_{09}^{b}saliency_{j} \cdot comp_{ij} + \gamma_{10}^{b}saliency_{j} \cdot resp_{ij} \\ +u_{1ij}comp_{ij} + u_{2ij}resp_{ij} + u_{1j}comp_{ij} + u_{2j}resp_{ij} \end{array} \right) \quad (9.17)
$$

Table 9.2 shows empirically what is derived in equations 9.9-9.12, that the two representations are equivalent. Since adding year and saliency directly is simpler, this is the preferred method.

If we have a number of outcomes, all related to a single theoretical construct or syndrome, directly adding an explanatory variable to the model results in a higher power than adding them as a set of interactions with all outcome variables. The reason is that in the former case we use a one-degree of freedom test, and in the latter a p-degree of freedom overall test. Adding an explanatory variable assumes that all interactions result in the same regression weight, which can subsequently be constrained to be equal. This assumption of a common effect size is strong, and it is not realistic if outcome variables are measured on different scales. Sammel, Lin and Ryan (1999) discuss the possibility of smoothing the regression coefficients. They suggest scaling the outcome variables prior to the analysis in such a way that they are measured on the same scale. With continuous variables a transformation to standardized scores is appropriate. Raudenbush, Rowan and Kang (1991) employ a transformation to correct for differences in measurement reliability. To arrive at comparable effect sizes this means that the outcomes are divided by the square root of the reliability coefficient, and then standardized.

9.3 EXAMPLE OF MULTIVARIATE MULTILEVEL ANALYSIS: MEASURING GROUP CHARACTERISTICS

Sometimes the interest may be in measuring characteristics of the context, that is, of the higher-level units, which can be individuals, groups, or organizations. For instance, we may be interested in school climate, and use a questionnaire that is answered by a sample of pupils from each of the schools. In this example we are not necessarily interested in the pupils, they are just used as informants to judge the school climate. Similar situations arise in health research, where patients may be used to express their satisfaction with their general practitioner, and community research, where samples from different neighborhoods evaluate various aspects of the neighborhood in which they live. In these cases, we may use individual characteristics to control for possible measurement bias, but the main interest is in measuring some aspect of the higher-level unit (cf. Paterson, 1998; Raudenbush & Sampson, 1999a; Sampson, Raudenbush & Earls, 1997).

Our example concerns data from an educational research study by Krüger (1994) In this study, male and female school managers were compared on a large number of characteristics. As part of the study, small samples of pupils from each school rated their school manager on six seven-point items that indicate a people-oriented approach toward leadership (the data are described in more detail in the appendix). There are ratings from 854 pupils within 96 schools, 48 with a male and 48 with a female school manager, on these six aspects. If we calculate the reliability coefficient, Cronbach's alpha, for the six items, we get a reliability of 0.80, which is commonly considered sufficient to sum the items to a scale (Nunnally & Bernstein, 1994). However, this reliability estimate is difficult to interpret, because it is based on a mixture of school level and individual pupil level variance. Since all judgments within the same school are ratings of the same school manager, within school variance does not give us information about the school manager. From the measurement point of view, we want to concentrate only on the between schools variance.

One convenient way to model data such as these is to use a multivariate multilevel model, with separate levels for the items, the pupils, and the schools. Thus, we create six dummy variables to indicate the six items, and exclude the intercept from the model. Hence, at the lowest level we have

$$Y_{hij} = \pi_{1ij}d_{1ij} + \pi_{2ij}d_{2ij} + \ldots + \pi_{6ij}d_{6ij} \qquad (9.18)$$

At the individual level we have

$$\pi_{pij} = \beta_{pj} + u_{pij} \tag{9.19}$$

At the group level (the third level in the multivariate model), we have

$$\beta_{pj} = \gamma_p + u_{pj} \tag{9.20}$$

By substitution, we obtain the single-equation version

$$
\begin{aligned}
Y_{hij} &= \gamma_1 \, d_{1ij} + \gamma_2 d_{2ij} + \ldots + \gamma_6 d_{pij} \\
&+ u_{1ij} d_{1ij} + u_{2ij} d_{2ij} + \ldots + u_{6ij} d_{pij} \\
&+ u_{1j} d_{1ij} + u_{2j} d_{2ij} + \ldots + u_{6j} d_{pij}
\end{aligned}
\tag{9.21}
$$

Using sum notation, we have:

$$Y_{hij} = \sum_{h=1}^{6} \gamma_h d_{hij} + \sum_{h=1}^{6} u_{hij} d_{hij} + \sum_{h=1}^{6} u_{hj} d_{hij} \tag{9.22}$$

The model described by equations (9.21) and (9.22), provides us with estimates of the six item means, and of their variances and covariances at the pupil and school level. Since in this application we are mostly interested in the variances and covariances, Restricted Maximum Likelihood (RML) estimation is preferred to Full Maximum Likelihood (FML) estimation. Table 9.3 below presents the RML estimates of the covariances and the corresponding correlations at the pupil level, and Table 9.4 presents the same at the school level.

Table 9.3	Covariances and correlations at the pupil level					
	1	**2**	**3**	**4**	**5**	**6**
item 1	1.19	*.57*	*.44*	*.18*	*.25*	*.44*
item 2	.67	1.13	*.52*	*.18*	*.26*	*.38*
item 3	.49	.57	1.07	*.19*	*.23*	*.43*
item 4	.17	.17	.17	.74	*.60*	*.30*
item 5	.22	.23	.20	.42	.66	*.38*
item 6	.48	.41	.45	.26	.31	1.00
Note: the italic entries in the upper diagonal are the correlations						

Table 9.4	Covariances and correlations at the school level				
	1	2	3	4	5	6
item 1	.24	*.91*	*.87*	*.57*	*.93*	*.96*
item 2	.30	.45	*.98*	*.14*	*.58*	*.88*
item 3	.24	.36	.31	*.07*	*.53*	*.87*
item 4	.12	.04	.02	.19	*.89*	*.57*
item 5	.15	.13	.10	.13	.11	*.90*
item 6	.16	.20	.17	.09	.10	.12

Note: the italic entries in the upper diagonal are the correlations

Tables 9.3 and 9.4 show that most of the variance of the six items is pupil level variance, that is, variance between pupils within schools. Since within the same school all pupils are evaluating the same school manager, this variance must be regarded as systematic measurement bias. Apparently, the pupils differ systematically in the way they use the six items. The pattern of covariation in Table 9.3 shows how they differ. We can add pupil level variables to the model, to investigate whether we can model this covariation. However, what we model in that case is individual idiosyncrasies in the way the measurement instrument is used. From the perspective of measurement, we are mostly interested in Table 9.4, because this shows how the items perform on the school level. Although the variances at the school level are lower, the correlations are generally much higher. The mean correlation at the pupil level is 0.36, and at the school level 0.71. This is reassuring, because it means that at the school level the consistency of the measurement instrument is higher than at the individual level.

We can use the covariances or correlations in Table 9.4 to carry out an item-analysis on the student or the school level. We can use standard formula's from classical measurement theory to calculate the internal consistency reliability coefficient alpha. For instance, a convenient way to estimate the internal consistency given the results in Table 9.3 or 9.4 is to use the mean correlation (e.g., Nunnally & Bernstein, 1994). We can estimate the internal consistency of the scale from the mean correlation, using the Spearman-Brown formula for test length. With p items, the reliability of the p-item scale is given by

$$\alpha = p\bar{r}/\left(1 + (p-1)\bar{r}\right) \tag{9.23}$$

where $\bar{r}$ is the mean correlation of the items, and p is the scale length. The mean correlation at the school level is 0.71, and using the Spearman-Brown formula, we can estimate the school-level coefficient alpha internal consistency as 0.94. This is not a very accurate estimate, since it ignores the differences in the variance of the items, but it produces a reasonable approximation. For a more accurate estimate, we could use the covariances in Table 9.3 or Table 9.4 as input in a software program for reliability or factor analysis, for a more formal analysis of the relationships between the items. If we do this, coefficient alpha is estimated as 0.92, and the item-analysis further informs is that we should consider removing item 4 from the scale, because of its low correlations with the other items.

There is one important consideration. On the pupil level, coefficient alpha correctly indicates the internal consistency reliability of measuring differences in evaluation between pupils within schools. On the school level, however, coefficient alpha is the internal consistency reliability of measuring differences in evaluation between schools, using a single randomly selected pupil from each school. Of course, we have more than one pupil in each school, and normally we would combine the evaluations of these pupils into one single school-level score. We have ratings from 854 pupils within 96 schools, or about 8.9 pupils per school. Combining the evaluations from all pupils within a school should increase the reliability. We can use the Spearman-Brown formula a second time, this time plugging in 0.92 (the more accurate estimate) as the internal consistency estimate $\bar{r}$, and 8.9 as the multiplication factor p. If we do this, the school level internal consistency is estimated as 0.99. This is very high, but consistent with the high school-level correlations in Table 9.4.

Raudenbush, Rowan and Kang (1991) give an extensive discussion of the issues involved in multilevel measurement. They provide (pp. 309-312) equations to calculate both the pupil level and school level internal consistency directly, using the intercept variances at the three available levels estimated in an intercept only model. This model can be written as

$$Y_{hij} = \gamma_{000} + u_{0hij} + u_{0ij} + u_{0j} \tag{9.24}$$

The model in equation (9.24) is the intercept-only model with three levels: the item, pupil, and school level. For our example, the variances are in Table 9.5, using an obvious notation for the subscripts of the variance components:

Table 9.5 Intercept and variances for school manager data		
Fixed part	coefficient	standard error
intercept	2.57	0.05
Random part		
σ^2_{item}	0.179	0.03
σ^2_{pupil}	0.341	0.03
σ^2_{school}	0.845	0.02

In Table 9.5, σ^2_{item} can be interpreted as an estimate of the variation due to item inconsistency, σ^2_{pupil} as an estimate of the variation of the scale score (mean item score) between different pupils within the same school, and σ^2_{school} as an estimate of the variation of the scale score between different schools. These variances can be used to produce the internal consistency reliability on the pupil and school level. If we have p items, the error variance in the scale score (computed as the mean of the items) is given by $\sigma^2_e = \sigma^2_{item}/p = 0.179/6 = 0.030$.

The item level exists only to produce an estimate of the variance due to item inconsistency. We are in fact using a scale score that is computed as the mean of the items. Thus, the intraclass correlation of the scale score for the schools is given by $\rho_I = \sigma^2_{school}/(\sigma^2_{school}+\sigma^2_{pupil})$, which for our example is $0.179/(0.179+0.341)=0.344$. Therefore, for the scale score, about 34% of the variance is between schools.

The pupil level internal consistency is given by $\alpha_{pupil} = \sigma^2_{pupil}/(\sigma^2_{pupil} + \sigma^2_{item}/p)$. For our example data this gives $\alpha_{pupil} = 0.341/(0.341+0.179/6) = 0.92$. This reflects consistency in the variability of the ratings of the same school manager, by different pupils in the same schools. The high internal consistency coefficient indicates that this variability is not random error, but that it is highly systematic. It could be systematic error, for instance response bias such as a halo effect in the judgments made by the pupils, or it could be based on different experiences of pupils with the same manager. This could be explored further by adding pupil characteristics to the model.

The school level internal consistency is (Raudenbush et al., 1991, p. 312):

$$\alpha_{school} = \sigma^2_{school} / \left[\sigma^2_{school} + \sigma^2_{pupil}/n_j + \sigma^2_{item}/\left(p \cdot n_j\right) \right] \tag{9.25}$$

In equation (9.25), p is the number of items in the scale, and n_j is the number of pupils in school j. Since the number of pupils varies across schools, the school level variability also varies. Raudenbush, Rowan and Kang (1991, p. 312) suggest using the mean of the schools' internal consistencies as a measure of the internal consistency reliability. A simpler approach is to use equation (9.25) with the mean number of teachers for n_j. In our example we have on average 8.9 pupils in each school, and the school level internal consistency as α_{school} = 0.845/[0.845+0.341/8.9+0.179/(8.9×6)]= 0.95. The school level internal consistency coefficient indicates that the school managers' leadership style is measured with high consistency.[1] The number of pupils per class varies between 4 and 10. If we plug these values into the equation, we find a reliability of 0.90 with four pupils, and 0.96 with ten pupils. It appears that even in schools with only four pupils, we still have a high internal consistency.

The school level internal consistency depends on four factors: the number of items in the scale, the mean correlation between the items on the school level, the number of pupils sampled in the schools, and the intraclass correlation at the school level. The school level reliability as a function of these quantities as follows

$$\alpha_{school} = \frac{kn_j \rho_I \bar{r}}{kn_j \rho_I \bar{r} + \left[(k-1)\bar{r} + 1\right](1 - \rho_I)} \tag{9.26}$$

where $\bar{r}$ is the mean item intercorrelation at the school level, which can be estimated using the variances in the intercept-only model by $\bar{r} = \sigma^2_{pupil} / \left(\sigma^2_{pupil} + \sigma^2_{item}\right)$.

Equation (9.26) shows that the internal consistency reliability can be improved by including more items in the scale, but also by taking a larger sample of pupils in each school. Raudenbush, Rowan and Kang (1991) demonstrate that increasing the number of pupils in the schools increases the school level reliability faster than increasing the number of items in the scale. Even with a low inter-item correlation and a low intraclass correlation, increasing the number of pupils to infinity (admittedly hard to do) will in the end produce a reliability equal to one, whereas increasing the number of items to infinity will in general not.

In an analysis presented by Raudenbush, Rowan and Kang (1991), the measurement model is extended by combining items from several different scales in one analysis. The constant in the multilevel model is then replaced by a set of dummy variables that indicate to which scale each item belongs. This is similar to a confirmative factor analysis, with the restriction that the loadings of all items that belong to the same scale are equal, and that there is one common error variance. These are strong restrictions, which are often expressed as the assumption that the items are parallel (Lord & Novick, 1968). The usual assumptions for the internal consistency index are considerably weaker. For a multivariate analysis of complex relationships on a number of distinct levels, multilevel structural equation modeling is both more powerful and less restrictive. These models are discussed in detail in Chapter Twelve.

---

[1] The difference with the estimate of 0.99 obtained using classical psychometric methods earlier reflects mostly rounding error by using the values in Table 9.4, which are presented in two decimals. The method presented here is more accurate because it is based on a much simpler model, and avoids intermediate rounding.

Note that the covariance matrices on the pupil and school level in Tables 9.3 and 9.4 could be used as input for such modeling.

If we want to predict the evaluations scores of the school manager using school-level variables, for instance the experience or gender of the school manager, or type of school, we can simply include these variables as explanatory variables in the multilevel model. Sometimes it is useful to have actual evaluation scores, for instance if we want to use these as explanatory variables in a different type of model. We can estimate the school managers' evaluation scores using the school level residuals. Since these are centered on the school mean, the school mean must be added again to these residuals, to produce so-called posterior means for the evaluation scores. Since the posterior means are based on the empirical Bayes residuals, they are not simply the observed mean evaluation scores in the different schools, but they are shrunken toward the overall mean. The amount each score is shrunken toward the overall mean depends on the reliability of that score, which depends among others on the number of pupils used in that particular school. The result is that we are using an estimate of the school-level true score of each school manager (cf. Lord & Novick, 1968; Nunnally & Bernstein, 1994). We can add pupil-level explanatory variables to the model, which would lead to evaluation scores that are conditional on the pupil-level variables. This corrects the evaluation scores for inequalities in the composition of the pupil population across schools, which is important if the schools attract different types of students.

A nice feature of using multilevel models for measurement scales is that it automatically accommodates for incomplete data. If some of the item scores for some of the pupils are missing, this is compensated in the model. The model results and estimated posterior means are the correct ones, under the assumption that the data are Missing At Random (MAR). This is a weaker assumption than the Missing Completely At Random (MCAR) assumption than is required with simpler methods, such as using only complete cases or replacing missing items by the mean of the observed items.

The measurement procedures just outlined are based on classical test theory, which means that they assume continuous multivariate normal outcomes. Most test items are categorical. If the items are dichotomous, we can use the logistic multilevel modeling procedures described in Chapter Six. If there are two levels, the item level and the person level, using multilevel logistic regression is equivalent to a Rasch model (Andrich, 1988). Kamata (2001) shows that the two-level multilevel model logistic model is equivalent to the Rasch model, and discusses extensions to three-level models. If we have items with more than two categories, a multinomial multilevel can be used. Adams, Wilson and Wu (1997) tie such models to Item-Response Theory (IRT) models in general. In the interest of accurate measurement, exact Maximum Likelihood (cf. Chapter Six) or Bayesian estimation procedures (cf. Chapter Eleven) are preferable, especially with dichotomous items.

10

Sample Sizes and Power Analysis in Multilevel Regression

10.1 SAMPLE SIZE AND ACCURACY OF ESTIMATES

The maximum likelihood estimation methods used commonly in multilevel analysis are asymptotic, which translates to the assumption that the sample size is large. This arouses questions about the accuracy of the various estimation methods with relatively small sample sizes. Most research on this problem uses simulation methods, and investigates the accuracy of the fixed and random parameters with small sample sizes at either the individual or the group level. Comparatively less research investigates the accuracy of the standard errors used to test specific model parameters.

10.1.1 Accuracy of fixed parameters and their standard errors

The estimates for the regression coefficients are generally unbiased, for Ordinary Least Squares (OLS), Generalized Least Squares (GLS), and Maximum Likelihood (ML) estimation (Van der Leeden & Busing, 1994; Van der Leeden, Busing & Meijer, 1997; Maas & Hox, 2001). OLS estimates are less efficient because they often have a larger sampling variance. Kreft (1996) reports that OLS estimates are about 90% efficient.

As illustrated in Chapter Two, the OLS based standard errors are severely biased downward. The asymptotic Wald tests, used in most multilevel software to test fixed effects, assume large samples. A large simulation by Maas and Hox (2001) finds that the standard errors for the fixed parameters are slightly biased downward if the number of groups is less than fifty. With thirty groups, they report an operative alpha level of 6.4% while the nominal significance level is 5%. Similarly, simulations by Van der Leeden & Busing (1994) and Van der Leeden et al. (1997) suggest that when assumptions of normality and large samples are not met, the standard errors have a small downward bias. GLS estimates of fixed parameters and their standard errors are somewhat less accurate than ML estimates, but workable.

The power of the Wald test for the significance of the individual level regression coefficients depends on the total sample size. The power of tests of higher-level effects and cross-level interactions depends more strongly on the number of groups than on the total sample size. Both simulations (Mok, 1995; Van der Leeden & Busing. 1994) and analytic work (Cohen, 1998; Raudenbush & Liu, 2000; Snijders & Bosker, 1993; suggest a trade-off between sample sizes at different levels. For accuracy and high power a large number of groups appears more important than a large number of individuals per group.

10.1.2 Accuracy of random parameters and their standard errors

Estimates of the residual error at the lowest level are generally very accurate. The group level variance components are sometimes underestimated. Simulations by Busing (1993) and Van der Leeden and Busing (1994) show that GLS variance estimates are less accurate than ML estimates. The same simulations also show that for accurate group level variance estimates many groups (more than 100) are needed (cf. Afshartous, 1995). However, using later versions of the software MLn, Browne and Draper (2000) show that with as few as six to twelve groups, Restricted ML (RML) estimation can provide reasonable variance estimates. With 48 groups, Full ML (FML) estimation also produces good variance estimates. Maas and Hox (2001) report that with as low as thirty groups, RML estimation produces accurate variance estimates. When the number of groups is around ten, the variance estimates are much too small.

The asymptotic Wald test for the variance components implies the unrealistic assumption that they are normally distributed. For this reason, other approaches have been advocated, among which estimating the standard error for sigma (the square root of the variance, Longford, 1993), and using the likelihood ratio test. Bryk and Raudenbush (1992) advocate a chi-square test based on the OLS residuals. The literature contains no comparisons between these methods. Simulations by Van der Leeden et al. (1997) show that, especially with small numbers of small groups, the standard errors used for the Wald test are often estimated too small, with RML again more accurate than FML. Symmetric confidence intervals around the estimated value also do not perform well. Browne and Draper (2000), and Maas and Hox (2001) report similar results. Typically, with 24-30 groups, the operating alpha level was almost 9%, and with 48-50 groups about 8%. In the simulations by Maas and Hox (2001), with 100 groups the operating alpha level was 6%, which is close to the nominal 5%. Chapter Eleven of this book treats some alternatives to the asymptotic Wald tests, which may be preferable when small variance components are tested or when the number of groups is less than 50.

10.1.3 Accuracy and sample size

It is clear that with increasing sample sizes at all levels, estimates and their standard errors become more accurate. Kreft (1996) suggests a rule of thumb, which she calls the '30/30 rule.' To be on the safe side, researchers should strive for a sample of at least 30 groups with at least 30 individuals per group. From the various simulations, this seems sound advice if the interest is mostly in the fixed parameters. For certain applications, one may modify this rule of thumb. Specifically, if there is strong interest in cross-level interactions, the number of groups should be larger, which leads to a 50/20 rule: about fifty groups with about 20 individuals per group. If there is strong interest in the random part, the variance and covariance components and their standard errors, the number of groups should be considerably larger, which leads to a 100/10 rule: about 100 groups with about 10 individuals per group.

These rules of thumb take into account that there are costs attached to data collection, so if the number of groups is increased, the number of individuals per group decreases. In some cases, this may not be a realistic reflection of costs. For instance, in school research an extra cost will be incurred when an extra class is included. Testing only part of the class instead of all pupils will usually not make much difference in the data collection cost. Given a limited budget, an optimal design should reflect the various costs of data collection. Snijders and Bosker (1993), Cohen (1998), Raudenbush and Liu (2000) and Moerbeek, van Breukelen and Berger (2000) all discuss the problem of choosing sample sizes at two levels while considering costs. Moerbeek, van Breukelen and Berger (2001) discuss the problem of optimal design for multilevel logistic models. Essentially, optimal design is a question of balancing statistical power against data collection costs. Data collection costs depend on the details of the data collection method (cf. Groves, 1989). The problem of estimating power in multilevel designs is treated later in this chapter.

10.1.4 Accuracy and sample size with proportions and dichotomous data

Multilevel analysis of proportions generally uses generalized linear models with a logit link (cf. Chapter Six), which gives us the model:

$$\pi_{ij} = \text{logistic}(\gamma_{00} + \gamma_{10}X_{ij} + u_{0j}) \tag{10.1}$$

The observed proportions P_{ij} are assumed to have a binomial distribution with known variance

$$\text{var}(P_{ij}) = (\pi_{ij} (1 - \pi_{ij}))/n_{ij} \tag{10.2}$$

In the software, this variance is usually specified by including the predictor $s_{ij} = \sqrt{var\left(P_{ij}\right)}$ in the random part, with associated variance constrained to one. The π_{ij} are estimated by prediction from the current model. If the variance term is not constrained to one, but estimated, we can model over- and underdispersion. If the extrabinomial variation is significantly different from one, this is usually interpreted as an indication that the model is misspecified, for instance by leaving out relevant levels, interactions among predictors, or in time series data by not allowing autocorrelation in the error structure.

Most programs rely on a Taylor expansion to linearize the model. The program MLwiN uses a first-order Taylor expansion and marginal (quasi) likelihood (MQL1: P_{ij} predicted by fixed part only) as a default. MLwiN can also use a second-order expansion and predictive or penalized (quasi) likelihood (PQL2: P_{ij} predicted by both fixed and random part), while HLM uses first-order expansion and predictive or penalized (quasi) likelihood (PQL1).

Simulations by Rodriguez and Goldman (1995, 2001) show that marginal quasi likelihood with first-order Taylor expansion (MQL1) underestimates both the regression coefficients and the variance components, in some cases very severely. Goldstein and Rasbash (1996) compare MQL1 and PQL2 by simulating data according to the worst performing dataset of Rodriguez and Goldman. This is a three-level data set, with 161 communities that contain in total 1558 women who reported 2449 births. Therefore, each community has on average 9.7 women, who on average report on 1.6 births. In Goldstein and Rasbash's simulation, the means of the MQL1 estimates for the fixed effects, from 200 simulation runs, were underestimated by about 25%. The means of the MQL1 estimates for the random effects were underestimated by as much as 88%. Moreover, 54% of the level 2 variances were estimated as zero, while the population value is one. For the same 200 simulated datasets, the means of the PQL2 estimates for the fixed effects underestimated the population value by at most 3%, and for the random effects by at most 20%. None of the PQL2 variance estimates was estimated as zero.

Browne and Draper (2000) also report a simulation study based on the structure of the Rodriguez/Goldman data. In their simulation, the MQL1 method had an abysmal performance. The PQL2 method fares somewhat better: the regression coefficients are close, but the actual coverage of the 95% confidence interval is close to 95% only for the lowest-level predictor; for the predictors on the woman- and the community-level the actual coverage is about 90%. The variances are still not estimated very accurately: the PQL2 method underestimates the woman-level variance by 11%, and the community-level variance by 43%, and the actual coverage of the 95% confidence interval for the variance estimates is 78% for the woman-level and 27% for the community level.

If anything, the analysis of proportions and binomial data requires larger samples than the analysis of normally distributed data. The Rodriguez/Goldman data set is extreme, because the data are dichotomous, the variance components are large, and the sample size at the lowest level is very small. Consequently, the estimated proportions at the lowest level are very inaccurate. In less extreme cases, it appears that predictive quasi likelihood with second order Taylor expansion is usually sufficiently accurate for the regression coefficients and in many cases good enough for the random parameters. A review of the available literature shows that PQL-based estimates and tests for the regression coefficients are accurate with samples of modest sizes, but estimates and tests of the variances are not. However, with some data sets the PQL2 algorithm breaks down, and the MLwiN manual recommends to start with the simpler MQL1 approach to obtain good starting values for the more complicated PQL2 approach.

For problematic data structures, such as proportions very close to 0 or 1 and small numbers sample sizes, bootstrapping approaches and Bayesian estimation using Gibbs sampling offer improvements. These are described in Chapter Eleven.

10.2 ESTIMATING POWER IN MULTILEVEL REGRESSION DESIGNS

Statistical testing controls the risk of erroneously rejecting the null hypothesis (H_0) or committing a Type I error by setting a significance level α. The alpha level is the maximum probability tolerated for falsely rejecting the null hypothesis. By convention, it is usually set equal to $\alpha = 0.05$, and less often to the more rigorous $\alpha = 0.01$. Sometimes, as in explorative analyses, the more lenient $\alpha = 0.10$ is chosen.

When the null-hypothesis is false, it should be rejected in favor of the alternative hypothesis H_A, which states that a certain effect exists. Failure to reject the null-hypothesis in this case implies another error, denoted by β or Type II error. The probability of committing this error is as a rule discussed in terms of the *power* of the statistical test, the probability of rejecting the null-hypothesis when it is in fact not true. Power increases when α is set to a higher level, and with larger samples or larger effect sizes. In the so-called Newman-Pearson approach to hypothesis testing (Barnett, 1999), a specific value for the alternative hypothesis H_A is stipulated, and both α and β are chosen to balance the relative costs of committing a Type I or a Type II error. In the absence of clear conceptions of these costs, Cohen (1988, 1992) recommends using a power of 0.80 (corresponding to $\beta = 0.20$) as a conventional value for a high power, because this is an adequate power level, which still keeps the sample size requirements within acceptable limits. A power level of 0.50 is considered moderate.

The power of a statistical test is a function of the significance level, the sample size, and the population effect size. For decisions about the research design and sample size to be employed, it is useful to estimate the sample size that is needed to achieve a specific power for a given α and hypothesized effect size. This is called an *a priori* power analysis. The most difficult part is the specification of the population effect size. For a particular test, the effect size indicates the degree to which the null-hypothesis is false in the population. Since this population value is in general unknown, the effect size can be understood as the smallest departure from H_0 that we want to be able to detect with a given probability.

For a broad variety of statistical tests, Cohen (1988) presents indices of effect size, and procedures to determine the sample sizes needed to reach a specified power. Since researchers often have only a vague idea of what constitutes a plausible effect size, Cohen also proposes conventions that define 'small', 'medium', and 'large' effect sizes. For instance, for testing a correlation, the effect size is simply the value of the correlation in the population, and Cohen (1988, 1992) proposes 0.10, 0.30, and 0.50 as conventions for a 'small', 'medium', and 'large' correlation. These values correspond to 1, 9, and 25 percent of explained variance. Cohen remarks that a small effect is of a size that needs statistical analysis to detect it, while a medium effect is of an effect size that one would become aware of given daily experience. A large effect is an effect, which is immediately obvious.

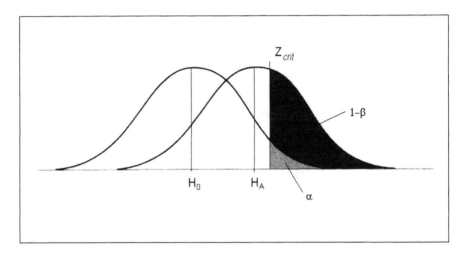

Figure 10.1. Significance and power in the Z-test

The general procedure to estimate the power of a statistical test is illustrated in Figure 10.1. Let us assume that we have a test that results in a standardized Z test statistic. Under the null-hypothesis, H_0, the critical value for a one-sided test at $\alpha = 0.05$ is $Z_{crit} = 1.65$. Under the alternative hypothesis, H_A, we have a Z distribution, which also has a variance equal to one, but its mean is shifted by $\delta = $(effect size)/(standard error). This distribution is known as the noncentral Z-distribution, with noncentrality parameter δ, which in this case is simply the mean of the Z-distribution under H_A. The power of the test is the probability of exceeding the critical value $Z_{crit} = 1.65$ in the noncentral z-distribution.

For example, the standard error of a correlation is approximately $1/\sqrt{N-3}$. If we assume a medium effect, the correlation in the population is assumed to be 0.30. For a sample of 50, the standard error of the correlation is approximately 0.15. The power of our test is the probability of exceeding $Z_{crit} = 1.65$ in the Z-distribution with mean 0.30/0.15=2. This is equal to the probability of exceeding $Z = 1.65$-$2 = $-0.35 in the standard normal Z-distribution, which turns out to be 0.64. Thus, our test has a power of 0.64.

A convenient formula for power analysis is (Snijders & Bosker, 1999, p. 142):

$$(\text{effect size})/(\text{standard error}) \approx (Z_{1-\alpha} + Z_{1-\beta}) \tag{10.3}$$

Equation (10.3) contains four quantities. If three of them are known, we can compute the fourth one. So, in our example, if we want a power of 0.80, which means that $\beta =0.20$, to detect a correlation of 0.30, the equation is:

$$(0.30)/(\text{standard error} = (Z_{0.95} + Z_{0.80}) = (1.65+0.84) = 2.48.$$

Thus, we need a standard error of (0.3/2.48=) 0.12. Calculating back to the sample size N from the formula $s.e._r = 1/\sqrt{N-3}$, we find we need at least $((1/0.12)^2+3=8.33^2+3=)$ 72.4 or a rounded 73 cases to achieve a 0.80 power.

To use equation (10.3) for power analysis, we need to know the standard error. This is simply available if we have analyzed available data, and wish to assess the power of a specific test. This is *post hoc* power analysis. Since this is a simple case, it will be treated first with an example in section 10.2.1, and the more difficult case of *a priori* power analysis is treated in section 10.2.2.

10.2.1 *Post hoc* power analysis

Chapter Eight contains the results of a meta-analysis using multilevel analysis techniques. Table 8.4, which is repeated here, presents the results of separately adding three explanatory study characteristics to the model. One of these is each study's total sample size N_{tot}. This variable is important, because if it shows a relationship with the effect size of the studies, this indicates that there may have been selective publication. The relationship is in fact not significant, with a regression coefficient estimated as 0.001 and a standard error of 0.01. However, there is the problem of power. There are only twenty studies, so it is possible that this nonsignificance is the result of low power, rather than the absence of a real effect in the population.

Table 8.4 (Rptd) Results meta-analysis example (Chapter Eight)					
Model:	intercept only	$+ N_{tot}$	$+$ reliability	$+$ weeks	$+$ all
intercept	.58 (.11)	.50 (.05)	.15 (1.23)	-.22 (.20)	.42 (.92)
N_{tot}		.001 (.01)			-.004 (.01)
reliability			.51 (1.47)		-.51 (1.18)
duration				.14 (.03)	.15 (.04)
variance σ_u^2	.14	.16	.16	.04	.05
p-value χ^2 test	$p < .001$	$p < .001$	$p < .001$	$p = .09$	$p = .07$

To investigate this possibility, we must specify what effect size we wish to be able to detect. For a correlation coefficient, a medium effect is defined as 0.30, or 9% explained variance. For a regression model, we may consider a predictor to have a medium effect if it explains 10% of the variance, which is a nice round figure. In the intercept-only model in Table 8.4, the between studies variance is estimated as $\sigma_u^2 = 0.14$. Ten percent of that variance equals 0.014. That variance must be explained using a term of the form γN_{tot}. In our data set in Table 8.4, we can calculate the variance of the total sample size N_{tot}, which turns out to have a variance of 155.305. To reduce that to 0.014, the regression coefficient gamma must be equal to $\gamma = \sqrt{0.14}/\sqrt{155.305} = 0.03$. Therefore, we want to test an effect size of $\gamma = 0.03$, with an associated standard error of 0.01 (the value of the standard error for N_{tot} in Table 8.4), and the significance level set at $\alpha = 0.05$. We again use equation (10.3): (effect size)/(standard error) $\approx (Z_{1-\alpha} + Z_{1-\beta})$, which in this case becomes $(0.03)/(0.01) = (1.64 + Z_{1-\beta})$. So, $Z_{1-\beta} = 3 - 1.64 = 1.36$. This leads to a *post hoc* power estimate of 0.91, which appears adequate. The failure to find a significant effect for the study sample size is not likely to be the result of insufficient power of the statistical test.

 Post hoc power analysis is not only useful in evaluation one's own analysis, as just shown, but also in the planning stages of a new study. By investigating the power of earlier studies, we find which effect sizes and intraclass correlations we may expect, which should help us to design our own study.

10.2.2 *A priori* power analysis: general issues

In an *a priori* power analysis, we want to estimate the power of our test for a specific effect size. Typically, we want to assess which sample size we need to achieve, say, a power of 0.80. In multilevel regression analysis, several factors complicate things. First, the multilevel regression model is a complex multivariate model, and to specify effect sizes and calculate standard errors we have to consider plausible values for many elements of that model. Secondly, we have sample sizes at different levels. The same or similar power values may be obtainable with different numbers of groups and group sizes. To decide which of these are going to be used, we must consider the cost of collecting data from more group members, or of collecting one more group. For example, assume that we want to assess the effect of an anti-smoking program, which is offered in school classes. In many cases, school research uses written questionnaires for data collection. In this case, once a class is selected for the study, it makes sense to collect data from all pupils in that class, since the extra cost of selecting one more pupil in a class is very low. Therefore, if the average class size is 20, we may decide to collect data from 10 experimental and 10 control classes, which give us 400 pupils. On the other hand, if the data collection is done by computer, and the teacher has to send the pupils one by one to the computer to respond to the questionnaire, the cost (if only in time) of collecting one more pupil in a selected class is considerable. It may be better to select only at random 10 pupils in each class, and compensate by collecting data from in total 40 classes. In fact, since the intervention is done on the class level, which means that the variable that codes for the intervention has no within-class variance, collecting data from more classes would certainly increase the power of our test. Since there are always cost considerations, the question of the best sample size always involves decisions about the optimal design.

For a large variety of classical statistical tests, Cohen (1992) presents procedures and tables that can be used for an *a priori* power analysis. For some special cases, similar procedures can be derived for power estimation in multilevel models. For instance, Cohen (1998) treats the problem of analyzing power in cluster samples, for the case that we have only lower level predictors and no random slopes. However, this case is more easily approached by using the standard tables in Cohen (1992) and correcting the results for the 'design effect' (Kish, 1965, 1987). This correction procedure, described in Chapter One of this book, uses the intraclass correlation between respondents within clusters to correct the sample size:

$$n_{eff} = n/\left[1+\left(n_{clus}-1\right)\rho\right] \tag{10.4}$$

In equation (10.4), n_{eff} is the effective sample size, n_{clus} is the cluster size, n is the total sample size, and ρ is the intraclass correlation. So, if we know the intraclass correlation, or can make a reasonable guess about its size, we can find the cluster size and the total sample size needed to give us a specific effective sample size. By rearranging the correction formula, we get:

$$n = n_{eff}\left(1+\left(n_{clus}-1\right)\rho\right) \tag{10.5}$$

Earlier, we calculated the sample size needed to detect a correlation of 0.30 with a power of 0.80 as 73 cases. Suppose that we collect our data using three school classes. We have no information about the intraclass correlation ρ, but school research often reports an intra class correlation $\rho = 0.1$. Taking that as a reasonable approximation, and using the (73/3=) 24.3 as the average class size, we find that with clustered data we need 243.3 or minimally 244 pupils, which implies about 10 classes. Considerably more than the 73 pupils who are needed if the data are collected as a simple random sample! Summarizing: when we have only a random intercept and no random slopes, we can use Cohen's (1992) procedures to estimate the power, and follow this by adjusting the sample size for the design effect. For group-level explanatory variables, the intraclass correlation is equal to 1.0, and the effective sample size is equal to the number of groups. Again, we can use Cohen's (1992) tables to assess the power.

Raudenbush and Liu (2000) treat the important problem of determining the optimal design for multisite randomized trials, where experimenters combine the results from an experiment conducted in a number of different sites. This is an important design in biomedical research, where the number of patients in any specific location may be too small to be useful. By combining data from experiments carried out at a number of different sites, the power of the statistical analysis of the treatment can be increased. Since the patients are nested within the sites, multisite studies have a multilevel structure (Woodruff, 1997). Raudenbush and Liu (2000) consider the problem of determining the power to confirm a treatment effect, given the possibility that the treatment effect varies across sites. In multilevel terminology, they assume that the treatment variable has a random slope across sites, and include potential cross-level interactions to model the influence of site characteristics on the treatment effect. Raudenbush (1997) treats the same problem when the intervention is not implemented within the sites, but at the site or cluster level. This means that some sites are treatment-sites, and others are control-sites. In this design, the intraclass correlation of the treatment variable is 1.0. Both approaches to power estimation are not completely general, because they do not include individual level explanatory variables. Snijders and Bosker (1993) present asymptotic formulae for the standard errors of fixed effects in two-level designs. The formulae are complicated, and they recommend using their program PinT (*Power in Two*-level models; Bosker, Snijders & Guldemond, 1996) for the calculations. The power problems considered by Raudenbush (1997) and Raudenbush and Liu (2000) can also be analyzed using PinT, but PinT also allows power calculations for the variance estimates.

When we consider power problems in multilevel designs, it is useful to translate the model under consideration into a standardized model. In a standardized model, the logic of power analysis, including decisions about effect sizes, does not depend on the arbitrary scales of the variables. In a standardized framework, it also becomes possible to establish rules of thumb about what may be considered small, medium, and large effects. Raudenbush and Liu (2000) propose to standardize the lowest level variance to $\sigma_e^2 = 1.0$. If there is an experimental treatment, we can imagine that the treatment variable is coded using a dummy variable with values – 0.5 and +0.5. This means that the intercept and the variance components reflect the average subject, and that the regression coefficient for the treatment dummy variable is equal to the standardized effect size d discussed in the meta-analysis chapter (Chapter Eight) in this book. In a two-group experiment, the effect size d is defined as $d = \left(\overline{Y}_E - \overline{Y}_C\right)/s$, which is precisely what we get if the within groups variance is standardized. Cohen (1988) defines $d=0.2$ as a small effect, $d=0.5$ as a medium effect, and $d=0.8$ as a large effect. These values roughly correspond to the correlation values of 0.10, 0.30, and 0.50 mentioned earlier, and they can be used to find matching values for the regression coefficients if we have continuous variables. If we define a small effect as an effect that explains 0.01 of the variance, this implies for a predictor variable with variance 1.0 a regression coefficient of 0.10. This adds $0.1^2 = 0.01$ to the total outcome variance, which leads to $0.01/(1.00+0.01)=0.01$ explained variance. In general, the standardized regression coefficient we seek is $b = \sqrt{r^2/\left(1-r^2\right)}$, where b is the regression coefficient, and r is the corresponding correlation. Similarly, a correlation of 0.30 between predictor variable and outcome variable, with lowest level error variance fixed at 1.0, implies a regression coefficient of 0.31, and a correlation of 0.50 between predictor variable and outcome variable, with lowest level error variance fixed at 1.0, implies a regression coefficient of 0.58. As a result, when we want to evaluate the power of a test of a fixed regression coefficient using standardized continuous explanatory variables, and $s_e^2 = 1.0$, conventional criteria lead to values of 0.10 for a small, 0.31 for a medium, and 0.58 for a large effect size.

In multilevel regression, we must also be concerned with the intraclass correlation and the variance of the random slopes. In multilevel regression analysis, it is useful to have rules-of-thumb about the variance components. Raudenbush and Liu (2000) suggest values of 0.05, 0.10, and 0.15 as small, medium, and large variances for the slope of an intervention dummy coded −0.5, +0.5. Such suggestions are of course tentative and study specific, but these values seem reasonable. For instance, Cohen (1988, 1992) views an intervention effect of 0.5 as a medium effect size. If the corresponding regression coefficient $\gamma=0.5$ has a slope variance of 0.05, this translates to a standard deviation of 0.22. Assuming normality, 95% of the slopes would be between 0.06 and 0.94[1]. The combination of a medium

---

[1] Note that this is not the 95% confidence interval. The 95% confidence interval relates to the precision of the estimate of the average effect across sites. In a random coefficient model, we assume variation around this average. The associated interval is the 95% predictive interval.

treatment effect and a small variance across treatment sites leads to the result that virtually all population intervention effects are positive. A small intervention effect of 0.20 combined with a medium slope variance of 0.10 leads to an interval for the intervention effects across sites between –0.42 and 0.82. In this situation, 26% of the intervention outcomes are expected to be zero or negative. This clearly underscores the importance of evaluating the treatment effect across sites. It also supports the rules of thumb chosen for small, medium, and large slope variances. The variance of the treatments across sites becomes important only if it has an effect size that is considerably larger than the effect size of the treatment.

For the variance of the intercept, the values of 0.05, 0.10, and 0.15 may be too small. They translate to intraclass correlations of 0.05, 0.09, and 0.13. In cluster sampling, variances are typically low (cf. Groves, 1989), and a value of 0.10 would be considered large in that context. In educational and organizational context, intraclass correlations of 0.10 seem reasonable, and 0.15 could indeed be considered high. However, in small group and family research, intraclass correlations are often much higher, and 0.15 would sooner be a medium effect, with 0.30 a large effect size. I suggest using 0.05, 0.10 and 0.15 as small, medium and large values for the intraclass correlation in general cases, and 0.10, 0.20, and 0.30 in those cases where on *a priori* grounds much higher intraclass correlations appear reasonable. These translate to intercept variances of 0.05, 0.11, and 0.18 in ordinary situations, and 0.11, 0.25, and 0.43 in situations where a high intraclass correlation can be expected.

With these considerations and suggestions set for rules of thumb, the next sections explain *a priori* power analysis by examples.

10.2.3 *A priori* power analysis: the intercept variance and intraclass correlation

In applications such as meta-analysis, it is important to be able to detect between-study heterogeneity, or between study variance. In the multilevel approach to meta-analysis (cf. Chapter Eight in this book), this translates to the significance of the second level intercept variance. Longford (1993, p. 58) shows that the sampling variance of the intercept variance σ_u^2 is equal to

$$\mathrm{var}\left(\sigma_u^2\right) = \frac{2\sigma_e^4}{k n_{clus}}\left(\frac{1}{n_{clus}-1} + 2\omega + n_{clus}\omega^2\right) \tag{10.6}$$

where k is the number of groups or clusters, n_{clus} is the cluster size, and ω is the ratio of the between and within studies variance: $\omega = \sigma_u^2/\sigma_e^2$. Equation (10.6) can be used to estimate the power of detecting any specific between study variance.

If we analyze standardized effect sizes, the first level variance is implicitly fixed to 1.0. Following Raudenbush and Liu (2000), we may use values of 0.05,

0.10, and 0.15 as small, medium, and large between-study variances for the standardized effect. We wish to be able to detect a medium variance of 0.10 with a power of 0.80.

Suppose we plan a meta-analysis on a specific topic. We have carried out a computerized literature search, and found 19 references on our topic. Three are available in the local library. We collect these three studies, and code their effect sizes and total sample sizes. The results are in Table 10.1.

Table 10.1 Three studies for an intended meta-analysis		
Study	d	N_{tot}
1	0.03	256
2	0.12	185
3	-0.14	144

The question is: given the results coded in the first three studies (actually, the first three studies in the meta-analysis example of Bryk & Raudenbush, 1992), is it worthwhile to go on, meaning retrieving and coding the remaining 16 studies? We can use an *a-priori* power analysis to formulate an answer to this question. Specifically, assume that we wish to test whether the studies are heterogeneous, i.e., whether the between studies variance σ_u^2 is significant. We require a power of 0.80 to detect the study-level variance at the conventional $\alpha=0.05$ significance level when the proportion between-study variance is at least 0.25 of the total variance, a value that Hunter and Schmidt (1990) consider an important lower limit. Because we meta-analyze standardized effect sizes, the within study variance is fixed at $\sigma_e^2=1.0$. For the proportion between-study variance to be 0.25, the between-study variance must be $\sigma_u^2=0.33$ (0.25=0.33/1.33), and therefore $\omega=0.33$. With $k=19$ studies, an average study sample size $n_{clus}=195$ (the average in Table 10.1), and $\omega=0.33$, we obtain var(σ_u^2)=0.012. Thus, the standard error of the second level variance estimate σ_u^2 is 0.11. Using formula (10.3), we find that the power of the test of $\sigma_u^2=0.33$ while the standard error is 0.11 is estimated as (assuming a one-sided test: $p(Z>(1.64-0.33/0.11)=p(Z>0-1.31)=)$ 0.91, which appears more than adequate. If the sample sizes of the three available studies are typical for all studies, it appears worthwhile to continue the meta-analysis.

Similar calculations using the *design effect* (cf. section 10.2.2) allow us to assess the power of the overall test for the effect size d. Suppose we are interested in detecting a combined small effect, meaning an effect size as low as $\delta=0.20$. This is small, but one of the advantages of meta-analysis is the possibility to detect small effects. If the sample sizes of the three available studies are typical for all studies, all studies together involve ($19 \times 195=$) 3705 subjects. However, we do not have one giant experiment with 3705 independent observations, we have 19 smaller experiments. We again assume that the between-studies variance is 0.25 of the total variance. In other words, we assume clustered data with 19 clusters of 195 subjects, and an intraclass correlation of 0.25. Using formula (10.3) to estimate the effective sample size from the intraclass correlation and the number of clusters, we obtain n_{eff} =3705/($1+18 \times 0.25$)= 674. Using the standard formula for the sampling error of the effect size (cf. Table 8.1 in Chapter 8), using 674 subjects with equal sample sizes for the experimental and control groups, we obtain an expected standard error for d of 0.077. Thus, the power estimate is (assuming a two-sided test: $p(Z>1.96-0.10/0.077)= p(Z>0.66)=$) 0.25. We conclude that the power of our meta-analysis for detecting a small experimental effect is poor. If we are interested in medium size effects, the power estimate is (assuming a two-sided test: $p(Z>1.96-0.30/0.077)= p(Z>-1.94)=$ 0.97, which is again more than adequate.

10.2.4 *A priori* power analysis: designing an intervention study

Suppose we plan an intervention study to evaluate a course given to general practitioners (GPs) to improve their communication skills. Fifty GPs will participate in the study. In such studies, there is an issue whether the randomization should take place at the patient level or at the GP level. In medical and organizational intervention studies, there is a similar issue whether the randomization should be within or between organizational centers. In medical research, this issue is discussed under the heading of 'cluster randomization.' Technically, randomization can be carried out at any of the available levels. Randomization within centers is generally more efficient, but it can also lead to 'treatment group contamination,' where information leaks from the experimental group to the control group (Moerbeek, 2000, p. 38). On the other hand, if randomization is at the organizational level, it is impossible to estimate a random component for the treatment variable. In our case, we choose a design in which all GP's are evaluated by a number of their patients, then they all follow a communication skill course, and after that they are evaluated again, using the same number of patients as before. Assuming the patients arrive at random, we have randomization at the patient level. The question is: how many patients do we need to interview?

   To answer this question, we must first decide on the effect size, and the desired power. For this example, we decide that a medium effect is the largest that we may reasonably expect from our intervention. We decide on a minimal power of 0.80 for a medium effect, and 0.60 for a small effect. The significance level is $\alpha=0.05$ and to maximize the power we will carry out a one-tailed test. For the moment, we assume that the second level sample size of 50 GPs is fixed by the study design, and we can increase the power only by using larger samples of patients within GPs. The calculations all assume equal group sizes. Since this is a planned study, we may assume that the investigators will aim to obtain equal numbers of patients per doctor.

Power of a simple *t*-test

The simplest analysis for this design is a *t*-test for independent groups after the intervention, which totally ignores the cluster effect of the GPs. To assess the power of a *t*-test for the difference between two means, we use the standardized difference, d, given by $d = (\bar{x}_1 - \bar{x}_2)/s$. Table 10.2 presents the power of the ordinary *t*-test for different combinations of effect size and sample size for each period, assuming 50 GPs and a spread of 9-15 patients for each GP in each period.

The power values in Table 10.2 assume that the patients are independent across GPs. However, it is reasonable to expect a dependency between observations collected from the same GP. The result is of course estimates for standard errors that are too small and spurious 'significant' results. The correction described by Kish (1965: p. 259) referred to in equation (10.4) computes the effective sample size in two-stage cluster sampling as $n_{eff} = n/[1 + (n_{clus} - 1)\rho]$, where n_{eff} is the effective sample size, n_{clus} is the cluster size, n is the total sample size, and ρ is the intraclass correlation.

Table 10.2 Power of simple *t*-test, intervention study				
		two-tailed		one-tailed
		small,	medium,	small,	medium,
n_{per}	n_{GP}	d=0.2	d=0.5	d=0.2	d=0.5
450	9	0.86	1.00	0.91	1.00
500	10	0.88	1.00	0.94	1.00
550	11	0.91	1.00	0.95	1.00
600	12	0.93	1.00	0.97	1.00
650	13	0.95	1.00	0.97	1.00
700	14	0.96	1.00	0.98	1.00
750	15	0.97	1.00	0.99	1.00

At this point, it is simple to calculate the effective sample size for different situations. For instance, suppose that we take a sample of 50 doctors, each with 9 patients for each period. This comes to a total sample size of 450 for each period, called n_{per} in Table

10.2, which is reasonable. Let us further suppose that we are interested in a variable, for which the intraclass correlation ρ is 0.10. We have defined this earlier, following Raudenbush and Liu (2000), as a medium size intraclass correlation. It is a reasonable value, which has also been found in other research on patients clustered within GPs. However, using Kish's formula, the effective sample size in this situation is 250, which is much less than the apparent sample size of 450!

Table 10.3 presents the power of the ordinary t-test assuming an intraclass correlation of ρ=0.10. It makes clear that in the presence of an intraclass correlation of 0.10, the effective sample size, given a fixed sample of 50 GPs, is relatively low, which leads to relatively low power values. However, medium effects can still be detected with ease in all cases, and even small effects have a reasonable probability of being detected. It appears that using only nine or ten patients for each GP is sufficient to meet our stated power criteria of 0.80 for a large and 0.60 for a small intervention effect. Using a one-sided test for the intervention effect is advisable if detection of small effects is important.

Table 10.3. Power of t-test, cluster sample, intervention study						
			two-tailed		one-tailed	
			small,	medium,	small,	medium,
n_{per}	n_{GP}	n_{eff}	d=0.2	d=0.5	d=0.2	d=0.5
450	9	250	0.61	1.00	0.72	1.00
500	10	263	0.63	1.00	0.74	1.00
550	11	275	0.65	1.00	0.76	1.00
600	12	286	0.67	1.00	0.77	1.00
650	13	295	0.68	1.00	0.78	1.00
700	14	304	0.69	1.00	0.79	1.00
750	15	312	0.70	1.00	0.80	1.00

Power in a variance component model

A test for the effectiveness of the intervention can conveniently be carried out using multilevel analysis, with patients defined as level 1, and GPs as level 2. The simplest multilevel model is a variance component model, which assumes a fixed effect size for the intervention for all GPs, but allows for differences between GP's in general effectiveness. If only a dummy variable for the intervention is included, this analysis is equivalent to the t-test with correction for the design effect. Since the multilevel analysis does not assume equal group sizes, it is slightly more accurate if group sizes are different. Otherwise, the power should be similar to the estimates in Table 10.3.

If we assume that the treatment effect is the same for all GPs, but allow for an intraclass correlation, we have a variance component model. Multilevel analysis of this model has the advantage that it allows simple modeling of additional covariates at the patient or GP level, similar to adding covariates in a multiple regression model. In both periods, the same GPs participate. If in both periods the same kinds of patients visit their GPs, we have effective randomization of patients over treatment and control period. This implies a correlation between patient characteristics and the intervention dummy that is close to zero. As a result, inclusion of a patient variable that explains significant residual variance leads to a larger power for the test of the intervention dummy, because the residual variance s_e^2 becomes smaller (Cohen, 1988). Furthermore, if GP level variables are added that explain variance, the partial intraclass correlation decreases, which (cf. the Kish equation) leads to a larger n_{eff}, and hence to a higher power. The increase in power can be estimated using procedures described by Cohen (1988) by including a correction for the design effect. These power estimates depend of course on ad hoc assumptions about the amount of variance explained and the correlations between the predictors. However, under realistic assumptions, adding effective explanatory variables on either the patient or the GP level leads to a higher power. Since the procedures described by Snijders and Bosker (1993) and later in this chapter include the variance component model as a special case, we will not look into the variance component model in more detail here.

Power in a random coefficient model

It is realistic to assume that the effect of the intervention may differ across GPs, which leads to a multilevel model with a random slope-coefficient for the intervention variable. The power of the test for the significance of the intervention coefficient in such models is addressed by Raudenbush and Liu (2000). They consider a multisite trial, where the average impact of an intervention is assessed across sites, and the moderating effect of site variables on the treatment efficacy. As mentioned before, Raudenbush and Liu propose 0.05 for a small, 0.1 for a medium, and 0.15 for a large slope variance. They note that when the intervention effect varies much across sites, the average effect of an intervention is a poor indicator of the importance of the treatment effect, and masks possible negative effects of the intervention.

Raudenbush and Liu note that the average treatment effect can be tested using an F-test. Under the null-hypothesis F has an F distribution described by $F(1, J-1)$, with the degrees of freedom for the numerator J equal to the number of groups, while under the alternative hypothesis F follows a noncentral F-distribution $F(1, J-1; \lambda)$, with λ the noncentrality parameter. This is analogous to the situation depicted in Figure 10.1, with the normal distribution replaced by the F-distribution. The noncentrality parameter is given by (following our notation):

$$\lambda = \frac{n_{tot}d^2}{n_{tot}\sigma_{u1}^2/J + 4\sigma_e^2} \qquad (10.7)$$

where σ_{u1}^2 is the slope variance, and σ_e^2 is the individual level residual variance. To find the power of the F-test, we must find the probability of exceeding the critical value for F in the non-central F-distribution with non-centrality parameter λ and degrees of freedom 1 and J-1. Standard software packages like SPSS or SAS can be used to find this probability, or a separate program like the freely available NCSS Probability Calculator (NCSS, 1995).

Table 10.4. Power of test on intervention, random slope model					
		two-tailed		one-tailed	
	var	small,	medium,	small,	medium,
n_{tot}	slope	d=0.2	d=0.5	d=0.2	d=0.5
450	0.05	0.50	1.00	0.63	1.00
450	0.10	0.47	1.00	0.60	1.00
500	0.05	0.54	1.00	0.67	1.00
500	0.10	0.50	1.00	0.63	1.00
550	0.05	0.58	1.00	0.70	1.00
550	0.10	0.53	1.00	0.66	1.00
600	0.05	0.61	1.00	0.73	1.00
600	0.10	0.56	1.00	0.68	1.00
650	0.05	0.64	1.00	0.75	1.00
650	0.10	0.58	1.00	0.71	1.00
700	0.05	0.67	1.00	0.78	1.00
700	0.10	0.61	1.00	0.73	1.00
750	0.05	0.69	1.00	0.80	1.00
750	0.10	0.63	1.00	0.74	1.00

Using Raudenbush and Liu's approach, we set up a power table for the intervention effect for two different postulated variances of the intervention slope across GP's. Table 10.4 again shows that for a medium effect all conditions result in sufficient power. For detection of a small effect, most power estimates are unsatisfactory. Using a one-tailed test improves the power appreciably.

The structure of the equation that leads to Table 10.4 again leads to the conclusion that in order to increase the power, increasing the sample of GPs is more effective than increasing the sample of patients. Inclusion of a patient variable that explains significant residual variance, leads to a larger power for the test of the intervention dummy. Furthermore, if GP level variables are added that explain residual variance, the partial intraclass correlation decreases, which again (cf. the Raudenbush/Liu equation) leads to a higher power. The increase in power can be estimated, but these power estimates again depend to a large degree on ad hoc assumptions about the amount of variance explained and the correlations between the predictors. Under realistic assumptions, adding effective explanatory variables on either the patient or the GP level leads to a higher power. Including GP variables improves the power primarily if they explain intervention slope variance σ_{u1}^2.

We have already concluded that the power of our intervention is sufficient, even without covariates. However, it is an interesting question whether adding covariates would give us a minimal power of 0.80 even for small intervention effects. To assess the effect of explanatory variables at both the patient or the GP level, we need an approach that is more general than the one described by Raudenbush and Liu (2000). Snijders and Bosker (1993) describe a very general approach to estimating standard errors and power for fixed effects in two-level models, based on asymptotic approximations to the necessary standard errors. If we restrict ourselves to the fixed effects, the models described by Raudenbush and Liu are a special case of the general model considered by Snijders and Bosker. However, using it requires specifying and entering into the program PinT (Bosker et al., 1996) information about the means and the variances and covariances at both levels, for all predictor variables, and the variances and covariances of all random effects. As mentioned earlier, this requires ad hoc assumptions about the amount of variance explained and the correlations between the predictors. Since patient and GP characteristics that are included as covariate correlate among themselves, only a limited number of covariates are useful. For simplicity, we assume that we can find at least one patient level and one GP level variable that have a small effect explaining intercept variance.

Since we use a standardized model, we can specify all means as equal to zero. The within patients variance σ_e^2 is standardized at 1.0. So far, we have assumed an intraclass correlation of 0.10, which translates to a second level intercept variance of 0.11. PinT does not ask for the regression coefficients, but requires specification of the variances of the explanatory variables and of all random effects in the model. Furthermore, explanatory variables at the lowest level are assumed to be group mean centered; their between groups variance must be specified by adding the aggregated group means as a different variable.

We have a treatment effect that is coded −0.5/+0.5, which is assumed to have a small effect, meaning a regression coefficient γ=0.2. The treatment dummy has a variance of 0.25, which is all within-GP variance.

Table 10.5 Comparison of different power estimation methods, variance component model			
n_{tot}	n_{GP}	adjusted t-test	PinT estimate
450	9	0.72	0.69
500	10	0.74	0.73
550	11	0.76	0.76
600	12	0.77	0.79
650	13	0.78	0.82
700	14	0.79	0.84
750	15	0.80	0.86

We have a variance component model, with a fixed treatment effect and an intraclass correlation of 0.10. We can use a t-test, and adjust the sample sizes for the cluster effect. Table 10.5 presents power estimates for a one-sided test of a small effect (δ=0.2) at α=0.05, using the t-test adjusted for the design effect and using PinT. Although the power estimates are not exactly the same, they are close.

Table 10.6 Comparison of different power estimation methods, random slope model			
n_{tot}	n_{GP}	Raudenbush & Liu	PinT estimate
450	9	0.60	0.61
500	10	0.63	0.64
550	11	0.66	0.67
600	12	0.68	0.69
650	13	0.71	0.72
700	14	0.73	0.74
750	15	0.74	0.76

Using PinT, we can expand our model by allowing for a varying treatment effect across the GPs. This is equivalent to the problem addressed by Raudenbush and Liu (2000). Assuming a value of 0.1 for the slope variance (a medium effect size), and zero covariance between the intercept and the slope, we can calculate the power using either Raudenbush and Liu's approach or using PinT. The results are in Table 10.6. The two sets of power estimates are very close.

The next question is whether the inclusion of patient or doctor level explanatory variables improves the power. First, assume that it is possible to find an explanatory variable at the patient level with a medium correlation with the outcome variable 'patient evaluation.' This means that 10% of the variance of the outcome variable is explained, and as a result, we expect the residual variance σ_e^2 to decrease to 0.90. The second level variance σ_{u0}^2 will probably also decrease, let us assume also 10% to 0.10. Second, assume that we also find a GP level variable that explains 10% of the variance of the intercepts, so σ_{u0}^2 decreases further to 0.09. Experience shows that it is often difficult to explain slope variance, but let us assume that our GP level variable also explains 5% of the slope variance, which then decreases from 0.10 to .095. To explain slope variance, we must build an interaction variable, so there are now four explanatory variables in the model: the intervention dummy, one patient variable, one GP variable, and the interaction term. To use PinT, we must specify all their (co)variances and the distribution over the two levels. The intervention variable has variance 0.25, on the patient level only. We assume that all other variables are standardized. The GP variable has all its variance on the GP level. If we assume an intraclass correlation of 0.10 for the outcome variable, we may as well assume the same for the explanatory patient variable, which gives us a patient level variance of 0.9 and a GP level variance of 0.10. The interaction variable is a multiplication of a variable with only patient level variance (0.25) and a variable with only GP level variance (1.0). We assume that, after standardization, its variance at the patient level is 0.20, and 0.80 at the GP level. Since we have approximate randomization, we assume no correlation between the intervention dummy and the other explanatory variables. For simplicity, we also assume zero correlations between the other variables. Only the interaction term correlates 0.60 with the two constituting variables. Since PinT expects covariances, we must calculate the ensuing covariances at both levels.

This is quite a bit of work, and it is clear that we must make some informed guesses about the explanatory variables. However, we do not need great precision here. The goal in a power analysis is to investigate whether adding explanatory variables is worthwhile for our objective of testing the intervention effect. Plausible values for the other variables are sufficient for that goal. If we have different objectives, for instance, if we are interested in the power for testing the interaction effect, we must be more specific about these values, and their justification.

Table 10.7 compares the results of the two PinT power estimates. It shows only modest increases in the power of the test of the intervention. Adding covariates at the patient or GP level makes sense only if the added cost of the data collection is small.

		Table 10.7 Comparison of power, random slope model, without and with covariates	
n_{tot}	n_{GP}	random slope, no covariates	random slope plus covariates
450	9	0.61	0.64
500	10	0.64	0.68
550	11	0.67	0.70
600	12	0.69	0.73
650	13	0.72	0.75
700	14	0.74	0.77
750	15	0.76	0.79

10.2.5 A general procedure for power analysis

All power estimation procedures discussed so far, proceed by estimating the standard error of a specific parameter, and then applying equation 10.3, or rather its reverse

$$Z_{1-\beta} = \frac{\text{effect size}}{\text{standard error}} - Z_{1-\alpha} \qquad (10.8)$$

The various formulas assume that the data are balanced, meaning that the group sizes are equal, and that any randomization into experimental and control groups results in a 50:50 ratio. Deviations from these assumptions generally lead to designs with less power, but unless the deviations are large the formulas yield good approximations.

We may have a design that is not covered by the models discussed earlier, or we may have very unbalanced data. There is a very general approach to estimate the needed standard errors, comparable to the approach used to estimate power in structural equation models (cf Satorra & Saris, 1985, Satorra, 1989). This can be summarized in three steps:

1. Specify a model that contains all variables and parameters of interest, including the parameter that is to be tested. All parameters are fixed at their (assumed) population values.

2. Generate data that reflect the population parameter values *exactly*.
3. Analyze the generated data using one of the available multilevel programs, and allow all parameters to be estimated.

The parameter estimates obtained in step *3* should be identical to the fixed values in step *1*. The standard errors produced by the program are the standard errors needed for power estimation.

The difficult step is step *2*: generate the data. In regression analysis, the explanatory variables are assumed fixed, so in theory we should know them. In practice the explanatory variables are usually also sampled. However, their precise distribution is not crucial. Unless they are dummy variables, as the intervention dummy used earlier, it makes sense to generate them as standardized variables with a multivariate normal distribution. It is more difficult to generate the residuals, since they must follow a specific multivariate normal distribution exactly. The solution is (Bollen & Stine, 1992) to generate a set of (centered) residuals **Y** with an arbitrary multivariate normal distribution characterized by covariance matrix **S,** and transform these to multivariate normal distributed residuals **Z** having the desired covariance matrix Σ, using the transformation

$$\mathbf{Z} = \mathbf{YS}^{-0.5}\mathbf{\Sigma}^{0.5} \tag{10.9}$$

A much simpler but approximate solution is to generate the residuals directly from Σ, skipping the transformation given by (10.9), and repeating the whole procedure three to five times to obtain an average standard error from the simulated distribution.

To use the exact solution for our example, we must set up an empty data set that has 50 GPs, and a specific number of patients for each GP. The equation for the model including the GP and patient variables is

$$Y_{ij} = \gamma_{00} + \delta D_{ij} + \gamma_{01}P_{ij} + \gamma_{10}G_j + \gamma_{11}D_{ij}G_j + u_{0j} + u_{1j}P_{ij} + e_{ij}, \tag{10.10}$$

where D is the intervention dummy coded -0.5, $+0.5$, P is the patient variable, and G is the GP variable.

Again, we assume that the explanatory variable P at the patient level has a medium correlation with the outcome variable 'patient evaluation.' This means that 10% of the variance of the outcome variable is explained, and as a result, we expect the residual variance σ_e^2 to decrease to 0.90. The second level variance σ^2_{u0} also decreases by 10% to 0.10. The GP level variable G explains another 10% of the variance of the intercepts, so σ_{u0}^2 decreases further to 0.09. We assume that our GP level variable also explains 5% of the slope variance, which then decreases from 0.10 to .095.

First, we must set up our simulated population data. The explanatory variables P and G are generated independently from a standard normal distribution. If we want P to have an intraclass correlation of 0.1, we must generate a group centered normal variable with a variance of 0.9, and a group level normal variable with a variance of 0.1, and add these. Since all this data generation is a random process, the mean and variance of the generated values for P and G will not be exactly zero and one, so they are standardized, and subsequently the product DG is calculated. Without loss of generality, we can set the intercept term γ_{00} to zero. In a standardized model, σ_e^2 is set to 1.0. The regression coefficient δ for the intervention dummy D is set to 0.2, to reflect a small effect. The regression coefficients γ_{01} and γ_{10} are set to 0.31, to reflect a medium effect (cf. par. 10.2.1). The residual intercept variance σ_{u0}^2 is set to 0.09, the residual slope variance σ_{u1}^2 is set to 0.095, and their covariance is set to zero. If we standardize DG, explaining 5% of the slope variance implies a value of 0.22 for γ_{11}. The lowest level residual variance σ_e^2 is set to 0.9. The residuals u_0 and u_1 are generated independently from a standard normal distribution. Again, since this data generation is a random process, their mean will not be exactly zero, and their variances will not be exactly equal to the theoretical values. In addition, their correlation will not be exactly zero, so we must apply the transformation given by (10.6) to make the residuals u_0 and u_1 follow the desired distribution exactly.

Estimating power using the general procedure outlined in this section implies much work. For problems that can be formulated within the PinT framework, using PinT is less complicated. For more general problems, it is convenient to use an approximate solution that generates the needed residuals directly from Σ and skips the transformation given by (10.9). Repeating the whole procedure three to five times to obtain an average standard error from the simulated distribution produces estimated standard errors that are accurate enough for an a priori power analysis (Hox, 2001).

11

Advanced Methods
for Estimation and Testing

The usual method to estimate the parameters of the multilevel regression model is Maximum Likelihood estimation. This produces parameter estimates and asymptotic standard errors, which can be used to test the significance of specific parameters, or to set a confidence interval around a specific parameter. Chapter Three mentions alternatives to this standard approach to estimation and testing. This chapter discusses some several alternatives in more detail: the profile likelihood method, robust standard errors, bootstrapping, and Bayesian methods.

To provide more insight into the details and show the effects of different estimation methods, two example data sets will be used throughout this chapter. The first is a small data set, containing 16 independent measurements of the estrone level in a single blood sample from five women (the data are described in the appendix). This data set is presented and discussed by Fears, Benichou and Gail (1996) to illustrate the fallibility of the Wald statistic (based on the parameter estimate divided by the estimated standard error) for testing variance components in certain situations. In this example data, the Wald test fails to detect a variance component for two reasons: first because the sample size is small (Fears et al., 1996), and second because the likelihood for the person-level variance is decidedly non-normal (Pawitan, 2000). In addition to this data set, which is known to be problematic, the pupil popularity data introduced in Chapter Two is used. This is a large data set (2000 pupils in 100 schools), which has been generated following the assumptions of the multilevel model using Maximum Likelihood. Given the generous sample size, this well-behaved data set should produce accurate estimates and standard errors for all estimation methods.

Since the problematic data set is balanced, standard analysis of variance methods (Stevens, 1996; Tabachnick & Fidell, 1996) produce exact results. One-way random effects analysis of variance can be used to assess whether the five women have significantly different average estrone levels. An analysis of variance on the estrone data yields the following results:

Table 11.1		Analysis of variance on estrone data, random effects model					
Source	df	SS	MS	var. comp.	F-ratio	p	
Individuals	4	1.133	0.2832	0.0175	87.0	<.0001	
Error	75	0.244	0.00325	0.0022			
Total	79	1.376					

The *F*-ratio is highly significant, providing strong evidence that estrone levels vary between individuals. Using the variance components as estimated by the analysis of variance method produces an intraclass correlation of ρ=0.84, which indicates that most of the variation in this data is between-person variation. Multilevel analysis using Maximum Likelihood estimation with the Restricted Maximum Likelihood (RML) method should lead to similar estimates. The multilevel approach estimates the variance components as s^2_{u0}=0.0176 on the person level and s^2_e=0.00323 on the measures (error) level. These estimates are close to the values obtained using analysis of variance, and the multilevel method produces an intraclass correlation of ρ=0.85. However, using the Wald test by dividing the variance estimate of 0.0176 by its estimated standard error of 0.0113 produces a standard normal variate Z=1.56, corresponding to a one-sided *p*-value of 0.059, which is not significant by conventional significance criteria. Clearly, the Wald test is not performing well with these data. The difference in the estimated variance components is trivial, so the problem is not the Maximum Likelihood estimation method, but the Wald test itself. The reason that the Wald test is performing badly in this example is simple. The Wald test depends on the assumption that the parameter tested has a normal sampling distribution, with a sampling variance that can be estimated from the information matrix. In the estrogen data, we are testing a variance component, with a very small sample, and close to its boundary value of zero.

Some simple alternatives discussed in Chapter Three work well for these data. For instance, Longford (1993) and Snijders and Bosker (1999) suggest basing the Wald test not on the variance, but on the standard deviation $s_{u_0} = \sqrt{s^2_{u_0}}$, with standard error equal to $s.e.\left(s_{u_0}\right) = s.e.\left(s^2_{u_0}\right)/\left(2s_{u_0}\right)$. The standard deviation is a square root transformation of the variance, and its distribution should be closer to normality. For our data, s_u is 0.133, with estimated standard error calculated as 0.0113/(2×0.133)=0.041. A Wald test on the standard deviation produces a test value Z=3.12, with *p*<0.001. So this test indeed performs better. However, in general, solving the problem by applying some transformation to the estimated variance is problematic. Fears, Benichou and Gail (1996) show that, since the Wald test depends on the parameterization of the model, by a judicious choice of a power transformation for s^2_{u0}, one can obtain any p-value between 0 and 1. This is awkward, and better methods than transforming the variance estimate are preferable.

If we use the chi-square test discussed in Chapter Three, and implemented in HLM, we find $\chi^2_{18} = 352.4$, with $p<0.001$. Similarly, if we use the deviance difference test discussed in Chapter Three, we find a deviance difference of 117.3 using RML, and 112.7 using FML. Since these are distributed as chi-square variates with one degree of freedom, they can be converted to standard normal Z-variates by taking their square roots. This produces a $Z=10.8$ using RML, and $Z=10.6$ using FML. Both Z values are highly significant. In effect, both the chi-square method and the test on the difference of the deviances work well on these data. However, these methods cannot be used if we wish to establish a confidence interval for the person-level variance. The next sections discuss some alternatives for the Wald test that allow the construction of a valid confidence interval for the variance components.

11.1 THE PROFILE LIKELIHOOD METHOD

For the estrone data, the (RML) estimate for the intercept is 1.418 (s.e.= 0.06). The estimate for the person-level variance σ^2_{u0} is 0.0176. The deviance for the model is calculated as -210.46[1]. If we restrict this variance component to zero, the deviance becomes -97.80. It has gone up by a considerable amount, and the difference of 112.66 can be tested against the chi-square distribution with one degree of freedom. Using the deviance test, the variance component is clearly significant. Since the Wald procedure is suspect for these data, a 95% confidence interval for the person-level variance based on the asymptotic standard error is also questionable. An alternative is a confidence interval that is based directly on the deviance test, similar to the procedures followed in the null-hypothesis test based on the deviance. Such a procedure exists, namely the *profile likelihood* method, and the resulting confidence interval is called a *profile likelihood* interval.

To construct a profile likelihood interval for the estrone data, we need a program that allows putting constraints on the fixed and random parameters in the model. First, we constrain the parameters to their estimated values. As a check, this should produce the same deviance as freely estimating them (within bounds of rounding error). Next, we constrain the value for the parameter that we wish to test to a different value. As a result, the deviance goes up. To reach significance, the increase in deviance must exceed the critical value in the chi-square distribution

---

[1] Using RML in MLwiN; using RML in HLM produces a slightly different estimate. The difference is that MLwiN 1.10 cannot calculate the RML deviance, so RML estimation is combined with values from the FML deviance.

with one degree of freedom. For a 95% confidence interval, this critical value is 3.8415. So, to establish a 95% confidence interval around the estimate s^2_{u0}=0.0176, we must find an upper limit $U(s^2_{u0})$ for which the deviance is –210.46+3.84=206.62, and a lower limit $L(s^2_{u0})$ for which the deviance is –210.46+3.84=206.62. These limits can be found by trial and error, or more efficiently by using a simple search method such as setting an interval that is on both sides of the limit we are looking for, and successively halving the interval until the limit is estimated with sufficient precision.

Using the profile likelihood method on the estrone data, we find a 95% confidence interval for σ^2_{u0}: 0.005<σ^2_{u0}<0.070. The profile likelihood confidence interval does not include zero, so the null hypothesis of no person-level variance is rejected. The profile likelihood interval is not symmetric around the estimated value of σ^2_{u0}=0.018. Of course, it is known that variance components follow a chi-square distribution, which is not symmetric, so a valid confidence interval should also be non-symmetric.

11.2 ROBUST STANDARD ERRORS

When the response variable does not have a normal distribution, the parameter estimates produced by the maximum likelihood method are still consistent and asymptotically unbiased, meaning that they tend to get closer to the true population values as the sample size becomes larger (Eliason, 1993). However, the asymptotic standard errors are incorrect, and they cannot be trusted to produce accurate significance tests or confidence intervals (Goldstein, 1995, p. 60). This problem does *not* vanish when the samples get larger.

Sometimes it is possible to obtain more nearly normal variables by transforming the outcome variable. If this is undesirable or even impossible, another method to obtain better tests and interval is to correct the asymptotic standard errors. One available correction method to produce robust standard errors is the so-called Huber/White or sandwich estimator (Huber, 1967; White, 1982). In maximum likelihood estimation, the usual estimator of the sampling variances and covariances is based on the Information matrix, or more general on the inverse of the so-called Hessian matrix (cf. Eliason, 1993). The standard errors used in the Wald test are simply the square root of the sampling variances that are found on the diagonal of this inverse. Thus, using matrix notation, the asymptotic variance-covariance matrix of the estimated regression coefficients can be written as:

$$\mathbf{V}_A\left(\hat{\beta}\right) = \mathbf{H}^{-1} \qquad\qquad (11.1)$$

where $\mathbf{V}_A$ is the asymptotic covariance matrix of the regression coefficients, and $\mathbf{H}$ is the Hessian matrix. The Huber/White estimator is given as

$$\mathbf{V}_R\left(\hat{\beta}\right) = \mathbf{H}^{-1}\mathbf{C}\mathbf{H}^{-1} \tag{11.2}$$

where $\mathbf{V}_R$ is the robust covariance matrix of the regression coefficients, and $\mathbf{C}$ is a correction matrix. In equation (11.2), the correction matrix is 'sandwiched' between the two $\mathbf{H}^{-1}$ terms, hence the name 'sandwich estimator' for the Huber/White standard errors. The correction term is based on the observed raw residuals. If the residuals follow a normal distribution, $\mathbf{V}_A$ and $\mathbf{V}_R$ are both consistent estimators of the covariances of the regression coefficients, but the model-based asymptotic covariance matrix $\mathbf{V}_A$ is more efficient because it leads to the smallest standard errors. However, when the residuals do not follow a normal distribution, the model-based asymptotic covariance matrix is not correct, while the observed residuals-based sandwich estimator $\mathbf{V}_R$ is still a consistent estimator of the covariances of the regression coefficients. This makes inference based on the robust standard errors less dependent on the assumption of normality, at the cost of sacrificing some statistical power. The precise form of the correction term is different in different models; for a technical discussion see Greene (1997). In the multilevel software MLwiN the correction is based on the cross-product matrix of the residuals, taking the multilevel structure of the data into account. MLwiN also contains robust sandwich estimators for the standard errors of the variance components (Goldstein, 1995, p. 60). The software aML (Lillard & Panis, 2000) also includes sandwich estimators. The robust standard errors are related to the Generalized Estimating Equations (GEE) estimation method described in Chapter Three, which uses the observed residuals to estimate the variance components in the model. In HLM, the robust standard errors automatically select GEE estimation.

When heteroscedasticity is involved due to non-normality, outliers, or misspecification of the model, the asymptotic standard errors are generally too small. Typically, the robust standard errors do not completely correct this, but they do result in more accurate significance tests and confidence intervals (Beck & Katz, 1997). So, when strong non-normality is suspected, it is prudent to use the sandwich standard errors. Since the robust standard errors are partly based on the observed residuals, they do need a reasonable level-two sample size to be accurate; single-level simulation results by Long and Ervin (1998) suggest a sample size of at least 100. In multilevel analysis, this would translate to a minimal second-level sample size of 100 for the robust standard errors to work well. Multilevel simulations with strongly non-normal two-level data (Hox & Maas, 2001a) confirm these recommendations.

Since the sandwich estimator needs a reasonable sample size to work well, the estrone data with $N=5$ are not a good example. We will use the pupil popularity data introduced in Chapter Two to illustrate the use of sandwich standard errors. The model that we use is a random component model. By omitting the significant variance for the slope of pupil gender we introduce a mis-specification in the model, which causes some heteroscedasticity in the second-level residuals. Figure 11.1 shows a plot of the second-level residuals u_0 against their ranks in this model. There is indeed some evidence of non-normality at the extremes.

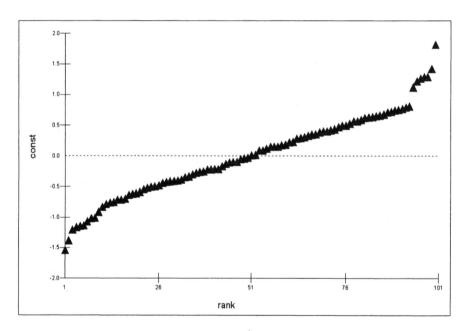

Figure 11.1. Popularity data: plot of 2nd level residuals against their rank

Table 11.1 presents the parameter estimates, standard errors, and 95% confidence intervals using both the asymptotic and the sandwich standard errors. The parameter estimates are the same, and most of the standard errors and confidence intervals are the same or very close. Only the robust standard error of the slope for pupil gender is clearly larger. Presumably, this reflects the misspecification caused by ignoring the random component for this slope.

Model:	Asymptotic standard errors (a.s.e.)		Robust standard errors (r.s.e.)	
Fixed part	coefficient a.s.e.	95% interval	coefficient r.s.e.	95% interval
intercept	3.56 0.17	3.23 / 3.89	3.56 0.16	3.24 / 3.88
pupil gender	0.85 0.03	0.78 / 0.91	0.85 0.06	0.73 / 0.96
teacher exp.	0.09 0.01	0.07 / 0.12	0.09 0.01	0.07 / 0.12
Random part				
σ^2_{u0}	0.48 0.07	0.34 / 0.62	0.48 0.06	0.35 / 0.60
σ^2_e	0.46 0.02	0.43 / 0.49	0.46 0.02	0.42 / 0.50

Table 11.1   Asymptotic and robust standard errors, popularity data

An approach related to the sandwich estimators is the *GEE* (generalized estimating equations) approach of Liang and Zeger (1986). GEE estimation is a quasi-likelihood approach that starts by estimating the variance components directly from the raw residuals, followed by GLS estimation for the regression coefficients. This results in estimates for the regression coefficients that are consistent, but less efficient than maximum likelihood estimates (cf. Goldstein, 1995, p. 22; for a discussion of the GEE and other approaches see Pendergast et al., 1996). If the second-level sample size is reasonable (N >100, cf. Long & Ervin, 1998, and Hox & Maas, 2001a), the GEE estimates for the standard errors are not very sensitive to misspecification of the variance component structure. The software HLM uses GEE to estimate robust standard errors for the regression coefficients. Raudenbush et al. (2000, p. 9) suggest that comparing the asymptotic standard errors calculated by the maximum likelihood method to the robust standard errors is a way to appraise the possible effect of model misspecification and non-normality. Used in this way, robust standard errors become an indicator for possible misspecification of the model or its assumptions. If the robust standard errors are much different from the asymptotic standard errors, this should be interpreted as a warning sign that some distributional assumption is violated, and an advice to look into the problem.

11.3 BOOTSTRAPPING ESTIMATES AND STANDARD ERRORS

In its simplest form, the *bootstrap* (Efron, 1982; Efron & Tibshirani, 1993) is a method to estimate the parameters of a model and their standard errors strictly from the sample, without reference to a theoretical sampling distribution. The bootstrap directly follows the logic of statistical inference. Statistical inference assumes that in repeated sampling, the statistics calculated in the sample will vary across samples. This sampling variation is modeled by a theoretical sampling distribution, for instance a normal distribution, and estimates of the expected value and the variability are taken from this distribution. In bootstrapping, we draw b times a sample (with replacement) from the observed sample at hand. In each sample, we calculate the statistic(s) of interest, and the observed distribution of the b statistics is used for the sampling distribution. Thus, estimates of the expected value and the variability of the statistics are taken from this empirical sampling distribution (Stine, 1989; Mooney & Duvall, 1993; Yung & Chan, 1999).

Since bootstrapping takes the observed data as the sole information about the population, it needs a reasonable original sample size. Good (1999, p. 107) suggests a minimum sample size of 50 when the underlying distribution is not symmetric. Yung and Chan (1999) review the evidence on the use of bootstrapping with small samples. They conclude that it is not possible to give a simple recommendation for the minimal sample size for the bootstrap method. However, in general the bootstrap appears to compare favorably over asymptotic methods. A large simulation study involving complex structural equation models (Nevitt & Hancock, 2001) suggests that, for accurate results despite large violations of normality assumptions, the bootstrap needs an observed sample of more than 150. Given such results, the bootstrap is probably not the best approach when the problem is a small sample size. When the problem is violations of assumptions, or establishing bias-corrected estimates and valid confidence intervals for variance components, the bootstrap appears to be a viable alternative to asymptotic estimation methods.

The number of bootstrap iterations b is typically large, with b between 1000 and 2000 (Booth & Sarkar, 1998; Carpenter & Bithell, 2000). If the interest is in establishing a very accurate confidence interval, we need an accurate estimate of percentiles close to 0 or 100, which requires an even larger number of iterations, such as $b > 5000$.[1]

The bootstrap is not without its own assumptions. A key assumption of the bootstrap is that the *resampling* properties of the statistic resemble its *sampling* properties (Stine, 1989). Bootstrapping does not work well for statistics that depend on a very "narrow feature of the original sampling process" (Stine, 1989, p. 286), such as the maximum value. Another key assumption is that the resampling scheme used in the bootstrap must reflect the actual sampling mechanism used to collect the data (Carpenter & Bithell, 2000). This assumption is of course very important in multilevel modeling, because in multilevel problems we have a hierarchical

---

[1] Typically, when bootstrapping is used to establish a confidence interval, b would be chosen as 999, 4999, 9999 or some such number, to avoid the need for interpolation in establishing the usual 95% or 99% confidence intervals.

sampling mechanism, which must be simulated correctly in the bootstrapping procedure.

11.3.1 A simple example of bootstrapping

To demonstrate the basic principles of the bootstrap, it is convenient to use a small example, omitting the complications of multilevel data for the moment. Table 11.2 presents test scores of twelve students on an algebra test and statistics test (Good, 1999, p. 89).

Table 11.2	Algebra and statistics scores of 12 students										
Algebra	80	71	67	72	58	65	63	65	68	60	60	59
Statistics	81	81	81	73	70	68	68	63	56	54	45	44

In this small data set, the correlation between algebra and statistics is r=0.677. The two-sided p-value provided by the usual t-test, which is exact in small samples, gives a p-value of 0.016. We conclude that knowing algebra apparently helps in getting a good grade in statistics. If we want to calculate a 95% confidence interval for the correlation, we face two problems. Firstly, it is known that the sampling distribution of correlations is not normal. Large correlations (such as 0.677) have a markedly skewed distribution (Hedges & Olkin, 1985, p225). The usual solution for this problem is to use a Fisher-Z transformation (cf. Hays, 1994)[1]. Secondly, the standard error for the Fisher-Z, which is given by $1/\sqrt{N-3}$, is a large sample estimate. For our N=12, the standard error is estimated as 0.333. If we apply the Fisher-Z transformation, establish the 95% confidence interval for Z, and transform back to correlations, we find a 95% confidence interval for the correlation r which runs from 0.151 to 0.897. The p-value based on the asymptotic method is p =0.042. However, N=12 is not a large sample, and the application of the large-sample standard error is questionable.

In a bootstrap approach, we resample the data set k=1000 times, each time computing the correlation between algebra and statistics (using Amos, cf. Arbuckle & Wothke, 1999). This produces 1000 correlations, with a mean of 0.668, and a standard deviation of 0.158. Establishing a confidence interval using the 1000 bootstrapped correlations is possible by means of two different techniques. One

---

[1] Fisher's Z is $Z = 0.5 \ln\left((1+r)(1-r)\right)$, and the inverse transformation is $r = \left(e^{2Z} - 1\right)/\left(e^{2Z} + 1\right)$.

approach is to take the mean value of the 1000 correlations as the point estimate, followed by establishing lower and upper limits for the 95% confidence interval using a normal approximation, with the standard deviation of the bootstrapped correlations as an estimate of the standard error (Mooney & Duval, 1993). When the statistic being bootstrapped is unbiased and follows an unbounded symmetric distribution, this method produces a valid confidence interval (Carpenter & Bithell, 2000; Stine, 1989). The other approach, which is much closer to the non-parametric spirit of the bootstrap method, is to use the 2.5[th] and 97.5[th] percentile of the observed bootstrap distribution as limits of the 95% confidence interval (Stine, 1989; Mooney & Duval, 1993). Since this needs a precise estimate of the 2.5[th] and 97.5[th] percentile, we should use a large number of bootstrap samples here, such as 4999. In our small example, the normal approximation produces a 95% confidence interval from 0.496 to 1.115. The normal approximation does not recognize boundaries such as 1.0 to the correlation; as a result, it produces an impossible value for the upper limit.[1] Since the sampling distribution of the correlation is skewed, the normal approximation is not a good choice. The 95% confidence interval using the percentile method runs from 0.295 to 0.906, with a p-value of 0.009.

The application of the bootstrap method to obtain standard errors for parameter estimates and establishing confidence intervals is straightforward. If we could sample, say, 1000 real samples from our population, we could calculate the sampling variance directly. Since this is not possible, we use the computer to *resample* 1000 samples from our sample data. This simulates the actual sampling, which is in practice not possible, and provides a simulated estimate of the sampling variance. In addition to providing parameter estimates and sampling variances, there are some less obvious refinements to the bootstrap method. For instance, it is possible to use the bootstrap method to correct the asymptotic parameter estimates. The mean of the bootstrapped parameters is not necessarily equal to the estimate in the original sample. On the contrary, it can be rather different. If that is the case, the assumption is that the statistic under consideration is biased. Whatever mechanism is operating to produce bias in the bootstrap samples is assumed to be operating in the original sample as well. To correct for this bias, we use the difference between the original estimate and the mean bootstrap estimate as an estimate of the amount of bias in the original estimate. In our example, the correlation in the original sample is 0.677, and the bootstrap mean is 0.668. Thus, the original correlation has a negative bias that is estimated as –0.009. Using this bias estimate, the original correlation is corrected to 0.677+0.009=0.686. Although this is a minute correction, the ordinary correlation coefficient has indeed a small negative bias in small samples (cf. Hedges

---

[1] Bootstrapping Fisher-Z transformed correlations would solve this problem, but the Amos program used for the bootstrap does not have this option.

& Olkin, 1985, p. 225). With our very small sample, the bias becomes noticeable, and the bootstrap procedure can be used to correct for it. Using a more complicated procedure (for details see Stine, 1989, and Mooney & Duval, 1993) the limits of the confidence interval can also be corrected for this bias. The 95% confidence interval using the bias-corrected percentile method runs from 0.234 to 0.892, with a *p*-value of 0.015. The bias-corrected or *BC p*-value is very close to the exact *p*-value of 0.016 given by the small-sample *t*-test.

11.3.2 Bootstrapping multilevel regression models

In bootstrapping regression models, we have two basic choices (Stine, 1989; Mooney & Duvall, 1993). First, we can resample complete cases, as in the previous example. This runs against the notion that in regression analysis the explanatory variables are viewed as fixed constants. This means that in any replication of the study, we expect that the predictor variables have *exactly* the same values and only the residual error and hence the outcome variable will be different. To simulate this situation, we should resample not entire cases, but only the residuals. To bootstrap residuals, we first perform a multiple regression analysis and estimate the regression coefficients and the residuals. Next, in each bootstrap iteration, the fixed values and regression coefficients are used to produce predicted outcomes, and to the predicted outcomes, a bootstrapped set of residuals is randomly added. These bootstrapped responses are then used to estimate the regression coefficients and other parameters of the model.

The choice between bootstrapping cases or residuals depends on the actual design and sampling process. Resampling residuals follows the statistical regression model more accurately. The statistical model behind multiple regression assumes that the predictor variables that are fixed by design, and that, if we replicate the study, the explanatory variables have exactly the same values. This can be appropriate if the study is an experiment, with the values of the explanatory variables fixed by the experimental design. However, in much social and behavioral science, the values of the explanatory variables are as much sampled as the responses. In a replication, we do not expect that the explanatory variables have exactly the same values. In this case, resampling cases would be justifiable.

In multilevel regression, bootstrapping cases is more complicated than in ordinary regression models, because it implies bootstrapping units at all available levels. This not only changes the values of the explanatory and outcome variables, but also the way the variance is partitioned over the different levels. This redistribution of the variance affects all the other estimates. Currently, none of the major software packages supports multilevel casewise bootstrapping. The program MLwiN supports bootstrapping residuals, in two different varieties. The first variety is the nonparametric bootstrap. In the nonparametric bootstrap, the multilevel regression estimation is carried out once on the total data set. The regression coefficients from this estimation are used to produce predicted values, and the residuals from this analysis are resampled in the bootstrap iterations.[1] This approach is called the nonparametric bootstrap because it preserves the possibly non-normal distribution of the residuals. The second approach, the parametric bootstrap, is to simulate the residuals using a multivariate normal distribution. In this approach, the residuals by definition always have a nice normal distribution.

If the observed residuals actually have a normal distribution, the parametric and non-parametric bootstrap are equivalent. In this case, both bootstrap methods can be used to obtain valid estimates of the sampling error in small samples, where the asymptotic standard errors may not be applicable. If the residuals do not have a normal distribution, the non-parametric bootstrap reproduces this irregularity in the bootstrap samples. In theory, this should produce valid standard errors and confidence intervals under these circumstances.

MLwiN contains the bootstrap-based bias correction described earlier, for both the non-parametric and the parametric bootstrap method. The bias correction can be repeated several times, by bootstrapping repeatedly using the corrected parameter estimates. This is called the iterated bootstrap; the complete bootstrap procedure is repeated several times, each time with new model parameters that include the bias corrections suggested by the earlier bootstraps.

Bootstrapping takes the observed data as the sole information about the population, and therefore it is best used with a reasonable level-two sample size. When we estimate variance components, a minimum of 50 second-level units is recommended for bootstrapping. If the interest is mainly in the fixed effects, which usually have a well-behaving symmetric distribution, we might get away with as few as 10 to 12 units (cf. Good, 1999, p. 109).

11.3.3 An example of the bootstrap

Since the bootstrap needs a reasonable sample size to work well, the estrone data with $N=5$ are not a good example. We will again use the pupil popularity data introduced in Chapter Two to illustrate bootstrapping. The model is a random component model. By omitting the significant variance for the slope of pupil gender,

---

[1] Since the observed residuals are themselves a sample, their variance is not exactly equal to the variance estimated by the maximum likelihood procedure. Therefore, before the residuals are resampled, MLwiN transforms them to make them conform exactly to the estimated variances and covariances at all levels, cf. Rasbash et al., 2000. Since a model is still needed to estimate the residuals, Carpenter and Bithell (2000) reserve the name 'nonparametric bootstrap' for the cases bootstrap, and call the residuals bootstrap 'semi-parametric'.

we misspecify the model, and as a result introduce some heteroscedasticity in the second-level residuals. The same model is used in section 11.2 for the robust standard errors.

Using MLwiN, there are several choices in the bootstrapping menu, such as setting the number of iterations for the bootstrap, or the number of iterated bootstraps. One choice is vital: allowing the program to estimate negative variance components. Many programs, including MLwiN, by default set negative variance estimates to zero, because negative variances are impossible. However, setting an offending variance estimate to zero may produce a better estimate, but it will also produce bias. To use bootstrapped estimates to estimate a parameter or establish a confidence interval, we need unbiased estimates in the bootstrap samples.

Table 11.3 presents the results of a parametric bootstrap using three iterated bootstrap runs of b=1000 iterations each. The 95% confidence interval for the bootstrap can be obtained in two different ways: by applying the usual procedure taking the bias-corrected estimate ± 1.96 times the bootstrapped standard error, or by taking the 2.5[th] and 97.5[th] percentile of the bootstrap distribution of the last of the three bootstraps. Especially when bootstrapping parameter estimates that do not have a normal sampling distribution, such as variances, using the percentile method is superior. For the purpose of comparison, Table 11.3 shows both bootstrap intervals: the normal and the percentile method.

Table 11.3	Asymptotic and bootstrapped results, parametric bootstrap					
Model:	Asymptotic results			Bootstrap results		
Fixed part	coeff.	a.s.e.	95% a.s.e. interval	coeff . b.s.e.		95% normal interval	95% perc. interval
intercept	3.56	0.17	3.23 / 3.89	3.56	0.17	3.23 / 3.90	3.22 / 3.89
pupil gender	0.85	0.03	0.78 / 0.91	0.85	0.03	0.78 / 0.91	0.78 / 0.91
teach. exp.	0.09	0.01	0.07 / 0.12	0.09	0.01	0.07 / 0.12	0.07 / 0.12
Random part							
σ^2_{u0}	0.48	.07	0.34 / 0.62	0.49	0.07	0.34 / 0.63	0.33 / 0.62
σ^2_e	0.46	.02	0.43 / 0.49	0.46	0.02	0.43 / 0.49	0.43 / 0.49

The bootstrap results in Table 11.3 are virtually identical to the asymptotic estimates. Since we have on purpose omitted a significant variance component for pupil gender, the second level residuals do not have a normal distribution. Therefore, simulating residuals from a normal distribution, as is done in the parametric bootstrap, is not optimal. The non-parametric bootstrap uses the non-normal residuals in the bootstrap samples, and for that reason produce estimates that are more valid. Table 11.4 shows the results of three iterated non-parametric bootstrap runs of 1000 iterations each.

Table 11.4	**Asymptotic and bootstrapped results, non-parametric bootstrap**						
Model:	Asymptotic results			Bootstrap results			
Fixed part	coeff.	a.s.e.	95% a.s.e. interval	coeff . b.s.e.		95% normal interval	95% perc. interval
intercept	3.56	0.17	3.23 / 3.89	3.57	0.17	3.23 / 3.90	3.22 / 3.89
pupil gender	0.85	0.03	0.78 / 0.91	0.85	0.03	0.78 / 0.91	0.78 / 0.91
teach. exp.	0.09	0.01	0.07 / 0.12	0.09	0.01	0.07 / 0.12	0.07 / 0.12
Random part							
σ^2_{u0}	0.48	0.07	0.34 / 0.62	0.50	0.07	0.35 / 0.64	0.35 / 0.63
σ^2_e	0.46	0.02	0.43 / 0.49	0.46	0.02	0.43 / 0.49	0.43 / 0.49

The bootstrapped results are very close to the asymptotic estimates, demonstrating that these data are closely following the assumptions for the asymptotic estimates. The bias-corrected estimates are close to the asymptotic estimates, indicating that there is no important bias in the asymptotic estimates. If there is a distinct difference between the asymptotic and the bias-corrected parameter estimates, the estimates of the successive iterated bootstraps should be monitored, to check that the series of iterated bootstraps has converged with sufficient accuracy. By way of example, Figure 11.2 shows the trend for the asymptotic and the bias-corrected estimate for the school-level variance component σ^2_{u0} in a series of three iterated bootstraps.

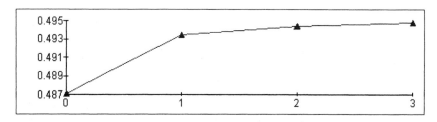

Figure 11.2. Bias-corrected estimate for σ_u^2 after three iterated bootstraps

There is a very small bias-correction visible in the first bootstrap iteration, and the second and third bootstraps do not change the estimate much. Therefore, we conclude that the iterated bootstrap has converged. The difference between the asymptotic estimate of 0.487 and the final bias-corrected estimate of 0.495 is of course trivial. It is as an indication of a real, but very small and therefore in practice negligible negative bias in the second level variance estimate.

11.4 BAYESIAN ESTIMATION METHODS

Statistics is about uncertainty. We estimate unknown population parameters by statistics, calculated in a sample. In classical statistical inference, we express our uncertainty about how well an observed statistic estimates the unknown population parameter by examining its sampling distribution over an infinite number of possible samples. Since we generally have only one sample, the sampling distribution is based on a mathematical sampling model. An alternative basis is bootstrapping, discussed in the previous section, which simulates the sampling process. The sampling variance, or rather its square root, the standard error, is used for significance testing and establishing confidence intervals.

In Bayesian statistics, we express the uncertainty about the population value of a model parameter by assigning to it a probability distribution of possible values. This probability distribution is called the *prior* distribution, because it is specified independently from the data. The Bayesian approach is fundamentally different from classical statistics (Barnett, 1999). In classical statistics, the population parameter has only one specific value, only we happen to not know it. In Bayesian statistics, we consider a probability distribution of possible values for the unknown population parameter. After we have collected our data, the prior distribution is combined with the Likelihood of the data to produce a *posterior* distribution, which describes our uncertainty about the population values after observing our data. Typically, the variance of the posterior distribution is smaller than the variance of the prior distribution, which means that observing the data has reduced our uncertainty about the possible population values.

In Bayesian statistics, each unknown parameter in the model must have an associated probability distribution. For the prior distribution, we have a fundamental choice between using an informative prior or an uninformative prior. An informative prior is a peaked distribution with a small variance, which expresses a strong belief about the unknown population parameter. An informative prior will, off course, strongly influence the posterior distribution, and hence our conclusions. For this reason, many statisticians prefer an uninformative or diffuse prior, which has very little influence, and only serves to produce the posterior. An example of an uninformative prior is the uniform distribution, which simply states that the unknown parameter value is between minus and plus infinity, with all values equally likely. Another example of an uninformative prior is a very flat normal distribution. Sometimes such a prior is called an ignorance prior, to indicate that we know nothing about the unknown parameter. However, this is not accurate, since total ignorance does not exist, at least not in Bayesian statistics. All priors add some information to the data, but diffuse priors add little information, and therefore do not have much influence on the posterior. One way to express the information added to the data is to view the prior as a certain number of hypothetical cases, which are added to the data set. Typically, an ignorance prior corresponds to less than ten of such hypothetical cases, which will have little influence unless the observed sample is very small.

If the posterior distribution has a mathematically simple form, such as a normal distribution, we can use the known characteristics of this distribution to calculate a point estimate and a confidence interval for the population parameter. In the case of a normal distribution, we could choose the mean as the point estimate, and base a confidence interval on the standard deviation of the posterior distribution. However, when Bayesian methods are applied to complex multivariate models, the posterior is generally a multivariate distribution with a complicated shape, which makes it difficult to use mathematical means to establish confidence intervals. When the posterior distribution is difficult to describe mathematically, it may be approximated using Markov Chain Monte Carlo simulation procedures. Markov Chain Monte Carlo (MCMC) procedures are simulation techniques that generate random samples from a complex posterior distribution. By producing a large number of random draws from the posterior distribution, we can closely approximate its true shape. The simulated posterior distribution is then used to compute a point estimate and a confidence interval (for an accessible introduction to Bayesian MCMC methods see Casella & George, 1992, and Smith & Gelfland, 1992). Typically, the marginal (univariate) distribution of each parameter is used. The mode of the marginal posterior distribution is an attractive point estimate of the unknown parameter, because it is the most likely value, and therefore the Bayesian equivalent of the maximum likelihood estimator. Since the mode is more difficult to determine than the mean, the mean of the posterior distribution is also often used. In skewed posterior distributions, the median is an attractive choice. The confidence interval generally uses the $100\text{-}\frac{1}{2}\alpha$ limits around the point estimate. In the Bayesian terminology, this is referred to as the $100\text{-}\alpha$ *central credibility interval*.

Bayesian methods have some advantages over classical methods. To begin, in contrast to the asymptotic maximum likelihood method, they are valid in small samples. Given the correct probability distribution, the estimates are always proper, which solves the problem of negative variance estimates. Finally, since the random draws are taken from the correct distribution, there is no assumption of normality when variances are estimated.

If we compare MCMC estimates for the popularity example data with the asymptotic FML estimates, the differences are small. Since the sample sizes for the example data are 2000 pupils within 100 classes, we may expect that the asymptotic estimates are close. The largest difference is an MCMC estimate of 0.49 for the level-2 intercept variance, compared to a value of 0.46 for the FML estimate. In such cases, the differences between asymptotic and MCMC estimates are small and inconsistent; sometimes asymptotic estimates are better, sometimes MCMC estimates are better (Browne, 1998). With small numbers of groups and especially with nonlinear models MCMC estimates tend to perform better than maximum likelihood using either FML or RML (Browne, 1998). However, Bayesian methods are computationally demanding, and the MCMC simulation procedure must be monitored to insure that it is working properly.

11.4.1 Simulating the posterior distribution

Different simulation methods are used to generate draws from the posterior distribution. Most methods use Markov Chain Monte Carlo (MCMC) sampling. Given a set of initial values from a specific multivariate distribution, MCMC procedures generate a new pseudorandom draw from the same distribution. Suppose that $Z^{(1)}$ is a draw from a target distribution $f(Z)$. Using MCMC methods, we generate a series of new draws: $Z^{(1)} \rightarrow Z^{(2)} \rightarrow \ldots \rightarrow Z^{(t)}$. MCMC methods are attractive because, even if $Z^{(1)}$ is not from the target distribution $f(Z)$, if t is sufficiently large, in the end $Z^{(t)}$ is a draw from the target distribution $f(Z)$. Having good initial values for $Z^{(1)}$ helps, because it speeds up the convergence on the target distribution, so the classical maximum likelihood estimates are often used as initial values for $Z^{(1)}$.

The number of iterations t needed before the target distribution is reached is referred to as the 'burn in' period of the MCMC algorithm. It is important that the burn in is complete. To check if enough iterations of the algorithm have passed to converge on the target distribution, several diagnostics are used. A useful diagnostic is a graph of the successive values produced by the algorithm. A different procedure is to start the MCMC procedure several times with widely different initial values. If essentially identical distributions are obtained after t iterations, we decide that t is large enough to converge on the target distribution (Gelman & Rubin, 1992).

An additional issue in MCMC methods is that successive draws are dependent. Depending on the distribution and the amount of information in the data, they can be strongly correlated. Logically, we would prefer independent draws to use as simulated draws from the posterior distribution. One way to reach independence is to throw away a number of successive estimates before a new draw is used for estimation. This process is called *thinning*. To decide how many iterations must be thrown away between two successive draws, it is useful to inspect the autocorrelations between successive draws. If the autocorrelations are high, we must throw away many estimates. Alternatively, since each draw still gives some information, we may keep all draws, but use a very large number of draws. Typically, the number of MCMC iterations is much higher than the number of bootstrap samples. Using 10000 or more MCMC iterations is common.

11.4.2 An example of Bayesian estimation using MLwiN: The estrone data

User-friendly software for MCMC estimation is still rare, most Bayesian modeling is executed using special software (see Zeger & Karim, 1991, and Kasim & Raudenbush, 1998, for multilevel applications of MCMC estimation). A very general but difficult program is *BUGS*, an acronym for Bayesian inference Using Gibbs Sampling (Spiegelhalter, 1994). At the time of writing, the only multilevel software that includes Bayesian methods is MLwiN. It is instructive to use the MCMC method in MLwiN to analyze the estrone data. The issues of determining the number of MCMC iterations, monitoring the convergence of the MCMC algorithm using plots and special statistics, and settling on estimates and confidence intervals are not dependent on the specific software used. Since the data set is very small (16 multiple measures on five women), asymptotic Maximum Likelihood does not work well for these data, and Bayesian methods may do better.

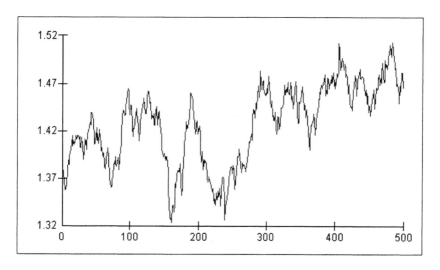

Figure 11.3. Plot of first 500 estimates of the intercept β_0, estrone data

By default, MLwiN uses non-informative priors. To start, we use a burn-in period of 500 iterations, and then monitor the next 5000 iterations. MLwiN produces a variety of plots and statistics to judge whether these quantities are sufficient. Figure 11.3 shows a plot of the first 500 MCMC estimates for the intercept β_0. It is clear from this figure that the series of estimates shows an upward trend, and that this trend has not yet flattened out after 500 initial iterations. This suggests that we need more than 500 initial iterations for the burn-in.

MLwiN also produces an *autocorrelation plot*, called the autocorrelation function or ACF in the output. This plot shows the correlation between two MCMC draws that are separated by 1, 2, 3, et cetera MCMC iterations. Figure 11.4 presents the autocorrelation plot for β_0.

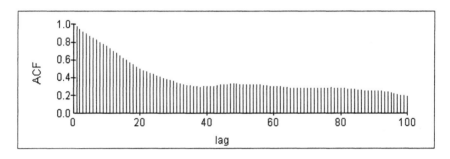

Figure 11.4. Autocorrelations for first 500 estimates of the intercept β_0, estrone data

Figure 11.4 shows strong autocorrelations between successive draws. When draws are more than 40 iterations apart, the autocorrelation is lower, but still considerable. Even after 100 iterations, the autocorrelation is still not close to zero. When we inspect the autocorrelation plots for the variance estimates σ^2_e and σ^2_{u0}, we observe similar problems, but not as severe as the problems in generating estimates for the intercept.

Based on the plots in Figure 11.3 and 11.4, we decide to try a burn-in period of 5000. Figure 11.5 shows the first 5000 estimates for the intercept. The plot of these 5000 estimates suggests that the series of estimates converges on the correct distribution after about 2000 iterations. Of course, the autocorrelations are still high. To obtain usable estimates, a burn-in of 5000 seems sufficient. To deal with the high autocorrelations, we call for 500000 MCMC iterations after the burn-in, and use a *thinning factor* of 100. That is, to reduce memory demands the program stores each 100th set of MCMC estimates, and discards the other estimates. This will give us 5000 MCMC estimates, which are each 100 MCMC iterations apart, which reduces the autocorrelations considerably.

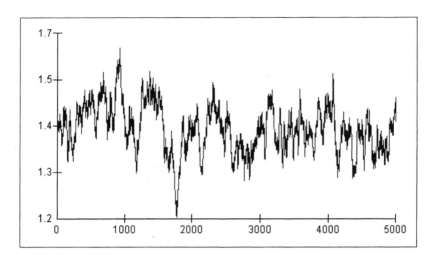

Figure 11.5. Plot of first 5000 estimates of the intercept β_0, estrone data

Figure 11.6 shows the last 500 estimates for the intercept. Note that these are the estimates taken at each 100th iteration. The plot looks horizontal and stable, but it still shows evidence of a considerable autocorrelation.

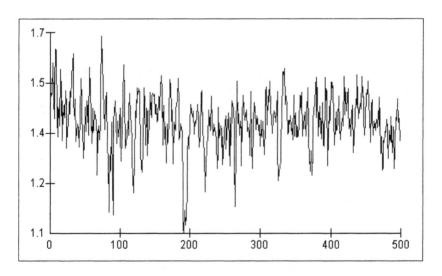

Figure 11.6. Plot of last 500 estimates of the intercept β_0, estrone data

Figure 11.7 shows some other diagnostic plots offered by MLwiN. The plot of the total chain of 5000 estimates looks quite stable, and the distribution of the generated values is nearly normal. There is still considerable autocorrelation. The last plot indicates how many MCMC iterations are needed to achieve a Monte Carlo Standard Error of a specific accuracy. MLwiN also produces a statistic, the Raftery-Lewis (Raftery & Lewis, 1992) statistic, which is an estimate of the number of MCMC iterations needed to be 95% confident that the 2.5[th] and 97.5[th] percentile are estimated with an error smaller than 0.005. Typically, the Raftery-Lewis statistics suggest a very large number of iterations to achieve this level of accuracy. For our example data, the Raftery-Lewis statistic indicates that we need to carry out about 1,000,000 MCMC iterations. This is an enormous number, especially since we are already using a thinning factor of 100. Given the normal distribution of the estimates, we can use the mode of 1.42 as a point estimate. The standard deviation of the MCMC estimates is 0.083, which we can use as a standard error in the usual way. This produces a Bayesian 95% confidence interval of 1.26-1.58. The Bayesian central 95% confidence interval determined from the 2.5[th] and 97.5[th] percentile of the 5000 observed estimates is 1.24-1.58, which is very close. The Maximum Likelihood point estimate is 1.42, with a standard error of 0.06, and a 95% confidence interval of 1.30-1.54. Since Maximum Likelihood is applied here in a very small sample, the MCMC confidence intervals are likely to be better.

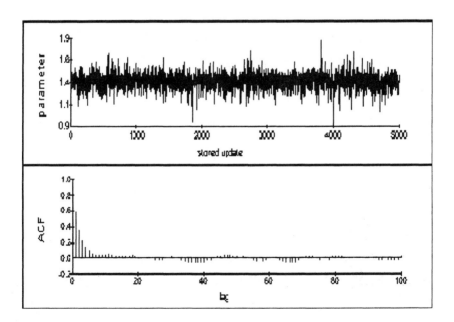

Figure 11.7. Diagnostic plots for 5000 estimates of the intercept β_0, estrone data

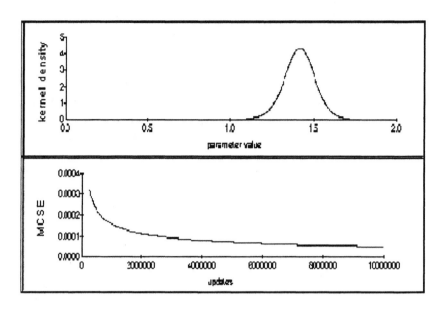

Figure 11.7., continued. Diagnostic plots for 5000 estimates of the intercept β_0, estrone data

In this example, we are mostly interested in the between-person variance estimate σ^2_{u0}. Figure 11.8 presents the plot of the last 500 estimates for σ^2_{u0}.

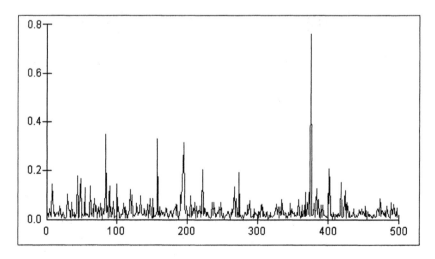

Figure 11.8 Plot of last 500 estimates of the variance σ^2_{u0}, estrone data

The plot of the variance appears stable, with a few spikes that indicate an occasional large estimate. Given the small sample of persons, this is normal.

Figure 11.9 presents the same diagnostic plots for all 5000 stored MCMC estimates for the estrone data. The diagnostic plots for the variance in Figure 11.9 highlight an important feature of the Bayesian estimation method used in MCMC: it always produces proper estimates. Thus, it will never produce a negative variance estimate. When we generate values for a variance that is actually zero, unbiased estimates should either be all equal to zero, or vary around this zero-value, with approximately half of the estimates being positive and the other half negative.

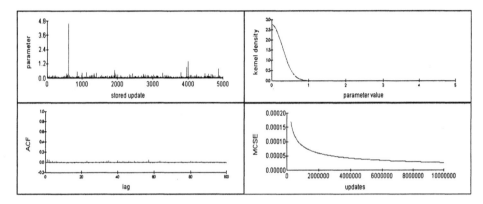

Figure 11.9. Diagnostic plots for 5000 estimates of the variance σ^2_0, estrone data

Since MCMC methods will never produce negative variance estimates, they have a positive bias. As a result, *no* central credibility interval will *ever* include the value zero. For instance, in the estrone example, the central 95% interval for the variance estimates is 0.01-0.14. If the variance term σ^2_{u0} indeed belongs in the model, the 0.01-0.14 interval is a reasonable 95% confidence interval, although the Raftery-Lewis statistic again indicates that we should use many more MCMC iterations for accuracy. However, since the value for the variance term is very small, we may well conclude that the between-person variance term is not significant, and can be omitted from the model. The fact that the value zero is outside the central 95% interval is no evidence that the variance term is significant, because when variances are estimated, the value zero will *always* lie outside the central 95% interval. To carry out a Bayesian significance test, to determine if σ^2_{u0} belongs in the model at all, we need different methods, which are not implemented in MLwiN. For an example of Bayesian *p*-values see Hoijtink (2000).

11.4.3 An example of Bayesian estimation using MLwiN: The popularity data

The estrone example illustrates that Bayesian methods do not solve all problems. Clearly, the MCMC method does not deal well with the estrone data set. The number of MCMC iterations that are required are very large, and the autocorrelations are high, especially in estimating the mean. This indicates that the data contain very little information about the parameter estimates, which is not surprising given the small sample size.

To illustrate Bayesian MCMC methods on a less extreme data set, they are also applied to the popularity data set, which consists of 2000 pupils in 100 schools. As in the section on bootstrapping, the model is a variance component model, on purpose omitting the significant variance term for pupil gender and the cross-level interaction. Using 500 iterations for the burn-in and a chain of 5000 for the estimates, MLwiN produces the following plots.

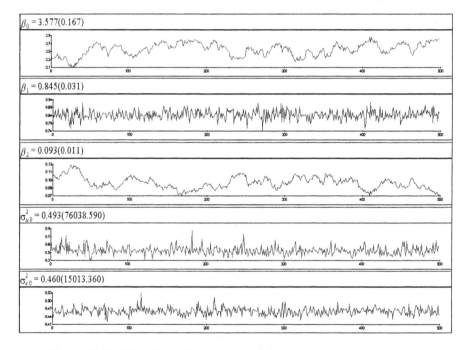

Figure 11.10. Plot of last 500 estimates of all parameters, popularity data

Figure 11.10 shows the plots of the last 500 estimates. All plots look well-behaved, meaning that no marked overall trend is visible, and the generating process appears stable. Both the intercept and the regression coefficient of teacher experience show rather strong autocorrelations (estimates close to each other are similar), and the plot of the intercept chain suggests a possible upward trend. All other plots look fine: chaotic, without obvious patterns or trends.

To examine the autocorrelation, we inspect the diagnostics for the slope of teacher experience. Figure 11.11 looks acceptable, but there is indeed a large autocorrelation.

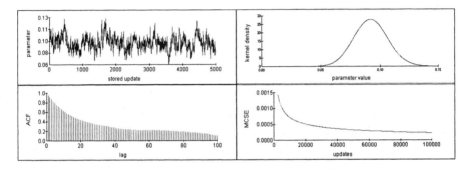

Figure 11.1.1 Diagnostic plots for 5000 estimates of the teacher experience slope

In addition to the plots, the convergence of the MCMC chain can also be studied by starting it with different initial values, and inspecting if and after how many MCMC iterations the different chains converge on the same distribution. For instance, we replace the customary Maximum Likelihood starting values by different values such as: intercept is 5 (FIML: 3.56); slope pupil gender is 0.5 (FIML: 0.85), slope teacher experience is 0.1 (FIML: 0.09), variance school level is 0.2 (FIML: 0.48), and pupil level is 0.8 (FIML: 0.46). These initial values are reasonable, but deviate noticeably from the Maximum Likelihood estimates. If we monitor the burn-in process that starts with these initial estimates, we find the plots given in Figure 11.12.

Figure 11.12 nicely illustrates what happens if we start the MCMC algorithm with poor starting values. It prolongs the burn-in period. In this case, it is clear that after about 200-400 iterations, the successive MCMC estimates have stabilized. Only the intercept term β_0 might need a longer burn-in.

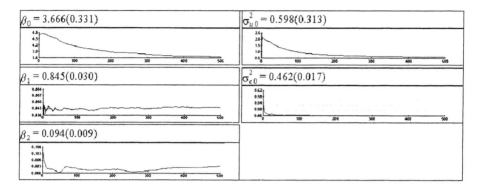

Figure 11.12 Plot of first 500 estimates, deviant initial values

For the final MCMC analysis, the analysis is repeated, with the burn-in set at 5000, and a MCMC chain of 50000 iterations, with a thinning factor of 10. In this analysis, all diagnostics look fine. Table 11.5 presents the results, with the asymptotic estimates. For the Bayesian results, the posterior mode is used as the point-estimate, because with normal data this is equivalent to the maximum likelihood estimate. The Bayesian central 95% credibility interval is based on the 2.5th and 97.5th percentile points of the posterior distribution.

Table 11.5	**Comparison of asymptotic and Bayesian results, popularity data**				
Model:	Asymptotic standard errors (a.s.e.)			MCMC estimates	
Fixed part	coefficient a.s.e.		95% interval	coefficient mode s.d.	95% central interval
intercept	3.56	0.17	3.23 / 3.89	3.57 0.18	3.22 / 3.90
pupil gender	0.85	0.03	0.78 / 0.91	0.84 0.03	0.78 / 0.91
teacher exp.	0.09	0.01	0.07 / 0.12	0.09 0.01	0.07 / 0.12
Random part					
σ^2_{u0}	0.48	0.07	0.34 / 0.62	0.49 0.06	0.37 / 0.67
σ^2_e	0.46	0.02	0.43 / 0.49	0.46 0.02	0.43 / 0.49

The Bayesian estimates in Table 11.5 are very close to the Maximum Likelihood estimates. Only the 95% central confidence interval for the school-level variance is somewhat different. Just as in the bootstrap example, the observed interval is not symmetric around the model estimate, which reflects the non-normal distribution of the variance parameter.

11.4.4 Some remarks on Bayesian estimation methods

The estrone example illustrates that Bayesian methods do not solve all problems. Clearly, the MCMC method does not deal very well with this data set. The number of MCMC iterations that are required are very large, and the autocorrelation is relatively high, especially in estimating the mean. This indicates that the data contain very little information about the parameter estimates, which is not surprising given the small sample size.

In the popularity example, the Bayesian method performs much better. But even in this well-behaved data set, the analyst must inspect the output carefully for indications of non-convergence or other problems. In the final analysis, with the burn-in set at 5000, and a MCMC chain of 50000 iterations, with a thinning factor of 10, the Raftery-Lewis statistic still indicates that more iterations are needed. However, the Raftery-Lewis statistic may be rather conservative. The Raftery-Lewis statistic is a lower-bound estimate (Raftery & Lewis, 1992) that often indicates huge numbers of MCMC iterations. It estimates the number of MCMC iterations needed to be 95% confident that the 2.5^{th} and 97.5^{th} percentile are estimated with an error smaller than 0.005. In essence, it requires that we are 95% confident that the end-points of the 95% confidence interval are correct in two decimal places. If several chains of far smaller numbers of iterations converge on the same confidence interval estimates, we may conclude that the smaller number is sufficient. In fact, if we analyze the pupil popularity data using the standard 500 iterations for the burn-in with 5000 consecutive iterations (no thinning) for monitoring, we find almost the same results. Only the intercept is estimated as 3.58 rather than 3.57. Although this is undeniably a difference larger than 0.005, for most applications such a difference would be negligible.

Bayesian estimation methods involve all the usual assumptions. They are *not* non-parametric, such as the non-parametric bootstrap. They use different methods to find point estimates and assess sampling variance, and they can be used in situations where asymptotic Maximum Likelihood methods are problematical.

As indicated earlier, all priors add some information to the data. As a result, Bayesian estimates are biased. When the sample size is reasonable, the amount of bias is usually small. This bias is accepted, because Bayesian methods promise more precision, and better estimates of the sampling variance. Simulation research (Browne, 1998, Browne & Draper, 2000) confirms this, especially when we are dealing with non-linear models.

In this section, all priors used are non-informative. This is useful, because with normal data and large datasets, the resulting estimates are equivalent to Maximum

Likelihood estimates. In addition, most analysts would be cautious in adding prior information to the data, because this could be interpreted as manipulating the outcome. However, sometimes we do have valid prior information. For instance, when we use a normed intelligence test as outcome variable, we know that its mean is in the neighborhood of 100, with a standard deviation of about 15. If we use a 10-point scale, we know that the mean must be somewhere between zero and ten, and the variance cannot be larger than 25. So, using a prior for the variance that implies that the variance can be any number between zero and infinity appears to be wasting real information. Novick and Jackson (1974) suggest in their excellent introduction to Bayesian methods that in a scientific debate it can be constructive to define two different priors that correspond to two different hypotheses about a phenomenon. After data are collected and analyzed, the two posterior distributions should be more similar than the two prior distributions, indicating that observing the data allows the conclusions to converge. An interesting example is given by Meyer (1964), and discussed in detail by Novick and Jackson (1974, pp. 177-182).

It is clear that Bayesian MCMC methods, like bootstrapping, are computationally intensive methods. However, given modern computer equipment and reasonably sized models, they are within present capabilities. The techniques presented in this section are all as programmed in MLwiN (vs. 1.1). However, the issues that are addressed, such as deciding on the length of the burn-in and monitoring chains, are general. These decisions must be made by the analyst, and should be based on careful inspection of relevant plots and statistics. The number of iterations is usually much larger than in bootstrapping. However, since MCMC methods are based on generating estimates, and bootstrap methods on generating or shuffling around raw data, MCMC methods are fast. As in bootstrapping, the rule is that, statistically speaking, there is no such thing as too many iterations. It may be worthwhile to repeat the analysis of the final model(s) using the very long MCMC-chains typically indicated by the Raftery-Lewis statistic.

12

Multilevel Factor Models

The models described in the previous chapters are all multilevel variants of the conventional multiple regression model. This is not as restrictive as it may seem, since the multiple regression model is very flexible and can be used in many different applications (for detailed examples see Cohen & Cohen, 1983). Still, there are models that cannot be analyzed with multiple regression, notably factor analysis and path analysis models.

A general approach that includes both factor and path analysis is *Structural Equation Modeling*, or *SEM*. The interest in structural equation modeling is usually on *theoretical constructs*, which are represented by the latent factors. The factor model, which is often called the measurement model, specifies how the latent factors are measured by the observed variables. The relationships between the theoretical constructs are represented by regression or path coefficients between the factors. The structural equation model implies a structure for the covariances between the observed variables, which explains the alternative name *Covariance Structure Analysis*. However, the model can be extended to include means of observed variables or factors in the model, which makes covariance structure analysis a less accurate name. Many researchers will simply think of these models as 'Lisrel-models,' which is also less accurate. LISREL is an abbreviation of LInear Structural RELations, and the name used by Jöreskog for one of the first and most popular SEM programs. Nowadays structural equation models need not be linear, and the possibilities of SEM extend well beyond the original LISREL program. Marcoulides and Schumacker (2001), for instance, discuss the possibility to fit nonlinear curves and interaction terms in SEM.

Structural equation modeling is a general and convenient framework for statistical analysis that includes as special cases several traditional multivariate procedures, such as factor analysis, multiple regression analysis, discriminant analysis, and canonical correlation. Structural equation models are often visualized by a graphical *path diagram*. The statistical model is usually represented in a set of matrix equations. In the early seventies, when this technique was first introduced in social and behavioral research, the software usually required setups that specify the model in terms of these matrices. Thus, researchers had to distill the matrix representation from the path diagram, and provide the software with a series of matrices for the different sets of parameters, such as factor loadings and regression coefficients. A recent development is software that allows the researchers to specify the model directly as a path diagram. Since the focus in this chapter is on structural equation models for multilevel data, and not on structural equation modeling itself, the models will generally be introduced using path diagrams.

Structural equation modeling has its roots in path analysis, which was invented by the geneticist Sewall Wright (Wright, 1921). It is customary to start a SEM analysis by drawing a path diagram. A path diagram consists of boxes and circles, which are connected by arrows. In Wright's notation, observed (or measured) variables are represented by a rectangle or square box, and latent (or unmeasured) factors by a circle or ellipse. Single-headed arrows or 'paths' are used to define causal relationships in the model, with the variable at the tail of the arrow causing the variable at the point. Double-headed arrows indicate covariances or correlations, without a causal interpretation. Statistically, the single-headed arrows or paths represent regression coefficients, and double-headed arrows covariances.

Often a distinction is made between the measurement model and the structural model. The measurement model, which is a confirmatory factor model, specifies how the latent factors are related to the observed variables. The structural model contains the relationships between the latent factors. In this chapter, I discuss multilevel factor analysis, and introduce the techniques currently available to estimate multilevel factor models. Multilevel path models, which are structural models that may or may not include latent factors, are discussed in Chapter Thirteen. For a general introduction in SEM, I refer to the introductory article by Hox and Bechger (1998) or introductory books such as Loehlin (1998) and Schumacker and Lomax (1996). A statistical treatment is presented by Bollen (1989). An interesting collection of introductory articles focusing on SEM models for multigroup and longitudinal data is found in Little, Schnabel and Baumert (2000).

Structural models for multilevel data have been elaborated by, among others, Goldstein and McDonald (Goldstein & McDonald, 1988; McDonald & Goldstein, 1989, McDonald, 1994), Muthén and Satorra (Muthén, 1989; Muthén & Satorra, 1989) and Longford and Muthén (Longford & Muthén, 1992). I refer to McArdle and Hamagami (1996) for a comparison between multilevel regression techniques and standard multigroup SEM. The approach by Muthén is particularly interesting, because he shows that structural equation modeling (SEM) of multilevel data is possible using available SEM software, such as LISREL (Jöreskog & Sörbom, 1996), EQS (Bentler, 1995), or AMOS (Arbucle & Wothke, 1999). For an introductory exposition of Muthén's method, see Muthén (1994), Hox (1995), Kaplan and Elliot (1997) and Li, Duncan, Harmer, Acock, and Stoolmiller (1998). Meanwhile, software has appeared that includes the multilevel extensions directly in the SEM program (MPLUS, see Muthén & Muthén, 1998; LISREL 8.5, see du Toit & du Toit, 2001) or acts as a front end for conventional SEM software (STREAMS, see Gustafsson & Stahl, 1999). Heck and Thomas (2000) present an extended example of multilevel SEM, which uses Muthén's method and discusses the implementation details for the programs LISREL, STREAMS, and MPLUS, and Heck (2001) explains multilevel SEM using MPLUS.

This chapter discusses two different approaches to multilevel SEM: the approach originally proposed by Muthén, as applied, e.g., by Härnqvist, Gustafsson, Muthén and Nelson (1994), and an approach that is based on direct estimation of the covariance matrices at the distinct levels, as proposed by Goldstein (1987, 1995) and applied, e.g., by Rowe and Hill (1998) and Rowe (2002).

12.1 DECOMPOSING MULTILEVEL VARIABLES

Multilevel structural models assume that we have a population of individuals that are divided into groups. The individual data are collected in a p-variate vector $\mathbf{Y}_{ig}$ (subscript i for individuals, g for groups). Cronbach and Webb (1975) propose to decompose the individual data $\mathbf{Y}_{ig}$ into a between groups component $\mathbf{Y}_B = \bar{\mathbf{Y}}_g$, and a within groups component $\mathbf{Y}_W = \mathbf{Y}_{ig} - \bar{\mathbf{Y}}_g$. In other words, for each individual we replace the observed *Total* score $\mathbf{Y}_T = \mathbf{Y}_{ig}$ by its components: the group component $\mathbf{Y}_B$ (the disaggregated group mean) and the individual component $\mathbf{Y}_W$ (the individual deviation from the group mean.) These two components have the attractive property that they are orthogonal and additive (cf. Searle, Casella & McCulloch, 1992):

$$\mathbf{Y}_T = \mathbf{Y}_B + \mathbf{Y}_W \tag{12.1}$$

This decomposition can be used to compute a between groups covariance matrix Σ_B (the population covariance matrix of the disaggregated group means $\mathbf{Y}_B$) and a within groups covariance matrix Σ_W (the population covariance matrix of the individual deviations from the group means $\mathbf{Y}_W$). These covariance matrices are also orthogonal and additive:

$$\Sigma_T = \Sigma_B + \Sigma_W \tag{12.2}$$

Following the same logic, we can also decompose the sample data. Suppose we have data from N individuals, divided into G groups (subscript i for individuals, $i=1...N$; subscript g for groups, $g=1...G$). If we decompose the sample data, we have for the sample covariance matrices:

$$\mathbf{S}_T = \mathbf{S}_B + \mathbf{S}_W \tag{12.3}$$

Multilevel structural equation modeling assumes that the population covariance matrices Σ_B and Σ_W can be described by separate models for the between groups and within groups structure. To estimate the model parameters, the factor loadings, path coefficients, and residual variances, we need maximum likelihood estimates of the population between groups covariance matrix Σ_B and the population within groups covariance matrix Σ_W. What we have is the observed between groups matrix S_B and the observed within groups matrix S_W. It would be nice, if we could simply construct a within groups model for S_W, and a between groups model for S_B. Unfortunately, we cannot simply use S_B as an estimate of Σ_B, and S_W for Σ_W. The situation is a bit more complicated.

12.2 MUTHÉN'S PSEUDOBALANCED APPROACH

In the special case of balanced groups, meaning that all groups are the same size, estimation is straightforward (Muthén, 1989). If we have G balanced groups, with G equal group sizes n and a total sample size $N=nG$, we define two sample covariance matrices: the pooled within covariance matrix S_{PW} and the scaled between covariance matrix S^*_B.

Muthén (1989) shows that an unbiased estimate of the population within groups covariance matrix Σ_W is given by the pooled within groups covariance matrix S_{PW}, calculated in the sample by:

$$S_{PW} = \frac{\sum_{g}^{G}\sum_{i}^{n}\left(Y_{gi}-\bar{Y}_{g}\right)\left(Y_{gi}-\bar{Y}_{g}\right)'}{N-G} \tag{12.4}$$

Equation (12.4) corresponds to the conventional equation for the covariance matrix of the individual deviation scores, with $N-G$ in the denominator instead of the usual $N-1$.

Since the pooled within groups covariance matrix S_{PW} is an unbiased estimate of the population within groups covariance matrix Σ_W, we can estimate the population within group structure directly by constructing and testing a model for S_{PW}.

The scaled between groups covariance matrix for the disaggregated group means S^*_B, calculated in the sample, is given by:

$$S^*_B = \frac{\sum_{g}^{G}n\left(\bar{Y}-\bar{Y}_{g}\right)\left(\bar{Y}-\bar{Y}_{g}\right)'}{G-1} \tag{12.5}$$

Muthén (1989, 1990) shows that S_{PW} is the maximum likelihood estimator of Σ_W, with sample size N-G, and S^*_B is the maximum likelihood estimator of the composite $\Sigma_W + c\Sigma_B$, with sample size G, and c equal to the common group size n:

$$S_{PW} = \hat{\Sigma}_W \tag{12.6}$$

and

$$S^*_B = \hat{\Sigma}_W + c\hat{\Sigma}_B \tag{12.7}$$

Equations 12.6 and 12.7 suggest using the multi-group option of conventional SEM software for a simultaneous analysis at both levels. However, if we model the between groups structure, we cannot simply construct and test a model for Σ_B, because S^*_B estimates a combination of Σ_W and Σ_B. Instead, we have to specify for the S^*_B 'group' two models: one for the within groups structure and one for the between groups structure. The procedure is that we specify two groups, with covariance matrices S_{PW} and S^*_B (based on N-G and G observations). The model for Σ_W must be specified for both S_{PW} and S^*_B, with equality restrictions between both 'groups' to guarantee that we are indeed estimating the same model in both covariance matrices, and the model for Σ_B is specified for S^*_B only, with the scale factor c built into the model.

The reasoning strictly applies only in the so-called *balanced* case, that is, if all groups have the same group size. In the balanced case, the scale factor c is equal to the common group size n. The unbalanced case, where the group sizes differ, with G groups of unequal sizes, is more complicated. In this case, S_{PW} is still the maximum likelihood estimator of Σ_W, but S^*_B now estimates a different expression for each set of groups with distinct group size d:

$$S^*_{Bd} = \hat{\Sigma}_W + c_d\hat{\Sigma}_B \tag{12.8}$$

where equation 12.8 holds for each distinct set of groups with a common group size equal to n_d, and $c_d=n_d$ (Muthén, 1990, 1994). Full Information Maximum Likelihood (FIML) estimation for unbalanced groups implies specifying a separate between-group model for each distinct group size. These between groups models have different scaling parameters c_d for each distinct group size, and require equality constraints across all other parameters and inclusion of a mean structure (Muthén, 1994, p. 385). Thus, using conventional SEM software for the unbalanced case requires a complicated modeling scheme that creates a different 'group' for each set of groups with the same group size. This results in large and complex models, with possibly groups with a sample size less than the number of elements in the corresponding covariance matrix. This makes full

Maximum Likelihood estimation problematic, and therefore Muthén (1989, 1990) proposes to ignore the unbalance, and to compute a single S^*_B. The model for S^*_B includes an ad hoc estimator c^* for the scaling parameter, which is close to the average sample size:

$$c^* = \frac{N^2 - \sum_{g}^{G} n_g^2}{N(G-1)} \qquad (12.9)$$

This solution is not a full maximum likelihood solution. The result is a Limited Information Maximum Likelihood (LIML) solution, which McDonald (1994) calls a pseudobalanced solution, and Muthén (1989, 1994) the MUML (for MUthén's ML) solution. Muthén (1989, 1990) shows that S^*_B is a consistent and unbiased estimator of the composite $\Sigma_W + c\Sigma_B$. This means that with large samples (of both individuals *and* groups!) S^*_B becomes a close estimate of Σ_B, and the pseudobalanced solution should produce a good approximation given adequate sample sizes.

Since S^*_B is not a maximum likelihood estimator, the analysis produces only approximate parameter estimates and standard errors. However, when the group sizes are not extremely different, the pseudobalanced estimates will be close enough to the full maximum likelihood estimates to be useful in their own right. Comparisons of pseudobalanced estimates with full maximum likelihood estimates or with known population values have been made by Muthén (1990, 1994), Hox (1993), and McDonald (1994). Their main conclusion is that the pseudobalanced parameter estimates and the standard errors are fairly accurate and useful for a variety of multilevel problems. A large simulation study by Hox and Maas (2001a) assesses the robustness of the pseudobalanced method against unequal groups and small sample sizes at both the individual and the group level, in the presence of a low or a high intraclass correlation (ICC). In this study, the within groups part of the model poses no problems in any of the simulated conditions. The most important problem in the between groups part of the model, is the occurrence of inadmissible estimates, when the group level sample size is small (50) and the intracluster correlation is low. When an admissible solution is found, the factor loadings are generally accurate. However, the residual variances are underestimated, and the standard errors are generally too small. Having more or larger groups or a higher ICC does not effectively compensate this. Therefore, while the nominal alpha level is 5%, the operating alpha level is about 8% in all simulated conditions with unbalanced groups. The strongest contributing factor is an inadequate sample size at the group level. Imbalance is also a problem for the overall goodness-of-fit test. For balanced data, the chi-square test for goodness-of-fit is accurate. For unbalanced data, the model is rejected too often, which again results in an operating alpha level of about 8%. The size of the biases is comparable to the effect of moderate non-normality in ordinary modeling. Hox and Maas conclude that the approximate solution is useful, provided that the group level sample size is at least 100, and keeping in mind that the operating alpha level is somewhat higher than the nominal alpha level.

The multilevel part of the structural equation model outlined above is simpler than that of the multilevel regression model. It is comparable to the multilevel regression model with random variation of the intercepts. There is no provision for randomly varying slopes (factor loadings and path coefficients). Although it would be possible to include cross-level interactions, introducing interaction variables of any kind in structural equation models is neither simple nor elegant (cf. Bollen, 1989; Marcoulides & Schumacker, 2001). An interesting approach is allowing different within groups covariance matrices in different subsamples.

The pseudobalanced approach needs the pooled within and the scaled between covariance matrices. Standard software does not provide these directly. One solution is to use special software that calculates these matrices directly, such as the freeware program SPLIT2 (Hox, 1994b) or the preprocessor STREAMS (Gustafsson & Stahl, 1999). A different solution is to use standard software such as SPSS to calculate the correlations and standard deviations of the deviation scores and the disaggregated means. The correlations are scale-free numbers, and therefore the correct ones. The standard deviations will be calculated using $N-1$ in the denominator, instead of the denominators $N-g$ for the pooled within covariances and $G-1$ for the scaled between groups covariances. In other words, the standard deviations of the pooled within matrix must be corrected by multiplying them by $\sqrt{N-1/N-G}$, and the standard deviations of the scaled between matrix must be corrected by multiplying them by $\sqrt{N-1/G-1}$. It is easy to make these corrections by hand, and then input the correlations with the corrected standard deviations into any standard SEM program.

Since the pseudobalanced approach needs the within groups model both for the pooled within groups and the scaled between groups model, and needs to incorporate the scaling factor for the between groups model, the actual model can become quite complicated. In addition, some software has difficulties finding good starting values. Several software writers have addressed these problems. The program STREAMS (Gustafsson & Stahl, 1999) acts as a preprocessor for standard SEM software. For two-level SEM, it calculates the pooled within and scaled between matrices, and writes the complicated setup, including starting values based on previous analyses. The program MPLUs (Muthén & Muthén, 1998) hides all the complications of the pseudobalanced approach from the user. It also uses by default robust estimators for the standard errors and adjusts the chi-square test statistic for the heterogeneity that results from mixing groups of different sizes (cf. Muthén & Satorra, 1995).

12.2.1 An Example of Pseudobalanced Multilevel Factor Analysis

The example data are taken from Van Peet (1992). They are the scores on six intelligence measures of 187 children from 37 families. The six intelligence measures are: word list, cards, matrices, figures, animals, and occupations. The data have a multilevel structure, with children nested within families. If intelligence is strongly influenced by shared genetic and environmental influences in the families, we may expect rather strong between family effects.

To begin, the individual scores on the six measures are decomposed into disaggregated group means and individual deviations from the group means. Table 12.1 shows the means and variances of the scores, and the Intra Class Correlation (ICC),[1] with the family and individual level variances calculated using standard formulas for the variances. Note that, within rounding errors, the family level variance and the individual level variance sum to the total variance.

Table 12.1	Means, variances and ICC for family data				
		Total	Family	Individual	
Measure	Mean	Variance	Variance	Variance	ICC
Word list	29.8	15.21	7.48	7.73	.38
Cards	32.7	28.47	13.65	14.82	.36
Matrices	31.7	16.38	5.24	11.14	.16
Figures	27.1	21.23	6.84	14.38	.16
Animals	28.7	22.82	8.46	14.36	.22
Occupations	28.3	21.42	9.11	12.31	.29

The results in Table 12.1 suggest that there are indeed sizeable family effects. To analyze the factor structure of the six measures on the individual and family level, we compute the pooled within family covariance matrix S_{PW} and the scaled between family covariance matrix S^*_B, using equations (12.4) and (12.5). The within family covariance matrix the scaled between family covariance matrix are in Tables 12.2 and 12.3.

---

[1]The ICC can be estimated by analysis of variance procedures (Hays, 1994), or from the intercept-only model using a multilevel approach. In Split2 and M*PLUS* it is estimated from the pooled within groups and between groups variances as $\rho = \sigma^2_B/(\sigma^2_B + \sigma^2_W)$.

Table 12.2 Pooled within families covariances and correlations						
	1	2	3	4	5	6
1 **Word list**	9.59	*.24*	*.30*	*.20*	*.09*	*.05*
2 **Cards**	3.16	18.37	*.49*	*.14*	*.14*	*.01*
3 **Matrices**	3.49	7.83	13.81	*.14*	*.11*	*.07*
4 **Figures**	2.64	2.56	2.12	17.38	*.26*	*.19*
5 **Animals**	1.15	2.45	1.74	4.66	17.81	*.45*
6 **Occupations**	0.60	0.15	1.02	3.10	7.42	15.27

Note: *italic* entries in upper diagonal are the correlations

Table 12.3 Scaled between families covariances and correlations						
	1	2	3	4	5	6
1 **Word list**	37.58	*.56*	*.58*	*.19*	*.60*	*.32*
2 **Cards**	28.45	68.62	*.66*	*.49*	*.41*	*.17*
3 **Matrices**	18.23	28.24	26.35	*.47*	*.55*	*.10*
4 **Figures**	6.74	23.70	14.27	34.41	*.31*	*.13*
5 **Animals**	23.79	21.91	18.54	11.82	42.52	*.35*
6 **Occupations**	13.33	9.70	3.44	5.25	15.31	45.77

Note: *italic* entries in upper diagonal are the correlations

The covariances in Table 12.3 seem very large, which is what they should be, because the covariance matrix in Table 12.3 is the *scaled* between groups matrix. This matrix equals the within groups matrix plus the between groups matrix multiplied by the average group size. The average group size for these family data, indicated by the scaling factor in equation (12.6), is 5.04. The correlations in Tables 12.2 and 12.3 suggest that the structure is much stronger at the family than at the individual level.

Typically, in multilevel SEM, there are many more individuals than groups, and hence the number of observations for the pooled within groups covariance matrix (N-G) is much larger than the number of observations for the between groups covariance matrix (G). In this case, the number of observations on the individual level is 187-37=150, while on the family level it is 37. Thus, it makes sense to start on the individual level by constructing a model for S_{PW} only, ignoring S^*_B.

An exploratory factor analysis on the correlations derived from S_{PW} suggests two factors, with the first three measures loading on the first factor, and the last three measures on the last. A confirmatory factor analysis on S_{PW} confirms this model (χ^2= 7.21, df=8, p=0.51). A model with just one general factor for S_{PW} is rejected (χ^2=44.87, df=9, p=0.00. Figure 12.1 presents the conventional graphic representation of the individual level (within families) model.

The next step is to specificy a family model. For this, we must analyze the matrices S_{PW} and S^*_B simultaneously with the multigroup procedure. First, we specify the individual model for both 'groups' with equality restrictions applied across both groups for all parameters. Next, we must specify an additional family model for S^*_B.

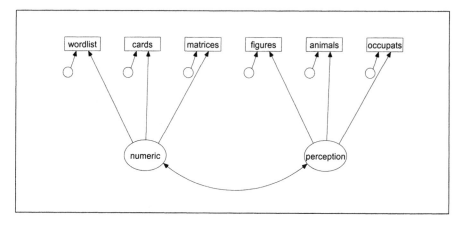

Figure 12.1. Within families model for Van Peet data

We start the analysis by estimating some 'benchmark' models, to test whether there is any between family structure at all. The simplest model is a null-model that completely leaves out the specification of a family level model. If the null-model holds, there is no family level structure at all; all covariances in S^*_B are the result of individual sampling variation. If this null-model holds, we may as well continue our analyses using simple single level analysis methods.

The next model tested is the independence model, which specifies only variances on the family level, but no covariances. A graphical representation of the independence model for S^*_B is given in Figure 12.2. The independence model estimates for the family level structure only the variances of the family level variables 'wl' to 'occ', If the independence model holds, there is family level variance, but no substantively interesting structural model. Nevertheless, in this case it is still useful to apply multilevel analysis, because this produces unbiased estimates of the individual model parameters.

Note that in Figure 12.2 the loadings for the family level variables (the six 'factors' in the circles going from 'wl' to 'occ') are not fixed to one, as is usual, but to 2.25, which is the square root of the scale factor. This is to transform the family level variables in the scaled between covariance matrix to their proper scale. Since this is a fixed value, it has no influence on the global fit of the model, but it is necessary for a correct interpretation of the factor loadings and path coefficients at the family level.

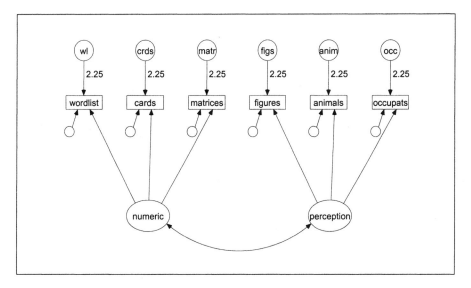

Figure 12.2. Within model+ independence model for between structure, Van Peet data

If the family-level independence model fits, there is no interesting between groups model, and we can simply analyze the pooled within matrix, at some cost in losing the within groups information from G observations that is contained in the between groups covariance matrix. If the independence model is rejected, there is some kind of structural model on the family level. To examine the best possible fit given the individual level model, we can estimate the saturated model; which fits a full covariance matrix to the family level observations. This places no restrictions on the family model.[1] Table 12.4 shows the results of estimating this sequence of benchmark models on the family level:

---

[1]To establish the within groups structure, we can specify the saturated model for the between structure, and then explore the within model simultaneously in both S_{PW} and S^*_B. However, since S_{PW} is usually based on many more observations than S^*_B little information is lost by only analyzing S_{PW}, while this makes the setups much simpler.

Table 12.4 Family level benchmark models			
Family model	Chi-square	df	p
Null	125.4	29	.00
Independence	52.5	23	.00
Saturated	7.2	8	.51

The null model and the independence model are both rejected. Next, we specify for the family level the same models we have used at the individual level. The two-factor model fits well. However, a one-factor model fits nearly as well, as Table 12.5 shows:

Table 12.5 Family level factor models			
Family model	Chi-square	df	P
1 Factor	21.3	17	.21
2 Factors	20.1	16	.22

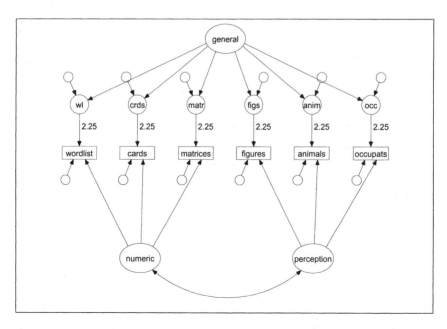

Figure 12.3. Final 2-level factor model for Van Peet data

The principle of using the simplest model that fits well, leads to acceptance of the one factor model on the family level. The resulting model for both the within-families and between-families structure is depicted in Figure 12.3. The model of Figure 12.3 shows reasonable to good 'goodness-of-fit' indices: the traditional fit index GFI is 0.88, which is too low, but the comparative fit index CFI is 0.97, and the root mean square error of approximation RMSEA is 0.04, both of which are acceptable values. The factor loadings and the residual error variances are in Table 12.6.

There is a small anomaly in Table 12.6: one of the error variances at the family level is negative. The value is very small, and this kind of problem tends to occur when the highest-level sample size is small (cf. Hox & Maas, 2001a). Thirty-seven families is indeed a small sample, and the usual treatment in SEM is to fix the small negative variance estimate to zero.

Table 12.6	Individual and family level estimates, standard SEM software					
	Individual level			Family level		
	Numeric	**Perception**	**resid. var.**	**General**		**resid. var.**
Word list	1*		8.13 (1.03)	1*		1.79 (1.14)
Cards	2.34 (.66)		10.76 (2.44)	1.24 (.36)		3.95 (1.84)
Matrices	2.39 (.74)		5.80 (2.28)	0.82 (.22)		-.03 (.66)
Figures		.63 (.21)	15.81 (1.97)	0.56 (.27)		2.45 (1.45)
Animals		1.51 (.55)	6.70 (3.92)	0.98 (.31)		1.36 (1.33)
Occupations		1*	10.43 (2.08)	0.41 $(.30)^{ns}$		5.69 (1.97)
Standard errors in parentheses. Correlation between individual factors: 0.22; * = fixed; ns = not significant						

Table 12.6 suggests an interpretation that on the family level, where the effects of the shared genetic and environmental influences are visible, one general (g) factor is sufficient to explain the covariances between the intelligence measures. On the individual level, where the effects of individual idiosyncratic influences are visible, we need two factors. These results could be fitted into Cattel's (1971) theory of fluid and crystallized intelligence, which states that, as a result of individual factors (education, physical and social environment), the general g-factor 'crystallizes' into specific individual competencies. The data do allow other interpretations; Gustafsson and Stahl (1999) also analyze this data set, and arrive at a somewhat different model.

The results given above were produced using standard SEM software on the pooled within and the scaled between covariance matrix, produced by the program

SPLIT2 (Hox, 1994b). Using MPLUS (Muthén & Muthén, 1998), we can analyze the multilevel factor model directly. If we use MPLUS to produce a Maximum Likelihood solution, the results are almost identical: a chi-square of 21.7 (df=17, p=0.20) and estimates and standard errors that are very close to the estimates given in Table 12.6. However, by default MPLUS produces for two-level models maximum likelihood estimates with robust standard errors (which are sandwich estimators, see Chapter Eleven) and a corrected chi-square test. The corrected chi-square is 24.0 (df=17, p=0.12), which is somewhat different from the standard chi-square. The MPLUS maximum likelihood estimates and robust standard errors are in Table 12.7.

Table 12.7	**Individual and family level estimates, MPLUS robust standard errors**				
	Individual level			Family level	
	Numeric	**Perception**	**resid. var.**	**General**	**resid. var.**
Word list	1*		8.13 (1.02)	1*	1.80 (1.42)
Cards	2.34 (.60)		10.75 (2.76)	1.24 (.43)	3.96 (1.55)
Matrices	2.39 (.86)		5.81 (2.51)	0.82 (.23)	-.04 (.56)
Figures		.63 (.17)	15.81 (1.51)	0.56 (.28)	2.46 (1.12)
Animals		1.51 (.55)	6.70 (3.91)	0.98 (.27)	1.37 (.88)
Occupations		1*	10.43 (1.74)	0.41 (.23)^{ns}	5.71 (2.18)
Standard errors in parentheses. Correlation between individual factors: 0.22; * = fixed; ns = not significant					

The results are not greatly different from the standard asymptotic standard errors. Still, using the MPLUS robust estimates, the covariance between the two within-families factors, which is barely significant using the asymptotic standard error (p=0.047), is clearly significant when the corrected standard error is used (p=0.034).

12.2.2 Goodness of Fit Using the Pseudobalanced Approach

Standard SEM programs, and specialized programs like STREAMS and MPLUS, produce in addition to the chi-square test a large number of goodness-of-fit indices that indicate how well the model fits the data. Statistical tests for model fit have the problem that their power varies with the sample size. If we have a very large sample, the statistical test will almost certainly be significant. Thus, with large samples, we will always reject our model, even if the model actually describes the data very well. Conversely, with a very small sample, the model will always be accepted, even if it fits rather badly.

Given the sensitivity of the chi-square statistic to the sample size, researchers have proposed a variety of alternative fit indices to assess model fit. All goodness-of-fit measures are some function of the chi-square and the degrees of freedom. Most of these fit indices do not only consider the fit of the model, but also its simplicity. A saturated model, that specifies all possible paths between all variables, always fits the data perfectly, but it is just as complex as the observed data. In general, there is a trade-off between the fit of a model and the simplicity of a model. Several goodness-of-fit indices assess simultaneously both the fit and the simplicity of a model. The goal is to produce a goodness-of-fit index that does not depend on the sample size or the distribution of the data. In fact, most goodness-of-fit indices still depend on sample size and distribution, but the dependency is much smaller than that of the routine chi-square test.

Modern SEM software computes a bewildering array of goodness-of-fit indices. All of them are functions of the chi-square statistic, but some include a second function that penalizes complex models. For instance, Akaike's information criterion (AIC), is twice the chi-square statistic minus the degrees of freedom for the model. For a detailed review and evaluation of a large number of fit indices, including those mentioned here, I refer to Gerbing and Anderson (1993).

Jöreskog and Sörbom (1989) have introduced two goodness-of-fit indices called GFI (Goodness of Fit) and AGFI (Adjusted GFI). The GFI indicates goodness-of-fit, and the AGFI attempts to adjust the GFI for the complexity of the model. Bentler (1990) introduces a similar index called the Comparative Fit Index CFI. Two other well-known measures are the Tucker-Lewis Index TLI (Tucker & Lewis, 1973), better known as the Non-Normed Fit Index or NNFI, and the Normed Fit Index NFI (Bentler & Bonett, 1980). Both the NNFI and the NFI adjust for complexity of the model. Simulation research shows that all these indices still depend somewhat on sample size and estimation method (e.g., ML or GLS), with the CFI and the TLI/NNFI showing the best overall performance (Chou & Bentler, 1995; Kaplan, 1995). If the model fits perfectly, these fit indices should have the value 1. Usually, a value of at least 0.90 is required to accept a model, while a value of at least 0.95 is required to judge the model fit as 'good.' However, these are just rules of thumb.

A relatively modern approach to model fit is to accept that models are only approximations, and that perfect fit may be too much to ask for. Instead, the problem is to assess how well a given model approximates the true model. This view led to the development of an index called RMSEA, for Root Mean Square Error of Approximation (Browne & Cudeck, 1992). If the approximation is good, the RMSEA should be small. Typically, a RMSEA of less than 0.05 is required, and statistical tests or confidence intervals can be computed to test if the RMSEA is significantly larger than this lower bound.

Given the many possible goodness-of-fit indices, the usual advice is to assess fit by inspecting several fit indices that derive from different principles. Therefore, for the confirmatory factor model for the family data, I report the chi-square test, and the fit indices GFI, CFI and RMSEA.

A general problem with these goodness-of-fit indices in multilevel SEM is that they apply to the entire model. Therefore, the goodness-of-fit indices reflect both the degree of fit in the within model and in the between model. Since the sample size for the within 'group' is generally the largest, this part of the model dominates the value of the fit indices. Clearly, we would prefer to assess the fit for both parts of the model separately.

Since the within groups sample size is usually much larger than the between groups sample size, we do not lose much information if we model the within groups matrix separately, and interpret the fit indices produced in this analysis separately.

A simple way to obtain goodness-of-fit indices for the between model is to specify a saturated model for the within groups matrix. The saturated model estimates all covariances between all variables. It has no degrees of freedom, and always fits the data perfectly. As a result, the degree of fit indicated by the goodness-of-fit indices, represents the fit of the between model. This is not the best way to assess the fit of the between model, because the perfect fit of the within model influences the value of the fit index. Fit indices that are mostly sensitive to the degree of fit will show a spuriously good fit, while fit indices that also reflect the parsimony of the model may even show a spurious lack of fit.

A better way to indicate the fit of the within and between model separately is to calculate these by hand. Most fit indices are a simple function of the chi-square, sample size N, and degrees of freedom df. Some consider only the current model, the target model M_t, others also consider a baseline model, usually the independence model M_I. By estimating the independence and the target model for the within matrix, with a saturated model for the between matrix, we can assess how large the contribution to the overall chi-square is for the various within models. In the same way, by estimating the independence and the target model for the between matrix, with a saturated model for the within matrix, we can assess how large the contribution to the overall chi-square is for the various between models. Using this information, we can calculate the most common goodness-of-fit indices. Most SEM software produces the needed information, and the references and formulas are in the user manuals and in the general literature (e.g., Gerbing & Anderson, 1992).[1]

Table 12.8 gives the separate chi-squares, degrees of freedom, and sample sizes for the independence model and the final model for the family intelligence example.

---

[1] The discussion here is based on the formulas in Arbuckle & Wothke, 1999, appendix C.

Table 12.8	Chi-squares and df separate for individual and family level models			
	Individual level, Between model saturated		Family level, Within model saturated	
	independence	**2 factors**	**independence**	**1 factor**
chi-square	148.26	7.27	45.23	13.96
Df	15	8	15	13
N	150	150	37	37

The calculation of the widely used goodness-of-fit index GFI is too complicated to be carried out by hand. The comparative fit index CFI (Bentler, 1990) is given by

$$CFI = 1 - \frac{\chi_t^2 - df_t}{\chi_I^2 - df_I} \tag{12.10}$$

In equation (12.10), χ_t^2 is the chi-square of the target model, χ_I^2 is the chi-square for the independence model, and df_t and df_I are the degrees of freedom for the target and the independence model. If the difference of the chi-square and the degrees of freedom is negative, it is replaced by zero. So, for example, the CFI for the family level model is given by $CFI = 1 - (13.96 - 13)/(45.23 - 15) = 0.90$.

The Tucker-Lewis index, TLI, which is also known as the Non-Normed Fit Index, NNFI, is given by

$$TLI = 1 - \frac{\dfrac{\chi_I^2}{df_I} - \dfrac{\chi_t^2}{df_t}}{\dfrac{\chi_I^2}{df_I} - 1} \tag{12.11}$$

Finally, the Root Mean Square Error of Approximation RMSEA is given by

$$RMSEA = \sqrt{\left(\frac{\chi_t^2 - df_t}{N df_t}\right)} \tag{12.12}$$

where N is the total sample size. Using equations (12.10) to (12.12) and the values in Table 12.8, we can calculate the CFI, TLI and RMSEA separately for the within and between models. The results are in Table 12.9.

Table 12.9	Fit indices for individual and family level models separately	
	Individual level, 2 factors	Family level, 1 factor
CFI	1.00	0.90
TLI	1.01	0.96
RMSEA	0.00	0.04

The goodness-of-fit indices in Table 12.9 indicate that the within groups model has an excellent fit, and the between groups model has a good fit. There is no need to modify our final two-level factor model for the family data.

12.3 DIRECT ESTIMATION OF THE COVARIANCES AT EACH LEVEL: THE MULTIVARIATE MULTILEVEL APPROACH

Goldstein (1987, 1995) suggests using the multivariate multilevel model described in Chapter Nine to produce a covariance matrix at the different levels, and to input these into a standard SEM program for further analysis. For our family data, we use a multivariate multilevel model with three separate levels for the six intelligence tests, the individual children, and the families. We create six dummy variables to indicate the six intelligence scales, and exclude the intercept from the model. Hence, at the lowest level we have

$$Y_{hij} = \pi_{1ij}d_{1ij} + \pi_{2ij}d_{2ij} + \ldots + \pi_{6ij}d_{6ij} \tag{12.13}$$

At the individual level we have

$$\pi_{pij} = \beta_{pj} + u_{pij} \tag{12.14}$$

And at the family level (the third level in the multivariate model), we have

$$\beta_{pj} = \gamma_p + u_{pj} \tag{12.15}$$

By substitution we obtain

$$\begin{aligned}Y_{hij} &= \gamma_1 d_{1ij} + \gamma_2 d_{2ij} + \ldots + \gamma_p d_{pij} \\ &+ u_{1ij}d_{1ij} + u_{2ij}d_{2ij} + \ldots + u_{pij}d_{pij} + u_{1j}d_{1ij} + u_{2j}d_{2ij} + \ldots + u_{pj}d_{pij}\end{aligned} \tag{12.16}$$

In sum notation, we have:

$$Y_{hij} = \sum_{h=1}^{6} \gamma_h d_{hij} + \sum_{h=1}^{6} u_{hij} d_{hij} + \sum_{h=1}^{6} u_{hj} d_{hij} \qquad (12.17)$$

The model described by equation (12.16) provides us with estimates of the six test means, and of their variances and covariances at the pupil and school level. Since in this application we are mostly interested in the variances and covariances, RML estimation is preferred to FML estimation. Table 12.10 presents the RML estimates of the covariances and the corresponding correlations at the individual level, and Table 12.11 presents the same at the family level.

Table 12.10	Covariances and correlations at the individual level					
	1	2	3	4	5	6
Word list	9.65	.24	.31	.20	.08	.05
Cards	3.21	18.38	.49	.14	.13	.01
Matrices	3.57	7.89	13.92	.14	.10	.06
Figures	2.59	2.56	2.13	17.93	.26	.19
Animals	1.03	2.41	1.61	4.74	18.03	.45
Occupations	0.55	0.12	0.93	3.19	7.52	15.35
Note: *italic* entries in upper diagonal are the correlations						

Table 12.11	Covariances and correlations at the family level					
	1	2	3	4	5	6
1 **Word list**	5.92	.68	.77	.20	.90	.45
2 **Cards**	5.29	10.37	.81	.72	.58	.25
3 **Matrices**	3.02	4.18	2.57	.84	1.01	.59
4 **Figures**	0.89	4.29	2.50	3.42	.34	.07
5 **Animals**	4.91	4.18	3.64	1.43	5.06	.27
6 **Occupations**	2.77	2.08	0.59	0.35	1.57	6.49
Note: italic entries in upper diagonal are the correlations						

Table 12.10 is equivalent to the pooled within families covariance matrix in Table 12.2. The actual values in both tables are certainly very close. In contrast, Table 12.11, the between families matrix, is *not* equivalent to the scaled between families matrix in Table 12.3. The covariance matrix in Table 12.3 is the scaled between groups matrix, S^*_B which is equal to the within groups matrix plus the between groups

matrix multiplied by the average group size. The average group size for these family data, indicated by the scaling factor in equation (12.9) is 5.04, and as a result the actual values in Table 12.3 are rather large. Table 12.11 is a direct estimate of the between family covariance matrix S_B itself. It is a maximum likelihood estimator of the population between family covariance matrix, and can be entered directly into a standard SEM program for analysis. As a result, if we are interested in the population structure of the within families or between families covariances, we can input the corresponding sample matrix from Table 12.10 or 12.11 directly into a SEM program. There is no need to analyze them simultaneously, using the two-group option, unless we want to impose constraints across the two levels.

There is one problematic entry in the family level matrix; the correlation between 'matrices' and 'animals' is estimated as 1.01, an impossible value. It is interesting to note that this impossible value is associated with the scale 'matrices', which in the pseudobalanced estimates in Table 12.6 has a small negative variance on the family level. Both impossible values point to the same variable, and the source of the problem is in both cases the small sample size at the family level. In the case of the negative variance estimate, the usual solution is to fix its value to zero. Some SEM programs can continue estimation with an improper input matrix (e.g., AMOS, cf. Arbuckle & Wothke, 1999). For our data, the result will be a negative variance estimate, which subsequently must be fixed at zero. If a SEM program cannot accommodate an improper covariance matrix, a practical solution is the *ridge* option, which is to multiply the diagonal of the covariance matrix with a number slightly larger than one (the LISREL program does this automatically, cf. Jöreskog & Sörbom, 1996). In our case, the automatic ridge option in LISREL multiplies all diagonal values by 2.0 to obtain a proper input matrix.[1]

If we analyze the individual level and family level covariance matrices separately, we find the parameter estimates reported all together in Table 12.12. For the individual level, the chi-square is 7.12 (df=8, p=.52), with all fit indices indicating a good fit. For the family level (after the ridge-correction) the chi-square is 6.47 (df=9, p=.69), with all fit indices indicating a good fit.

The estimates in Table 12.12 are all close to the pseudobalanced estimates presented earlier. The residual variances at the family level are very large, but this is the consequence of the large ridge multiplication factor.

---

[1] The ridge factor chosen automatically by LISREL is rather large. LISREL can be instructed to use a smaller value, such as 1.2, which would be sufficient. The effect of a ridge correction is that all error variances become larger. The AMOS estimates on the improper matrix are close to the LISREL estimates, but for an improper matrix Amos does not calculate the chi-square test. The ridge-solution presented here can be implemented using any of the available SEM software. For simplicity, the analysis here uses the LISREL default ridge factor.

Table 12.12	Individual and family level estimates, via direct estimation				
	Individual level			Family level	
	Numeric	**Perception**	**resid. var.**	**General**	**resid. var.**
Word list	1*		8.15 (1.04)	1*	8.26 (2.26)
Cards	2.23 (.61)		10.91 (2.38)	1.32 (.56)	14.51 (3.96)
Matrices	2.34 (72)		5.64 (2.32)	0.93 (.34)	2.06 (0.92)
Figures		.66 (.21)	15.78 (1.99)	0.61 (.30)	5.49 (1.40)
Animals		1.50 (.53)	6.86 (3.86)	1.07 (.42)	6.03 (0.19)
Occupations		1*	10.39 (2.07)	0.34 (.37)^{ns}	12.58 (2.99)

Standard errors in parentheses. Correlation between individual factors: 0.21^{ns}; * = fixed; ns = not significant

The fact that the individual level (within families) and family level (between families) covariances are estimated directly, and consequently can be modeled directly and separately by any SEM program, is a distinct advantage of the multivariate multilevel approach. As a result, we get separate model tests and fit indices at all levels. The multivariate multilevel approach to multilevel SEM also generalizes straightforwardly to more than two levels. There are other advantages as well. First, since the multilevel multivariate model does not assume that we have a complete set of variables for each individual, incomplete data are accommodated without special effort. Second, if we have dichotomous variables, we can use the multilevel generalized linear model to produce the covariance matrices, again without special effort.

There are some disadvantages to the multivariate multilevel approach as well. An important disadvantage is that the covariances produced by the multivariate multilevel approach are themselves estimated values. They are not directly calculated, as the pooled within groups and scaled between groups covariances are, but they are estimates produced by a complex statistical procedure. If the data have a multivariate normal distribution, the pooled within groups and scaled between groups covariances can be viewed as observed values, which have a known sampling distribution. This sampling distribution is used by SEM programs to estimate the chi-square model test and the standard errors of the parameter estimates. It is unknown how well the sampling distribution of the multivariate multilevel covariance estimates follows the sampling distribution of the observed covariances. This is, of course, especially true when we analyze incomplete data or dichotomous variables. In the case of incomplete data it is unclear what the proper sample size is, and in the case of dichotomous variables we know that the underlying distribution is not normal, and that the data in general contain less information than normally distributed variables do. The covariances estimated using the multivariate multilevel approach are consistent estimates, meaning that as the sample sizes increase they will approach the population values more closely. Most likely, the chi-square model test is upwardly biased, and the standard errors are probably downwardly biased. If the direct approach is used, it seems prudent to use other goodness-of-fit indices in addition to the chi-square test, and to interpret borderline significances with some care.

The advantage of the direct approach when data are incomplete can be illustrated with the Van Peet family data. The data set used so far is just the subset of the data that has no missing values on the six intelligence scales. The full data set does in fact contain many missing values. The main reason for this is that the two last tests 'naming animals' and 'naming occupations' are very time consuming, and for that reason these tests were dropped in the course of the data collection. So, for these two tests, there are 37 families and 187 children, while for the whole (but incomplete) data set there are 49 families and 269 children. Table 12.12 shows the pairwise sample sizes for the individual level correlations. At the family level, there are data on 49 families except for the correlations that involve the two last tests. The mean number of individual children is 231 across all entries in the table, and the mean number of families is 43. In this case, using the direct estimation approach on the incomplete data set appears an attractive choice, because we can incorporate far more data in our analysis.

Table 12.13 Pairwise sample sizes for family data, individual level						
	1	2	3	4	5	6
Word list	265					
Cards	265	269				
Matrices	265	269	269			
Figures	265	269	269	269		
Animals	187	191	191	191	191	
Occupations	187	191	191	191	191	191

Tables 12.14 and 12.15 present the covariances and correlations based on the whole data set. Especially for the family level covariances and correlations, the values for the entire data set appear somewhat different. Since most values in Table 12.15 are based on about 30% more families, the covariances presented here are presumably more accurate.

Table 12.14   Covariances and correlations at the individual level, entire data set

	1	2	3	4	5	6
1 Word list	9.07	.22	.30	.24	.09	.06
2 Cards	2.82	17.79	.46	.22	.15	.02
3 Matrices	3.36	7.09	13.60	.18	.11	.08
4 Figures	3.04	3.76	2.71	17.13	.27	.20
5 Animals	1.12	2.75	1.67	4.70	18.06	.46
6 Occupations	0.69	0.38	1.12	3.23	7.59	15.30

Note: *italic* entries in upper diagonal are the correlations

Table 12.15   Covariances and correlations at the family level, entire data set

	1	2	3	4	5	6
1 Word list	6.30	.57	.81	.27	.91	.52
2 Cards	4.12	8.20	.62	.69	.46	.21
3 Matrices	3.61	3.15	3.14	.66	1.02	.34
4 Figures	1.33	3.91	2.33	3.96	.37	.23
5 Animals	5.46	3.15	4.31	1.77	5.74	.41
6 Occupations	3.64	1.73	1.72	1.28	2.75	7.91

Note: *italic* entries in upper diagonal are the correlations

Given that there is no single number for the sample size, the mean sample size will be used as an indicator for the effective sample size. Thus, the sample size for the family level covariance matrix is 43, and for the individual level covariance matrix the sample size is set equal to 231- 43= 188. The results are combined in Table 12.16.

For the individual level, the chi-square is 15.00 (df=8, p=.06), with the fit indices indicating an acceptable fit. For the family level (after the ridge-correction) the chi-square is 75.54 (df=9, p=.00), with all fit indices indicating a poor fit. Earlier we saw that the direct estimation approach on the complete data produces almost the same results as the pseudobalanced approach. The large difference in the family level results when the incomplete cases are added to the analysis, must be the effect of adding extra cases. Given the small sample size at the family level, no further exploration of these data is attempted.

Table 12.16 Individual and family level estimates, via direct estimation

	Individual level			Family level	
	Numeric	**Perception**	**resid. var.**	**General**	**resid. var.**
Word list	1*		7.64 (.89)	1*	3.12 (.70)
Cards	2.15 (.56)		11.17 (2.05)	0.87 (.23)	6.15 (1.35)
Matrices	2.29 (65)		6.08 (2.01)	0.95 (.14)	0.01 (.14)
Figures		.67 (.18)	14.81 (1.70)	0.64 (.16)	2.80 (.61)
Animals		1.42 (.41)	7.55 (3.00)	1.19 (.18)	0.91 (.29)
Occupations		1*	10.06 (1.80)	0.48 (.23)	7.83 (1.71)

Standard errors in parentheses. Correlation between individual factors: 0.26^{ns}; * = fixed; ns = not significant

12.4 STANDARDIZING PARAMETER ESTIMATES IN MULTILEVEL STRUCTURAL EQUATION MODELING

The estimates discussed are all unstandardized estimates. For interpretation, it is often useful to inspect the standardized estimates as well, because these can be used to compare the loadings and residual variances for variables that are measured in a different metric. A convenient standardization is to standardize both the latent factors and the observed variables on each level separately. When MPLUS is used, it can provide such standardization. If conventional SEM software is used in a multiple group solution, it can also provide such standardization. In LISREL this is called the within groups completely standardized solution. However, conventional SEM software also provides a so-called 'completely standardized common metric solution.' This standardizes the variables using a common metric across the two groups. In multilevel SEM, this solution produces estimates that have no meaningful interpretation. So, although conventional SEM software can be used to produce both unstandardized and standardized estimates, some care is needed in choosing the correct standardization method. Heck and Thomas (2000) provide a clear and extensive discussion of the choices available in LISREL and the corresponding program output. Table 12.17 presents the within groups standardized estimates produced by MPLUS.

Table 12.17 Individual and family level completely standardized estimates

	Individual level			Family level	
	Numeric	**Perception**	**resid. var.**	**General**	**resid. var.**
Word list	0.38		0.85	0.83	0.31
Cards	0.64		0.59	0.78	0.38
Matrices	0.76		0.89	0.58	0.66
Figures		0.56	0.42	1.01	-.01
Animals		0.79	0.38	0.86	0.26
Occupations		0.33	0.69	0.32	0.90

The program STREAMS has a different approach to standardization (cf. Gustafsson & Stahl, 1999; Heck & Thomas, 2000). STREAMS standardizes the latent variables at each separate level, but uses the total variance of a variable to standardize both the within groups and the between groups level. This provides a better insight into how much variance each effect explains at the different levels. This multilevel standardization can also be accomplished by hand calculation using other SEM software. Table 12.18 presents the multilevel standardized estimates.

Table 12.18 Individual and family level multilevel standardized estimates

	Individual level			Family level	
	Numeric	**Perception**	**resid. var.**	**General**	**resid. var.**
Word list	0.30		0.54	0.52	0.12
Cards	0.52		0.38	0.47	0.14
Matrices	0.70		0.35	0.41	0.12
Figures		0.47	0.75	0.24	-.00
Animals		0.69	0.29	0.42	0.06
Occupations		0.30	0.49	0.18	0.27

The squares of the standardized loadings of a variable are the proportion of variance that this variable shares with each factor. Table 12.18 shows that most variables have more systematic variance on the individual level, than on the family level. At the same time, the amount of residual error variance is much larger on the individual level than on the family level. This information is not available from the within groups standardized estimates in Table 12.16. The multilevel standardized estimates in Table 12.17 can be used to compute intraclass correlations for the variables based only on the systematic variance. Thus, the intraclass correlation of the first variable, 'Wordlist', is estimated as 0.39 using the scores on the raw variable (see Table 12.1), but as $0.52^2/(0.30^2+0.52^2)= 0.75$ if we look only at the systematic variance, excluding the residual error variances from the computation. 'Wordlist' has more variance on the individual level than on the family level, but most of this variance must be considered measurement error.

13

Multilevel Path Models

Path models are structural equation models that consist of complex paths between latent and/or observed variables, often including both direct and indirect effects, or reciprocal effects between variables. As mentioned in Chapter Twelve, often a distinction is made between the structural and the measurement part of a model. The measurement model specifies how the latent factors are measured by the observed variables, and the structural model specifies the structure of the relationships between the theoretical constructs, which may be latent factors or observed variables in the model.

A multilevel path model uses the same approaches outlined in Chapter Twelve for multilevel factor analysis. We decompose the individual variables into disaggregated group means and individual deviations from the group means, and calculate the pooled within groups covariance matrix S_{PW} and the scaled between groups covariance matrix S^*_B. Next, we construct models for Σ_W and Σ_B, and use the multigroup approach as illustrated in Chapter Twelve. Conversely, we may use the direct estimation method to obtain direct estimates of the within groups and between groups covariance matrices Σ_W and Σ_B, and model these directly.

With multilevel path models, we often have the complication that we have pure group level variables (*global* variables in the terminology of Chapter One). An example would be the global variable *group size*. This variable simply does not exist on the individual level. We can of course disaggregate group size to the individual level. However, this disaggregated variable is constant within each group, and as a result the variance and covariances with the individual deviation scores are all zero. Actually, what we have in this case is a different set of variables at the individual and the group level. Some SEM-software (e.g., AMOS or EQS) does not require that both groups in a multi-group analysis have the same variables. Estimation using the two-group approach described in Chapter Twelve is not a problem with such software. There is also no problem if we use the direct estimation approach outlined in Chapter Twelve. Since this approach models the two levels separately, having different sets of variables at the distinct levels is not an issue. However, if we use the pseudobalanced approach, we may encounter a problem, because some SEM-software (e.g., LISREL) requires that both groups in a multi-group analysis have the same variables. This problem can be solved by viewing the group level variable as a variable that is systematically missing in the individual level data. Bollen (1989) and Jöreskog and Sörbom (1989) describe how systematically missing variables can be handled in Lisrel.[1] The details will be discussed in the next section.

13.1 EXAMPLE OF A MULTILEVEL PATH ANALYSIS

The data for this example are from a study by Schijf and Dronkers (1991). They analyzed data from 1377 pupils in 58 schools. We have the following pupil level variables: father's occupational status *focc*, father's education *feduc*, mother's education *meduc*, pupil sex *sex*, the result of GALO school achievement test *GALO*, and the teacher's advice about secondary education *advice*. On the school level we have only one variable: the school's denomination *denom*. Denomination is coded 1= Protestant, 2= Nondenominational, 3= Catholic (categories based on optimal scaling). The research question is whether the school's denomination affects the GALO score and the teacher's advice, after the other individual variables have been accounted for.[2]

We can use a sequence of multilevel regression models to answer this question. The advantage of a path model is that we can specify one model that describes all hypothesized relations between independent, intervening, and dependent variables. However, we have multilevel data, with one variable on the school level, so we must use a multilevel model to analyze these data.

There is one global variable: *denomination*. This variable does not exist on the individual level. If we disaggregate denomination to the individual level, we will find that this disaggregated variable is constant within each school, and that the variance and all the covariances with the other individual deviation scores are zero. In software that requires the same number of variables in both groups, this problem is solved by viewing the school level variable denomination as a variable that is systematically missing in the pupil level data. The trick is that the variable denomination is included in the (school level) scaled between schools covariance matrix in the usual way. In the (pupil level) pooled within schools covariance matrix, we include denomination as a variable with a variance equal to one and all covariances with other variables equal to zero. In the within school models, there are no paths pointing to or from this observed variable. Subsequently, we fix for this variable the residual error variance to 1.00. Since this produces a perfect fit for this 'ghost' variable, inclusion of this variable has

---

[1] Bollen gives a more detailed description of the procedure, but Jöreskog and Sörbom's account is to be preferred when a model must be specified, because they use some LISREL features that were not yet available when Bollen wrote his book.

[2] The data were collected in 1971. The example uses only those pupils with complete data on all variables. The same data were analyzed in Hox (1995) using a different model. The current model was suggested by the analyses presented by Gustafsson & Stahl (1999).

no influence on the within school estimates or the overall chi-square. There is only one problem; LISREL assumes that this variable represents a real observed variable, and will include it when it enumerates the degrees of freedom for the within schools model. As a result, the *df* and *p*-values (and most fit-indices) in the LISREL output are incorrect, and must be corrected by hand (cf. Jöreskog & Sörbom, 1989). Again, some software can handle multigroup models with different numbers of observed variables in the various groups, which makes this kind of modeling much simpler.

	school	sex	galo	advice	feduc	meduc	focc	denom	nmis
19	1	1	85	2	1	1	9	2	1
20	1	1	108	2	1	1	9	2	1
21	2	1	110	2	4	3	2	3	0
22	2	2	111	4	5	3	6	3	0
23	2	1	100	2	4	5	3	3	0
24	2	1	79	0	4	2	2	3	0
25	2	2	111	4	2	1	3	3	0
26	2	1	92	2	7	5	5	3	0
27	2	1	97	2	5	1	3	3	0
28	2	1	120	5	7	2	3	3	0
29	2	1	134	6	2	6	3	3	0
30	2	1	114	4	4	6	3	3	0
31	2	1	109	4	7	6	6	3	0
32	2	1	109	4	7	2	3	3	0
33	3	1	119	5	5	5	4	2	0
34	3	2	106	4	2	5	4	2	0

Figure 13.1 Part of data file for school example

Figure 13.1 shows part of the school data. Note that the school variable *denom* does not vary within schools. If a program like SPLIT2 (Hox, 1994b) is used to produce the pooled within and scaled between covariance matrices, the program will report an intraclass correlation of 1.00 for this variable. In this specific example, there is another problematic variable, which is *pupil sex*. This variable turns out to have an intraclass correlation of 0.005, which is very small, and obviously not significant. This means that there is almost no variation between schools in the gender composition; all schools have about the same proportion of girls and boys. As a result of this empirical finding, the variable *pupil sex* can only be used at the pupil level, and must be omitted from the school level. Again, with software that can handle multigroup models with different numbers of observed variables in the various groups, this poses no special problem, and in software that does, we give this variable the same treatment as the school level variable *denom*.

After calculating the pooled within and scaled between groups covariance matrices, the first step in modeling the Schijf/Dronkers data is again to construct a within schools (pupil level) model. Figure 13.2 below depicts the pupil level model. The problematic variable *pupil sex* is removed completely from the model, since it has no significant relations with any of the other variables.

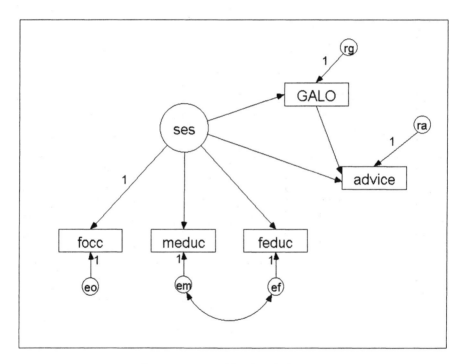

Figure 13.2 Pupil level path diagram

The pupil level path model has one latent factor 'SES' measured by the observed variables *focc*, *fedu* and *medu*. An analysis of the pooled within schools matrix S$_{PW}$ only with this model gives a chi-square of 1.7, with *df*=3 and *p*=0.64. The goodness-of-fit indices are all excellent. Given the large sample size (the pupil level data have 1377-

58=1319 independent observations), the high goodness-of-fit and the absence of large modification indices in the output, we accept this model.

The next step is specifying a school level model for S^*_B. First, we specify the pupil level model constructed earlier for both S_{PW} and S^*_B, with equality restrictions across the two 'groups' for all corresponding parameters. We start the analysis of the between groups matrix S_{SB} by specifying two benchmark models to explore whether there is any school level structure: the null model, which specifies *no* school level structure, and the independence model, which specifies only variances at the school level, and the maximum model, which specifies a full covariance matrix at the school level. This produces the following results:

Table 13.1   School level benchmark models

Family model	Chi-square	df	p
Null	259.9	18	.00
Independence	218.7	13	.00
Saturated	9.9	3	.02

Table 13.1 shows that the null and independence model are rejected, there is some kind of school level covariance structure. The maximum model specifies a saturated model for S^*_B, meaning that it produces an estimate of the full covariance matrix Σ_B. This model does not fit completely, since the *p*-value of 0.02 is significant. Since the maximal model fits perfectly on the group level, the amount of mis-fit is due to adding the within groups information that is part of the scaled between groups covariances. However, since the various goodness-of-fit measures are still good, we continue to accept the pupil level model established earlier.[1] Inspection of the estimated between schools covariance matrix reveals that on the school level the three SES indicators *focc*, *feduc* and *meduc* have extremely high correlations (all intercorrelations are larger than .98). A school-level factor model for these three indicators does not converge, and is therefore replaced by a component model. Thus, on the school level we have a path model without latent variables (other than having latent variables to represent the school level).

---

[1]The null and maximum model can be used to define separate goodness-of-fit measures, as discussed in Chapter 11. Since the maximum model has a *p*-value of .02, it is likely that all school level models will also be significant. In such situations, goodness-of-fit indices are a useful alternative to significance testing.

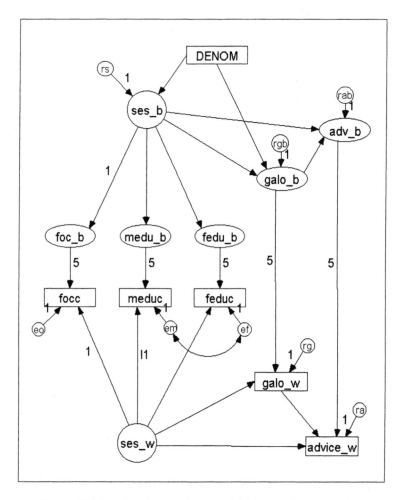

Figure 13.3 Pupil and school level model for school example data

The school level model resembles the individual level model, but with *SES* as a component instead of a latent factor. As a result, there are no residual measurement errors for the latent variables *foc_b*, *fedub* and *medu_b* that are the school level indicators of *SES*. The fit of this model is acceptable (chi-square=28.1, *df*=10, *p*=.0.002), with goodness-of-fit indicated as acceptable by a CFI of 1.00 and an RMSEA of 0.04.

The school level variable *denomination* turns out to have an effect on the school level *SES* and on the GALO test score. The graphical representation of this final model (chi-squared=64, *df*=47, *p*=.05) is given in Figure 13.4, including standardized path coefficients. The effect of school denomination on SES can be interpreted as a selection effect; denominational schools attract pupils with on average higher SES.

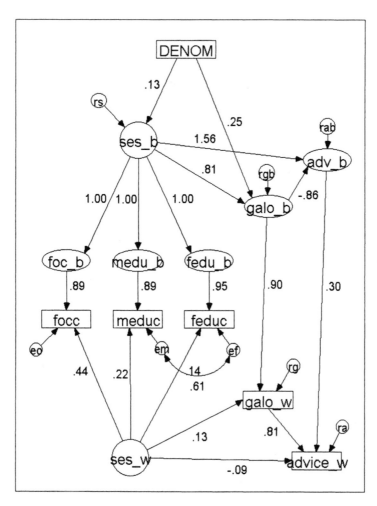

Figure 13.4 Final model for the school data

In the multilevel regression analyses presented by Schijf and Dronkers (1991), denomination has a significant effect on both the teachers' advice and on the GALO test score. The path model presented here shows that the main influence is through the GALO test score; the different advice given by teachers in schools of different denominations are apparently the result of differences in GALO test scores between such schools. This is precisely the kind of result that a sequence of separate regression analyses cannot show.

Figure 13.4 also shows that SES has a school level effect on the variables GALO and advice. The interpretation is *not* that some schools simply happen to have more high SES pupils and therefore perform better; sampling differences between schools in SES composition are accounted for in the pupil model that is also fitted for the school level covariances. Instead, the substantive interpretation of the school level results must be in terms of some kind of contextual or systematic selection effect. It appears that the concentration of high or low SES pupils has its own effect on the school career variables. It is interesting to note that, on the school level, the effect of the school average on the GALO test on the average advice is negative. This can be interpreted as a typical context effect, in which the GALO score is apparently interpreted differently by teachers if the overall score of a school on the test is high..

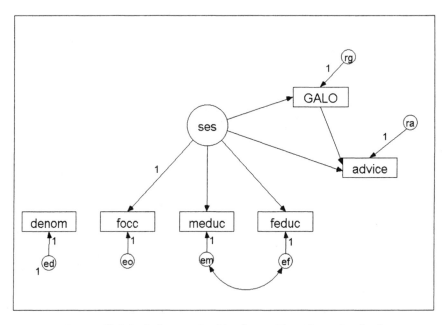

Figure 13.5 Including a school level variable at the within-level

Figure 13.5 shows how a school level variable like *denom* is handled in a program like Lisrel. It is included in the pooled within groups covariance matrix as a 'virtual' variable with a variance of one, and the covariances with the other variables all set to zero. In the pupil level model, which is the model for the pooled within groups covariance matrix, the observed variable *denom* is modeled as independent from all other variables in the model, with an error term *ed* that has a variance fixed at 1. This of course exactly models the variance of one and the covariances of zero that were added to the pooled within groups covariance matrix. The problem is that a program like LISREL counts an extra variance plus five covariances in the input matrix, which means that it counts an extra six degrees of freedom. Since these nonexistent variance and covariances are necessarily estimated perfectly, the fit of the model appears spuriously good. For this reason, the degrees of freedom *df* must be corrected by subtracting 6, and the *p*-value and all goodness-of-fit indices that depend on the degrees of freedom must also be corrected.

13.2 STATISTICAL AND SOFTWARE ISSUES
IN MULTILEVEL FACTOR AND PATH MODELS

It should be noted that multilevel factor and path models differ from multilevel regression models, because they do not have random regression slopes. The variation and covariation on the group level is intercept variation. There are also no cross-level and interaction effects. In multilevel factor models, the group level variation can properly be interpreted as group level variance of the group means of the latent factors. In path analysis, the interpretation of group level path coefficients is in terms of contextual effects, which are added to the individual effects. Inclusion of cross-level and other interaction terms in structural equation models is possible, but they are difficult to specify and estimate in current SEM software (cf. Jöreskog & Yang, 1996; Schumacker & Marcoulides, 1998; Marcoulides & Schumacker, 2001).

The direct estimation approach does not need special SEM software. The Muthén pseudobalanced approach can be followed in any SEM software that supports multiple group analysis. Both Muthén's pseudobalanced approach and direct estimation of the within and between covariance matrices have strong limitations. Direct estimation of the covariance matrices, followed by standard SEM analyses, ignores the fact that these covariances are themselves estimates, and that with incomplete data it is misleading to assign a single sample size to each matrix. The pseudobalanced approach, although consistent, is not a maximum likelihood method. For a full Maximum Likelihood solution using standard SEM software, we must model as many groups as there are distinct sample sizes, which is impractical and sometimes impossible.

Raudenbush and Sampson (1999b) advocate a different method to analyze multilevel models with latent variables, using standard multilevel regression software. They represent measurement error in a separate 'variables' level (Raudenbush, Rowan & Kang, 1991), a method described in the multivariate multilevel measurement models section in Chapter Nine of this book. The random regression coefficients at the second level are interpreted as latent variables or factors, indicated by the variables to which they are linked by sets of dummy variables. Using the means and covariances at the higher levels, path coefficients can be estimated with the corresponding standard errors. This approach can be used to estimate both factor and path models. The major advantages of their approach are that it can include random regression coefficients, and it works fine with incomplete data, which are difficult to handle in the pseudobalanced approach. The major disadvantage is the simplicity of the measurement model. The model requires that all the factor loadings are known; typically they are all set equal to one. This is a strong assumption, which implies that all observed variables that load on the same factor are measured on the same scale and have the same error variance. There are also no fit indices, so information on how well the factor or path model fits is not readily available.

A full Maximum Likelihood solution to the problem of multilevel factor and path analysis requires maximization of a very complicated likelihood function. Some progress has been made in that direction. Lee and Poon (1992) describe an exact method for multilevel confirmatory factor analysis. Bentler & Liang (2001) describe a different approach to maximize the multilevel likelihood that can estimate both confirmatory factor and path models. Finally, the software LISREL 8.5 (du Toit & du Toit, 2001) includes a full maximum likelihood estimation procedure for multilevel confirmatory factor and path models, including an option to analyze incomplete data. The LISREL 8.5 user's manual (du Toit & du Toit, 2001) cautions that this procedure still has some problems; it frequently encounters convergence problems, and needs good starting values. These are promising developments. In theory, these methods should produce better estimates than either the pseudobalanced or the direct estimation approach. In practice, this advantage will depend on the precise way the methods are actually be implemented in the software. So far, the pseudobalanced approach has been shown to produce highly accurate parameter estimates with reasonable standard errors (Hox & Maas, 2001b). The direct estimation method is probably less accurate. However, since LISREL 8.5 also includes a powerful three-level regression module, a preliminary analysis using direct estimation would be an excellent method to find good starting values for the full maximum likelihood method.

Many more complex types of multilevel path models with latent variables, for instance including random slopes and cross-level effects, can be estimated using Bayesian methods. Bayesian models for continuous data are described by Goldstein and Browne (2001) and Jedidi and Ansari (2001), and models for binary data by Ansari and Jedidi (2000). These methods are not yet implemented in generally available software. Many multilevel structural equation models can be estimated using Bayesian methods and the software BUGS (Spiegelhalter, 1994), but this requires an intimate knowledge of both structural equation modeling and Bayesian estimation methods. Finally, Rabe-Hesketh et al. (Rabe-Hesketh, Pickles & Taylor, 2000; Rabe-Hesketh,

Pickles & Skrondal, 2001a) describe a very general procedure that allows fitting multilevel structural equation models with random coefficients, regressions among latent variables varying at different levels, and mixtures of continuous and ordered or dichotomous data. Maximum Likelihood estimation of all such models is implemented in a procedure called GLLAMM (for Generalized Linear Latent And Mixed Models) that runs in the statistical package STATA (Statacorp, 2001). The program and manual are available for free (Rabe-Hesketh, Pickles & Skrondal, 2001b), but the commercial package STATA is needed to run it. Specifying a model in GLLAMM requires detailed knowledge of statistical modeling in general. It is clear that there are many developments in multilevel factor and path analysis, but most require sophisticated and detailed statistical knowledge. I consider them beyond the scope of this book, especially since it will take time before these methods find their way in generally available and user-friendly software packages.

The analysis issues in multilevel path models, whether analyzed using Muthén's pseudobalanced approach, using directly estimated within and between groups covariance matrices, or full maximum likelihood estimation, are comparable to the issues in multilevel factor analysis. Thus, the recommendations given in Chapter Twelve about inspecting goodness-of-fit indices separately for the distinct levels that exist in the data, and about the separate standardization, also apply to multilevel path models.

All approaches to multilevel factor and path analysis model only one single within groups covariance matrix. In doing so, they commonly assume that the within groups covariances are homogeneous, i.e., that all groups have the same within groups covariance matrix. This is not necessarily the case. The effect of violating this assumption is currently unknown. Simulation studies on the assumption of homogeneous covariance matrices in MANOVA show that MANOVA is robust against moderate differences in the covariances, provided the group sizes are not too different (Stevens, 1996). Strongly different group sizes pose a problem in MANOVA. When larger variability exists in the smaller group sizes, the between group variation is overestimated; when larger variability exists in the larger group sizes, the between group variation is underestimated.

If we assume that the covariance matrices differ in different groups, one possible solution is to divide the groups in two or more separate subsets, with each subset having its own within groups model. For instance, we may assume that within group covariances differ for male and female respondents. Or, in the situation where we have larger variances in small groups and vice versa, we may divide the data into a set of small and a set of large groups. Then we model a different within groups model for each set of groups, and a common between groups model. If the pseudobalanced approach is used, this means that for separate groups of males and females we must specify a four-group analysis: two groups for the within and between groups model for the males, and two more groups for the within and between groups model for the females. The result is a rather complicated model. For that reason, we must make very sure that we specify the correct collection of equality constraints to estimate the exact model that we intend to estimate. The program M*PLUS* (Muthén & Muthén, 1998) handles this analysis in a somewhat simpler way, by hiding all the multilevel complications from the user. Using direct estimation in a four-group analysis is also much simpler, because in that approach we do not need the complex equality constraints that are required in the pseudobalanced approach.

14

Latent Curve Models

An interesting structural equation model for fixed occasion panel data is the Latent Curve Model (LCM). This model has been applied mainly to developmental or growth data, hence the usual name Latent Growth Curve Model. In the latent curve model, the time variable is defined in the measurement model of the latent factors. For instance, in a linear growth model, consecutive measurements are modeled by a latent variable for the intercept of the growth curve, and a second latent variable for the slope of the curve.

Figure 14.1 shows the path diagram of a simple latent curve model for panel data with five occasions, and one time-independent explanatory variable Z. In Figure 14.1, Y_0, Y_1, Y_2, Y_3 and Y_4 are the observations of the response variable at the five consecutive time points. In the latent curve model, the expected score at time point zero is modeled by a latent *intercept* factor. The intercept is constant over time, which is modeled by constraining the loadings of all time points on the intercept factor equal to one. The latent slope factor is the slope of a linear curve, modeled by constraining the loadings of the five time points on this factor to be equal to 0, 1, 2, 3 and 4 respectively. Following the usual custom in the graphical model presentation in SEM, the one path that is constrained to zero is not drawn. Obviously, a quadratic trend would be specified by a third latent variable, with successive loadings constrained to be equal to 0, 1, 4, 9 and 16. What is not immediately obvious from the path diagram in Figure 14.1 is that the latent curve model *must* include the means of the variables and the factors in the model. Therefore, the regression equations that predict the observed variables from the latent factors, depicted by the single-headed arrows towards the observed variables in Figure 14.1, also contain terms for the intercept.

In the latent curve model, the intercepts of the response variable at the five time points are constrained to zero, and as a result, the mean of the intercept factor is an estimate of the common intercept. In Figure 14.1, which uses the Amos representation (Arbuckle & Wothke, 1999), this is visible in the zeros placed close to the latent and observed variables; these indicate means and intercepts that are constrained to zero.

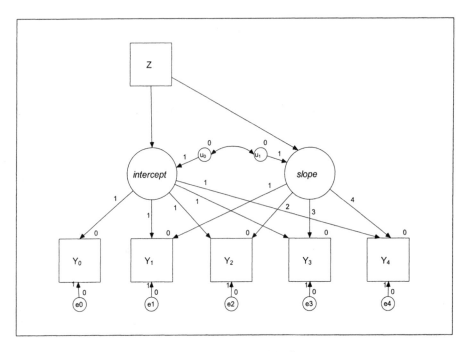

Figure 14.1. Latent Curve Model for five occasions

The successive loadings for the slope factor define the slope as the linear trend over time (note that, as is common in SEM, the first path from the slope factor to variable Y_0, which is equal to zero, is omitted from the diagram). The mean of the slope factor is an estimate of the common slope (c.f. Meredith & Tisak, 1990; Muthén, 1991; Willet & Sayer, 1994, Duncan & Duncan, 1995, Maccallum & Kim, 2000). Individual deviations from the common intercept are modeled by the variance of the intercept factor, and individual deviations in the slope of the curve are modeled by the variance of the slope factor. Both the intercept and slope factor can be modeled by a path model including explanatory variables, in our example the one explanatory variable Z.

The latent curve model is a random coefficient model for change over time, completely equivalent to the multilevel regression model for longitudinal data that is described in Chapter Five. To clarify the relationship between the two models, we write the equations for both specifications. In the multilevel linear growth model, the model described by Figure 14.1 can be expressed as a multilevel regression model, with at the lowest level, the occasion level:

$$Y_{tj} = \pi_{0i} + \pi_{1i}T_{ti} + e_{ti} \tag{14.1}$$

where T_{ti} is an indicator for the occasions, which is set to 0, 1, 2, 3, 4 to indicate the five occasions, with subscript t indicating occasions, and subscript i the individuals.. At the second level, the individual level, we have

$$\pi_{0i} = \beta_{00} + \beta_{01}Z_i + u_{0i} \tag{14.2}$$

$$\pi_{1i} = \beta_{10} + \beta_{11}Z_i + u_{1i} \tag{14.3}$$

By substitution, we get the single equation model:

$$Y_{ti} = \beta_{00} + \beta_{10}T_{ti} + \beta_{01}Z_i + \beta_{11}Z_iT_{ti} + u_{1i}T_{ti} + u_{0i} + e_{ti} \tag{14.4}$$

In a typical SEM notation, we can express the path model in Figure 14.1 as:

$$Y_{ti} = \lambda_{0t} \, \text{intercept}_i + \lambda_{1t} \, \text{slope}_i + e_{ti} \tag{14.5}$$

where λ_{0t} are the factor loadings for the intercept factor, and λ_{1t} are the factor loadings for the slope factor.

Note the similarity between the equations (14.5) and (14.1). In both cases, we model an outcome variable that varies across times t and individuals i. In equation (14.1), we have the intercept term π_{0i}, which varies across individuals. In equation (14.5), we have a latent intercept factor, which varies across individuals, and is multiplied by the factor loadings λ_{0t} to predict the Y_{tj}. Since the factor loadings λ_{0t} are all set equal to one, it can be left out of equation (14.5), and we see that the intercept factor in equation (14.5) is indeed equivalent to the regression coefficient π_{0i} in equation (14.1). Next, in equation (14.1), we have the slope term π_{1i}, which varies across individuals, and is multiplied by the 0, ..., 4 values for the occasion indicator T_{ti}. In equation (14.5), we have a latent slope factor, which varies across individuals, and gets multiplied by the factor loadings λ_{0t} to predict the Y_{tj}. Since the factor loadings λ_{1t} are set to 0, ..., 4, we see that the slope factor in equation (14.5) is indeed equivalent to the regression coefficient π_{1i} in equation (14.1). Therefore, the fixed factor loadings for the slope factor play the role of the time variable T_{ti} in the multilevel regression model and the slope factor plays the role of the slope coefficient π_{1i} in the multilevel regression model.

In a manner completely analogous to the second level equations (14.2) and (14.3) in the multilevel regression model, we can predict the intercept and the slope factor using the time-independent variable Z. For these equations, using for consistency the same symbols for the regression coefficients, we have

$$intercept_i = \beta_{00} + \beta_{01}Z_i + u_{0i} \qquad\qquad (14.6)$$

$$slope_j = \beta_{10} + \beta_{11}Z_i + u_{1i} \qquad\qquad (14.7)$$

which lead to a combined equation

$$Y_{ti} = \beta_{00} + \beta_{10}\,\lambda_{1t} + \beta_{01}Z_i + \beta_{11}Z_i\,\lambda_{1t} + u_{1i}\,\lambda_{1t} + u_{0i} + e_{ti} \qquad\qquad (14.8)$$

Keeping in mind that the factor loadings 0, ..., 4 in λ_{1t} play the role of the occasion indicator variable in T_t, we see that the multilevel regression model and the latent curve model are indeed highly similar. The only difference so far is that multilevel regression analysis generally assumes one common variance for the lowest level errors e_{ti}, while structural equation analysis typically estimates different residual error variances for all observed variables. However, this is easily solved by imposing a constraint on the latent curve model that the variances for e_0, ..., e_4 are all equal. If we impose this constraint, we have indeed the same model. Full maximum likelihood estimation, using either approach, should give essentially the same results.

14.1 EXAMPLE OF LATENT CURVE MODELING

The longitudinal *GPA* data from Chapter Five are used again, with a standard latent curve model as in Figure 14.1 applied to the data. The example data are a longitudinal data set, with longitudinal data from 200 college students. The students' Grade Point Average (GPA) has been recorded for six successive semesters. At the same time, it was recorded whether the student held a job in that semester, and for how many hours. This is recorded in a variable 'job' (with categories 0=no job, 1=1 hour, 2=2 hours, 3=3 hours, 4=4 or more hours), which for the purpose of this example is treated as an interval level variable. In this example, we also use the student variables high school GPA and sex (1=male, 2=female).

In a statistical package such as SPSS or SAS, such data are typically stored with the students defining the cases, and the repeated measurements as a series of variables, such as GPA1, GPA2, ..., GPA6, and JOB1, JOB2, ..., JOB6. As explained in Chapter Five, most multilevel regression software requires a different data structure. Latent curve analysis views the successive time point as different variables, and thus we can use such a data file as it is. We start with a model that includes only the linear trend over time. Figure 14.2 shows the path diagram for this model.

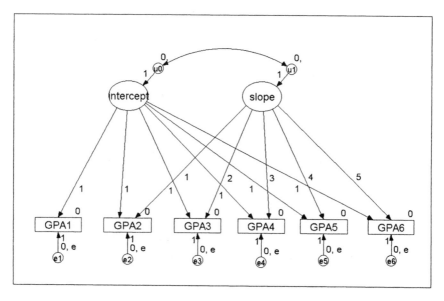

Figure 14.2. Path diagram for linear model GPA example data

The model in Figure 14.2 is equivalent to a multilevel regression model with a linear predictor coded 0, ..., 5 for the successive occasions, and a random intercept and slope on the student level. To make the models completely equivalent, the error variances of the residual errors e_1, ..., e_6 for the successive occasions are all constrained to be equal to e. In the graphical model in Figure 14.2 this is symbolized by the letter e next to each residual error variable. The means of the intercept and slope factor are freely estimated; all other means and intercepts in the model are constrained to zero, which is symbolized by placing a zero next to the constrained variable. The mean of the intercept is freely estimated as 2.60, and the mean of the slope is estimated as 0.11. This is identical to the estimates of the intercept and slope in the (fixed effects) multilevel regression model in Table 5.3 in Chapter Five.

For simplicity, we omit the time varying *JOB* variable for the moment, and start with specifying a latent curve model using only the six *GPA* scores, and the time-independent (student level) variables *high school GPA* and *student sex*. The path diagram, which includes the unstandardized parameter estimates obtained by standard SEM estimation, is shown in Figure 14.3.

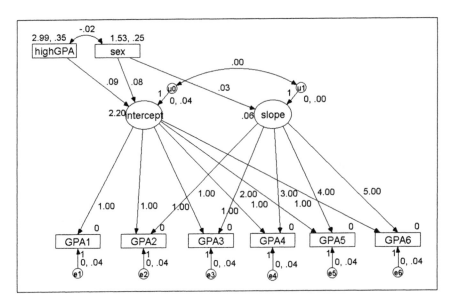

Figure 14.3. Path diagram and parameter estimates
for linear curve model with two predictors

In the path diagram we see that in this model, which includes an interaction between the slope of the linear development over time and the student's sex, the average slope over time is 0.06. The slope variance in the figure is given in two decimals as 0.00, in the text output it is given as 0.004, with standard error 0.001. This is identical to the estimates in the similar multilevel regression model presented in Table 5.4 in Chapter Five.

The SEM analysis of the latent curve model gives us some information that is not available in the equivalent multilevel analyses. The fit indices produced by the SEM-software tell us that the models depicted in Figures 14.2 and 14.3 do not describe the data well. The model in Figure 14.2 has a chi-square of 190.8 (df=21, p <0.001) and a RMSEA fit index of 0.20, and the model in Figure 14.3 has a chi-square of 195.6 (df=30, p <0.001) and a RMSEA fit index of 0.17.[1] The SEM analysis also provides us with diagnostic information of the locus of the fit problem. The program output contains so called *modification indices* that signify constraints that decrease the fit of the model. All large modification indices indicate that the constraint of equal error variances for the residual errors e_1, ..., e_6 does not fit well, and that the implicit constraint of no correlations between the residual errors e_1, ..., e_6 does not fit well

---

[1] The GFI, CFI and TLI fit indices are problematic when the model includes means, because it is not clear what a proper null model would imply for the means. The RSMEA does not have this limitation. An RMSEA smaller than 0.05 is judged as satisfactory (Browne & Cudeck, 1992).

either. Presumably, the multilevel regression models presented in Chapter Five also have these problems. Since in Chapter Five we did not carry out a residuals analysis or some other procedure to check for model misspecifications, we do not have any information about model fit. In SEM, we do have such information; it is automatically provided by all current SEM-software. If we remove the equality constraint on the residual errors, the model fit becomes much better, as indicated by a chi-square of 47.8 (df=25, p=0.01) and an RMSEA fit index of 0.07. Allowing correlated errors between the two first measurement occasions improves the fit to a chi-square of 42.7 (df=24, p= 0.01) and an RMSEA of 0.06. Since the other estimates do not change much because of these modifications, the last model is accepted.

To bring the time varying variable *job status* into the model, we have several choices. Equivalent to the multilevel regression models for these data, which are treated in Chapter Five, we can add the variables *job₁*, ..., *job₆* as explanatory variables to the model. These predict the outcomes GPA_1, ..., GPA_6, and since the multilevel regression model estimates only one single regression for the effect of *job status* on *GPA*, we must add equality constraints for these regression coefficients.

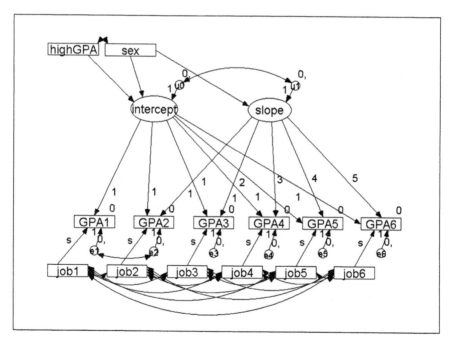

Figure 14.5. Path diagram for GPA example, including effects for job status

The path diagram for this model is given in Figure 14.5. Note the zeros that indicate means and intercepts constrained to zero. The variances of these variables are not constrained, which is visible in the diagram because there are no constraints visible next to the zeros.. The common regression coefficient for *job status* on the *GPA* is estimated as –0.12 (s.e. 0.01), which is close to the multilevel regression estimates in Table 5.4. However, the model including all the job status variables does not fit well, with a chi-square of 202.1 (df=71, p<0.001) and an RMSEA of 0.10. There are no large modification indices, which indicates that there exists no single model modification, which substantially improves the model. We probably need many small modifications to make the model fit better.

An advantage of latent curve analysis over multilevel regression analysis of repeated measures is that it can be used to analyze structures that are more complex. For instance, we may attempt to model the changes in hours spend on a job using a second latent curve model. The path diagram for the latent curve model for *job status* at the six time points is presented in Figure 14.6.

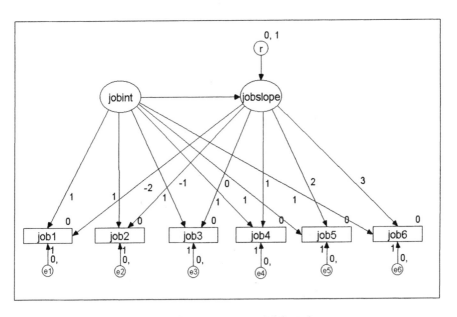

Figure 14.6. Latent curve model for job status

Figure 14.6 has some features that merit discussion. To ensure that the variances of the job intercept and slope factors are positive, the variance is modeled by an error term *r* with the variance set at 1, and the path to *jobslope* estimated. In this specific case, the more usual procedure of setting the path at 1 and estimating the error variances resulted in negative variance estimates. The model specification in Figure 14.6 leads to a latent curve model that fits quite well, with a chi-square of 17.8 (df=17, p= 0.40) and an RMSEA of 0.02. All estimates in this model are acceptable. A powerful feature of structural equation modeling, compared to standard multilevel regression models, is that both models can be combined into one large model for change of both job status and GPA over time. Figure 14.7 shows one such model.

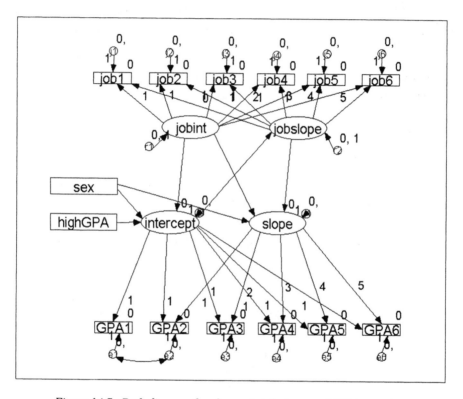

Figure 14.7. Path diagram for change in job status and GPA over time

The model depicted by the path diagram in Figure 14.7 has a moderate fit. The chi-square is 166.0 (df=85, p <.001) and the RMSEA is 0.07. The AIC for the model in Figure 14.5, which is equivalent to a multilevel regression model, is 298.3. In comparison, the AIC for the model in Figure 14.5, which is *not* equivalent to a multilevel regression model, is 243.1. Although the complex latent curve model does not show an extremely good fit, it fits better than the related multilevel regression model.

Figure 14.7 also illustrates that with complicated models with constraints on intercepts and variances, a path diagram quickly becomes cluttered and difficult to read. At some point, presenting the model by describing a sequence of equations becomes simpler. Table 14.1 presents the estimates for the regression weights for the predictor variables *sex* and *high school GPA*, and the intercepts and slopes.

Table 14.1	Path coefficients for structural model in Figure 14.7		
Predictor	**Job slope (s.e.)**	**GPA intercept (s.e.)**	**GPA slope (s.e.)**
sex		0.07 (.03)	0.02 (.01)
high sch. GPA		0.07 (.02)	
job intercept		1.06 (.04)	0.03 (.01)
job slope			-0.46 (.11)
GPA intercept	-0.29 (.06)		

Figure 14.8 presents the same information, but now as standardized path coefficients with only the structural part of the path diagram shown.

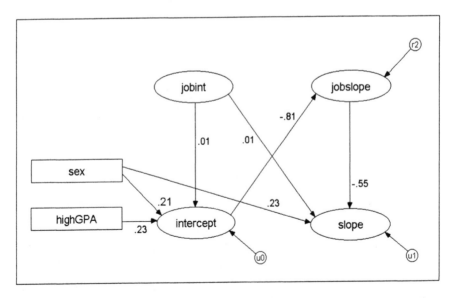

Figure 14.8. Standardized path coefficients for structural model in Figure 14.7

Figure 14.8 shows results similar to the results obtained with the multilevel regression analyses in Chapter Five. Females have a higher GPA to begin with, and their GPA increases over the years at a faster rate than the male students do. The relations between the intercepts and slopes in Figure 14.8 show the mutual effects of changes over time in both job status and GPA. Initial job status has virtually no effect. Changes in job status, as reflected in the slope for job status, have a negative effect on the GPA. If the job status changes in the direction of spending more time on the job, the overall increase in GPA ends, and in fact can become negative. There is also an effect of initial GPA on job status: students with a high initial GPA increase their job workload less than other students do.

14.2 A BRIEF COMPARISON OF MULTILEVEL REGRESSION ANALYSIS AND LATENT CURVE MODELING OF LONGITUDINAL DATA

When equivalent multilevel regression analysis and latent curve modeling are applied to the same data set, the results are identical (Chou, Bentler & Penz, 2000). Plewis (2001) compares three different approaches to longitudinal data, including multilevel regression and latent curve models. Using empirical examples, he concludes that multilevel and latent curve models are very useful in testing interesting hypotheses about longitudinal data, for which they share many strengths and limitations.

A clear advantage of multilevel regression analysis is that adding more levels is straightforward. Modeling development over time of pupils nested within classes, nested in schools, is a simple procedure when multilevel regression is used, provided the analysis software can deal with more than three levels. When latent curve models and SEM software are used, adding a third (group) level is possible (cf. Muthén, 1997), but requires complicated program setups, or a specialized program (Muthén & Muthén, 1998). Adding a fourth level is virtually impossible. Multilevel regression also allows varying relationships at different levels, and modeling this variation by cross-level interactions with explanatory variables at the higher levels.

As remarked earlier in Chapter Five, multilevel regression copes automatically with missing data due to panel dropout. Since there is no requirement that each person has the same number of measurements, or even that the measures are taken at the same occasions, multilevel regression works very well on incomplete data. The latent curve model is a fixed occasions model. If different respondents are measured at different occasions, the latent curve model can deal with this only by specifying paths for all possible measurement occasions that occur in the data set, and regarding individuals observed at different measurement occasions as instances of incomplete data. Modern SEM software can estimate model parameters using

Maximum Likelihood estimation on incomplete data (Arbucle, 1996; Arbucle & Wothke, 1999; Muthén & Muthén, 1998; du Toit & du Toit, 2001), but when there are many and varying time points, the setup becomes complicated, and the estimation procedure may have convergence problems.

Latent curve models estimated with SEM software, on the other hand, have the advantage that it is straightforward to embed them in more complex path models. For instance, in latent growth methodology it is simple to specify a path model where the slope factor is itself a predictor of some outcome. This represents a hypothesis that the rate of growth is a predictor of some outcome variable. An example of such a path model was given in the previous section, where the rate of change in the latent slope for job status is a predictor for the rate of change indicated by the GPA slope factor. This model combines two latent curve models in one larger model, to investigate whether the rate of change in one process depends on the rate of change in a second process. Although the program HLM allows some limited means to model latent variables and path models (Raudenbush et al., 2000), this kind of hypothesis is difficult to model in standard multilevel software. Hoeksma and Knol (2001) present an example of a model, where the slope factor is a predictor of an outcome variable, using in MLwiN. Their discussion makes clear that these models can be specified in the multilevel regression framework, but also that it is difficult and leads to complicated software setups. Using the latent curve approach, the model is a straightforward extension of the basic latent curve model.

In the SEM latent growth curve approach, it is also simple to allow for different errors or correlated errors over time, which is possible in multilevel regression analysis, but more difficult to set up in the current software. A second interesting extension of the latent curve model is adding a measurement model for the variable that is measured over time or for the explanatory variables. To add a measurement model to the variable that is measured over time, it is indicated by a set of observed variables, and the variable that is modeled using the latent curve defined by the intercept and slope factors is then itself a latent variable. A final advantage of the latent curve model is that standard SEM software provides information on goodness-of-fit, and suggests model changes that improve the fit.

Appendix:
Data and Stories

This appendix describes the data used for the examples in *MULTILEVEL ANALYSIS.*
TECHNIQUES AND APPLICATIONS. Some of the example data sets are real data; other
data sets have been simulated especially for their use in this book. The simulated
data sets have been constructed following some hypothetical but plausible real-
world scenario. This appendix describes the various data sets, giving either a
reference to the study where they come from, or the 'story' that has been used as a
template to generate the data.

Data are available on the Internet in SPSS system-file and portable file format.
Most analyses in this book can be carried out by most of the available multilevel
software. Obviously, there is a limit to the number of computer packages one can
master. Most of the multilevel regression analyses in this book have been carried out
in both HLM and MLwiN, and the multilevel SEM analyses have been carried out
using AMOS, LISREL and MPLUS. System files and setups using these packages,
where present, will also be made available on the Internet (currently at:
http://www.fss.uu.nl/ms/jh). I invite users of other multilevel software to use these
data for their own learning or teaching. I appreciate receiving data sets and setups
that have been transferred to other software systems, so I can make them also
available to other users.

POPULARITY DATA

The popularity data in the file POPULAR are simulated data for 2000 pupils in 200
schools. Their purpose is to offer a very simple example for multilevel regression
analysis. The main outcome variable is the *pupil popularity*, a popularity rating on a
scale of 1-10 derived by a sociometric procedure. Typically, a sociometric procedure
asks all pupils in a class to rate all the other pupils, and then assigns the average
received popularity rating to each pupil. Because of the sociometric procedure, group
effects as apparent from higher level variance components are rather strong. There is a
second outcome variable: pupil popularity as rated by their teacher, on a scale from 1-
7. The explanatory variables are pupil gender (boy=0, girl=1) and teacher experience in
years. The pupil popularity data are used as the main example in chapter two. It could
also be used with both outcome variables as an example for the multilevel multivariate
analysis in chapter 9 (chapter 9 uses the survey meta-analysis data for that purpose; a
multivariate multilevel analysis of the popularity data is left as an exercise for the

reader). It is also used as the vehicle to compare the different estimation and testing procedures described in chapter 3 and chapter 11. The popularity data have been generated to be a 'nice' well-behaved data set: the sample sizes at both levels are sufficient, the residuals have a normal distribution, and the multilevel effects are strong.

GPA DATA

The GPA data are a longitudinal data set, where 200 college students have been followed 6 consecutive semesters. The data are simulated. In this data set, there are GPA measures on 6 consecutive occasions, with a JOB status variable (how many hours worked) for the same 6 occasions. There are two student-level explanatory variables: the gender (1= male, 2= female) and the high school GPA. These data are used in the longitudinal analyses in chapter 5, and again in the latent curve analysis in chapter 14. There is also a dichotomous student-level outcome variable, which indicates whether a student has been admitted to the university of their choice. Since not every student applies to a university, this variable has many missing values. The outcome variable 'admitted' is not used in any of the examples in this book.

These data come in several varieties. The basic data file is GPA. In this file, the 6 measurement occasions are represented by separate variables. Some software packages (HLM, Prelis) use this format. Other multilevel software packages (MLwiN, MixReg, SAS) require that the separate measurement occasions are different data records. The GPA data, arranged in this 'flat' data format are in the data file GPAFLAT. A second data set based on the GPA data is data where a process of panel attrition is simulated. Students were simulated to drop out, partly based on having a low GPA in the previous semester. This dropout process leads to data that are Missing At Random (MAR). A naive analysis on the incomplete date gives biased results. A sophisticated analysis using multilevel longitudinal modeling or SEM with the modern raw data likelihood (available in AMOS, M*PLUS* and MX, and in recent versions of LISREL) should give unbiased results. Comparing analyses on the complete and the incomplete data sets gives an impression of the amount of bias. This analysis is referred to in chapter 5, but not presented. The incomplete data are in files GPAMISS and MISFLAT.

CHILDREN'S VOCABULARY DATA

The children's vocabulary growth data are longitudinal data, one of the example data sets that are included with the software HLM (also in the student version of HLM). They are discussed at length in Bryk and Raudenbush (1992) and in the HLM user's manual. The data are a combination of the data from two different studies. Since the two studies use different time periods between vocabulary measurements, and there are some other missing data as well, the result is a very unbalanced data set. This data set is used in chapter 5 to illustrate the issues in longitudinal modeling using 'real time' instead of fixed occasions. The data are in file VOCAGRWT. They contain an identification variable for the measurement occasion, the child's age in months at that occasion, and the vocabulary size at that measurement occasion. Since the vocabulary size at age zero is undefined, it makes sense to center the age variable on some sensible time point. The data set includes a variable 'age12', the age centered on 12 months, and 'age12sq' which is the square of 'age12'. Time invariant covariates are the child's gender (0= boy, 1= girl) and the amount of maternal speech measured at one specific occasion. These variables are not used in this book; Bryk and Raudenbush (1992) model the vocabulary growth using these variables as well. In the course of analyzing these data for this book, I found that they are an interesting example, because they are difficult to analyze, most probably because of their small sample size and small variances at time zero. MLwiN (vs. 1.10) has problems analyzing the more complicated models, HLM (vs. 5.02) does not. This shows that with marginally sufficient data (small samples, complex models) the details of the software implementation can become important. With sufficiently large data sets, such occurrences are rare; Kreft, de Leeuw and van der Leeden (1994) found almost no differences in their review of five multilevel software packages.

THAILAND EDUCATION DATA

The Thailand education data are one of the example data sets that are included with the software HLM (also in the student version of HLM). They are discussed at length in the HLM user's manual. They stem from a large survey of primary education in Thailand (Raudenbush & Bhumirat, 1992). The outcome variable is dichotomous, an indicator whether a pupil has ever repeated a class (0= no, 1= yes). The explanatory variables are pupil gender (0= girl, 1= boy), pupil pre-primary education (0 =no, 1= yes) and the school's mean SES. The example in chapter 6 of this book uses only pupil gender as explanatory variable. There are 8582 cases in the file THAIEDUC, but school mean SES is missing in some cases; there are 7516 pupils with complete data.

SURVEY RESPONSE META-ANALYSIS DATA

The survey response data used to analyze proportions in chapter 6 are from a meta-analysis by Hox & de Leeuw (1994). The basic data file is METARESP. This file contains an identification variable for each study located in the meta-analysis. A mode-identification indicates the data collection mode (face-to-face, telephone, mail). The main response variable is the proportion of sampled respondents who participate. Different studies report different types of response proportions: we have the completion rate (the proportion of participants from the total initial sample) and the response rate (the proportion of participants from the sample without ineligible respondents (moved, deceased, address nonexistent). Obviously, the response rate is usually higher than the completion rate. The explanatory variables are the year of publication and the (estimated) saliency of the survey's main topic. The file also contains the denominators for the completion rate and the response rate, if known. Since most studies report only one of the response figures, the variables 'comp' and 'resp' and the denominators have many missing values.

Some software (e.g., MLwiN) expects the *proportion* of 'successes' and the denominator on which it is based, other software (e.g., HLM) expects the *number* of 'successes' and the corresponding denominator. The file contains the proportion only, the number of successes must be computed from the proportion if the software needs that. The file MULTRESP contains the same information, but now in a three-level format useful if the data are analyzed using the multivariate outcome, which is demonstrated in chapter 9.

PUPCROSS DATA

This data file is used to demonstrate the cross-classified data with pupils nested within both primary and secondary schools. These are simulated data. One thousand pupils have gone to 100 primary and subsequently 30 secondary schools. There is no complete nesting structure; the pupils are nested within the cross-classification of primary and secondary schools. The file PUPCROSS contains the secondary school-achievement score, which is the outcome variable, and the explanatory pupil-level variables gender (0= boy, 1= girl) and SES. School-level explanatory variables are the denomination of the primary and the secondary school (0= no, 1 =yes). These data are used for the example of a cross-classified analysis in chapter 7.

SOCIOMETRIC SCORES DATA

The sociometric data are simulated data, intended to demonstrate a data structure where the cross-classification is at the lowest level, with an added group structure because there are several groups. The story is that in small groups all members are asked to rate each other. Since the groups are of different sizes, the usual data file organized by case in SOCSCORS has many missing values. The data are rearranged in data file SOCSFLAT for the multilevel analysis. In SOCSFLAT each record is defined by the sender-receiver pairs, with explanatory variables age and sex defined separately for the sender and the receiver. The group variable 'group size' is added to this file.

SOCIAL SKILLS META-ANALYSIS DATA

The social skills meta-analysis data in file META20 contain the coded outcomes of 20 studies that investigate the effect of social skills training on social anxiety. All studies use an experimental group/control group design. Explanatory variables are the duration of the training in weeks, the reliability of the social anxiety measure used in each study (2 values, taken from the official test manual), and the studies' sample size. The data are simulated.

SCHOOL MANAGER DATA

The school manager data are from an educational research study (Krüger, 1994). In this study, male and female school managers from 98 schools were rated by 854 pupils. The data are in file MANAGER. These data are used to demonstrate the use of multilevel regression modeling for measuring context characteristics (here: the school manager's management style). The questions about the school manager are question 5, 9, 12, 16, 21 and 25; in chapter 9 of the book these are renumbered 1...6. These data are used only to demonstrate the multilevel psychometric analyses in chapter 9. They can also be analyzed using one of the multilevel factor analysis procedures outlined in chapter 12. The data set also contains the pupils' and school manager's gender (1= female, 2= male), which is not used in the example. The remaining questions in the data set are all about various aspects of the school climate; a full multilevel exploratory factor analysis is a useful approach to these data.

ESTRONE DATA

The estrone data are 16 independent measurements of the estrone level of 5 post-menopausal women (Fears et al., 1996). The data file ESTRONEX contains the data in the usual format, the file ESTRFLAT contains the data in the format used for multilevel analysis. Although the data structure suggests a temporal order in the measurements, there is none. Before the analysis, the estrone levels are transformed by taking the natural logarithm of the measurements. The estrone data are used in chapter

11 to illustrate the use of advanced estimation and testing methods on difficult data. The difficulty of the estrone data lies in the extremely small sample size and the small value of the variance components.

GOOD89 DATA

The file GOOD89 (from Good, 1999, p. 89) contains the very small data set used to demonstrate the principles of bootstrapping in chapter 11.

VAN PEET DATA

The van Peet data are from a study of intelligence in large families (van Peet, 1992). They are the scores on six subscales from an intelligence test. They are used in chapter 12 to illustrate multilevel factor analysis. There are two files: PEETCOMP contains the complete data for 187 children from 37 families, and PEETMIS contains in addition the incomplete data. This data file is interesting because the data set is actually rather small for a SEM analysis, which shows up in (small, insignificant) negative variance estimates. The data file contains the additional variable gender, which is not used in the analyses in this book.

GALO DATA

The GALO data in file GALO are from an educational study by Schijf & Dronkers (1991). They are data from 1377 pupils within 58 schools. We have the following pupil level variables: father's occupational status *focc*, father's education *feduc*, mother's education *meduc*, pupil sex *sex*, the result of GALO school achievement test *GALO*, and the teacher's advice about secondary education *advice*. On the school level we have only one variable: the school's denomination *denom*. Denomination is coded 1= Protestant, 2= Nondenominational, 3= Catholic (categories based on optimal scaling). The data file GALO contains both complete and incomplete cases, and an indicator variable that specifies whether a specific case in the data file is complete or not.

References

Adams, R.J., Wilson, M., & Wu, M. (1997). Multilevel item response models: an approach to errors in variables regression. *Journal of Educational and Behavioral Statistics, 22*, 1, 47-76.

Afshartous, D. (1995): Determination of sample size for multilevel model design. Paper, AERA Conference, San Francisco, 18-22 April 1995.

Agresti, A. (1984). *Analysis of ordinal categorical data.* New York: Wiley.

Aiken, L.S., & West, S.G. (1991). *Multiple regression: Testing and interpreting interaction.* Newbury Park, CA: Sage.

Aitkin, M., Anderson, D., Francis, B., & Hinde, J. (1989). *Statistical modelling in GLIM.* Oxford: Clarendon Press.

Akaike, H. (1987). Factor analysis and the AIC. *Psychometrika, 52*, 317-332.

Alba, R.D., & Logan, J.R. (1992). Analyzing locational attainments: constructing individual-level regression models using aggregate data. *Sociological Methods & Research, 20*, 3, 367-397.

Alker, H.R. (1969). A typology of fallacies. In M. Dogan & S. Rokkan (Eds.), *Quantitative ecological analysis in the social sciences.* Cambridge, Ma.: M.I.T. Press.

Algina, J. (2000). Intraclass correlation – 3 level model (message on Internet Discussion List, 7 December 2000). Multilevel Discussion List, Archived at listserv@jiscmail.ac.uk.

Andrich, D. (1988). Rasch-models for measurement. Newbury Park, CA: Sage.

Ansari, A., & Jedidi, K. (2000). Bayesian factor analysis for multilevel binary observations. *Psychometrika, 65*, 475-496.

Anscombe, F.J. (1973). Graphs in statistical analysis. *American Statistician, 27*, 17-21.

Arbuckle, J.L. (1996). Full information estimation in the presence of incomplete data. In G.A. Marcoulides & R.E. Schumacker (Eds.), *Advanced structural equation modeling.* Mahwah, NJ: Lawrence Erlbaum Associates.

Arbuckle, J.L., & Wothke, W. (1999). *Amos 4.0 user's guide.* Chicago: SmallWaters.

Arnold, C.L. (1992). An introduction to hierarchical linear models. *Measurement and Evaluation in Counseling and Development, 25*, 58-90.

Barbosa, M.F. & Goldstein, H. (2000). Discrete response multilevel models for repeated measures: an application to voting intentions data. *Quality & Quantity, 34*, 323-330.

Barnett, V. (1999). *Comparative statistical inference.* New York: Wiley.

Bechger, T.M., van Schooten, E., de Glopper, C., & Hox, J.J. (1998). The validity of international surveys of reading literacy: the case of the IEA reading literacy study. *Studies in Educational Evaluation, 24*, 2, 99-125.

Beck, N., & Katz, J.N. (1997). The analysis of binary time-series-cross-section data and/or the democratic peace. Paper, Annual Meeting of the Political Methodology Group, Columbus, Ohio, July, 1997.

Bentler, P.M. (1990). Comparative fit indices in structural models. *Psychological Bulletin, 107*, 238-246.

Bentler, P.M. (1995). *EQS structural equations program manual.* Encino, CA: Multivariate Software.

Bentler, P.M., & Bonett, D.G. (1980). Significance tests and goodness-of-fit in the analysis of covariance structures. *Psychological Bulletin, 88*, 588-606.

Bentler, P.M., & Liang, J. (2001). General two level mean and covariance structure models: Maximum likelihood via EM-type algorithms. In J. Blasius, J. Hox, E. de Leeuw & P. Schmidt (Eds.), *Social science methodology in the new millennium. Proceedings of the Fifth International conference on logic and methodology.* Opladen, FRG: Leske + Budrich.

Berkhof, J. & Snijders, T.A.B. (2001). Variance component testing in multilevel models. *Journal of Educational end Behavioral Statistics, 26*, 133-152.

Berkey, C.S., Hoaglin, D.C., Antczak-Bouckoms, A., Mosteller, F., & Colditz, G.A. (1998). Meta-analysis of multiple outcomes by regression with random effects. *Statistics in Medicine, 17*, 2537-2550.

Biggerstaff, B.J., Tweedy, R.L., & Mengersen, K.L. (1994). Passive smoking in the workplace: classical and Bayesian meta-analyses. *International Archives of Occupational and Environmental Health, 66*, 269-277.

Blalock, H.M. (1990). Auxiliary measurement theories revisited. In J.J. Hox & J. De Jong-Gierveld (Eds.), *Operationalization and research strategy.* Amsterdam: Swets & Zeitlinger.

Bollen, K.A. (1989). *Structural equations with latent variables*. New York: Wiley.

Bollen, K.A., & Stine, R.A. (1992). Bootstrapping goodness-of-fit measures in structural equation models. *Sociological Methods & Research, 21*, 205-229.

Booth, J.G., & Sarkar, S. (1998). Monte Carlo approximation of bootstrap variances. *American Statistician, 52*, 354.

Bosker, R.J., Snijders, T.A.B., & Guldemond, H. (1996). *User's manual PINT*. Program and manual available at http://www.ppsw.rug.nl/~sem/staff/snijders.html.

Boyd, L. H., & Iversen, G. R. (1979). *Contextual analysis: concepts and statistical techniques*. Belmont, CA: Wadsworth Publ. Co.

Brockwell, S.E. & Gordon, I.R. (2001). A comparison of statistical methods for meta-analysis. *Statistics in Medicine, 20*, 825-840.

Browne, M.W., & Cudeck, R. (1992). Alternative ways of assessing model fit. *Sociological Methods & Research, 21*, 230-258.

Browne, W.J. (1998). Applying MCMC methods to multilevel models. University of Bath, UK.

Browne, W.J., & Draper, D. (2000). Implementation and performance issues in the Bayesian and likelihood fitting of multilevel models. *Computational Statistics, 15*, 391-420.

Bryk, A.S., & Raudenbush, S.W. (1987). Application of hierarchical linear models to assessing change. *Psychological Bulletin, 101*, 147-158.

Bryk, A.S., & Raudenbush, S.W. (1992). *Hierarchical linear models*. Newbury Park, CA: Sage.

Burchinal, M., & Appelbaum, M.I. (1991). Estimating individual developmental functions: Methods and their assumptions. *Child Development, 62*, 23-43.

Burton, P., Gurrin, L., & Sly, P. (1998). Extending the simple regression model to account for correlated responses: an introduction to generalized estimating equations and multi-level mixed modeling. *Statistics in Medicine, 17*, 1261-1291.

Busing, F. (1993). Distribution characteristics of variance estimates in two-level models. Unpublished manuscript. Leiden: Department of Psychometrics and Research Methodology, Leiden University.

Camstra, A., & Boomsma, A. (1992). Cross-validation in regression and covariance structure analysis: an overview. *Sociological Methods & Research, 21*, 89-115.

Carlin, B.P., & Louis, T.A. (1996). *Bayes and empirical Bayes methods for data analysis*. London: Chapman & Hall.

Carpenter, J., & Bithell, J. (2000). Bootstrap confidence intervals: when, which, what? A practical guide for medical statisticians. *Statistics in Medicine, 19*, 1141-1164.

Casella, G., & George, E. (1992). Explaining the Gibbs sampler. *American Statistician, 46*, 167-174.

Cattell, R.B. (1971). *Abilities: their structure, growth, and action*. Boston: Houghton Mifflin.

Chan, D. (1998). Functional relations among constructs in the same content domain at different levels of analysis: a typology of composition models. *Journal of Applied Psychology, 83*, 2, 234-246.

Chou, C.-P., & Bentler, P.M. (1995). Estimates and tests in structural equation modeling. In R.H. Hoyle (Ed.), *Structural equation modeling: concepts, issues, and applications*. (Pp. 37-55). Newbury Park, CA: Sage.

Chou, C.-P., Bentler, P.M., & Pentz, M.A. (2000). Comparisons of two statistical approaches to study growth curves: the multilevel model and latent curve analysis. *Structural Equation Modeling, 5*, 3, 247-267.

Cnaan, A., Laird, N.M. & Slasos, P. (1997). Using the general linear mixed model to analyse unbalanced repeated measures and longitudinal data. *Statistics in Medicine, 16*, 2349-2380.

Cohen, J. (1988). *Statistical power analysis for the behavioral sciences*. Mahwah, NJ: Lawrence Erlbaum Associates.

Cohen, J. (1992). A power primer. *Psychological Bulletin, 112*, 1, 155-159.

Cohen, J., & Cohen, P. (1975, 1983). *Applied Multiple Regression Analysis for the Behavioral Sciences*. Hillsdale, NJ: Lawrence Erlbaum Associates.

Cohen, M.P. (1998). Determining sample sizes for surveys with data analyzed by hierarchical linear models. *Journal of Official Statistics, 14*, 267-275.

Cooper, H., & Hedges, L.V. (Eds.), (1994). *The handbook of research synthesis*. New York: Russel Sage Foundation.

Cornell, J., & Mulrow, C. (1999). Meta-analysis. In H.J. Ader and G.J. Mellenbergh (Eds.), *Research methodology in the social, behavioral, and life sciences*. London: Sage.

Cronbach, L.J. (1976). Research in classrooms and schools: formulation of questions, designs and analysis. Occasional paper: Stanford Evaluation Consortium.

Cronbach, L.J., & Webb, N. (1979). Between class and within class effects in a reported aptitude × treatment interaction: a reanalysis of a study by G.L. Anderson. *Journal of Educational Psychology*, *67*, 717-724.

Cronbach, L.J., Gleser, G.C., Nanda, H., & Rajaratnam, N. (1972). *The dependability of behavioral measures*. New York: Wiley.

Davidson, R., & MacKinnon, J.G. (1993). Estimation and inference in econometrics. New York: Oxford University Press.

Davis, P., & Scott, A. (1995). The effect of interviewer variance on domain comparisons. *Survey Methodology*, *21*, 2, 99-106.

De Leeuw, E.D. (1992). *Data quality in mail, telephone, and face-to-face surveys*. Amsterdam: TT-Publikaties.

De Leeuw, J., & Kreft, I.G.G. (1986). Random coefficient models for multilevel analysis. *Journal of Educational Statistics, 11*, 57-85.

Delucchi, K., & Bostrom, A. (1999). Small sample longitudinal clinical trials with missing data: a comparison of analytic methods. *Psychological Methods*, *4*, 2, 158-172.

DiPrete, T.A., & Forristal, J.D. (1994). Multilevel models: methods and substance. *Annual Review of Sociology*, *20*, 331-357.

DiPrete, T.A., & Grusky, D.B. (1990). The multilevel analysis of trends with repeated cross-sectional data. In C.C. Clogg (Ed.) *Sociological methodology*, 1990. London: Blackwell.

DuMouchel, W.H. (1989). Bayesian meta-analysis. In D. Berry (Ed.), *Statistical methodology in pharmaceutical sciences.*, p.509-529. New York: Marcel Dekker.

DuMouchel, W.H. (1994). *Hierarchical Bayesian linear models for meta-analysis*. Unpublished report, Research Triangle Park, NC: National Institute of Statistical Sciences.

Duncan, T.E., & Duncan, S.C. (1995). Modeling the processes of development via latent variable growth curve methodology. *Structural Equation Modeling*, *2*, 3, 187-213.

du Toit, M., du Toit, S. (2001). *Interactive LISREL: User's guide*. Chicago: Scientific Software Inc.

Efron, B. (1982). *The Jackknife, the bootstrap and other resampling plans*. Philadelphia: Society for Industrial and Applied Mathematics.

Efron, B., & Tibshirani, R.J. (1993). *An introduction to the bootstrap*. New York: Chapman & Hall.

Eliason, S.R. (1993). *Maximum Likelihood estimation*. Newbury Park, CA: Sage.

Engels, E.A., Schmidt, C.H., Terrin, N., Olkin, I., & Lau, J. (2000). Heterogeneity and statistical significance in meta-analysis: an empirical study of 125 meta-analyses. *Statistics in Medicine*, *19*, 13, 1707-1728.

Erbring, L., & Young, A.A. (1979). Contextual effects as endogenous feedback. *Sociological Methods & Research*, *7*, 396-430.

Evans, M., Hastings, N., & Peacock, B. (1993). *Statistical distributions*. New York: Wiley.

Fears, T.R., Benichou, J., & Gail, M.H. (1996). A reminder of the fallibility of the Wald statistic. *American Statistician*, *50*, 3, 226-227.

Fielding, A. (1999). Why use arbitrary points scores? Ordered categories in models of educational progress. *Journal of the Royal Statistical Society, Series A*, *162*, 303-328.

Fotiu, R.P. (1989): A comparison of the EM and data augmentation algorithms on simulated small sample hierarchical data from research on education. Unpublished doctoral dissertation, Michigan State University, East Lansing.

Galtung, J. (1969). *Theory and methods of social research*. New York: Columbia University Press.

Gelman, A., & Rubin, D.B. (1992). Inference from iterative simulation using multiple sequences. *Statistical Science*, *7*, 457-511.

Gerbing, D.W., & Anderson, J.C. (1992). Monte Carlo evaluations of goodness-of-fit indices for structural equation models. *Sociological Methods & Research*, *21*, 132-161.

Gill, J. (2000). *Generalized linear models*. Thousand Oaks, CA: Sage.

Glass, G.V. (1976). Primary, secondary and meta-analysis of research. *Educational Researcher*, *10*, 3-8.

Goldstein, H. (1986). Efficient statistical modelling of longitudinal data. *Annals of Human Biology*, *13*, 129-141.

Goldstein, H. (1987). *Multilevel Models in Educational and Social Research*. London: Griffin.

Goldstein, H. (1989). Efficient statistical modelling of longitudinal data. In R.D. Bock (Ed.), *Multilevel Analysis of Educational Data*. San Diego: Academic Press.

Goldstein, H. (1991) Non-linear multilevel models, with an application to discrete response data.

Biometrika, 78, 45-51.

Goldstein, H. (1994). Multilevel cross-classified models. *Sociological Methods & Research, 22,* 364-376.

Goldstein, H. (1995). *Multilevel Statistical Models.* London: Edward Arnold/New York: Halsted.

Goldstein, H., & Browne, W. (2001). Multilevel factor analysis modeling using Markov Chain Monte Carlo (MCMC) estimation. In G.A. Marcoulides & I. Moustaki (Eds.). *Latent variable and latent structure models.* Mahwah: NJ: Lawrence Erlbaum Associates.

Goldstein, H., & Healy, M.J.R. (1995). The graphical representation of a collection of means. *Journal of the Royal Statistical Society, A, 158,* 175-177.

Goldstein, H., Healy, M.J.R., & Rasbash, J. (1994). Multilevel time series models with applications to repeated measures data. *Statistics in Medicine, 13,* 1643-1656.

Goldstein, H., & McDonald, R. (1988). A general model for the analysis of multilevel data. *Psychometrika, 53,* 455-467.

Goldstein, H., & Rasbash, J. (1996). Improved approximations to multilevel models with binary responses. *Journal of the Royal Statistical Society,* Series A, *159,* 505-513.

Goldstein, H., Rasbash, J., Plewis, I., Draper, D., Browne, W., Yang, M., Woodhouse, G., & Healy, M. (1998). *A user's guide to MlwiN.* London: Institute of Education, University of London.

Goldstein, H., & Silver, R. (1989). Multilevel and multivariate models in survey analysis. In C. Skinner, D. Holt, & F. Smith (Eds.), *The analysis of complex surveys.* New York: Wiley.

Goldstein, H., & Spiegelhalter, D.J. (1996). League tables and their limitations: statistical issues in comparisons of institutional performance. *Journal of the Royal Statistical Society, A, 159,* 505-513.

Goldstein, H., Yang, M., Omar, R., Turner, R. & Thompson, S. (2000). Meta-analysis using multilevel models with an application to the study of class sizes. *Applied Statistics, 49,* 399-412.

Good, P.I. (1999). *Resampling methods: a practical guide to data analysis.* Boston/Berlin: Birkhäuser.

Green, S.B. (1991). How many subjects does it take to do a regression analysis? *Multivariate Behavior Research, 26,* 499-510.

Greene, W.H. (1997). *Econometric analysis.* Upper Saddle River, NJ: Prentice Hall.

Groves, R.M. (1989). *Survey cost and survey error.* New York: Wiley.

Gulliford, M.C., Ukoumunne, O.C., & Chinn, S. (1999). Components of variance and intraclass correlations for the design of community-based surveys and intervention studies. *American Journal of Epidemiology, 149,* 876-883.

Gustafsson, J.-E., & Stahl, P.E. (1999). *Streams user's guide, Vs. 2.0.* Mölndal, Sweden: MultivariateWare.

Härnqvist, K., Gustafsson, J.-E., Muthén, B.O., & Nelson, G. (1994). Hierarchical models of ability at individual and class level. *Intelligence, 18,* 165-187.

Hartford, A., & Davidian, M. (2000). Consequences of misspecifying assumptions in nonlinear mixed effects models. *Computational Statistics & Data Analysis, 34,* 139-164.

Harwell, M. (1997). An empirical study of Hedges' homogeneity test. *Psychological Methods, 2,* 2, 219-231.

Hays, W.L. (1994). *Statistics.* New York: Harcourt Brace College Publishers.

Heck, R.H., & Thomas, S.L. (2000). *An introduction to multilevel modeling techniques.* Mahwah, NJ: Lawrence Erlbaum Associates.

Heck, R.H. (2001). Multilevel modeling with SEM. In G.A. Marcoulides & R.E. Schumacker (Eds.). *New developments and techniques in structural equation modeling.* Mahwah, NJ: Lawrence Erlbaum Associates. (Pp. 89-127).

Hedeker, D., & Gibbons, R.D. (1996a). MIXOR: A computer program for mixed effects ordinal regression analysis. *Computer Methods and Programs in Biomedicine, 49,* 157-176.

Hedeker, D., & Gibbons, R.D. (1996b). MIXREG: A computer program for mixed effects regression analysis with autocorrelated errors. *Computer Methods and Programs in Biomedicine, 49,* 229-252. Available at: http://tigger.uic.edu/%7Ehedeker/mix.html.

Hedeker, D., & Gibbons, R.D. (1997). Application of random-effects pattern-mixture models for missing data in longitudinal studies. *Psychological Methods, 2,* 1, 64-78. Available at: http://tigger.uic.edu/%7Ehedeker/mix.html.

Hedges, L.V., & Olkin, I. (1985). *Statistical methods for meta-analysis.* San Diego, CA: Academic Press.

Hedges, L.V., & Vevea, J.L. (1998). Fixed- and random effects models in meta-analysis. *Psychological Methods, 3,* 486-504.

Higgins, J.P.T., Whitehead, A., Turner, R.M., Omar, R.Z. & Thompson, S.G. Meta-analysis of continuous outcome data from individual patients. *Statistics in Medicine, 20,* 2219-2241.

Hill, P.W., & Goldstein, H. (1998). Multilevel modeling of educational data with cross-classification and missing identification for units. *Journal of Educational and Behavioral Statistics*, *23*, 2, 117-128.

Hoeksma, J.B. & Knol, D.L. (2001). Testing predictive developmental hypotheses. *Multivariate Behavior Research*, *36*, 227-248.

Hofmann, D.A., & Gavin, M.B. (1998). Centering decisions in hierarchical linear models: implications for research in organizations. *Journal of Management*, *24*, 5, 623-641.

Hoijtink, H. (2000). Posterior inference in the random intercept model based on samples obtained with Markov chain Monte Carlo methods. *Computational Statistics*, *15*, 315-336.

Holm, S. (1979). A simple sequentially rejective multiple test procedure. *Scandinavian Journal of Statistics*, *6*, 65-70.

Hox, J.J. (1993). Factor analysis of multilevel data: Gauging the Muthén model. In J.H.L. Oud & R.A.W.van Blokland-Vogelesang (Eds.), *Advances in longitudinal and multivariate analysis in the behavioral sciences*. Pp.141-156. Nijmegen: ITS.

Hox, J.J. (1994a). Hierarchical regression models for interviewer and respondent effects. *Sociological Methods & Research*, *22*, 300-318.

Hox, J.J. (1994b, revised 2000). *Split2*. Computer Program, available at: http://www.fss.uu.nl/ms/jh.

Hox, J.J. (1995). *Applied multilevel analysis. (Second edition)*. Amsterdam: TT-Publikaties. Available at: http://www.fss.uu.nl/ms/jh.

Hox, J.J. (1998). Multilevel modeling: when and why. In I. Balderjahn, R. Mathar & M. Schader (Eds.), *Classification, data analysis, and data highways*. Pp. 147-154. New York: Springer Verlag.

Hox, J.J. (2000). Multilevel analysis of grouped and longitudinal data. In T.D. Little, K.U. Schnabel & J. Baumert (Eds.), *Modeling longitudinal and multiple-group data. Practical issues, applied approaches, and specific examples*. Hillsdale, NJ: Lawrence Lawrence Erlbaum Associates.

Hox, J.J. (2001). Estimating power in multilevel models: A general approach. Paper presented at the 3th Amsterdam multilevel conference, Amsterdam, April 9-10, 2001.Hox, J.J., & Bechger, T.M. (1998). An introduction to structural equation modeling. *Family Science Review*, *11*, 354-373.

Hox, J.J., & de Leeuw, E.D.. (1994). A comparison of nonresponse in mail, telephone, and face-to-face surveys. Applying multilevel modeling to meta-analysis. *Quality & Quantity*, *28*, 329-344.

Hox, J.J., & de Leeuw, E.D.. (2001). Multilevel Models for meta-Analysis. In N. Duan & S. Reise (Eds.), *Multilevel Modeling: Methodological advances, issues and applications*. Mahwah, NJ: Lawrence Erlbaum Associates.

Hox, J.J., de Leeuw, E.D., & Kreft, G.G. (1991). The effect of interviewer and respondent characteristics on the quality of survey data: a multilevel model. In P.P. Biemer, R.M. Groves, L.E. Lyberg, N.A. Mathiowetz, & S. Sudman (Eds.), *Measurement errors in surveys*. New York: Wiley.

Hox, J.J., Kreft, G.G., & Hermkens, P.L.J. (1991). The analysis of factorial surveys. *Sociological Methods & Research*, *19*, 493- 510.

Hox, J.J., & Lagerweij, N. (1993). Using hierarchical models to analyze facet-data. In *Proceedings of the 4th International Facet Theory conference*. Prague: Facet Theory Association, Pp. 198-207.

Hox, J.J., & Maas, C.J.M. (2001a). The accuracy of multilevel structural equation modeling with pseudobalanced groups and small samples. *Structural Equation Modeling*, *8*, 157-174.

Hox, J.J., & Maas, C.J.M. (2001b). The accuracy of asymptotic and robust standard errors for fixed coefficients when data are strongly non-normal. Paper presented at the 3rd Amsterdam Multilevel Conference, Amsterdam, April 2001.

Huber, P.J. (1967). The behavior of maximum likelihood estimates under non-standard conditions. In *Proceedings of the Fifth Berkeley symposium on mathematical statistics and probability*. Pp. 221-233. Berkeley, CA: University of California Press.

Hunter, J.E., & Schmidt, F.L. (1990). *Methods of meta-analysis*. Newbury Park, CA: Sage.

Hunter, J.E., & Schmidt, F.L. (1994). Correcting for sources of artifact variation. In H. Cooper & L.V. Hedges (Eds.), *The handbook of research synthesis*. New York: Russel Sage Foundation.

Huttenlocher, J.E., Haight, W., Bryk, A.S., & Seltzer, M. (1991). Early vocabulary growth: Relation to language input and gender. *Developmental Psychology*, *27*, 2, 236-249.

Hüttner, H.J.M., & van den Eeden, P. (1993). *The multilevel design. A guide with an annotated bibliography, 1980-1993*. London: Greenwood Press.

Jaccard, J., Turrisi, R., & Wan, C.K. (1990). *Interaction effects in multiple regression*. Newbury Park, CA: Sage.

Jedidi, K., & Ansari, A. (2001). Bayesian structural equation models for multilevel data. In G.A.

Marcoulides & R.E. Schumacker (Eds.). *New developments and techniques in structural equation modeling.* Mahwah, NJ: Lawrence Erlbaum Associates. (Pp. 129-157).

Jöreskog, K.G., & Sörbom, D. (1989*). Lisrel 7: A guide to the program and applications.* Chicago: SPSS Inc.

Jöreskog, K.G., & Sörbom, D. (1996). *Lisrel 8: User's reference guide. 2nd Edition.* Chicago: Scientific Software International Inc.

Jöreskog, K.G., Sörbom, D., du Toit, S., & du Toit, M. (1999). *Lisrel 8: New statistical features.* Chicago: Scientific Software Inc.

Jöreskog, K.G., & Yang, F. (1996). Non-linear structural equation models: the Kenny-Judd model with interactions. In G.A. Marcoulides & R.E. Schumacker (Eds.), *Advanced structural equation modeling.* Mahwah, NJ: Lawrence Erlbaum Associates.

Kalaian, H.A., & Raudenbush, S.W. (1996). A multivariate mixed linear model for meta-analysis. *Psychological Methods, 1,* 227-235.

Kamata, A. (2001). Item analysis by the hierarchical generalized linear model. *Journal of Educational Measurement, 38,* 79-93.

Kaplan, D. (1995). Statistical power in SEM. In R.H. Hoyle (Ed.), *Structural equation modeling: concepts, issues, and applications.* (Pp. 100-117). Newbury Park, CA: Sage.

Kaplan, D., & Elliot, P.R. (1997). A didactic example of multilevel structural equation modeling applicable to the study of organizations. *Structural Equation Modeling, 4,* 1-24.

Kasim, R.M., & Raudenbush, S.W. (1998). Application of Gibbs sampling to nested variance components models with heterogeneous within-group variance. *Journal of Educational and Behavioral Statistics, 23,* 2, 93-116.

Kef, S., Habekothé, H.T., & Hox, J.J. (2000). Social networks of blind and visually impaired adolescents: structure and effect on well-being. *Social Networks, 22,* 73-91.

Kendall, M.G. (1959). Hiawatha designs an experiment. *American Statistician, 13,* 23-24.

King, G. (1997). *A solution to the ecological inference problem: reconstructing individual behavior from aggregate data.* Princeton, NJ: Princeton University Press.

Kirk, R.E. (1968). *Experimental design: procedures for the behavioral sciences.* Belmont, Calif: Brooks/Cole.Kish, L. (1965): *Survey Sampling.* Wiley, New York.

Kish, L. (1965). *Survey sampling.* NY: Wiley.

Kish, L. (1987). *Statistical design for research.* New York: Wiley.

Kreft, I.G.G. (1996): Are multilevel techniques necessary? An overview, including simulation studies. Unpublished Report, California State University, Los Angeles. Available at http://ioe.ac.uk/multilevel.

Kreft, Ita G.G., & de Leeuw, E.D. (1987). The see-saw effect: a multilevel problem? A reanalysis of some findings of Hox and De Leeuw. *Quality & Quantity,* 22, 127-137.

Kreft, I., & de Leeuw, J. (1998). *Introducing multilevel modeling.* Newbury Park, CA: Sage.

Kreft, I.G.G., de Leeuw, J., & Aiken, L. (1995). The effect of different forms of centering in hierarchical linear models. *Multivariate Behavioral Research, 30,* 1-22.

Kreft, I.G.G., de Leeuw, J., & van der Leeden, R. (1994). Review of five analysis programs: BMDP-5V, GENMOD, HLM, ML3, VARCL. *American Statistician, 48,* 324-335.

Krüger, M. (1994). Sekseverschillen in schoolleiderschap. Alphen a/d Rijn: Samson. [Gender differences in school leadership.]

Langford, I. and Lewis, T. (1998). Outliers in multilevel data. *Journal of the Royal Statistical Society, Series A, 161,* 121-160.

Lazarsfeld, P.F., & Menzel, H. (1961). On the relation between individual and collective properties. In A. Etzioni (Ed.), *Complex organizations: A sociological reader.* New York: Holt, Rhinehart & Winston.

Lee, S.Y., & Poon, W.Y. (1992). Two level analysis of covariance structures for unbalanced designs with small level one samples. *British Journal of Mathematical and Statistical Psychology, 45,* 109-123.

Lesaffre, E. & Spiessens, B. (2001). On the effect of the number of quadrature points in a logistic random-effects model: an example. *Applied Statistics, 50,* 325-335.

Li, F., Duncan, T.E., Harmer, P., Acock, A., & Stoolmiller, M. (1998). Analyzing measurement models of latent variables through multilevel confirmatory factor analysis and hierarchical linear modeling approaches. *Structural Equation Modeling, 5,* 3, 294-306.

Liang, K., & Zeger, S.L. (1986). Longitudinal data analysis using generalized linear models. *Biometrica,* 73, 45-51.

Light, R.J., & Pillemer, D.B. (1984). *Summing up: The science of reviewing research.* Cambridge, MA:

Harvard University Press.

Light, R.J., Singer, J.D., & Willet, J.B. (1994) The visual presentation and interpretation of meta-analyses. In H. Cooper & L.V. Hedges (Eds.), *The handbook of research synthesis.* New York: Russell Sage Foundation.

Lillard, L.A., & Panis, C.W.A. (2000). *aML. Multilevel multiprocess statistical software, release 1.* Los Angeles, CA: EconWare.

Lindley, D.V., & Novick, M.R. (1981). The role of exchangeability in inference. *Annals of Statistics, 9,* 45-58.

Lindley, D.V., & Smith, A.F.M. (1972). Bayes estimates for the linear model. *Journal of the Royas Statistical Society, Series B, 34,* 1-41.

Lipsey, M.W., & Wilson, D.B. (2001). *Practical meta-analysis.* Thousand Oaks, CA: Sage.

Littell, R.C., Milliken, G.A., Stroup, W.W., & Wolfinger, R.D. (1996). *SAS system for mixed models.* Cary: NC: SAS Institute, Inc.

Little, T.D., Schnabel K.U., & Baumert J. (2000) (Eds.), *Modeling longitudinal and multiple-group data. Practical issues, applied approaches, and specific examples.* Hillsdale, NJ: Lawrence Erlbaum Associates.

Little, R.J.A. (1995). Modeling the drop-out mechanism in repeated measures studies. *Journal of the American Statistical Association, 90,* 1112-1121.

Little, R.J.A., & Rubin, D.B. (1987). *Statistical analysis with missing data.* New York: Wiley.

Little, R.J.A., & Rubin, D.B. (1989). The treatment of missing data in multivariate analysis. *Sociological Methods & Research, 18,* 292-326.

Loehlin, J.C. (1998). *Latent variable models: An introduction to factor, path, and structural analysis.* Mahwah, NJ: Lawrence Erlbaum Associates.

Long, J.S. (1997). *Regression models for categorical and limited dependent variables.* Thousand Oaks, CA: Sage.

Long, J.S., & Ervin, L.H. (1998). Correcting for heteroscedasticity with heteroscedasticity consistent standard errors in the linear regression model: small sample considerations. Unpublished manuscript, Indiana University, Bloomington, Indiana.

Longford, N.T. (1987). A fast scoring algorithm for maximum likelihood estimation in unbalanced mixed models with nested random effects. *Biometrika, 74,* 817-827.

Longford, N.T. (1988). A quasi-likelihood adaptation for variance component analysis. Proceedings of the Section on Statistical Computing of the American Statistical Association. Alexandria, VA: American Statistical Association.

Longford, N.T. (1990) VARCL. Software for variance component analysis of data with nested random effects (Maximum Likelihood). Princeton, NJ: Educational Testing Service.

Longford, N.T. (1993). *Random coefficient models.* Oxford: Clarendon Press.

Longford, N.T., & Muthén, B.O. (1992). Factor analysis for clustered observations. *Psychometrika, 57,* 581-597.

Lord, F.M., & Novick, M.R. (1968). *Statistical theories of mental test scores.* Reading, MA: Addison-Wesley.

Maas, C.J.M., & Hox, J.J. (2001). Robustness of multilevel parameter estimates against non-normality and small sample sizes. In J. Blasius, J. Hox, E. de Leeuw & P. Schmidt (Eds.), *Social science methodology in the new millennium. Proceedings of the Fifth International conference on logic and methodology.* Opladen, FRG: Leske + Budrich.

Maas, C.J.M., & Snijders, T.A.B. (2002). The multilevel approach to repeated measures with missing data. *Quality & Quantity,* in press.

Macaskill, P., Walter, S.D. & Irwig, L. (2001). A comparison of methods to detect publication bias in meta-analysis. *Statistics in Medicine, 20,* 641-654.

MacCallum, R.C., & Kim, C. (2000) Modeling multivariate change. In T.D. Little, K.U. Schnabel & J. Baumert (Eds.), *Modeling longitudinal and multiple-group data. Practical issues, applied approaches, and specific examples.* Pp. 51-68. Hillsdale, NJ: Lawrence Erlbaum Associates.

Marcoulides, G.A., & Schumacker, R.E. (Eds.), (2001). *New developments and techniques in structural equation modeling.* Mahwah, NJ: Lawrence Erlbaum Associates.

Maxwell, S.E. (1998). Longitudinal designs in randomized group comparisons: when will intermediate observations increase statistical power? *Psychological Methods, 3,* 275-290.

McArdle, J.J., & Hamagami, F. (1996). Multilevel models from a multiple group structural equation perspective. In G.A. Marcoulides & R.E. Schumacker (Eds.), *Advanced Structural Equation Modeling*. Pp. 89-125. Mahwah, NJ: Lawrence Erlbaum Associates.

McCullagh, P., & Nelder, J.A. (1989). *Generalized linear models*. Second Edition. London: Chapman & Hall.

McDonald, R.P. (1994). The bilevel reticular action model for path analysis with latent variables. *Sociological Methods & Research, 22*, 399-413.

McDonald, R., & Goldstein, H. (1989). Balanced versus unbalanced designs for linear structural relations in two-level data. *British Journal of Mathematical and Statistical Psychology, 42*, 215-232.

Meredith, W., & Tisak, J. (1990). Latent curve analysis. *Psychometrika, 55*, 107-122.

Meyer, D.K. (1964). A Bayesian school superintendent. *American Educational Research Journal, 1*, 219-228.

Mislevy, R.J., & Bock, R.D. (1989). A hierarchical item-response model for educational testing. In R.D. Bock (Ed.) *Multilevel analysis of educational data*. San Diego, CA: Academic Press.

Moerbeek, M. (2000). *The design and analysis of multilevel intervention studies*. Maastricht, the Netherlands, University of Maastricht, Ph.D. Thesis.

Moerbeek, M., van Breukelen, G.J.P., & Berger, M. (2000). Design issues for experiments in multilevel populations. *Journal of Educational and Behavioral Statistics, 25*, 271-284.

Moerbeek, M., van Breukelen, G.J.P., & Berger, M. (2001). Optimal experimental design for multilevel logistic models. *The Statistician, 50*, 17-30.

Mok, M. (1995). Sample size requirements for 2-level designs in educational research. Unpublished manuscript. London: Multilevel Models Project, Institute of Education, University of London. Available at http://multilevel.ioe.ac.uk.

Mooney, C.Z., & Duval, R.D. (1993). *Bootstrapping. A nonparametric approach to statistical inference*. Newbury Park, CA: Sage.

Mosteller, F., & Tukey, J.W. (1977). *Data analysis and regression*. Reading, Ma: Addison-Wesley.

Muthén, B. (1989). Latent variable modeling in heterogeneous populations. *Psychometrika, 54*, 557-585.

Muthén, B. (1990). *Means and covariance structure analysis of hierarchical data*. Los Angeles: UCLA Statistics series, #62.

Muthén, B.O. (1991). Analysis of longitudinal data using latent variable models with varying parameters. In L.C. Collins & J.L. Horn (Eds.), *Best methods for the analysis of change*. Washington, DC: American Psychological Association.

Muthén, B.O. (1994). Multilevel covariance structure analysis. *Sociological Methods & Research, 22*, 376-398.

Muthén, B.O. (1997). Latent growth modeling with longitudinal and multilevel data. In A.E. Raftery (Ed.) *Sociological Methodology, 1997*. Pp. 453-480. Boston: Blackwell.

Muthén, B.O., & Satorra, A. (1989). Multilevel aspects of varying parameters in structural models. In Bock, R.D. (Ed.), *Multilevel analysis of educational data*. San Diego: Academic Press.

Muthén, B., & Satorra, A. (1995). Complex sample data in structural equation modeling. In P.V. Marsden (Ed.), *Sociological Methodology, 1995*. Pp. 267-316. Oxford: Blackwell.

Muthén, L.K., & Muthén, B.O. (1998). *Mplus user's guide*. Los Angeles: Muthén & Muthén.

NCSS (1995). *NCSS probability calculator*. Available at http://www.icw.com/ncss.

Nevitt, J., & Hancock, G.R. (2001). Performance of bootstrapping approaches to model test statistics and parameter standard error estimation in structural equation modeling. *Structural Equation Modeling, 8*, 3, 353-377.

Novick, M.R., & Jackson, P.H. (1974). *Statistical methods for educational and psychological research*. New York: McGraw-Hill.

Nunnally, J.C., & Bernstein, I.H. (1994). *Psychometric theory*. New York: McGraw-Hill.

O'Brien, R.G., & Kaiser, M.K. (1985). MANOVA method for analyzing repeated measures designs: an extensive primer. *Psychological Bulletin, 97*, 316-333.

O'Muircheartaigh, C., & Campanelli, P. (1999). A multilevel exploration of the role of interviewers in survey non-response. *Journal of the Royal Statistical Society, Series A, 162*, 437-446.

Pan, H. & Goldstein, H. (1998). Multilevel repeated measures growth modeling using extended spline functions. *Statistics in Medicine, 17*, 2755-2770.

Paterson, L. (1998). Multilevel multivariate regression: an illustration concerning school teachers' perception of their pupils. *Educational Research and Evaluation, 4*, 126-142.

Pawitan, Y. (2000). A reminder of the fallibility of the Wald statistic: Likelihood explanation.

American Statistician, 54, 1, 54-56.

Pedhazur, E.J. (1997). *Multiple regression in behavioral research : Explanation and prediction.* Forth Worth, TA: Harcourt.

Pendergast, J., Gange, S., Newton, M., Lindstrom, M., Palta, M., & Fisher, M. (1996). A survey of methods for analyzing clustered binary response data. *International Statistical Review, 64*, 1, 89-118.

Pickery, J., & Loosveldt, G. (1998). The impact of respondent and interviewer characteristics on the number of 'no opinion' answers. *Quality & Quantity, 32*, 31-45.

Pickery, J., Loosveldt, G., & Carton, A. (2001). The effects of interviewer and respondent characteristics on response behavior in panel-surveys: A multilevel approach. *Sociological Methods & Research, 29*, 4, 509-523.

Plewis, I. (1985). *Analysing change.* New York: Wiley.

Plewis, I. (1996). Statistical methods for understanding cognitive growth: A review, a synthesis and an application. *British Journal of Mathematical and Statistical Psychology, 49*, 25-42.

Plewis, I. (2001). Explanatory models for relating growth processes. *Multivariate Behavior Research, 36*, 207-225.

Rabe-Hesketh, S. Pickles, A. & Taylor, C. (2000). Generalized linear latent and mixed models. *Stata Technical Bulletin, 53*, 47-57.

Rabe-Hesketh, S. Pickles, A. & Skrondal, A. (2001a). GLLAMM: a general class of multilevel models and a STATA program. *Multilevel Modelling Newsletter, 13*, 17-23.

Rabe-Hesketh, S. Pickles, A. & Skrondal, A. (2001b). GLLAMM Manual. Department of Biostatistics and Computing, Institute of Psychiatry, King's College, University of London. Available at: http://www.iop.kcl.ac.uk/iop/depatrments/biocomp/programs/gllamm.html.

Raftery, A.E. & Lewis,S.M. (1992). How many iterations in the Gibbs sampler? In J.M. Bernardo, J.O. Berger, A.P. Dawid and A.F M. Smith (Eds.), *Bayesian Statistics 4.* Pp.765-776. Oxford: Oxford University Press.

Rasbash, J., Browne, W., Goldstein, H., Yang, M., Plewis, I., Healy, M., Woodhouse, G., Draper, D., Langford, I., & Lewis, T. (2000). A user's guide to MlwiN. London: Multilevel Models Project, University of London.

Rasbash, J., & Goldstein, H. (1994). Efficient analysis of mixed hierarchical and cross-classified random structures using a multilevel model. *Journal of Educational and Behavioral Statistics, 19*, 4, 337-350.

Raudenbush, S.W. (1993a). Hierarchical linear models as generalizations of certain common experimental designs. In L. Edwards (Ed.), *Applied analysis of variance in behavioral science.* Pp. 459-496. New York: Marcel Dekker.

Raudenbush, S.W. (1993b). A crossed random effects model for unbalanced data with applications in cross-sectional and longitudinal research. *Journal of Educational Statistics, 18*, 4, 321-349.

Raudenbush, S.W. (1994). Random effects models. In H. Cooper & L.V. Hedges (Eds.), *The handbook of research synthesis.* New York: Russell Sage Foundation.

Raudenbush, S.W. (1995). Maximum likelihood estimation for unbalanced multilevel covariance structure models via the EM algorithm. *British Journal of Mathematical and Statistical Psychology, 48*, 359-370.

Raudenbush, S.W. (1997). Statistical analysis and optimal design for cluster randomized trials. *Psyhological Methods, 2*, 2, 173-185.

Raudenbush, S., & Bhumirat, C. (1992). The distribution of resources for primary education and its consequences for educational achievement in Thailand. *International Journal of Educational Research, 17*, 143-164.

Raudenbush, S.W., & Bryk, A.S. (1985). Empirical Bayes meta-analysis. *Journal of Educational Statistics, 10*, 75-98.

Raudenbush, S.W., & Bryk, A.S. (1986). A hierarchical model for studying school effects. *Sociology of Education, 59*, 1-17.

Raudenbush, S.W., & Bryk, A.S. (1987). Examining correlates of diversity. *Journal of Educational Statistics, 12*, 241-269.

Raudenbush, S.W., & Bryk, A.S. (1988). Methodological advances in studying effects of schools and classrooms on student learning. *Review of Research on Education, 15*, 423-476.

Raudenbush, S., Bryk, A., Cheong, Y.F., & Congdon, R. (2000). *HLM 5. Hierarchical linear and nonlinear modeling.* Chicago: Scientific Software International.

Raudenbush, S.W. & Chan, W.-S. (1993). Application of a hierarchical linear model to the study of adolescent deviance in an overlapping cohort design. *Journal of Consulting and Clinical Psychology*, *61*, 941-951.

Raudenbush, S.W., & Liu, X. (2000). Statistical power and optimal design for multisite randomized trials. *Psychological Methods*, *5*, 2, 199-213.

Raudenbush, S.W., Rowan, B., & Kang, S.J. (1991) A multilevel, multivariate model for studying school climate with estimation via the EM algorithm and application to U.S. high-school data. *Journal of Educational Statistics*, *16*, 4, 295-330.

Raudenbush, S.W., & Sampson, R. (1999a). Ecometrics: Toward a science of assessing ecological settings, with application to the systematic social observations of neighborhoods. *Sociological Methodology*, *29*, 1-41.

Raudenbush, S. W., & Sampson, R. (1999b). Assessing direct and indirect associations in multilevel designs with latent variables. *Sociological Methods and Research*, *28*, 123-153.

Raudenbush, S.W., Yang, M.-L., & Yosef, M. (2000). Maximum likelihood for generalized linear models with nested random effects via high-order, multivariate Laplace approximation. *Journal of Computational and Graphical Statistics*, *9*, 141-157.

Raudenbush, S.W., & Willms, J.D. (Eds.), (1991). *Schools, classrooms, and pupils: International studies of schooling from a multilevel perspective*. New York: Academic Press.

Roberts, K., & Burstein, L. (1980). *New directions for methodology for social and behavioral sciences. Vol. 6.* San Francisco: Jossey-Bass.

Robinson, W.S. (1950). Ecological correlations and the behavior of individuals. *American Sociological Review*, *15*, 351-357.

Rodriguez, G., & Goldman, N. (1995): An assessment of estimation procedures for multilevel models with binary responses. *Journal of the Royal Statistical Society, Series A*, *158*, 73-90.

Rosenthal, R. (1984). *Meta-analytic procedures for social research*. Newbury Park, CA: Sage.

Rosenthal, R. (1994). Parametric measures of effect size. In H. Cooper and L.V. Hedges (Eds.), *The handbook of research synthesis*. Pp. 231-244. New York: Russell Sage Foundation.

Rowe, K.J. (2002). Simultaneous estimation of interdependent effects among multilevel composite variables in psychosocial research: An annotated example of the application of multilevel structural equation modeling. In N. Duan & S. Reise (Eds.), *Multilevel Modeling: Methodological advances, issues and aplications*. Mahwah, NJ: Lawrence Erlbaum Associates.

Rowe, K.J., & Hill, P.W. (1998). Modeling educational effectiveness in classrooms: the use of multi-level structural equations to model students' progress. *Educational Research and Evaluation*, *4*, 307-347.

Sammel, M., Lin, X., & Ryan, L. (1999). Multivariate linear mixed models for multiple outcomes. *Statistics in Medicine*, *18*, 2479-2492.

Sampson, R., Raudenbush, S.W., & Earls, T. (1997). Neigborhoods and violent crime: A multilevel study of collective efficacy. *Science*, *227*, 918-924.

Sánchez-Meca, J., & Marín-Martínez, F. (1997). Homogeneity tests in meta analysis: a Monte Carlo comparison of statistical power and type I error. *Quality & Quantity*, *31*, 385-399.

Satorra, A. (1989). Alternative test criteria in covariance structure analysis: a unified approach. *Psychometrika*, *54*, 131-151.

Satorra, A., & Saris, W.E. (1985). Power of the likelihood ratio test in covariance structure analysis. *Psychometrika*, *50*, 83-90.

Schall, R. (1991). Estimation in generalized linear models with random effects. *Biometrika*, *78*, 719-727.

Schijf, B., & Dronkers, J. (1991). De invloed van richting en wijk op de loopbanen in de lagere scholen van de stad Groningen. In I.B.H. Abram, B.P.M. Creemers & A. van der Ley (Eds.), *Onderwijsresearchdagen 1991: Curriculum*. Amsterdam: University of Amsterdam, SCO. [The effect of denomination and neigborhood on education in basic schools in the city Groningen in 1971.]

Schumacker, R.E., & Lomax, R.G. (1996). *A beginner's guide to structural equation modeling*. Mahwah, NJ: Lawrence Erlbaum Associates.

Schumacker, R.E., & Marcoulides, G.A. (Eds.), (1998). *Interaction and nonlinear effects in structural equation modeling*. Mahwah, NJ: Lawrence Erlbaum Associates.

Schwarz, G. (1978). Estimating the dimension of a model. *Annals of Statistics*, *6*, 461-464.

Schwarzer, R. (1989). *Meta-analysis programs. Program manual*. Berlijn: Institüt für Psychologie, Freie Universität Berlin.

Searle, S.R., Casella, G., & McCulloch, C.E. (1992). *Variance components*. New York: Wiley.

Shrout, P.E., & Fleiss, J.L. (1979). Intraclass correlation: uses in assessing rater reliability. *Psychological Bulletin, 86,* 420-428.

Siddiqui, O., Hedeker, D., Flay, B.R., & Hu, F.B. (1996). Intraclass correlation estimates in a school-based smoking prevention study: outcome and mediating variables, by gender and ethnicity. *American Journal of Epidemiology, 144,* 425-433.

Singer, J.D. (1998). Using SAS PROC MIXED to fit multilevel models, hierarchical models, and individual growth models. *Journal of Educational and Behavioral Statistics, 23,* 323-355.

Skinner, C.J., Holt, D., & Smith, T.M.F. (Eds.), (1989). *Analysis of complex surveys.* New York: Wiley.

Smith, A.F.M., & Gelfland, A.E. (1992). Bayesian statistics without tears: a sampling-resampling perspective. *American Statistician, 46,* 2, 84-88.

Smith, T.C., Spiegelhalter, D., & Thomas, A. (1995). Bayesian approaches to random-effects meta-analysis: A comparative study. *Statistics in Medicine, 14,* 2685-2699.

Snijders, T.A.B. (1996). Analysis of longitudinal data using the hierarchical linear model. *Quality and Quantity, 30,* 405-426.

Snijders, T.A.B. (2001). Sampling. In A. Leyland & H. Goldstein (Eds.), *Multilevel modelling of health statistics.* New York: Wiley.

Snijders, T.A.B., & Bosker, R. (1993). Standard errors and sample sizes for two-level research. *Journal of Educational Statistics, 18,* 237-259.

Snijders, T.A.B., & Bosker, R. (1994). Modeled variance in two-level models. *Sociological Methods & Research, 22,* 342-363.

Snijders, T.A.B., & Bosker, R. (1999). *Multilevel analysis. An introduction to basic and advanced multilevel modeling.* Thousand Oaks, CA: Sage.

Snijders, T.A.B., & Kenny, D.A. (1999). Multilevel models for relational data. *Personal Relationships, 6,* 471-486.

Snijders, T.A.B., Spreen, M., & Zwaagstra, R. 1994. Networks of cocaine users in an urban area: the use of multilevel modelling for analysing personal networks. *Journal of Quantitative Anthropology, 5,* 85-105.

Spiegelhalter, D. (1994). *BUGS: Bayesian inference Using Gibbs Sampling.* MRC Biostatistics Unit, Cambridge, UK. Available at: http://www.mrc-bsu.cam.ac.uk/bugs.

Spreen, M., & Zwaagstra, R. (1994). Personal network sampling, outdegree analysis and multilevel analysis: Introducing the network concept in studies of hidden populations. *International Sociology, 9,* 475-491.

StataCorp (2001). *Stata Statistical Software: Release 7.* College Station, TX.

Stevens, J. (1996). *Applied multivariate statistics for the social sciences.* Mahwah, NJ: Lawrence Erlbaum Associates.

Stinchcombe, A.L. (1968). *Constructing social theories.* New York: Harcourt.

Stine, R. (1989). An introduction to bootstrap methods. *Sociological Methods & Research, 18,* 2-3, 243-291.

Stoel, R., & van den Wittenboer, G. (2001). Prediction of initial status and growth rate: incorporating time in linear growth curve models. In J. Blasius, J. Hox, E. de Leeuw & P. Schmidt (Eds.), *Social science methodology in the new millennium. Proceedings of the Fifth International conference on logic and methodology.* Opladen, FRG: Leske + Budrich.

Sullivan, L.M., Dukes, K.A., & Losina, E. (1999). An introduction to hierarchical linear modeling. *Statistics in Medicine, 18,* 855-888.

Sutton, A.J., Abrams, K.R., Jones, D.R., Sheldon, T.A., & Song, F. (2000). *Methods for meta-analysis in medical research.* New York: Wiley.

Tabachnick, B.G., & Fidell, L.S. (1996). *Using multivariate statistics.* New York: HarperCollins Publishers Inc.

Taris, T.W. (2000). *A primer in longitudinal data analysis.* Thousand Oaks, CA: Sage.

Tate, R.L., & Hokanson, J.E. (1993). Analyzing individual status and change with hierarchical linear models: illustration with depression in college students. *Journal of Personality, 61,* 181-206.

Tucker, C., & Lewis, C. (1973). A reliability coefficient for maximum likelihood factor analysis. *Psychometrika, 38,* 1-10.

Turner, R.M., Omar, R.Z., Yang, M., Goldstein, H. & Thompson, S.G. (2000). A multilevel model framework for meta-analysis of clinical trials with binary outcomes. *Statistics in Medicine, 19,* 3417-3432.

Van den Eeden, P., & Hüttner, H.J.M. (1982). Multi-level Research. *Current Sociology, 30,* 3, 1-117.

Van der Leeden, R. (1998). Multilevel analysis of repeated measures data. *Quality & Quantity, 32,* 15-29.

Van der Leeden, R., & Busing, F. (1994). First iteration versus IGLS/RIGLS estimates in two-level models: A Monte Carlo study with ML3. Unpublished manuscript. Leiden: Department of Psychometrics and Research Methodology, Leiden University.

Van der Leeden, R., Busing, F., & Meijer, E. (1997): Applications of bootstrap methods for two-level models. Paper, Multilevel Conference, Amsterdam, April 1-2, 1997.

van Duijn, M.A.J. (1995). Estimation of a random effects model for directed graphs. In: T.A.B. Snijders (Ed.), *SSS'95. Symposium Statistische Software, nr.7. Toeval zit overal: programmatuur voor random-coefficient modellen* (pp. 113-131). [Chance everywhere. Software for random coefficient models] Groningen: iec ProGAMMA.

Van Duijn, M.A.J., van Busschbach, J.T., and Snijders, T.A.B., (1999). Multilevel analysis of personal networks as dependent variables. *Social Networks, 21*, 187-209

Van Peet, A.A.J. (1992). *De potentieeltheorie van intelligentie.* [The potentiality theory of intelligence] Amsterdam: University of Amsterdam, Ph.D. Thesis.

Verbeke, G., & Lesaffre, E. (1997). The effect of misspecifying the random-effects distribution in linear mixed models for longitudinal data. *Computational Statistics & Data Analysis, 23*, 541-556.

Villar, J., Mackey, M.E., Carroli, G. & Donner, A. (2001). Meta-analyses in systematic reviews of randomized controlled trials in perinatal medicine: comparison of fixed and random effects models. *Statistics in Medicine, 20*, 3635-3647.

Wald, A. (1943): Tests of statistical hypotheses concerning several parameters when the number of observations is large. *Transactions of the American Mathematical Society, 54*, 426-482.

Wasserman, S., & Faust, K. (1994). *Social network analysis.* Cambridge, UK: Cambridge University Press.

White, H. (1982). Maximum likelihood estimation of misspecified models. *Econometrica, 50*, 1-25.

Willett, J.B. (1988). Questions and answers in the measurement of change. In E. Rothkopf (Ed.) *Review of Research in Education.* Pp. 345-422. Washington, DC: AERA.

Willett, J.B. (1989). Some results on reliability for the longitudinal measurement of change: implications for the design of studies of individual growth. *Educational and Psychological Measurement, 49*, 587-602.

Willett, J.B., & Sayer, A.G. (1994). Using covariance structure analysis to detect correlates and predictors of individual change over time. *Psychological Bulletin, 116*, 363-381.

Wolfinger, R.W. (1993). Laplace's approximation for nonlinear mixed models. *Biometrika, 80*, 791-705.

Wong, G.Y., & Mason, W.M. (1985) The hierarchical logistic regression model for multilevel analysis. Extensions of the hierarchical normal linear model for multilevel analysis. *Journal of the American Statistical Association, 80*, 513-524.

Woodruff, S.I. (1997). Random-effects models for analyzing clustered data from a nutrition education intervention. *Evaluation Review, 21*, 688-697.

Wright, D.B. (1997). Extra-binomial variation in multilevel logistic models with sparse structures. *British Journal of Mathematical and Statistical Psychology, 50*, 21-29.

Wright, S. (1921). Correlation and causation. *Journal of Agricultural Research, 20*, 557-585.

Yang, M., Rasbash, J., & Goldstein, H. (1998). *MlwiN macros for advanced multilevel modelling.* London: Institute of Education, University of London.

Yung, Y.-F., & Chan, W. (1999). Statistical analyses using bootstrapping: Concepts and implementation. In R. Hoyle (Ed.), *Statistical strategies for small sample research.* Pp. 82-108. Thousand Oaks, CA: Sage.

Zeger, S.L., & Karim, M.R. (1991). Generalized linear models with random effects; a Gibbs sampling approach. *Journal of the American Statistical Association, 86*, 79-86.

Zeger, S., Liang, K., & Albert, P. (1988). Models for longitudinal data: a generalised estimating equation approach. *Biometrics, 44*, 1049-1060.

Author Index

A

Abrams, K.R., 139, 153, 291
Acock, A., 226, 286
Adams, R.J., 172, 281
Afshartous, D., 172, 281
Agresti, A., 107, 281
Aiken, L., see Aiken L.S.
Aiken, L.S., 58, 62, 281, 286
Aitkin, M., 103, 107, 116, 281
Akaike, H., 45, 181
Alba, R.D., 8, 281
Albert, P., 40, 292
Algina, J., 32, 281
Alker, H.R., 4, 281
Anderson, D., 103, 107, 116, 281
Anderson, J.C., 239, 240,283
Andrich, D., 172, 281
Ansari, A., 260, 281, 285
Anscombe, F.J., 26, 281
Antczak-Boucoums, A., 152, 281
Appelbaum, M.I., 93, 94, 282
Arbuckle, J.L., 205, 226, 240, 244, 263, 274, 281
Arnold, C.L., 35, 281, 284

B

Barbosa, M.F., 102, 281
Barnett, V., 175, 211, 281
Baumert J., 226 , 287
Bechger, T.M., 73, 226, 281, 285
Beck, N., 201, 281
Benichou, J., 197, 198, 279, 283
Bentler, P.M., 226, 239, 241, 260, 273, 281, 282
Berger, M., 173, 288, 289
Berkey, C.S., 152, 153, 281
Berkhof, J., 45, 281
Bernstein, I.H., 149, 150, 166, 168, 172, 288
Bhumirat, C., 110, 277, 289
Biggerstaff, B.J., 154, 281

Bithell, J., 204, 208, 282
Blalock, H.M., 7, 138, 281
Bock, R.D., 8, 107, 284, 288
Bollen, K.A., 193, 231, 252, 282
Bonett, D.G., 239, 281
Boomsma, A., 53, 282
Booth, J.G., 204, 282
Bosker, R., see Bosker, R.J.
Bosker, R.J., 30, 34, 66, 67, 68, 81, 94, 135, 172, 173, 177, 180, 187, 189, 198, 282, 291
Bostrom, A., 97, 283
Boyd, L. H., 4, 282
Brockwell, S.E., 145, 282
Browne, M.W., 239, 268, 282
Browne, W., see Browne, W.J.
Browne, W.J., 34, 38, 43, 109, 132, 137, 153, 213, 172, 173, 223, 260, 282, 284, 289
Bryk, A.S., 8, 11, 12, 22, 29, 30, 33, 34, 38, 40, 43, 52, 54, 64, 65, 69, 70, 75, 86, 87, 90, 91, 93, 95, 96, 97, 141, 142, 143, 148, 149, 1532, 153, 172, 203, 274, 276, 277, 282, 285, 289
Burchinal, M., 93, 94, 282
Burstein, L., 4, 290
Burton, P., 40, 282
Busing, F., 40, 42, 43, 171, 172, 282, 292

C

Campanelli, P., 8, 124, 288
Camstra, A., 53, 282
Carlin, B.P., 29, 282
Carpenter, J., 204, 208, 282
Carroli, G., 145, 292
Carton, A., 124, 289
Casella, G., 38, 212, 227, 282, 290
Cattell, R.B., 237, 282
Chan, D., 7, 282
Chan, W., 204, 292
Chan, W.-S., 74, 289

Subject Index

A

Adjusted goodness-of-fit index, *see* Evaluation of SEM fit, AGFI
Aggregation, 2, 7
AIC, *see* Evaluation of multilevel regression fit, Akaike's information criterion
Akaike's criterion, *see* Evaluation of multilevel regression fit
Akaike's information criterion, *see* Evaluation of multilevel regression fit
AMOS, *see* computer programs
ANCOVA, 52
Assumptions
  - checking normality, 23
Atomistic fallacy, 4
Autocorrelation, *see* longitudinal model, complex covariance structure
Autocorrelation plot in MCMC, *see* MCMC, diagnostic plots
Autoregression, *see* longitudinal model, complex covariance structure

B

Balanced data, 228, 229
Bayes estimators, *see* Estimation methods
Bernouilli distribution, *see* Data, dichotomous
Between-groups covariance matrix, *see* Covariance matrix
BIC, *see* Schwarz's Bayesian Information Criterion
Binary response, *see* Data, dichotomous
Binomial data, *see* Data, proportions
Binomial distribution, *see* Data, proportions
Bonferroni correction, 53
Bootstrap, 201, 207
  - bias correction, 206, 210
  - iterated bootstrap, 210
  - number of iterations, 204, 206
  - nonparametric, 208
  - parametric, 208
  - sample size, 204, 208
BUGS, *see* computer programs, BUGS

C

Causal analysis, *see* Structural equation modeling
Centering, 54
  - grand mean, 56
  - group mean, 58, 61
Chi-square test in meta-analysis, 153
Chi-square test in multilevel regression, 148, 153
Chi-square test in multilevel SEM, *see* Evaluation of SEM fit
Comparative fit index, *see* Evaluation of SEM fit
Compound symmetry, *see* Longitudinal model
Computer programs
  - aML, 110, 137, 201
  - AMOS, 226, 251, 263
  - BUGS, 154, 214
  - EQS, 226, 251
  - GLLAMM, 261
  - HLM, 33, 34, 35, 43, 91, 102, 110, 137, 152, 176, 201, 274
  - LISREL, 226, 248, 251, 260
  - META, 145, 155
  - Mixor/Mixreg, 102, 110
  - MLwiN, 34, 91, 102, 137, 153, 176, 201, 214, 220, 274
  - Mplus, 226, 231, 237, 248, 262
  - PinT, 182, 191
  - PRELIS, 102, 137
  - SAS Proc Mixed, 34, 35, 153
  - SPLIT2, 231, 237, 253
  - SPSS, 35
  - STATA, 261
  - STREAMS, 227, 231, 249
Confidence interval, 18, 42, 200, 212
Confirmatory factor analysis, *see* Structural equation modeling